FINANCIAL MANAGEMENT

Theory and

Practice

STUDY GUIDE *to accompany*

FINANCIAL MANAGEMENT

Theory and Practice

Eighth Edition

EUGENE F. BRIGHAM
UNIVERSITY OF FLORIDA

LOUIS C. GAPENSKI
UNIVERSITY OF FLORIDA

THE DRYDEN PRESS
HARCOURT BRACE COLLEGE PUBLISHERS

FORT WORTH   PHILADELPHIA   SAN DIEGO   NEW YORK   AUSTIN   ORLANDO   SAN ANTONIO
TORONTO   MONTREAL   LONDON   SYDNEY   TOKYO

Address for Editorial Correspondence
The Dryden Press, 301 Commerce Street, Suite 3700, Fort Worth, TX 76102

Address for Orders
The Dryden Press, 6277 Sea Harbor Drive, Orlando, FL 32887
1-800-782-4479, or 1-800-433-0001 (in Florida)

ISBN: 0-03-018689-7

Printed in the United States of America

6 7 8 9 0 1 2 3 4 5   066   9 8 7 6 5 4 3 2 1

The Dryden Press
Harcourt Brace College Publishers

PREFACE

This *Study Guide* is designed primarily to help you develop a working knowledge of the concepts and principles of financial management. Additionally, it will familiarize you with the types of true/false and multiple-choice test questions that are being used with increasing frequency in introductory finance courses.

The *Study Guide* follows the outline of *Financial Management: Theory and Practice.* You should read carefully the next section, "How to Use This *Study Guide*," to familiarize yourself with its specific contents and to gain some insights into how it can be used most effectively.

We would like to thank Dana Aberwald Clark, Carol Stanton, and Susan Sternberg for their considerable assistance in the preparation of this edition and Bob LeClair for his helpful ideas in prior editions which we carried over to this one.

We have tried to make the *Study Guide* as clear and error-free as possible. However, some mistakes may have crept in, and there are almost certainly some sections that could be clarified. Any suggestions for improving the *Study Guide* would be greatly appreciated and should be addressed to us. Since instructors almost never read study guides, we address this call for help to students!

Eugene F. Brigham
Louis C. Gapenski
College of Business Administration
University of Florida
Gainesville, FL 32611-7167

June 1996

HOW TO USE THIS STUDY GUIDE

Different people will tend to use the *Study Guide* in somewhat different ways. This is natural because both introductory finance courses and individual students' needs vary widely. However, the tips contained in this section should help all students use the *Study Guide* more effectively, regardless of these differences.

Each chapter contains (1) an overview, (2) an outline, (3) definitional self-test questions, (4) conceptual self-test questions, (5) self-test problems, and (6) answers and solutions to the self-test questions and problems. You should begin your study by reading the overview; it will give you an idea of what is contained in the chapter and how this material fits into the overall scheme of things in financial management.

Next, read over the outline to get a better fix on the specific topics covered in the chapter. It is important to realize that the outline does not list every facet of every topic covered in the textbook—the *Study Guide* is intended to highlight and summarize the textbook, not to supplant it. Also, note that appendix material is clearly marked as such within the outline. Thus, if your instructor does not assign a particular appendix, you may not want to study that portion of the outline.

The definitional self-test questions are intended to test your knowledge of, and also to reinforce your ability to work with, the terms and concepts introduced in the chapter. If you do not understand the definitions thoroughly, review the outline prior to going on to the conceptual questions and problems.

The conceptual self-test questions focus on the same kinds of ideas that the textbook end-of-chapter questions address, but in the *Study Guide*, the questions are set out in a true/false or multiple-choice format. Thus, for many students these questions can be used to practice for the types of tests that are being used with increasing frequency. However, regardless of the types of tests you must take, working through the conceptual questions will help drive home the key concepts of financial management.

The numeric problems are also written in a multiple-choice format. Generally, the problems are arranged in order of increasing difficulty. Also, note that some of the *Study Guide* problems are convoluted in the sense that information normally available to financial managers is withheld and information normally unknown is given. Such problems are designed to test your knowledge of a subject, and you must work "backwards" to solve them. Furthermore, such problems are included in the *Study Guide* in part because they provide a good test of how well you understand the material and in part because you may well be seeing similar problems on your exams.

Finally, each *Study Guide* chapter provides the answers and solutions to the self-test questions and problems. The rationale behind a question's correct answer is explained where necessary, but the problem solutions are always complete. Note that the problems in the early chapters generally provide both "table-based" and "financial calculator" solutions. In later chapters, only calculator solutions are shown. You should not be concerned if your answer differs from ours by a small amount which is caused by rounding errors.

Of course, each student must decide how to incorporate the *Study Guide* in his or her overall study program. Many students begin an assignment by reading the *Study Guide* overview and outline to get the "big picture," then read the chapter in the textbook. Naturally, the *Study Guide* overview and outline is also used extensively to review for exams. Most students work the textbook questions and problems, using the latter as a self-test and review tool. However, if you are stumped by a text problem, try the *Study Guide* problems first because their detailed solutions can get you over stumbling blocks.

CONTENTS OF THE STUDY GUIDE

Chapter 1

An Overview of Financial Management

Overview

This chapter provides an overview of financial management and should give you a better understanding of the following: (1) what forces will affect financial management in the future, (2) how businesses are organized, (3) how finance fits into the structure of a firm's organization, (4) how financial managers relate to their counterparts in other departments, (5) what the goals of a firm are, and (6) how financial managers can contribute to the attainment of these goals.

Outline

Finance consists of three interrelated areas: money and capital markets, investments, and financial management. Career opportunities within each field are varied and numerous, but financial managers must have a knowledge of all three areas.

- Many finance majors go to work for financial institutions, including banks, insurance companies, investment companies, savings and loans, and credit unions. The bank officer trainee is the most common entry-level job in this area.

- Finance graduates who go into investments generally work for a brokerage house in sales or as a security analyst; for a bank, a mutual fund, or an insurance company in the management of their investment portfolios; or for a financial consulting firm, advising individual investors or pension funds on how to invest their funds.

- Financial management, the broadest of the three areas, and the one with the greatest number of job opportunities, is important to all types of businesses. The types of jobs one encounters in this area range from decisions regarding plant expansions to the choice of stocks or bonds to finance expansion.

The two most important trends for financial management during the 1990s are likely to be the continued globalization of business and a further increase in the use of information technology.

- Four factors have led to the increased globalization of many businesses.
  - ☐ Transportation and communications improvements have lowered shipping costs and made international trade more feasible.
  - ☐ Increased political clout of consumers has helped lower trade barriers.
  - ☐ New technology has raised development costs, necessitating worldwide marketing to increase unit sales.
  - ☐ Competitive pressures have forced companies to shift manufacturing operations to lower-cost countries.

- Continued advances in information technology are revolutionizing the way financial decisions are made. Thus, the new generation of financial managers will need stronger computer and quantitative skills than were required in the past.

The historical trends discussed above have greatly increased the importance of financial management. Today the financial manager must make decisions in a much more coordinated manner, and he or she generally has direct responsibility for the control process. Because there are financial implications in virtually all business decisions, nonfinancial executives must know enough finance to work these implications into their own specialized analyses.

The financial manager's task is to acquire and use funds so as to maximize the value of the firm. Some specific activities follow.

- Financial managers use *forecasting and planning* to shape the firm's future position.

- Financial managers make *major investment and financing decisions*.

- Financial managers *coordinate and control* when interacting with other executives so that the firm operates as efficiently as possible.

- The financial manager must *deal with the financial markets*.

The three main forms of business organization are the sole proprietorship, the partnership, and the corporation. About 80 percent of businesses operate as sole proprietorships, but when based on dollar value of sales, 80 percent of all business is conducted by corporations.

■ A *sole proprietorship* is an unincorporated business owned by one individual.
  □ Advantages are: (a) it is easily and inexpensively formed, (b) it is subject to few government regulations, and (c) it pays no corporate income taxes (however, all business earnings are taxed as personal income to the owner).
  □ Disadvantages are: (a) it is limited in its ability to raise large sums of capital, (b) the proprietor has unlimited personal liability for the business' debts, and (c) it has a life limited to the life of the individual who created it.

■ A *partnership* exists when two or more persons associate to conduct a noncorporate business.
  □ Its major advantage is its low cost and ease of formation.
  □ Disadvantages are: (a) unlimited liability, (b) limited life, (c) difficulty in transferring ownership, and (d) difficulty of raising large amounts of capital.

■ A *corporation* is a legal entity created by a state, and it is separate and distinct from its owners and managers.
  □ Advantages are: (a) unlimited life, (b) ownership which is easily transferred through the exchange of stock, and (c) limited liability. Because of these three factors, it is much easier for corporations to raise money in the capital markets.
  □ Disadvantages are: (a) corporate earnings are subject to double taxation and (b) setting up a corporation and filing required state and federal reports are more complex than for a sole proprietorship or partnership.
  □ A charter must be filed with the state where the firm is incorporated, and bylaws which govern the management of the company must be prepared.

■ The value of any business, other than a very small one, will probably be maximized if it is organized as a corporation for these three reasons:
  □ Limited liability reduces risks borne by investors, thus, other things constant, the lower the firm's risk, the higher its value.
  □ A firm's value is dependent on growth opportunities, which, in turn, are dependent on the firm's ability to attract capital.
  □ The value of an asset depends on its liquidity. An investment in the stock of a corporation is much more liquid than a similar investment in a proprietorship or partnership.

■ Although the three basic types of organization dominate the business scene, several hybrid forms are gaining popularity.
  □ It is possible to limit the liabilities of some of a firm's partners by establishing a *limited partnership*, wherein certain partners are designated *general partners* and others *limited partners*.

- ☐ The *limited liability partnership (LLP)*, sometimes called a *limited liability company (LLC)*, combines the limited liability advantage of a corporation with the tax advantages of a partnership.
- ☐ The *professional corporation (PC)*, or *professional association (PA)*, was established to provide a way for groups of professionals to incorporate and thus avoid certain types of unlimited liability, yet still be held responsible for professional liability.
- ☐ If certain requirements are met, particularly with regard to size and number of stockholders, one (or more) individuals can establish a corporation but elect to be taxed as if the business were a proprietorship or partnership. This form of organization is called an *S corporation*.

Maximizing the price of the firm's common stock is the primary goal of most corporations.

- ■ Other objectives, such as personal satisfaction, employee welfare, and the good of the community, also have an influence, but for publicly-owned companies, they are less important than stock price maximization.

- ■ Social responsibility raises the question of whether businesses should operate strictly in their stockholders' best interests or also be responsible for the welfare of their employees, customers, and the communities in which they operate.
  - ☐ Any voluntary, socially responsible acts that raise costs will be difficult, if not impossible, in industries that are subject to keen competition.
  - ☐ Even firms with above-average profits will be constrained in exercising social responsibility by capital market forces because investors will normally prefer a firm that concentrates on profits over one excessively devoted to social action.
  - ☐ Socially responsible actions that increase costs may have to be put on a mandatory, rather than a voluntary, basis to insure that the burden falls uniformly on all businesses.
  - ☐ Industry and government must cooperate in establishing rules for fair hiring, product safety, environmental protection, and other programs that affect all businesses.

- ■ The same actions that maximize stock price also benefit society. To maximize stock price, a firm must provide a low-cost, high-quality product to consumers. This, in itself, is a benefit to society.

Business ethics can be thought of as a company's attitude and conduct toward its employees, customers, community, and stockholders. Most firms today have in place strong codes of ethical behavior; however, it is imperative that top management be openly committed to ethical behavior and that they communicate this commitment through their own personal actions as well as company policies.

An agency relationship exists when one or more individuals (called principals) hire another individual (called an agent) to perform some service and then delegate decision-making authority to that agent. Primary agency relationships exist (1) between stockholders and managers and (2) between debtholders and stockholders.

■ A potential *agency problem* exists whenever a manager owns less than 100 percent of the firm's common stock. Since the firm's earnings do not go solely to the manager, he or she may not concentrate exclusively on maximizing shareholder wealth.

■ Several mechanisms are used to ensure that managers act in shareholders' best interests: (1) performance-based incentive plans, (2) direct intervention by shareholders, (3) the threat of firing, and (4) takeovers.

■ Another agency problem involves conflicts between stockholders and creditors (debtholders).
  □ Conflicts arise if (a) management, acting for its stockholders, takes on projects that have greater risk than was anticipated by creditors or (b) the firm increases debt to a level higher than was anticipated. Both of these actions decrease the value of the debt outstanding.
  □ It is in the firm's best interest to deal fairly with its creditors in order to assure future access to debt markets at reasonable interest costs.

The financial manager can affect the firm's stock price by influencing the following factors: (1) projected earnings per share, (2) timing of the earnings stream, (3) riskiness of these projected earnings, (4) use of debt, and (5) dividend policy. Every significant corporate decision should be analyzed in terms of its effects on these factors and, through them, on the price of the firm's stock.

■ Other things held constant, if management is interested in the well-being of its current stockholders, it should concentrate on earnings per share rather than on total corporate profits. However, the timing of earnings is an important reason to concentrate on wealth as measured by the stock price rather than on earnings alone.

■ The financial manager must decide exactly how much of the current earnings to pay out as dividends rather than to retain and reinvest. This is called the *dividend policy decision*.

Although managerial actions affect the value of a firm's stock, external factors also influence stock prices. Included among them are legal constraints, the general level of economic activity, the tax laws, and conditions in the stock market.

SELF-TEST QUESTIONS

Definitional

1. Finance consists of three interrelated areas: (1) _____ ___ _____ _____, which deals with securities markets and financial institutions; (2) _____, which focuses on the decisions of individuals and financial institutions as they choose securities for their investment portfolios; and (3) _____ _____ or "business finance."

2. In the 1990s, two of the most important trends affecting financial management are likely to be the continued _____ of business and a further increase in the use of _____ _____.

3. Sole proprietorships are easily formed, but often have difficulty raising _____, they subject proprietors to unlimited _____, and they have a limited _____.

4. Partnership profits are taxed as _____ income in proportion to each partner's proportionate ownership.

5. A partnership is dissolved upon the withdrawal or _____ of any one of the partners. In addition, the difficulty in _____ ownership is a major disadvantage of the partnership form of business organization.

6. A(n) _____ is a legal entity created by a state, and it is separate from its owners and managers.

7. The concept of _____ _____ means that a firm's stockholders are not personally liable for the debts of the business.

8. Modern financial theory operates on the assumption that the goal of management is the _____ of shareholder _____. This goal is accomplished if the firm's _____ _____ is maximized.

9. Socially responsible activities that increase a firm's costs will be most difficult in those industries where _____ is most intense.

10. Firms with above-average profit levels will find social actions _____ by capital market factors.

11. A(n) _____ relationship exists when one or more individuals (the principals) hire another individual (an agent) to act on their behalf.

12. Potential agency problems exist between a firm's shareholders and its _____ and also between shareholders and _____.

13. A firm's stock price depends on several factors. Among the most important of these are the level of projected _____ _____ _____ and the riskiness of these projections.

Conceptual

14. The primary objective of the firm is to maximize EPS.

   a. True   b. False

15. The types of actions that help a firm maximize stock price are generally not directly beneficial to society at large.

   a. True   b. False

16. There are factors that influence stock price over which managers have virtually no control.

   a. True   b. False

17. Which of the following factors affect stock price?

   a. Level of projected earnings per share.
   b. Riskiness of projected earnings per share.
   c. Timing of the earnings stream.
   d. The manner of financing the firm.
   e. All of the above factors.

18. Which of the following factors tend to encourage management to pursue stock price maximization as a goal?

   a. Shareholders link management's compensation to company performance.
   b. Managers' reactions to the threat of tender offers and proxy fights.
   c. Managers do not have goals other than stock price maximization.
   d. Statements a and b are both correct.
   e. Statements a, b, and c are all correct.

19. The primary contribution of finance to total social welfare is its

   a. Function as a productive resource.
   b. Contribution to the efficient allocation and use of resources.
   c. Role as an exogenous variable.
   d. Positive impact on the externalities of "other variables."
   e. Contribution to environmental protection.

20. Shareholder agency costs include

   a. Expenditures to monitor managerial actions.
   b. Managerial salaries.
   c. Opportunity costs associated with managerial restrictions.
   d. All of the above.
   e. Answers a and c.

21. Which of the following represents a significant *disadvantage* to the corporate form of organization?

   a. Difficulty in transferring ownership.
   b. Exposure to taxation of corporate earnings and stockholder dividend income.
   c. Degree of liability to which corporate owners and managers are exposed.
   d. Level of difficulty corporations face in obtaining large amounts of capital in financial markets.
   e. None of the above is a significant disadvantage.

22. Which of the following statements is most *correct*?

   a. The corporate bylaws are the set of rules drawn up by the state to enable managers to run the firm in accordance with state laws.
   b. Procedures for electing corporate directors are contained in the bylaws while the declaration of the activities that the firm will pursue and the number of directors are included in the corporate charter.
   c. Procedures which govern changes in the bylaws of the corporation are contained in the corporate charter.
   d. Although most companies design a charter, only the bylaws are legally required to be filed with the secretary of state in order for a corporation to be in official existence.
   e. Statements b and d.

ANSWERS TO SELF-TEST QUESTIONS

1. money and capital markets; investments; financial management
2. globalization; information technology
3. capital; liability; life
4. personal
5. death; transferring
6. corporation
7. limited liability
8. maximization; wealth; stock price
9. competition
10. constrained
11. agency
12. managers; creditors (or debtholders)
13. earnings per share

14. b. An increase in earnings per share will not necessarily increase stock price. For example, if the increase in earnings per share is accompanied by an increase in the riskiness of the firm, stock price might fall. *The primary objective is the maximization of stock price.*

15. b. The actions that maximize stock price generally also benefit society by promoting efficient, low-cost operations; encouraging the development of new technology, products, and jobs; and requiring efficient and courteous service.

16. a. Managers have no control over factors such as (1) external constraints (for example, antitrust laws and environmental regulations), (2) the general level of economic activity, (3) taxes, and (4) conditions in the stock market, all of which affect the price of the firm's stock.

17. e. The firm's stock price is dependent on all the factors mentioned. One additional factor not mentioned is dividend policy.

18. d. Mechanisms which tend to force managers to act in the shareholders' best interests include (1) performance-based incentive plans, (2) direct intervention by shareholders, (3) the threat of firing, and (4) takeovers.

19. b. Financial management plays a crucial role in the operation of successful firms because of finance's contribution to the efficient allocation and use of resources. Successful firms are absolutely necessary for a healthy, productive economy.

20. e. Shareholder agency costs include expenditures to monitor managerial actions and the opportunity costs associated with restrictions placed on managers.

21. b. The double taxation of corporate earnings is a significant disadvantage of the corporate form of organization. The corporations' earnings are taxed, and then any earnings paid out as dividends are taxed again as income to the stockholders.

22. b. The firm's charter is filed with the secretary of state in which the firm will be incorporated, and, when it is approved, the corporation is officially in existence. The charter includes such information as the types of activities the firm will pursue and the number of directors. On the other hand, the bylaws are a set of rules drawn up by the founders of the corporation to aid in governing the internal management of the company.

CHAPTER 2

ANALYSIS OF FINANCIAL STATEMENTS

OVERVIEW

Financial analysis is designed to determine the relative strengths and weaknesses of a company. Investors need this information to estimate both future cash flows from the firm and the riskiness of those cash flows. Financial managers need the information provided by analysis both to evaluate the firm's past performance and to map future plans. Financial analysis concentrates on *financial statement analysis*, which highlights the key aspects of a firm's operation. Financial statement analysis involves a study of the relationships between income statement and balance sheet accounts, how these relationships change over time (trend analysis), and how a particular firm compares with other firms in its industry (comparative analysis). Although financial analysis has limitations, when used with care and judgment, it can provide some very useful insights into the operations of a company.

OUTLINE

A firm's annual report to shareholders presents two important types of information. The first is a verbal statement of the company's recent operations and its expectations for the coming year. The second is a set of quantitative financial statements which report what actually happened to the firm's financial position, earnings, and dividends over the past few years. The information contained in an annual report is used by investors to form expectations about future earnings and dividends.

■ The *income statement* summarizes the firm's revenues and expenses over the past year. Earnings per share (EPS) is called "the bottom line," denoting that of all the items on the income statement, EPS is the most important.

■ The *balance sheet* shows the firm's assets and the claims against those assets. It portrays the financial condition at a point in time.

- ☐ Assets, found on the left-hand side of the balance sheet, are typically shown in the order of their liquidity. Claims, found on the right-hand side, are generally listed in the order in which they must be paid.
- ☐ Only cash represents actual money. Noncash assets should produce cash flows eventually, but they do not represent cash in hand.
- ☐ Claims against the assets consist of liabilities and stockholders' equity. Thus, Assets – Liabilities – Preferred stock = Common stockholders' equity (Net worth).
- ☐ The common equity section of the balance sheet is divided into three accounts: common stock, paid-in capital, and retained earnings. Common stock and paid-in capital accounts arise from the issuance of stock to raise capital. Retained earnings are built up over time as the firm "saves" a part of its earnings rather than paying all earnings out as dividends.
- ☐ Companies often use the most accelerated permissible method to calculate depreciation for tax purposes but use straight line depreciation, which results in a lower expense, for stockholder reporting.
- ☐ The balance sheet may be thought of as a snapshot of the firm's financial position *at a point in time* (for example, end of year), while the income statement reports on operations *over a period of time* (for example, one calendar year).

- ■ The *statement of retained earnings* reports changes in the equity accounts between balance sheet dates.
  - ☐ The balance sheet account "retained earnings" represents a claim against assets, not assets per se.
  - ☐ Retained earnings as reported on the balance sheet do not represent cash and are not "available" for the payment of dividends or anything else. Retained earnings represent funds which have already been reinvested in operating assets of the firm.

- ■ In finance the emphasis is on the *cash flows* which the company is expected to generate. The firm's net income is important, but cash flows are even more important because dividends must be paid in cash, and cash is also necessary to purchase the assets required to continue operations.
  - ☐ A firm's cash flows are generally equal to cash from sales, minus cash operating costs, minus interest charges, and minus taxes.
  - ☐ Depreciation is a noncash charge, so it must be added back to net income to obtain an estimate of the cash flow from operations.
  - ☐ A stock's value is based on the *present value of the cash flows* which investors expect it to provide in the future. The cash flow provided by the stock itself is the expected future dividend stream, and that expected dividend stream provides the fundamental basis for the stock's value. There are two classes of cash flows:

- ▸ Operating cash flows arise from normal operations, and they are the difference between sales revenues and cash expenses, including taxes paid.
- ▸ Other cash flows arise from the issuance of stock, from borrowing, or from the sale of fixed assets.

■ To understand how timing of cash flows influences the financial statements, one must understand the *cash flow cycle* within a firm. It shows the way in which actual net cash, as opposed to accounting net income, flows into or out of the firm during some specified period.

■ The *statement of cash flows* reports the impact of a firm's operating, investing, and financing activities on cash flows over an accounting period.

The real value of financial statements is to help predict the firm's future earnings and dividends. From an investor's standpoint, predicting the future is what financial statement analysis is all about. From management's standpoint, financial statement analysis is useful both as a way to anticipate future conditions and, more important, as a starting point for planning actions that will influence the future course of events. An analysis of the firm's ratios is the first step in a financial analysis.

■ *Liquidity ratios* are used to measure a firm's ability to meet its current obligations as they come due.
- ☐ The *current ratio* measures the extent to which the claims of short-term creditors are covered by short-term assets. It is determined by dividing current assets by current liabilities.
- ☐ The *quick,* or *acid test, ratio* is calculated by deducting inventories from current assets and then dividing the remainder by current liabilities. Inventories are excluded because it may be difficult to liquidate them at their full book value.

■ *Asset management ratios* measure how effectively a firm is managing its assets and whether or not the level of those assets is properly related to the level of operations as measured by sales.
- ☐ The *inventory turnover ratio* is defined as sales divided by inventories. It is often necessary to use the average inventory figure rather than the year-end figure, especially if a firm's business is highly seasonal.
- ☐ The *days sales outstanding (DSO)* is used to appraise accounts receivable, and it is calculated by dividing average daily sales into accounts receivable to find the number of days' sales tied up in receivables. Thus, the DSO represents the average length of time that the firm must wait after making a sale before receiving cash.

- ☐ The *fixed assets turnover ratio* is the ratio of sales to net fixed assets, or the amount of sales generated by each dollar of fixed assets. It measures how effectively the firm uses its plant and equipment.
- ☐ The *total assets turnover ratio* is calculated by dividing sales by total assets. It measures the utilization of all the firm's assets.

- ■ *Debt management ratios* measure the extent to which a firm is using debt financing, or *financial leverage*, and the degree of safety afforded to creditors.
  - ☐ The *debt ratio*, or ratio of total debt to total assets, measures the proportion of funds provided by creditors. The lower the ratio, the greater the protection afforded creditors in the event of liquidation.
  - ☐ The *times-interest-earned (TIE) ratio* is determined by dividing earnings before interest and taxes (EBIT) by the interest charges. The TIE measures the extent to which operating income can decline before the firm is unable to meet its annual interest costs.
  - ☐ The *fixed charge coverage ratio* is similar to the TIE ratio, but it is more inclusive because it recognizes that many firms incur long-term obligations under lease contracts and sinking funds.

- ■ *Profitability ratios* show the combined effects of liquidity, asset management, and debt management on operating results.
  - ☐ The *profit margin on sales* is calculated by dividing net income by sales.
  - ☐ The *basic earning power (BEP) ratio* is calculated by dividing earnings before interest and taxes (EBIT) by total assets. It shows the raw earning power of the firm's assets, before the influence of taxes and leverage.
  - ☐ The *return on total assets (ROA)* is the ratio of net income to total assets; it measures the return on all the firm's assets after interest and taxes.
  - ☐ The *return on common equity (ROE)* measures the rate of return on the common stockholders' investment. It is equal to net income divided by common equity.

- ■ *Market value ratios* relate the firm's stock price to its earnings and book value per share, and thus give management an indication of what investors think of the company's past performance and future prospects.
  - ☐ The *price/earnings (P/E) ratio*, or price per share divided by earnings per share, shows how much investors are willing to pay per dollar of reported profits. P/E ratios are higher for firms with high growth prospects, other things held constant, but they are lower for riskier firms.
  - ☐ The *market/book (M/B) ratio*, defined as market price per share divided by book value per share, gives another indication of how investors regard the company. Higher M/B ratios are generally associated with firms that have a high rate of return on common equity.

Trend analysis looks at the trend of a single ratio over time. Trend analysis can provide clues as to whether the firm's financial situation is improving, holding constant, or deteriorating. Comparative analysis compares the firm's ratios with industry average ratios and/or the ratios of leading competitors. Such analysis provides insights into the firm's relative performance.

The Du Pont equation shows the relationship among four key ratios:

$$ROE = \text{Profit margin} \times \text{Total assets turnover} \times \text{Equity multiplier}$$
$$= \frac{\text{Net income}}{\text{Sales}} \times \frac{\text{Sales}}{\text{Total assets}} \times \frac{\text{Total assets}}{\text{Common equity}}.$$

This relationship allows analysts to easily summarize a firm's financial condition because it decomposes stockholder profitability into three important determinants: (1) expense control, (2) asset utilization, and (3) debt utilization.

Common size analysis is another technique for analyzing a firm's financial statements.

■ To create common size statements, all income statement items are divided by sales, and all balance sheet items are divided by total assets. Thus, a common size income statement shows each item as a percentage of sales, and a common size balance sheet shows each item as a percentage of total assets.

■ The advantage of common size statements is that they facilitate comparisons of balance sheets and income statements over time and across companies.

■ Common size and ratio analyses provide the same types of information about a firm, but, since they look at the data from different perspectives, they should both be used in a complete financial statement analysis, along with a Du Pont analysis.

A final technique used to help analyze a firm's financial statements is percentage change analysis. In this type of analysis, growth rates are calculated for all income statement items and balance sheet accounts. The conclusions reached in common size and percentage change analysis generally parallel those derived from ratio analysis.

Two non-accounting measures that are widely used to measure profitability and assess managerial performance are market value added (MVA) and economic value added (EVA).

- Shareholder wealth is maximized by maximizing the difference between the market value of equity and the amount of equity capital that investors have supplied to the firm. The difference is called *market value added (MVA)*.

- Whereas MVA measures the effect of managerial actions to enhance shareholder wealth since the inception of the company, *economic value added (EVA)* focuses on managerial effectiveness in a given year. The basic formula for EVA is operating profit minus cost of capital.
  - □ EVA is an estimate of a business's true economic profit for the year.
  - □ EVA represents the residual income that remains after the opportunity cost of all capital has been deducted. It depends on both operating efficiency and balance sheet management: without operating efficiency, operating profits will be low, and without efficient balance sheet management, there will be too many assets, hence too much capital, which results in higher-than-necessary capital costs.

- In the past few years, many highly successful firms have adopted incentive compensation systems based on EVA. The primary rationale is that EVA is linked both theoretically and empirically to shareholder wealth.

Industry data to be used in comparative analyses can be found in external sources such as Dun & Bradstreet's *Key Business Ratios*, Robert Morris Associates' *Annual Statement Studies*, and *The Value Line Investment Survey*. Larger firms will generally create their own comparative data using a computerized data base supplied by a financial services firm.

Financial statement analysis is useful, but there are a number of limitations which analysts must recognize.

- Ratios are often not useful for analyzing the operations of conglomerate firms which operate in many different industries because comparative ratios are from single industries.

- The use of industry averages may not provide a very challenging target for high-level performance.

- Inflation affects depreciation charges, inventory costs, and therefore the value of both balance sheet items and net income. For this reason, the analysis of a firm over time, or a comparative analysis of firms of different ages, can be misleading. Also, ratios may be distorted by seasonal factors.

- Different operating policies, such as the decision to lease rather than to buy equipment, may have an impact on financial ratios. Information on the firm's noncapitalized lease agreements, on its pension plan, on its recent acquisitions and divestitures, on its accounting policies, and so forth, can be found in the notes to the financial statements and should be considered by the analyst.

- Many ratios can be interpreted in different ways, and whether a particular ratio is "good" or "bad" should be based upon a complete financial analysis rather than the level of a single ratio at a single point in time.

- Different accounting practices can distort ratio comparisons. However, most firms in a given industry use similar procedures.

- Window dressing is sometimes used to make financial statements look better to analysts.

SELF-TEST QUESTIONS

Definitional

1. Of all its communications with shareholders, a firm's _____ report is generally the most important.

2. The income statement reports the results of operations during the past year, the most important item being _____ _____ _____.

3. The _____ _____ lists the firm's assets as well as claims against those assets.

4. Typically, assets are listed in order of their _____, while liabilities are listed in the order in which they must be paid.

5. Assets – Liabilities – Preferred stock = _____ worth, or _____ _____ equity.

6. The three accounts which normally make up the common equity section of the balance sheet are common stock, _____ - ___ capital, and _____ _____.

7. _____ _____ as reported on the balance sheet represent income earned by the firm in past years that has not been paid out as dividends.

8. Retained earnings are generally reinvested in _____ _____ and are not held in the form of cash.

9. The _____ ____ _____ _____ is designed to show how the firm's operations have affected its cash position.

10. The three major categories of the Statement of Cash Flows are cash flows associated with _____ activities, _____-_____ _____ activities, and _____ activities.

11. The current ratio and acid-test ratio are examples of _____ ratios. They measure a firm's ability to meet its _____-_____ obligations.

12. The days sales outstanding (DSO) ratio is found by dividing average sales per day into accounts _____. The DSO is the length of time that a firm must wait after making a sale before it receives _____.

13. Debt management ratios are used to evaluate a firm's use of financial _____.

14. The debt ratio, which is the ratio of _____ _____ to _____ _____, measures the proportion of funds supplied by creditors.

15. The _____-_____-_____ ratio is calculated by dividing earnings before interest and taxes by the amount of interest charges.

16. The combined effects of liquidity, asset management, and debt management are measured by _____ ratios.

17. Dividing net income by sales gives the _____ _____ on sales.

18. The _____/_____ ratio measures how much investors are willing to pay for each dollar of a firm's current income.

19. Firms with higher rates of return on stockholders' equity tend to sell at relatively high ratios of _____ price to _____ value.

20. Individual ratios are of little value in analyzing a company's financial condition. More important are the _____ of a ratio over time and the comparison of the company's ratios to _____ average ratios.

21. The ___ _____ equation shows how debt utilization, total assets turnover, and profit margin combine to produce return on equity.

22. Return on assets is a function of two variables, the profit _____ and _____ _____ turnover.

23. Analyzing a particular ratio over time for an individual firm is known as _____ analysis.

24. To create _____ _____ _____, all income statement items are divided by sales, and all balance sheet items are divided by total assets.

25. In _____ _____ _____, growth rates are calculated for all income statement items and balance sheet accounts.

26. Two non-accounting measures that are widely used to measure profitability and assess managerial performance are _____ _____ _____ and _____ _____ _____.

27. Shareholder wealth is maximized by maximizing the difference between the market value of equity and the amount of equity capital that investors have supplied to the firm. The difference is called _____ _____ _____.

28. The basic formula for _____ _____ _____ is operating profit minus cost of capital.

Conceptual

29. The equity multiplier can be expressed as 1 – (Debt/Assets).

   a. True   b. False

30. A high quick ratio is *always* a good indication of a well-managed liquidity position.

   a. True   b. False

31. International Appliances Inc. has a current ratio of 0.5. Which of the following actions would improve (increase) this ratio?

    a. Use cash to pay off current liabilities.
    b. Collect some of the current accounts receivable.
    c. Use cash to pay off some long-term debt.
    d. Purchase additional inventory on credit (accounts payable).
    e. Sell some of the existing inventory at cost.

32. Refer to Self-Test Question 31. Assume that International Appliances has a current ratio of 1.2. Now, which of the following actions would improve (increase) this ratio?

    a. Use cash to pay off current liabilities.
    b. Collect some of the current accounts receivable.
    c. Use cash to pay off some long-term debt.
    d. Purchase additional inventory on credit (accounts payable).
    e. Use cash to pay for some fixed assets.

33. Examining the ratios of a particular firm against the same measures for a group of firms from the same industry, at a point in time, is an example of

    a. Trend analysis.
    b. Comparative analysis.
    c. Du Pont analysis.
    d. Simple ratio analysis.
    e. Industry analysis.

34. Which of the following statements is most *correct*?

a. Having a high current ratio and a high quick ratio is always a good indication that a firm is managing its liquidity position well.

b. A decline in the inventory turnover ratio suggests that the firm's liquidity position is improving.

c. If a firm's times-interest-earned ratio is relatively high, then this is one indication that the firm should be able to meet its debt obligations.

d. Since ROA measures the firm's effective utilization of assets (without considering how these assets are financed), two firms with the same EBIT must have the same ROA.

e. If, through specific managerial actions, a firm has been able to increase its ROA, then, because of the fixed mathematical relationship between ROA and ROE, it must also have increased its ROE.

35. Which of the following statements is most *correct*?

a. Suppose two firms with the same amount of assets pay the same interest rate on their debt and earn the same rate of return on their assets and that ROA is positive. However, one firm has a higher debt ratio. Under these conditions, the firm with the higher debt ratio will also have a higher rate of return on common equity.

b. One of the problems of ratio analysis is that the relationships are subject to manipulation. For example, we know that if we use some cash to pay off some of our current liabilities, the current ratio will always increase, especially if the current ratio is weak initially, for example, below 1.0.

c. Generally, firms with high profit margins have high asset turnover ratios and firms with low profit margins have low turnover ratios; this result is exactly as predicted by the Du Pont equation.

d. Firms A and B have identical earnings and identical dividend payout ratios. If Firm A's growth rate is higher than Firm B's, then Firm A's P/E ratio must be greater than Firm B's P/E ratio.

e. Each of the above statements is false.

SELF-TEST PROBLEMS

(The following financial statements apply to the next six problems.)

Roberts Manufacturing Balance Sheet
December 31, 1996
(Dollars in Thousands)

Cash	$ 200	Accounts payable	$ 205
Receivables	245	Notes payable	425
Inventory	625	Other current liabilities	115
Total current assets	$1,070	Total current liabilities	$ 745
Net fixed assets	1,200	Long-term debt	420
		Common equity	1,105
Total assets	$2,270	Total liabilities and equity	$2,270

Roberts Manufacturing
Income Statement for Year Ended December 31, 1996
(Dollars in Thousands)

Sales		$2,400
Cost of goods sold:		
Materials	$1,000	
Labor	600	
Heat, light, and power	89	
Indirect labor	65	
Depreciation	80	1,834
Gross profit		$ 566
Selling expenses		175
General and administrative expenses		216
Earnings before interest and taxes (EBIT)		$ 175
Less interest expense		35
Earnings before taxes (EBT)		$ 140
Less taxes (40%)		56
Net income (NI)		$ 84

1. Calculate the liquidity ratios, that is, the current ratio and the quick ratio.

    a. 1.20; 0.60   **b.** 1.20; 0.80   **c.** 1.44; 0.60   **d.** 1.44; 0.80   **e.** 1.60; 0.60

2. Calculate the asset management ratios, that is, the inventory turnover ratio, fixed assets turnover, total assets turnover, and days sales outstanding.

    a. 3.84; 2.00; 1.06; 36.75 days   **d.** 3.84; 2.00; 1.24; 34.10 days
    b. 3.84; 2.00; 1.06; 35.25 days   **e.** 3.84; 2.20; 1.48; 34.10 days
    c. 3.84; 2.00; 1.06; 34.10 days

3. Calculate the debt management ratios, that is, the debt and times-interest-earned ratios.

    a. 0.39; 3.16   **b.** 0.39; 5.00   **c.** 0.51; 3.16   **d.** 0.51; 5.00   **e.** 0.73; 3.16

4. Calculate the profitability ratios, that is, the profit margin on sales, return on total assets, return on common equity, and basic earning power of assets.

    a. 3.50%; 4.25%; 7.60%; 8.00%   **d.** 3.70%; 3.50%; 8.00%; 8.00%
    b. 3.50%; 3.70%; 7.60%; 7.71%   **e.** 4.25%; 3.70%; 7.60%; 8.00%
    c. 3.70%; 3.50%; 7.60%; 7.71%

5. Calculate the market value ratios, that is, the price/earnings ratio and the market/book value ratio. Roberts had an average of 10,000 shares outstanding during 1996, and the stock price on December 31, 1996, was $40.00.

    a. 4.21; 0.36   **b.** 3.20; 1.54   **c.** 3.20; 0.36   **d.** 4.76; 1.54   **e.** 4.76; 0.36

6. Use the Du Pont equation to determine Roberts' return on equity.

    a. 6.90%   **b.** 7.24%   **c.** 7.47%   **d.** 7.60%   **e.** 8.41%

7. Lewis Inc. has sales of $2 million per year, all of which are credit sales. Its days sales outstanding is 42 days. What is its average accounts receivable balance?

    a. $233,333   **b.** $266,667   **c.** $333,333   **d.** $350,000   **e.** $366,667

8. Southeast Jewelers Inc. sells only on credit. Its days sales outstanding is 60 days, and its average accounts receivable balance is $500,000. What are its sales for the year?

   a. $1,500,000   **b.** $3,000,000   **c.** $2,000,000   **d.** $2,750,000   **e.** $3,225,000

9. A firm has total interest charges of $20,000 per year, sales of $2 million, a tax rate of 40 percent, and a profit margin of 6 percent. What is the firm's times-interest-earned ratio?

   a. 10   **b.** 11   **c.** 12   **d.** 13   **e.** 14

10. Refer to Self-Test Problem 9. What is the firm's TIE, if its profit margin decreases to 3 percent and its interest charges double to $40,000 per year?

    a. 3.0   **b.** 2.5   **c.** 3.5   **d.** 4.2   **e.** 3.7

11. A fire has destroyed many of the financial records at Anderson Associates. You are assigned to piece together information to prepare a financial report. You have found that the firm's return on equity is 12 percent and its debt ratio is 0.40. What is its return on assets?

    a. 4.90%   **b.** 5.35%   **c.** 6.60%   **d.** 7.20%   **e.** 8.40%

12. Refer to Self-Test Problem 11. What is the firm's debt ratio if its ROE is 15 percent and its ROA is 10 percent?

    a. 67%   **b.** 50%   **c.** 25%   **d.** 33%   **e.** 45%

13. Rowe and Company has a debt ratio of 0.50, a total assets turnover of 0.25, and a profit margin of 10 percent. The president is unhappy with the current return on equity, and he thinks it could be doubled. This could be accomplished (1) by increasing the profit margin to 14 percent and (2) by increasing debt utilization. Total assets turnover will not change. What new debt ratio, along with the 14 percent profit margin, is required to double the return on equity?

    a. 0.55   **b.** 0.60   **c.** 0.65   **d.** 0.70   **e.** 0.75

14. Altman Corporation has $1,000,000 of debt outstanding, and it pays an interest rate of 12 percent annually. Altman's annual sales are $4 million, its federal-plus-state tax rate is 25 percent, and its net profit margin on sales is 10 percent. If the company does not maintain a TIE ratio of at least 5 times, its bank will refuse to renew the loan, and bankruptcy will result. What is Altman's TIE ratio?

    a. 3.33   **b.** 4.44   **c.** 2.50   **d.** 4.00   **e.** 5.44

15. Refer to Self-Test Problem 14. What is the maximum amount Altman's EBIT could decrease and its bank still renew its loan?

    a. $53,333   **b.** $45,432   **c.** $66,767   **d.** $47,898   **e.** $57,769

16. Pinkerton Packaging's ROE last year was 2.5 percent, but its management has developed a new operating plan designed to improve things. The new plan calls for a total debt ratio of 50 percent, which will result in interest charges of $240 per year. Management projects an EBIT of $800 on sales of $8,000, and it expects to have a total assets turnover ratio of 1.6. Under these conditions, the federal-plus-state tax rate will be 40 percent. If the changes are made, what return on equity will Pinkerton earn?

    a. 12.50%   **b.** 13.44%   **c.** 13.00%   **d.** 14.02%   **e.** 14.57%

(The following financial statement applies to the next three problems.)

Baker Corporation Balance Sheet
December 31, 1996

Cash and marketable securities	$ 50	Accounts payable	$ 250
Accounts receivable	200	Accruals	250
Inventory	250	Notes payable	500
Total current assets	$ 500	Total current liabilities	$1,000
Net fixed assets	1,500	Long-term debt	250
		Common stock	400
		Retained earnings	350
Total assets	$2,000	Total liabilities and equity	$2,000

17. What is Baker Corporation's current ratio as of December 31, 1996?

    a. 0.35   **b.** 0.65   **c.** 0.50   **d.** 0.25   **e.** 0.75

18. If Baker uses $50 of cash to pay off $50 of its accounts payable, what is its new current ratio?

    a. 0.47   **b.** 0.44   **c.** 0.54   **d.** 0.33   **e.** 0.62

19. If Baker uses its $50 cash balance to pay off $50 of its long-term debt, what is its new current ratio?

    a. 0.35   **b.** 0.50   **c.** 0.55   **d.** 0.60   **e.** 0.45

(The following financial statements apply to the next problem.)

Whitney Inc. Balance Sheet
December 31, 1996

Total current assets	$250	Total current liabilities	$100
Fixed assets	500	Long-term debt	250
		Common stockholders' equity	400
Total assets	$750	Total liabilities and equity	$750

Whitney Inc. Income Statement
for Year Ended December 31, 1996

Sales		$1,000
Cost of goods sold (excluding depreciation)	$550	
Other operating expenses	100	
Depreciation	50	
Total operating costs		700
Earnings before interest and taxes (EBIT)		$ 300
Less interest expense		25
Earnings before taxes (EBT)		$ 275
Less taxes (40%)		110
Net income		$ 165

20. What are Whitney Inc.'s basic earning power and ROA ratios?

a. 30%; 22%   **b.** 40%; 30%   **c.** 50%; 22%   **d.** 40%; 22%   **e.** 40%; 40%

(The following financial statements apply to the next problem.)

Cotner Enterprises Balance Sheet
December 31, 1996

Total current assets	$ 417	Total current liabilities	$ 300
Fixed assets	833	Long-term debt	500
		Common stockholders' equity	450
Total assets	$1,250	Total liabilities and equity	$1,250

Cotner Enterprises Income Statement
for Year Ended December 31, 1996

Sales		$1,700
Cost of goods sold (excluding depreciation)	$1,190	
Other operating expenses	135	
Depreciation	75	
Total operating costs		1,400
Earnings before interest and taxes (EBIT)		$ 300
Less interest expense		54
Earnings before taxes (EBT)		$ 246
Less taxes (34%)		84
Net income		$ 162

21. What are Cotner Enterprise's basic earning power and ROA ratios?

a. 20%; 12.96%   **d.** 17.5%; 12.96%
b. 24%; 12.96%   **e.** 24%; 10.5%
c. 24%; 15.75%

22. Dauten Enterprises is just being formed. It will need $2 million of assets, and it expects to have an EBIT of $400,000. Dauten will own no securities, so all of its income will be operating income. If it chooses to, Dauten can finance up to 50 percent of its assets with debt which will have a 9 percent interest rate. Dauten has no other liabilities. Assuming a 40 percent federal-plus-state tax rate on all taxable income, what is the difference between the expected ROE if Dauten finances with 50 percent debt versus the expected ROE if it finances entirely with common stock?

    a. 7.2%   **b.** 6.6%   **c.** 6.0%   **d.** 5.8%   **e.** 9.0%

ANSWERS TO SELF-TEST QUESTIONS

1. annual
2. earnings per share
3. balance sheet
4. liquidity
5. Net; Common stockholders'
6. paid-in; retained earnings
7. Retained earnings
8. operating assets
9. Statement of Cash Flows
10. operating; long-term investing; financing
11. liquidity; short-term (or current)
12. receivable; cash
13. leverage
14. total debt; total asset

15. times-interest-earned
16. profitability
17. profit margin
18. price/earnings
19. market; book
20. trend; industry
21. Du Pont
22. margin; total assets
23. trend
24. common size statements
25. percentage change analysis
26. market value added; economic value added
27. market value added
28. economic value added

29. b. 1 − (Debt/Assets) = Equity/Assets. The equity multiplier is equal to Assets/Equity.

30. b. Excess cash resulting from poor management could produce a high quick ratio. Similarly, if accounts receivable are not collected promptly, this could also lead to a high quick ratio.

31. d. This question is best analyzed using numbers. For example, assume current assets equal $50 and current liabilities equal $100; thus, the current ratio equals 0.5. For answer a, assume $5 in cash is used to pay off $5 in current liabilities. The new current ratio would be $45/$95 = 0.47. For answer d, assume a $10 purchase of inventory on credit (accounts payable). The new current ratio would be $60/$110 = 0.55, which is an increase over the old current ratio of 0.5. (Self-Test Problems 17 through 19 were set up to help visualize this question.)

32. a. Again, this question is best analyzed using numbers. For example, assume current assets equal $120 and current liabilities equal $100; thus, the current ratio equals 1.2. For answer a, assume $5 in cash is used to pay off $5 in current liabilities. The new current ratio would be $115/$95 = 1.21, which is an increase over the old current ratio of 1.2. For answer d, assume a $10 purchase of inventory on credit (accounts payable). The new current ratio would be $130/$110 = 1.18, which is a decrease from the old current ratio of 1.2.

33. b. The correct answer is comparative analysis. A trend analysis compares the firm's ratios over time, while a Du Pont analysis shows the relationships among return on equity, assets turnover, profit margin, and leverage.

34. c. Excess cash resulting from poor management could produce high current and quick ratios; thus statement a is false. A decline in the inventory turnover ratio suggests that either sales have decreased or inventory has increased—which suggests that the firm's liquidity position is *not* improving; thus statement b is false. ROA = Net income/Total assets, and EBIT does not equal net income. Two firms with the same EBIT could have different financing and different taxes resulting in different net incomes. Also, two firms with the same EBIT do not necessarily have the same total assets; thus statement d is false. ROE = ROA × Assets/Equity. If ROA increases because total assets decrease, then the equity multiplier decreases, and depending on which effect is greater, ROE may or may not increase; thus statement e is false. Statement c is correct; the TIE ratio is used to measure whether the firm can meet its debt obligation, and a high TIE ratio would indicate this is so. (Self-Test Problems 20 and 21 were set up to help visualize statement d of this question.)

35. a. Ratio analysis is subject to manipulation; however, if the current ratio is less than 1.0 and we use cash to pay off some current liabilities, the current ratio will decrease, *not* increase; thus statement b is false. Statement c is just the reverse of what actually occurs. Firms with high profit margins have low turnover ratios and vice versa. Statement d is false; it does not necessarily follow that if a firm's growth rate is higher that its stock price will be higher. Statement a is correct. From the information given in statement a, one can determine that the two firms' net incomes are equal; thus, the firm with the higher debt ratio (lower equity ratio) will indeed have a higher ROE.

SOLUTIONS TO SELF-TEST PROBLEMS

1. c. $\text{Current ratio} = \dfrac{\text{Current assets}}{\text{Current liabilities}} = \dfrac{\$1,070}{\$745} = 1.44.$

$\text{Quick ratio} = \dfrac{\text{Current assets} - \text{Inventory}}{\text{Current liabilities}} = \dfrac{\$1,070 - \$625}{\$745} = 0.60.$

2. a. $\text{Inventory turnover} = \dfrac{\text{Sales}}{\text{Inventory}} = \dfrac{\$2,400}{\$625} = 3.84.$

$\text{Fixed assets turnover} = \dfrac{\text{Sales}}{\text{Net fixed assets}} = \dfrac{\$2,400}{\$1,200} = 2.00.$

$\text{Total assets turnover} = \dfrac{\text{Sales}}{\text{Total assets}} = \dfrac{\$2,400}{\$2,270} = 1.06.$

$\text{DSO} = \dfrac{\text{Accounts receivable}}{\text{Sales}/360} = \dfrac{\$245}{\$2,400/360} = 36.75 \text{ days.}$

3. d. $\text{Debt ratio} = \text{Total debt}/\text{Total assets} = \$1,165/\$2,270 = 0.51.$

$\text{TIE ratio} = \text{EBIT}/\text{Interest} = \$175/\$35 = 5.00.$

4. b. $\text{Profit margin} = \dfrac{\text{Net income}}{\text{Sales}} = \dfrac{\$84}{\$2,400} = 0.0350 = 3.50\%.$

$\text{ROA} = \dfrac{\text{Net income}}{\text{Total assets}} = \dfrac{\$84}{\$2,270} = 0.0370 = 3.70\%.$

$\text{ROE} = \dfrac{\text{Net income}}{\text{Common equity}} = \dfrac{\$84}{\$1,105} = 0.0760 = 7.60\%.$

$\text{BEP} = \dfrac{\text{EBIT}}{\text{Total assets}} = \dfrac{\$175}{\$2,270} = 0.0771 = 7.71\%.$

5. e. $\text{EPS} = \dfrac{\text{Net income}}{\text{Number of shares outstanding}} = \dfrac{\$84,000}{10,000} = \$8.40.$

$\text{P/E ratio} = \dfrac{\text{Price}}{\text{EPS}} = \dfrac{\$40.00}{\$8.40} = 4.76.$

$\text{Market/book value} = \dfrac{\text{Market price}}{\text{Book value}} = \dfrac{\$40(10,000)}{\$1,105,000} = 0.36.$

6. d. $\text{ROE} = \text{Profit margin} \times \text{Total assets turnover} \times \text{Equity multiplier}$

$= \dfrac{\$84}{\$2,400} \times \dfrac{\$2,400}{\$2,270} \times \dfrac{\$2,270}{\$1,105} = 0.035 \times 1.057 \times 2.054 = 0.0760 = 7.60\%.$

7. a. $\text{DSO} = \dfrac{\text{Accounts receivable}}{\text{Sales/360}}$

$42 \text{ days} = \dfrac{\text{AR}}{\$2,000,000/360}$

$\text{AR} = \$233,333.$

8. b. $\text{DSO} = \text{Accounts receivable/(Sales/360)}$

$60 \text{ days} = \$500,000/(\text{Sales}/360)$

$60(\text{Sales}/360) = \$500,000$

$\text{Sales} = \$3,000,000.$

9. b. Net income = \$2,000,000(0.06) = \$120,000.
Earnings before taxes = \$120,000/(1 − 0.4) = \$200,000.
EBIT = \$200,000 + \$20,000 = \$220,000.
TIE = EBIT/Interest = \$220,000/\$20,000 = 11.

10. c. Net income= \$2,000,000(0.03) = \$60,000.
Earnings before taxes = \$60,000/(1 − 0.4) = \$100,000.
EBIT = \$100,000 + \$40,000 = \$140,000.
TIE = EBIT/Interest = \$140,000/\$40,000 = 3.5.

11. d. If Total debt/Total assets = 0.40, then Total equity/Total assets = 0.60, and the equity multiplier (Assets/Equity) = 1/0.60 = 1.667.

$$\frac{NI}{E} = \frac{NI}{A} \times \frac{A}{E}$$

ROE = ROA × EM

12% = ROA × 1.667

ROA = 7.20%.

12. d. ROE = ROA × Equity multiplier

15% = 10% × TA/Equity

1.5 = TA/Equity

Equity/TA = 0.67.

Debt/TA = 1 − Equity/TA = 1 − 0.67 = 0.33 = 33%.

13. c. If Total debt/Total assets = 0.50, then Total equity/Total assets = 0.50 and the equity multiplier (Assets/Equity) = 1/0.50 = 2.0.

ROE = PM × Total assets turnover × EM.

Before: ROE = 10% × 0.25 × 2.00 = 5.00%.

After: 10.00% = 14% × 0.25 × EM; thus EM = 2.8571.

$$\text{Equity multiplier} = \frac{\text{Assets}}{\text{Equity}}$$

$$2.8571 = \frac{1}{\text{Equity}}$$

$$0.35 = \text{Equity}.$$

Debt = Assets − Equity = 100% − 35% = 65%.

14. e. TIE = EBIT/Interest, so find EBIT and Interest.

Interest = $1,000,000(0.12) = $120,000.

Net income = $4,000,000(0.10) = $400,000.

Pre-tax income = $400,000/(1 − T) = $400,000/(0.75) = $533,333.

EBIT = $533,333 + $120,000 = $653,333.

TIE = $653,333/$120,000 = 5.44×.

15. a. TIE = EBIT/INT
         5 = EBIT/$120,000
         EBIT = $600,000.

         From Self-Test Problem 14, EBIT = $653,333, so EBIT could decrease by $653,333 –
         $600,000 = $53,333.

16. b. ROE = Profit margin × Total assets turnover × Equity multiplier
             = NI/Sales × Sales/TA × TA/Equity.

         Now we need to determine the inputs for the equation from the data that were given. On
         the left we set up an income statement, and we put numbers in it on the right:

Sales (given)	$8,000
– Cost	NA
EBIT (given)	$ 800
– Interest (given)	240
EBT	$ 560
– Taxes (40%)	224
Net income	$ 336

         Now we can use some ratios to get some more data:

         Total assets turnover = S/TA = 1.6.

         D/A = 50%, so E/A = 50%, and therefore TA/E = 1/(E/A) = 1/0.5 = 2.00.

         Now we can complete the Du Pont equation to determine ROE:

         ROE = $336/$8,000 × 1.6 × 2.0 = 13.44%.

17. c. Baker Corporation's current ratio equals Total current assets/Total current liabilities =
         $500/$1,000 = 0.50.

18. a. Baker Corporation's new current ratio equals ($500 – $50)/($1,000 – $50) = $450/$950 =
         0.47.

19. e. Only the current asset balance is affected by this action. Baker's new current ratio = ($500 − $50)/$1,000 = $450/$1,000 = 0.45.

20. d. Whitney's BEP ratio equals EBIT/Total assets = $300/$750 = 40%.
Whitney's ROA equals Net income/Total assets = $165/$750 = 22%.

21. b. Cotner's BEP ratio equals EBIT/Total assets = $300/$1,250 = 24%.
Cotner's ROA equals Net income/Total assets = $162/$1,250 = 12.96%.

22. b. Known data: Total assets = $2,000,000, EBIT = $400,000, k_d = 9%, T = 40%.

D/A = 0.5 = 50%, so Debt = 0.5($2,000,000) = $1,000,000. Equity = Total assets - Debt = $2,000,000 - $1,000,000 = $1,000,000. At a 9 percent interest rate, INT = 0.09($1,000,000) = $90,000.

	D/A = 0%	D/A = 50%
EBIT	$400,000	$400,000
Interest	0	90,000
Taxable income	$400,000	$310,000
Taxes (40%)	160,000	124,000
Net income (NI)	$240,000	$186,000

For D/A = 0%, ROE = NI/Equity = $240,000/$2,000,000 = 12%. For D/A = 50%, ROE = $186,000/$1,000,000 = 18.6%. Difference = 18.6% - 12.0% = 6.6%.

CHAPTER 3

THE FINANCIAL ENVIRONMENT: MARKETS, INSTITUTIONS, INTEREST RATES, AND TAXES

OVERVIEW

It is critical that financial managers understand the environment and markets within which they operate. In this chapter, we examine the markets where capital is raised, securities are traded, and stock prices are established. We examine the institutions that operate in these markets and hence through which securities transactions are conducted. In the process, we shall see how money costs are determined, and we shall explore the principal factors that determine both the general level of interest rates in the economy and the interest rate on a particular debt security. We also examine the federal income tax system and its effect on financial management.

OUTLINE

Financial markets bring together people and organizations wanting to borrow money with those having surplus funds. A healthy economy is dependent on efficient transfers of funds from people who are net savers to firms and individuals who need capital.

■ There are many different financial markets in a developed economy, each dealing with a different type of instrument, serving a different set of customers, or operating in a different part of the country.

■ The major types of financial markets include the following:
  □ *Physical asset markets* are the markets for tangible or real assets.
  □ *Financial asset markets* are the markets that deal with stocks, bonds, and other claims on real assets.
  □ *Money markets* are the markets for short-term debt securities, those securities that mature in less than one year.
  □ *Capital markets* are the markets for long-term debt and corporate stocks.

☐ *Primary markets* are the markets in which corporations sell newly issued securities to raise capital.

☐ *Secondary markets* are the markets in which existing, outstanding securities are bought and sold.

Transfers of capital between savers and borrowers take place in three different ways.

■ *Direct transfers* of money and securities occur when a business sells its stock or bonds directly to savers, without going through any type of financial institution.

■ Transfers through an *investment banking house* occur when a brokerage firm, such as Merrill Lynch, serves as a middleman. These middlemen help corporations design securities that will be attractive to investors, buy these securities from the corporations, and then resell them to savers in the primary markets.

■ Transfers through a *financial intermediary* occur when a bank or mutual fund obtains funds from savers, issues its own securities in exchange, and then uses these funds to purchase other securities.

☐ Some major classes of intermediaries include commercial banks, savings and loan (S&L) associations, mutual savings banks, credit unions, mutual funds, pension funds, and life insurance companies.

☐ Ongoing regulatory changes have resulted in a blurring of distinctions between the different types of financial institutions. As a result, in the United States the trend has been toward huge *financial service corporations*, which own any number of financial intermediaries with national and even global operations.

The stock market is one of the most important markets to financial managers because it is here that the price of each stock, and hence the value of all publicly-owned firms, is established. There are two basic types of stock markets.

■ The *organized exchanges*, typified by the New York Stock Exchange (NYSE) and the American Stock Exchange (AMEX), are tangible, physical entities.

■ The *over-the-counter (OTC) market* is, basically, all the dealers, brokers, and communications facilities that provide for security transactions not conducted on the organized exchanges.

■ There has been a rise in the so-called "third market," where large financial institutions use computers to trade both listed and unlisted stocks among themselves on a 24-hour basis. Buyers and sellers in this market are located all around the globe.

Capital in a free economy is allocated through the price system. The interest rate is the price paid to borrow debt capital, whereas in the case of equity capital, investors expect to receive dividends and capital gains.

■ The four most fundamental factors affecting the cost of money are *production opportunities, time preferences for consumption, risk,* and *inflation.*

■ The rate of return producers expect on their business investments sets an upper limit on how much they can pay for savings, while consumers' time preferences for consumption establish how much consumption they are willing to defer, hence how much they will save at different levels of interest offered by producers. Higher risk and higher inflation also lead to higher interest rates.

■ Firms with the most profitable investment opportunities are willing and able to pay the most for capital, so they tend to attract it away from inefficient firms or from those whose products are not in demand.

The quoted (or nominal) interest rate on a debt security, k, is composed of a real risk-free rate of interest, k*, plus several premiums that reflect inflation, the riskiness of the security, and the security's marketability: $k = k^* + IP + DRP + LP + MRP$.

■ The *real risk-free rate of interest (k*)* is the interest rate that would exist on a riskless security if no inflation were expected, and it may be thought of as the rate of interest that would exist on short-term U.S. Treasury securities in an inflation-free world.

■ The *nominal, or quoted, risk-free rate of interest* (k_{RF}) is the real risk-free rate plus a premium for expected inflation: $k_{RF} = k^* + IP$. The actual rate of interest on short-term Treasury bills is normally used to measure k_{RF}, although the rate on long-term Treasury bonds is also used.

■ The *inflation premium (IP),* which is the average inflation rate expected over the life of the security, compensates investors for the expected loss of purchasing power.

■ The *default risk premium (DRP)* compensates investors for the risk that a borrower will default and hence not pay the interest or principal on a loan.

■ A security which can be sold and quickly converted into cash at a fair market value is said to be *liquid*. A *liquidity premium (LP)* is also added to the real rate for securities that are not liquid.

■ Long-term securities are more price sensitive to interest rate changes than are short-term securities. Therefore, a *maturity risk premium (MRP)* is added to longer-term securities to compensate investors for interest rate risk.

The term structure of interest rates is the relationship between yield to maturity and time to maturity for bonds of a given default risk class.

■ When plotted, this relationship produces a *yield curve*.

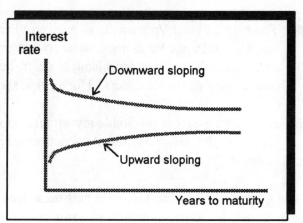

■ Yield curves have different shapes depending on expected inflation rates and supply and demand conditions.
  □ The "normal" yield curve is *upward sloping* because investors charge higher rates on longer term bonds, even when inflation is expected to remain constant.
  □ An inverted, or *downward sloping*, yield curve signifies that investors expect inflation to decrease.

Three theories have been proposed to explain the shape of the yield curve, or the term structure of interest rates.

■ The *expectations theory* states that the yield curve depends on expectations about future inflation rates. If the rate of inflation is expected to decline, the curve will be downward sloping, and if the rate of inflation is expected to increase, the curve will be upward sloping.

■ The *liquidity preference theory* states that long-term bonds normally yield more than short-term bonds (that is, the yield curve tends to be upward sloping) for two reasons:
  □ Investors prefer short-term to long-term securities due to the interest rate risk associated with long-term securities. Investors will, therefore, generally accept lower yields on short-term securities.

☐ Borrowers generally prefer long-term debt because short-term debt exposes them to the risk of having to repay the debt under adverse conditions. Accordingly, borrowers are willing to pay a higher rate, other things held constant, for long-term funds than for short-term funds.

■ The *market segmentation theory* states that the slope of the yield curve depends on supply and demand conditions in the long-term and short-term markets. Under this theory, the curve could, at any time, be either upward or downward sloping.

■ Various test of the term structure theories indicate all three theories have merit; that is, actual yield curves are influenced by all three sets of factors. However, these tests also indicate that inflation, hence the expectations theory, has the strongest influence.

There are other factors that influence both the general level of interest rates and the shape of the yield curve.

■ Expansionary monetary policy (growth in monetary supply) by the Federal Reserve initially lowers the interest rate but inflationary pressures could cause a rise in the interest rate in the long term. Contractionary monetary policy has the opposite effect.

■ Federal budget deficits drive interest rates up due to increased demand for loanable funds, while surpluses drive rates down due to increased supply of loanable funds.

■ Foreign trade deficits push interest rates up because deficits must be financed from abroad and rates must be high enough relative to world interest rates to draw foreign investors.

■ In relation to the business cycle, there is a general tendency for interest rates to decline during a recession.

The level of interest rates also has a significant effect on stock prices.

■ Since interest is a cost to companies, interest rates have a direct effect on corporate profits.

■ Stocks and bonds compete in the marketplace for investors' capital. Therefore, a rise in interest rates will increase the rate of return on bonds, causing investors to transfer funds from the stock market to the bond market. The resultant selling of stocks lowers stock prices.

Interest rate movements have a significant impact on business decisions.

■ Wrong decisions, such as using short-term debt to finance long-term projects just before interest rates rise, can be very costly.

■ It is extremely difficult, if not impossible, to predict future interest rate levels.

■ Sound financial policy calls for using a mix of long-term and short-term debt, and equity, so that the firm can survive in almost any interest rate environment.

Individuals pay taxes on wages and salaries, on investment income (dividends, interest, and profits from the sale of securities), and on the profits of proprietorships and partnerships.

■ U.S. income taxes are *progressive*; that is, the higher the income, the larger the percentage paid in taxes. *Marginal tax rates* begin at 15 percent and can go up to 39.6 percent.
  □ The marginal tax rate is the tax applicable to the last unit of income.
  □ The *average tax rate* is calculated as taxes paid divided by taxable income.

■ Because dividends are paid from corporate income that has already been taxed (at rates going up as high as 39 percent), there is double taxation of corporate income. Interest on most state and local government securities, which are often called "municipals," is not subject to federal income taxes. This creates a strong incentive for individuals in high tax brackets to purchase such securities.

■ Gains and losses on the sale of *capital assets* such as stocks, bonds, and real estate have historically received special tax treatment. Currently, all *long-term capital gains* income is taxed as if it were ordinary income, with a maximum tax rate capped at 28 percent.

Corporations pay taxes on profits.

■ Corporate tax rates are also progressive up to $18,333,333 of taxable income, but are constant thereafter. Marginal tax rates range from 15 to 39 percent.

■ Interest and dividend income received by a corporation are taxed.
  □ Interest is taxed as ordinary income at regular corporate tax rates.
  □ However, 70 percent of the dividends received by one corporation from another is excluded from taxable income. The remaining 30 percent is taxed at the ordinary rate. Thus, the effective tax rate on dividends received by a 35 percent marginal tax bracket corporation is $0.30(35\%) = 10.5\%$.

- The tax system favors debt financing over equity financing.
  - ☐ Interest paid is a tax-deductible business expense.
  - ☐ Dividends on common and preferred stock are not deductible. Thus, a 40 percent federal-plus-state tax bracket corporation must earn $1/(1.0 - 0.40) = $1/0.60 = $1.67 before taxes to pay $1 of dividends, but only $1 of pretax income is required to pay $1 of interest.

- Before 1987, long-term corporate capital gains were taxed at lower rates than ordinary income. However, at present, long-term capital gains are taxed as ordinary income.

- Ordinary corporate operating losses can be carried back to each of the preceding 3 years and forward for the next 15 years in the future to offset taxable income in those years. The purpose of permitting this loss treatment is to avoid penalizing corporations whose incomes fluctuate substantially from year to year.

- The Internal Revenue Code imposes a penalty on corporations that improperly accumulate earnings if the purpose of the accumulation is to enable stockholders to avoid personal income tax on dividends.

- If a corporation owns 80 percent or more of another corporation's stock, it can aggregate profits and losses and file a consolidated tax return. Thus, losses in one area can offset profits in another.

- Small businesses which meet certain restrictions may be set up as *S corporations* which receive benefits of the corporate form—especially limited liability—yet are taxed as proprietorships or partnerships rather than as corporations. This treatment would be preferred by owners of small corporations in which all or most of the income earned each year is distributed as dividends because the income would be taxed only once at the individual level.

SELF-TEST QUESTIONS

Definitional

1. Markets for short-term debt securities are called _____ markets, while markets for long-term debt and equity are called _____ markets.

2. Firms raise capital by selling newly issued securities in the _____ markets, while existing, outstanding securities are traded in the _____ markets.

3. An institution which issues its own securities in exchange for funds and then uses these funds to purchase other securities is called a financial _____.

4. A(n) _____ _____ firm facilitates the transfer of capital between savers and borrowers by acting as a middleman.

5. The two basic types of stock markets are the _____ _____, such as the NYSE, and the _____-____-_____ market.

6. The risk that a borrower will not pay the interest or principal on a loan is _____ risk.

7. _____ _____ _____ bonds have zero default risk.

8. A(n) _____ premium is added to the real risk-free rate to protect investors against loss of purchasing power.

9. The nominal rate of interest is determined by adding a(n) _____ premium plus a(n) _____ risk premium plus a(n) _____ premium plus a(n) _____ risk premium to the real risk-free rate of return.

10. The relationship between yield to maturity and time to maturity for bonds in a given default risk class is called the _____ _____ of interest rates, while the resulting plotted curve is the _____ curve.

11. The "normal" yield curve has a(n) _____ slope.

12. Three theories have been proposed to explain the term structure of interest rates. They are the market _____ theory, the _____ preference theory, and the _____ theory.

13. Because interest rates fluctuate, a sound financial policy calls for using a mix of _____-_____ and _____-_____ debt and _____.

14. A(n) _____ tax system is one in which tax rates are higher at higher levels of income.

15. A progressive tax structure, which when combined with inflation increases the government's share of GNP without any change in tax rates, is called _____ _____.

16. The marginal tax rate on the largest corporations, those with taxable incomes exceeding $18,333,333, is ___ percent, while that on the wealthiest individuals can go up as high as ___ percent.

17. Interest received on _____ bonds is generally not subject to federal income taxes. This feature makes them particularly attractive to investors in _____ tax brackets.

18. In order to qualify as a long-term capital gain or loss, an asset must be held for more than ___ months.

19. Gains or losses on assets held less than one year are referred to as _____ - _____ transactions.

20. Interest income received by a corporation is taxed as _____ income. However, only ___ percent of dividends received from another corporation is subject to taxation.

21. Another important distinction exists between interest and dividends paid by a corporation. Interest payments are ____ _____, while dividend payments are not.

22. Ordinary corporate operating losses can first be carried back ___ years and then forward ___ years.

23. A firm that refuses to pay dividends in order to help stockholders avoid personal income taxes may be subject to a penalty for _____ _____ of earnings.

24. A corporation that owns 80 percent or more of another corporation's stock may choose to file _____ tax returns.

25. The Tax Code permits a corporation (that meets certain restrictions) to be taxed at the owners' personal tax rates and to avoid the impact of _____ taxation of dividends. This type of corporation is called a(n) ____ corporation.

Conceptual

26. If management is sure that the economy is at the peak of a boom and is about to enter a recession, a firm which needs to borrow money should probably use short-term rather than long-term debt.

    a. True   **b.** False

27. Long-term interest rates reflect expectations about future inflation. Inflation has varied greatly from year to year over the last 10 years, and, as a result, long-term rates have fluctuated more than short-term rates.

    a. True   **b.** False

28. The fact that 70 percent of intercorporate dividends received by a corporation is excluded from taxable income has encouraged debt financing over equity financing.

    a. True   **b.** False

29. Suppose the Fed takes actions which lower expectations for inflation this year by 1 percentage point, but these same actions raise expectations for inflation in Years 2 and thereafter by 2 percentage points. Other things held constant, the yield curve becomes steeper.

    a. True   **b.** False

30. An individual with substantial personal wealth and income is considering the possibility of opening a new business. The business will have a relatively high degree of risk, and losses may be incurred for the first several years. Which legal form of business organization would probably be best?

    a. Proprietorship   **d.** S corporation
    b. Corporation   **e.** Limited partnership
    c. Partnership

31. Assume interest rates on 30-year government and corporate bonds were as follows: T-bond = 6.5%: AAA = 7.3%; A = 7.8%; BBB = 8.6%. The differences in rates among these issues are caused primarily by:

a. Tax effects.

b. Default risk differences.

c. Maturity risk differences.

d. Inflation differences.

e. Both b and d.

32. Which of the following statements is most *correct*?

a. The introduction of a new technology, such as computers, might be expected to improve labor productivity, making businesses more able and willing to pay a higher price for capital. This would put upward pressure on interest rates. However, the productivity improvements might give rise to lower inflationary expectations, which would put downward pressure on interest rates. Thus, the net effect of the new technology on interest rates might be uncertain.

b. If future inflation were expected to remain constant at 6 percent for all future years, then for all bonds (government and corporate combined) we could measure the maturity risk premium as the difference between the yields on 30-year and 1-year bonds.

c. If investors expect the inflation rate to *decrease* over time, e.g., the expected inflation rate in Year t exceeds the expected rate in Year t+1 for all values of t, then we can be *certain* that the yield curve for U.S. Treasury securities will be downward sloping.

d. Each of the above statements is correct.

e. Statements a and c are both correct.

33. Which of the following statements is most *correct*?

   a. Suppose financial institutions, such as savings and loans, were required by law to make long-term, fixed interest rate mortgages, but, at the same time, they were largely restricted, in terms of their capital sources, to taking deposits that could be withdrawn on demand. Under these conditions, these financial institutions should prefer a "normal" yield curve to an inverted curve.

   b. You are considering establishing a new firm, the University Assistance Company (UAC). UAC would obtain funds in the short-term money market and write long-term mortgage loans to students so that they might buy condominiums rather than rent. A downward sloping yield curve, if it persisted over time, would be best for UAC.

   c. The yield curve is upward sloping, or normal, if short-term rates are higher than long-term rates.

   d. All of the above statements are correct.

   e. Only statements a and b are correct.

34. Which of the following statements is most *correct*?

   a. In order to avoid double taxation and to escape the frequently higher tax rate applied to capital gains, stockholders generally prefer to have corporations pay dividends rather than to retain their earnings and reinvest the money in the business. Thus, earnings should be retained only if the firm needs capital very badly and would have difficulty raising it from external sources.

   b. Under our current tax laws, when investors pay taxes on their dividend income, they are being subjected to a form of double taxation.

   c. The fact that a percentage of the interest received by one corporation, which is paid by another corporation, is excluded from taxable income has encouraged firms to use more debt financing relative to equity financing.

   d. If the tax laws stated that $0.50 out of every $1.00 of interest paid by a corporation was allowed as a tax-deductible expense, this would probably encourage companies to use more debt financing than they presently do, other things held constant.

   e. Statements b and d are both correct.

35. Which of the following statements is most *correct*?

   a. One of the major benefits of well-developed stock markets such as the New York Stock Exchange is that they increase liquidity, which makes it easier for firms to raise capital.
   b. In the United States, we have a number of specialized financial institutions, but, according to the text, the trend is toward larger, more diversified institutions which offer broad arrays of financial services.
   c. If the expected rate of inflation rose by 2 percentage points, from 5 to 7 percent, then the *real* risk-free rate (k*) would also rise by 2 percentage points.
   d. Statements a, b, and c are all true.
   e. Only statements a and b are true.

SELF-TEST PROBLEMS

1. You have determined the following data for a given bond: Real risk-free rate (k*) = 3%; inflation premium = 8%; default risk premium = 2%; liquidity premium = 2%; and maturity risk premium = 1%. What is the nominal risk-free rate, k_{RF}?

   a. 10%   **b.** 11%   **c.** 12%   **d.** 13%   **e.** 14%

2. Refer to Self-Test Problem 1. What is the interest rate on long-term Treasury securities, or T-bonds, of the relevant maturity?

   a. 10%   **b.** 11%   **c.** 12%   **d.** 13%   **e.** 14%

3. Assume that a 3-year Treasury note has no maturity risk nor liquidity risk and that the real risk-free rate of interest falls to 2 percent. A 3-year T-note carries a yield to maturity of 12 percent. If the expected inflation rate is 12 percent for the coming year and 10 percent the year after, what is the implied expected inflation rate for the third year?

   a. 8%   **b.** 9%   **c.** 10%   **d.** 11%   **e.** 12%

4. Assume that the real risk-free rate is 2 percent, that the expected inflation rate during Year 2 is 3 percent, and that 2-year T-bonds yield 5.5 percent. If the maturity risk premium is zero, what is the inflation rate during Year 1?

   a. 3.0%   **b.** 5.0%   **c.** 3.5%   **d.** 4.0%   **e.** 2.5%

5. Refer to Self-Test Problem 4. Given the same information, what is the rate of return on 1-year T-bonds?

   a. 5.5%   **b.** 6.0%   **c.** 5.0%   **d.** 6.5%   **e.** 4.5%

6. Wayne Corporation had income from operations of $385,000, it received interest payments of $15,000, it paid interest of $20,000, it received dividends from another corporation of $10,000, and it paid $40,000 in dividends to its common stockholders. What is Wayne's federal income tax?

   a. $122,760   **b.** $130,220   **c.** $141,700   **d.** $155,200   **e.** $163,500

7. A firm purchases $10 million of corporate bonds which paid a 16 percent interest rate, or $1.6 million in interest. If the firm's marginal tax rate is 35 percent, what is the after-tax interest yield?

   a. 7.36%   **b.** 8.64%   **c.** 10.40%   **d.** 13.89%   **e.** 14.32%

8. Refer to Self-Test Problem 7. The firm also invests in the common stock of another company having a 16 percent before-tax dividend yield. What is the after-tax dividend yield?

   a. 7.36%   **b.** 8.64%   **c.** 10.40%   **d.** 13.89%   **e.** 14.32%

9. The Carter Company's taxable income and income tax payments are shown below for 1993 through 1996:

Year	Taxable Income	Tax Payment
1993	$10,000	$1,500
1994	5,000	750
1995	10,000	1,500
1996	5,000	750

   Assume that Carter's tax rate for all 4 years was a flat 15 percent; that is, each dollar of taxable income was taxed at 15 percent. In 1997, Carter incurred a loss of $17,000. Using corporate loss carry-back, what is Carter's adjusted tax payment for 1996?

   a. $850   **b.** $750   **c.** $610   **d.** $550   **e.** $450

10. A firm can undertake a new project which will generate a before-tax return of 20 percent or it can invest the same funds in the preferred stock of another company which yields 13 percent before taxes. If the only consideration is which alternative provides the highest relevant (after-tax) return and the applicable tax rate is 35 percent, should the firm invest in the project or the preferred stock?

    a. Preferred stock; its relevant return is 12 percent.
    b. Project; its relevant return is 1.36 percentage points higher.
    c. Preferred stock; its relevant return is 0.22 percentage points higher.
    d. Project; its before-tax return is 20 percent.
    e. Either alternative can be chosen; they have the same relevant return.

11. Assume that the real risk-free rate, k^*, is 4 percent and that inflation is expected to be 7 percent in Year 1, 4 percent in Year 2, and 3 percent thereafter. Assume also that all Treasury bonds are highly liquid and free of default risk. If 2-year and 5-year Treasury bonds both yield 11 percent, what is the difference in the maturity risk premiums (MRPs) on the two bonds; that is, what is $MRP_5 - MRP_2$?

    a. 0.5%   **b.** 1.0%   **c.** 2.25%   **d.** 1.5%   **e.** 1.25%

12. Cooley Corporation has $20,000 which it plans to invest in marketable securities. It is choosing between MCI bonds which yield 10 percent, state of Colorado municipal bonds which yield 7 percent, and MCI preferred stock with a dividend yield of 8 percent. Cooley's corporate tax rate is 25 percent, and 70 percent of its dividends received are tax exempt. What is the after-tax rate of return on the highest yielding security?

    a. 7.4%   **b.** 7.0%   **c.** 7.5%   **d.** 6.5%   **e.** 6.0%

13. Due to the recession, the rate of inflation expected for the coming year is only 3.5 percent. However, the rate of inflation in Year 2 and thereafter is expected to be constant at some level above 3.5 percent. Assume that the real risk-free rate is $k^* = 2\%$ for all maturities and that the expectations theory fully explains the yield curve, so there are no maturity premiums. If 3-year Treasury bonds yield 3 percentage points (0.03) more than 1-year bonds, what rate of inflation is expected after Year 1?

    a. 4%   **b.** 5%   **c.** 7%   **d.** 6%   **e.** 8%

ANSWERS TO SELF-TEST QUESTIONS

1. money; capital
2. primary; secondary
3. intermediary
4. investment banking
5. organized exchanges;
   over-the-counter (OTC)
6. default
7. U.S. Treasury
8. inflation
9. inflation; default; liquidity; maturity
10. term structure; yield
11. upward
12. segmentation; liquidity; expectations

13. short-term; long-term; equity
14. progressive
15. bracket creep
16. 35; 39.6
17. municipal; high
18. 12
19. short-term
20. ordinary; 30
21. tax deductible
22. 3; 15
23. improper accumulation
24. consolidated
25. double; S

26. a. The firm should borrow short-term until interest rates drop due to the recession, then go long-term. Predicting interest rates is extremely difficult, for managers can rarely be sure about what is going to happen to the economy.

27. b. Fluctuations in long-term rates are smaller because the long-term inflation premium is an average of inflation expectations over many years, and hence the IP on long-term bonds is quite stable relative to the IP on short-term bonds. Also, short-term rates fluctuate as a result of Federal Reserve policy (the Fed intervenes in the short-term rather than the long-term market).

28. b. Debt financing is encouraged by the fact that interest payments are tax deductible while dividend payments are not.

29. a. The yield curve becomes steeper. Although interest rates in Year 1 decrease by 1 percent, interest rates in the following years increase by 2 percent, making the yield curve steeper.

30. d. The S corporation limits the liability of the individual, but permits losses to be deducted against personal income.

31. b. $k = k^* + IP + DRP + LP + MRP$. Since each of these bonds has a 30-year maturity, the MRP and IP would all be equal. Thus, the differences in the interest rates among these issues are the default risk and liquidity premiums.

32. a. Statement b is false because $k = k^* + IP + DRP + LP + MRP$. $k^* + IP$ would be the same for the two bonds; however, the default risk premium and liquidity premium would not be the same for the two bonds. Thus, you could not simply subtract the two yields to determine the MRP. Statement c is false because the expectations theory is not the only theory proposed to explain the shape of the yield curve. The market segmentation theory states that the slope depends on supply/demand conditions, and the liquidity preference theory states that under normal conditions a positive maturity risk premium exists. So, we cannot be certain that the yield curve would be downward sloping.

33. a. Statement b is incorrect. If a downward-sloping yield curve existed, long-term interest rates would be lower than short-term rates. This would be very serious for UAC: UAC receives as income the interest it charges on its long-term mortgage loans, but it has to pay out interest for obtaining funds in the short-term money market. Therefore, UAC would be receiving low interest income, but it would be paying out even higher interest. Statement c is incorrect. An upward-sloping yield curve would indicate higher interest rates for long-term securities than for short-term securities.

34. b. Statement a is incorrect. To avoid double taxation, stockholders would prefer that corporations retain more of its earnings because capital gains are taxed at a maximum tax rate of 28 percent. Statement c is incorrect. Debt financing has been encouraged by the fact that interest on debt is tax deductible. Statement d is incorrect. Currently, interest on debt is fully tax deductible; allowing 50 percent of interest to be tax deductible would discourage debt financing.

35. e. Statement c is incorrect because the nominal rate ($k_{RF} = k^* + IP$) would increase (not the real rate, k^*) if inflation increased by 2 percentage points.

SOLUTIONS TO SELF-TEST PROBLEMS

1. b. $k_{RF} = k^* + IP = 3\% + 8\% = 11\%$.

2. c. There is virtually no risk of default on a U.S. Treasury security, and they trade in active markets, which provide liquidity, so

$$
\begin{aligned}
k &= k^* + IP + DRP + LP + MRP \\
&= 3\% + 8\% + 0\% + 0\% + 1\% \\
&= 12\%.
\end{aligned}
$$

3. a. $k = k^* + IP + DRP + LP + MRP$
$12\% = 2\% + IP + 0\% + 0\% + 0\%$
$IP = 10\%$.

Thus, the average expected inflation rate over the next 3 years (IP) is 10 percent. Given that the average expected inflation rate over the next three years is 10%, we can find the implied expected inflation rate for the third year by solving the equation that sets the two known plus the one unknown expected inflation rates equal to 10%:

$$\frac{12\% + 10\% + I_3}{3} = 10\%$$

$$I_3 = 8\%.$$

4. d.

Year	k^*	Inflation	Average Inflation	k_t
1	2%	?	$I_1/1 = ?$	?
2	2%	3	$(I_1 + 3\%)/2$	5.5%

$k_2 = 2\% + (I_1 + 3\%)/2 = 5.5\%$. Solving for I_1, we find I_1 = Year 1 inflation = 4%.

5. b. $I_1 = IP = 4\%$. $k_1 = k^* + IP = 2\% + 4\% = 6\%$.

6. b. The first step is to determine taxable income:

Income from operations	$385,000
Interest income (fully taxable)	15,000
Interest expense (fully deductible)	(20,000)
Dividend income (30% taxable)	3,000
Taxable income	$383,000

(Note that dividends are paid from after-tax income and do not affect taxable income.)

Based on the current corporate tax table, the tax calculation is as follows:

Tax = $113,900 + 0.34($383,000 - $335,000) = $113,900 + $16,320 = $130,220.

7. c. The after-tax yield (or dollar return) equals the before-tax yield (or dollar return) multiplied by one minus the effective tax rate, or AT = BT(1 - Effective T). Therefore, AT = 16%(1 - 0.35) = 16%(0.65) = 10.40%.

8. e. Since the dividends are received by a corporation, only 30 percent are taxable, and the Effective T = Tax rate × 30%:

$$
\begin{aligned}
AT &= BT(1 - \text{Effective T}) \\
&= 16\%[1 - 0.35(0.30)] \\
&= 16\%(1 - 0.105) \\
&= 16\%(0.895) \\
&= 14.32\%.
\end{aligned}
$$

9. e.

Year	Taxable Income	Tax Payment	Adjusted Taxable Income	Adjusted Tax Payment
1993	$10,000	$1,500	$10,000	$1,500
1994	5,000	750	0	0
1995	10,000	1,500	0	0
1996	5,000	750	3,000	450

The carry-back can only go back 3 years. Thus, there was no adjustment made in 1993. After a $5,000 adjustment in 1994 and $10,000 in 1995, there was a $2,000 loss remaining to apply to 1996. The 1996 adjusted tax payment is $3,000(0.15) = $450. Thus, Carter received a total of $2,550 in tax refunds after the adjustment.

10. b. The project is fully taxable; thus its after-tax return is as follows:

$$AT = 20\%(1 - 0.35) = 20\%(0.65) = 13.0\%.$$

But only 30 percent of the preferred stock dividends are taxable; thus its after-tax yield is $AT = 13\%[1 - 0.35(0.30)] = 13\%(1 - 0.105) = 13\%(0.895) = 11.64\%$. Therefore, the new project should be chosen since its after-tax return is 1.36 percentage points higher.

11. d. First, note that we will use the equation $k_t = 4\% + IP_t + MRP_t$. We have the data needed to find the IPs:

$$IP_5 = (7\% + 4\% + 3\% + 3\% + 3\%)/5 = 20\%/5 = 4\%.$$

$$IP_2 = (7\% + 4\%)/2 = 5.5\%.$$

Now we can substitute into the equation:

$$k_2 = 4\% + 5.5\% + MRP_2 = 11\%.$$

$$k_5 = 4\% + 4\% + MRP_5 = 11\%.$$

Now we can solve for the MRPs, and find the difference:

$$MRP_5 = 11\% - 8\% = 3\%.$$

$$MRP_2 = 11\% - 9.5\% = 1.5\%.$$

$$\text{Difference} = 3\% - 1.5\% = 1.5\%.$$

12. c. AT yield on Colorado bond = 7%.

AT yield on MCI bond = 10% – Taxes = 10% – 10%(0.25) = 7.5%.

Check: Invest $20,000 at 10% = $2,000 interest.

Pay 25% tax, so AT income = $2,000(1 – T) = $2,000(0.75) = $1,500.

AT rate of return = $1,500/$20,000 = 7.5%.

AT yield on MCI preferred stock = 8% – Taxes = 8% – 0.3(8%)(0.25) = 8% – 0.6% = 7.4%.

Therefore, invest in MCI bonds.

13. e. Basic relevant equations:

$k_t = k* + IP_t + DRP_t + MRP_t + LP_t$. But $DRP_t = MRP_t = LP_t = 0$, so

$k_t = k* + IP_t$

$$IP_t = \frac{\text{Average}}{\text{inflation}} = \frac{I_1 + I_2 + \cdots}{N}.$$

We know that $I_1 = IP_1 = 3.5\%$, and $k* = 2\%$. Therefore,

$k_1 = 2\% + 3.5\% = 5.5\%$.

$k_3 = k_1 + 3\% = 5.5\% + 3\% = 8.5\%$.

But $k_3 = k* + IP_3 = 2\% + IP_3 = 8.5\%$, so

$IP_3 = 8.5\% - 2\% = 6.5\%$.

We also know that $I_t = $ Constant after t = 1.

Avg. $I = IP_3 = (3.5\% + 2I)/3 = 6.5\%$; $2I = 16\%$, so $I = 8\%$.

We can set up this table:

Year	k*	I_t	Avg. I = Ip_t	k = k* + Ip_t
1	2%	3.5%	3.5%/1 = 3.5%	5.5%
2	2%	I	(3.5% + I)/2 = IP_2	
3	2%	I	(3.5% + I + I)/3 = IP_3	8.5%, so IP_3 = 8.5% - 2% = 6.5%.

CHAPTER 4

RISK AND RETURN: THE BASICS

OVERVIEW

Risk is an important concept in financial analysis, especially in terms of how it affects security prices and rates of return. Investment risk is associated with the probability of low or negative future returns.

The riskiness of an asset can be considered in two ways: (1) on a *stand-alone basis*, where the asset's cash flows are analyzed all by themselves, or (2) in a *portfolio context*, where the cash flows from a number of assets are combined, and then the consolidated cash flows are analyzed.

In a portfolio context, an asset's risk can be divided into two components: (1) a *diversifiable risk component*, which can be diversified away and hence is of little concern to diversified investors, and (2) a *market risk component*, which reflects broad market movements and which cannot be eliminated by diversification, and therefore, is of concern to investors. Only market risk is *relevant*; diversifiable risk is irrelevant because it can be eliminated.

An attempt has been made to quantify market risk with a measure called *beta*. Beta is a measurement of how a particular firm's stock returns move relative to overall movements of stock market returns. The *Capital Asset Pricing Model (CAPM)*, using the concept of beta and investors' aversion to risk, specifies the relationship between market risk and the required rate of return. This relationship can be visualized graphically with the Security Market Line (SML). The slope of the SML can change, or the line can shift upward or downward, in response to changes in risk or required rates of return.

OUTLINE

Risk refers to the chance that some unfavorable event will occur. Investment risk is related to the probability of actually earning less than the expected return; thus, the greater the chance of low or negative returns, the riskier the investment.

■ An asset's risk can be analyzed in two ways: (1) on a *stand-alone basis,* where the asset is considered in isolation, and (2) on a *portfolio basis,* where the asset is held as one of a number of assets in a portfolio.

■ The relationship between risk and return is such that no investment will be made unless the expected rate of return is high enough to compensate the investor for the perceived risk of the investment.

■ The *probability distribution* for an event is the listing of all the possible outcomes for the event, with mathematical probabilities assigned to each.
  □ The sum of the probabilities for a particular event must equal 1.0.

■ The *expected rate of return* ($\hat{k}$) is the sum of the products of each possible outcome times its associated probability—it is a weighted average of the various possible outcomes, with the weights being their probabilities of occurrence:

$$\text{Expected rate of return} = \hat{k} = \sum_{i=1}^{n} P_i k_i.$$

  □ Where the number of possible outcomes is virtually unlimited, *continuous probability distributions* are used in determining the expected rate of return of the event.
  □ The tighter, or more peaked, a distribution, the more likely it is that the actual outcome will be closer to the expected value, and thus, the smaller is the risk.

■ One measure for determining the tightness of a distribution is the *standard deviation,* σ.

$$\text{Standard deviation} = \sigma = \sqrt{\sum_{i=1}^{n} (k_i - \hat{k})^2 P_i}.$$

  □ Thus, the standard deviation is a probability-weighted average deviation from the expected value, and it gives you an idea of how far above or below the expected value the actual value is likely to be. The standard deviation is a measure of dispersion around the mean.

■ Another useful measure of risk is the *coefficient of variation (CV)*, which is the standard deviation divided by the expected return. It shows the risk per unit of return and provides a more meaningful basis for comparison when the expected returns on two alternatives are not the same:

$$\text{Coefficient of variation (CV)} = \frac{\sigma}{\hat{k}}.$$

■ Most investors are *risk averse*. This means that for two alternatives with the same expected rate of return, investors will choose the one with the lower risk. Therefore, in market equilibrium, riskier securities must have higher expected returns than less risky ones, for if this situation does not hold, buying and selling in the market will force it to occur.

An asset held as part of a portfolio is less risky than the same asset held in isolation. This is important, because most financial assets are not held in isolation; rather, they are held as parts of portfolios. From the investor's standpoint, what is important is the return on his or her portfolio, and the portfolio's risk—not the fact that a particular stock goes up or down. Thus, the risk and return of an individual security should be analyzed in terms of how it affects the risk and return of the portfolio in which it is held.

■ The expected return on a portfolio, $\hat{k}_p$, is the weighted average expected return of the individual stocks in the portfolio, with the weights being the fraction of the total portfolio invested in each stock:

$$\hat{k}_p = \sum_{i=1}^{n} w_i \hat{k}_i.$$

■ The riskiness of a portfolio, σ_p, is generally *not* a weighted average of the standard deviations of the individual securities in the portfolio. The riskiness of a portfolio depends not only on the standard deviations of the individual stocks, but also on the *correlation between the stocks*.
  □ The correlation coefficient, r, measures the tendency of two variables to move together. With stocks, these variables are the individual stock returns.
  □ Diversification does nothing to reduce risk if the portfolio consists of *perfectly positively correlated* stocks; however, when stocks are *perfectly negatively correlated*, all risk can be diversified away.
  □ A correlation coefficient of zero suggests that two stocks' returns are not related to each other—that is, changes in one are independent of changes in the other.
  □ As a rule, the riskiness of a portfolio will be reduced as the number of stocks in the portfolio increases.
  □ However, in the typical case, where the correlation among the individual stocks are positive, but less than +1.0, some, but not all, risk can be eliminated.

■ While very large portfolios end up with a substantial amount of risk, it is not as much risk as if all the money were invested in only one stock. Almost half of the riskiness inherent in an average individual stock can be eliminated if the stock is held in a reasonably well-diversified portfolio, which is one containing 40 or more stocks.

☐ Diversifiable risk is that part of the risk of a stock which can be eliminated. It is caused by events particular to the firm.

☐ Market risk is that part of the risk which cannot be eliminated, and it stems from factors which systematically affect all firms, such as war, inflation, recessions, and high interest rates. It can be measured by the degree to which a given stock tends to move up and down with the market. Thus, market risk is the *relevant* risk, which reflects a security's contribution to the portfolio's risk.

☐ The Capital Asset Pricing Model is an important tool for analyzing the relationship between risk and rates of return. The model is based on the proposition that a stock's required rate of return is equal to the risk-free rate of return plus a risk premium, where risk reflects diversification.

The tendency of a stock to move with the market is reflected in its beta coefficient, b, which is a measure of the stock's volatility relative to that of an average stock.

■ An average-risk stock is defined as one that tends to move up and down in step with the general market. By definition it has a beta of 1.0.

■ A stock that is twice as volatile as the market will have a beta of 2.0, while a stock that is half as volatile as the market will have a beta coefficient of 0.5.

■ The beta coefficient of a portfolio of securities is the weighted average of the individual securities' betas:

$$b_p = \sum_{i=1}^{n} w_i b_i.$$

■ Since a stock's beta measures its contribution to the riskiness of a portfolio, beta is the appropriate measure of the stock's relevant risk.

The Capital Asset Pricing Model (CAPM) employs the concept of beta, which measures risk as the relationship between a particular stock's movements and the movements of the overall stock market. The CAPM uses a stock's beta, in conjunction with the average investor's degree of risk aversion, to calculate the return that investors require, k_s, on that particular stock.

■ The *Security Market Line (SML)* shows the relationship between risk as measured by beta and the required rate of return for individual securities. The SML equation can be used to find the required rate of return on Stock i:

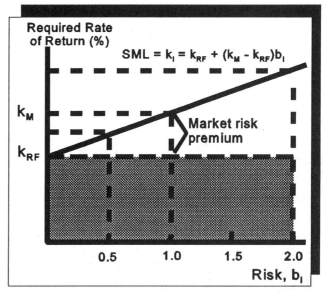

$$\text{SML: } k_i = k_{RF} + (k_M - k_{RF})b_i.$$

Here k_{RF} is the rate of interest on risk-free securities, b_i is the ith stock's beta, and k_M is the return on the market or, alternatively, on an average stock.

☐ The term $k_M - k_{RF}$ is the *market risk premium, RP_M.* This is a measure of the additional return over the risk-free rate needed to compensate investors for assuming an average amount of risk.

☐ In the CAPM the market risk premium, $k_M - k_{RF}$, is multiplied by the stock's beta to determine the additional premium over the risk-free rate that is required to compensate investors for the risk inherent in a particular stock.

☐ This premium may be larger or smaller than the premium required on an average stock, depending on the riskiness of that stock in relation to the overall market as measured by the stock's beta.

☐ The risk premium calculated by $(k_M - k_{RF})b_i$ is added to the risk-free rate, k_{RF} (the rate on Treasury securities), to determine the total rate of return required by investors on a particular stock, k_s.

■ The risk-free (also known as the nominal, or quoted) rate of interest consists of two elements: (1) a real inflation-free rate of return, k^*, and (2) an inflation premium, IP, equal to the anticipated rate of inflation.

☐ The real risk-free rate on long-term Treasury bonds has historically ranged from 2 to 4 percent.

☐ As the expected rate of inflation increases, a higher premium must be added to the real risk-free rate of return to compensate for the loss of purchasing power.

■ The slope of the Security Market Line reflects the extent to which investors are averse to risk. As risk aversion increases, so does the risk premium and, thus, the slope of the SML.

■ Many factors can affect a company's beta. A firm can affect its market risk, hence its beta, through changes in the composition of its assets and also through its use of debt financing. A company's beta can also change as a result of external factors such as increased competition in its industry, the expiration of basic patents, and the like. When such changes occur, the required rate of return also changes. Any change which affects the required rate of return on a security will have an impact on the price of the security.

A word of caution is in order regarding betas and the Capital Asset Pricing Model. The entire theory is based on ex ante, or expected, conditions, yet we have available only ex post, or past, data. Thus, the betas we calculate show how volatile a stock has been in the past, but conditions may change, and its future volatility, which is the item of real concern to investors, might be quite different from its past volatility.

■ Practitioners and academicians have long recognized the limitations of the CAPM, and they are constantly working on ways to improve it. Procedures have been developed to calculate "adjusted" betas, which provide a better indication of a stock's future relative volatility than purely historical betas.

SELF-TEST QUESTIONS

Definitional

1. Investment risk is associated with the _____ of low or negative returns; the greater the chance of loss, the riskier the investment.

2. A listing of all possible _____, with a probability assigned to each, is known as a probability _____.

3. Weighting each possible outcome of a distribution by its _____ of occurrence and summing the results give the expected _____ of the distribution.

4. One measure of the tightness of a probability distribution is the _____ _____.

5. One measure of risk is the _____ ____ _____, which is the standard deviation divided by the expected return.

6. Investors who prefer outcomes with a high degree of certainty to those that are less certain are described as being _____ _____.

7. Owning a portfolio of securities enables investors to benefit from _____.

8. Diversification of a portfolio can result in lower _____ for the same level of return.

9. Diversification of a portfolio is achieved by selecting securities that are not perfectly _____ correlated with each other.

10. A correlation coefficient of _____ suggests that two stocks' returns are not related to each other—that is, changes in one are independent of changes in the other.

11. That part of a stock's risk that can be eliminated is known as _____ risk, while the portion that cannot be eliminated is called _____ risk.

12. The _____ coefficient measures a stock's relative volatility as compared with a stock market index.

13. A stock that is twice as volatile as the market would have a beta coefficient of ____, while a stock with a beta of 0.5 would be only _____ as volatile as the market.

14. The beta coefficient of a portfolio is the _____ _____ of the betas of the individual stocks.

15. The minimum expected return that will induce investors to buy a particular security is the _____ rate of return.

16. The security used to measure the _____ - _____ rate is the return available on U.S. Treasury securities.

17. The risk premium for a particular stock may be calculated by multiplying the market risk premium times the stock's _____ _____.

18. A stock's required rate of return is equal to the _____ - _____ rate plus the stock's _____ _____.

19. The risk-free rate on a short-term Treasury security is made up of two parts: the _____ _____ - _____ rate of return plus a(n) _____ premium.

20. Changes in investors' risk aversion alter the _____ of the Security Market Line.

Conceptual

21. The Y-axis intercept of the Security Market Line (SML) indicates the required rate of return on an individual stock with a beta of 1.0.

    a. True   **b.** False

22. If a stock has a beta of zero, it will be riskless when held in isolation.

    a. True   **b.** False

23. A group of 200 stocks each has a beta of 1.0. We can be certain that each of the stocks was positively correlated with the market.

    a. True   **b.** False

24. Refer to Self-Test Question 23. If we combined these same 200 stocks into a portfolio, market risk would be reduced below the average market risk of the stocks in the portfolio.

    a. True   **b.** False

25. Refer to Self-Test Question 24. The standard deviation of the portfolio of these 200 stocks would be lower than the standard deviations of the individual stocks.

    a. True   **b.** False

26. Suppose $k_{RF} = 7\%$ and $k_M = 12\%$. If investors became more risk averse, k_M would be likely to decrease.

    a. True   **b.** False

27. Refer to Self-Test Question 26. The required rate of return for a stock with b = 0.5 would increase more than for a stock with b = 2.0.

   a. True   **b.** False

28. Refer to Self-Test Questions 26 and 27. If the expected rate of inflation increased, the required rate of return on a b = 2.0 stock would rise by more than that of a b = 0.5 stock.

   a. True   **b.** False

29. Which is the best measure of risk for an asset held in a well-diversified portfolio?

   a. Variance   **d.** Semi-variance
   b. Standard deviation   **e.** Expected value
   c. Beta

30. In a portfolio of three different stocks, which of the following could *not* be true?

   a. The riskiness of the portfolio is less than the riskiness of each stock held in isolation.
   b. The riskiness of the portfolio is greater than the riskiness of one or two of the stocks.
   c. The beta of the portfolio is less than the beta of each of the individual stocks.
   d. The beta of the portfolio is greater than the beta of one or two of the individual stocks.
   e. The beta of the portfolio is equal to the beta of one of the individual stocks.

31. If investors expected inflation to increase in the future, and they also became more risk averse, what could be said about the change in the Security Market Line (SML)?

   a. The SML would shift up and the slope would increase.
   b. The SML would shift up and the slope would decrease.
   c. The SML would shift down and the slope would increase.
   d. The SML would shift down and the slope would decrease.
   e. The SML would remain unchanged.

32. Which of the following statements is most *correct*?

    a. The SML relates required returns to firms' market risk. The slope and intercept of this line *cannot* be controlled by the financial manager.

    b. The slope of the SML is determined by the value of beta.

    c. If you plotted the returns of a given stock against those of the market, and if you found that the slope of the regression line was negative, then the CAPM would indicate that the required rate of return on the stock should be less than the risk-free rate for a well-diversified investor, assuming that the observed relationship is expected to continue on into the future.

    d. If investors become less risk averse, the slope of the Security Market Line will increase.

    e. Statements a and c are both true.

33. Which of the following statements is most *correct*?

    a. Normally, the Security Market Line has an upward slope. However, at one of those unusual times when the yield curve on bonds is downward sloping, the SML will also have a downward slope.

    b. The market risk premium, as it is used in the CAPM theory, is equal to the required rate of return on an average stock minus the required rate of return on an average company's bonds.

    c. If the marginal investor's aversion to risk decreases, then the slope of the yield curve would, other things held constant, tend to increase. If expectations for inflation also increased at the same time risk aversion was decreasing—say the expected inflation rate rose from 5 percent to 8 percent—the net effect could possibly result in a parallel upward shift in the SML.

    d. According to the text, it is theoretically possible to combine two stocks, each of which would be quite risky if held as your only asset, and to form a 2-stock portfolio that is riskless. However, the stocks would have to have a correlation coefficient of expected future returns of -1.0, and it is hard to find such stocks in the real world.

    e. Each of the above statements is false.

34. Which of the following statements is most *correct*?

    a. The expected future rate of return, $\hat{k}$, is always *above* the past realized rate of return, $\bar{k}$, except for highly risk-averse investors.

    b. The expected future rate of return, $\hat{k}$, is always *below* the past realized rate of return, $\bar{k}$, except for highly risk-averse investors.

    c. The expected future rate of return, $\hat{k}$, is always *below* the required rate of return, k, except for highly risk-averse investors.

    d. There is no logical reason to think that any relationship exists between the expected future rate of return, $\hat{k}$, on a security and the security's required rate of return, k.

    e. Each of the above statements is false.

35. Which of the following statements is most *correct*?

    a. Someone who is highly averse to risk should invest in stocks with high betas (above +1.0), other things held constant.

    b. The returns on a stock might be highly uncertain in the sense that they could actually turn out to be much higher or much lower than the expected rate of return (that is, the stock has a high standard deviation of returns), yet the stock might still be regarded by most investors as being less risky than some other stock whose returns are less variable.

    c. The standard deviation is a better measure of risk when comparing securities than the coefficient of variation. This is true because the standard deviation "standardizes" risk by dividing each security's variance by its expected rate of return.

    d. Market risk can be reduced by holding a large portfolio of stocks, and if a portfolio consists of all traded stocks, market risk will be completely eliminated.

    e. The market risk in a portfolio declines as more stocks are added to the portfolio, and the risk decline is linear, that is, each additional stock reduces the portfolio's risk by the same amount.

SELF-TEST PROBLEMS

1. Stock A has the following probability distribution of expected returns:

Probability	Rate of Return
0.1	-15%
0.2	0
0.4	5
0.2	10
0.1	25

What is Stock A's expected rate of return and standard deviation?

a. 8.0%; 9.5% **b.** 8.0%; 6.5% **c.** 5.0%; 3.5% **d.** 5.0%; 6.5% **e.** 5.0%; 9.5%

2. If k_{RF} = 5%, k_M = 11%, and b = 1.3 for Stock X, what is k_X , the required rate of return for Stock X?

a. 18.7% **b.** 16.7% **c.** 14.8% **d.** 12.8% **e.** 11.9%

3. Refer to Self-Test Problem 2. What would k_X be if investors expected the inflation rate to increase by 2 percentage points?

a. 18.7% **b.** 16.7% **c.** 14.8% **d.** 12.8% **e.** 11.9%

4. Refer to Self-Test Problem 2. What would k_X be if an increase in investors' risk aversion caused the market risk premium to increase by 3 percentage points? k_{RF} remains at 5 percent.

a. 18.7% **b.** 16.7% **c.** 14.8% **d.** 12.8% **e.** 11.9%

5. Refer to Self-Test Problem 2. What would k_X be if investors expected the inflation rate to increase by 2 percentage points *and* their risk aversion increased by 3 percentage points?

a. 18.7% **b.** 16.7% **c.** 14.8% **d.** 12.8% **e.** 11.9%

6. Jan Middleton owns a 3-stock portfolio with a total investment value equal to $300,000.

Stock	Investment	Beta
A	$100,000	0.5
B	100,000	1.0
C	100,000	1.5
Total	$300,000	

What is the weighted average beta of Jan's 3-stock portfolio?

a. 0.9   **b.** 1.3   **c.** 1.0   **d.** 0.4   **e.** 1.2

7. The Apple Investment Fund has a total investment of $450 million in five stocks.

Stock	Investment (Millions)	Beta
1	$130	0.4
2	110	1.5
3	70	3.0
4	90	2.0
5	50	1.0
Total	$450	

What is the fund's overall, or weighted average, beta?

a. 1.14   **b.** 1.22   **c.** 1.35   **d.** 1.46   **e.** 1.53

8. Refer to Self-Test Problem 7. If the risk-free rate is 12 percent and the market risk premium is 6 percent, what is the required rate of return on the Apple Fund?

a. 20.76%   **b.** 19.92%   **c.** 18.81%   **d.** 17.62%   **e.** 15.77%

9. Stock A has a beta of 1.2, Stock B has a beta of 0.6, the expected rate of return on an average stock is 12 percent, and the risk-free rate of return is 7 percent. By how much does the required return on the riskier stock exceed the required return on the less risky stock?

a. 4.00%   **b.** 3.25%   **c.** 3.00%   **d.** 2.50%   **e.** 3.75%

10. You are managing a portfolio of 10 stocks which are held in equal dollar amounts. The current beta of the portfolio is 1.8, and the beta of Stock A is 2.0. If Stock A is sold and the proceeds are used to purchase a replacement stock, what does the beta of the replacement stock have to be to lower the portfolio beta to 1.7?

   a. 1.4   **b.** 1.3   **c.** 1.2   **d.** 1.1   **e.** 1.0

11. Consider the following information for the Alachua Retirement Fund, with a total investment of $4 million.

Stock	Investment	Beta
A	$ 400,000	1.2
B	600,000	-0.4
C	1,000,000	1.5
D	2,000,000	0.8
Total	$4,000,000	

   The market required rate of return is 12 percent, and the risk-free rate is 6 percent. What is its required rate of return?

   a. 9.98%   **b.** 10.45%   **c.** 11.01%   **d.** 11.50%   **e.** 12.56%

12. You are given the following distribution of returns:

Probability	Return
0.4	$30
0.5	25
0.1	-20

   What is the coefficient of variation of the expected dollar returns?

   a. 206.2500   **b.** 0.6383   **c.** 14.3614   **d.** 0.7500   **e.** 1.2500

13. If the risk-free rate is 8 percent, the expected return on the market is 13 percent, and the expected return on Security J is 15 percent, then what is the beta of Security J?

   a. 1.40   **b.** 0.90   **c.** 1.20   **d.** 1.50   **e.** 0.75

ANSWERS TO SELF-TEST QUESTIONS

1. probability
2. outcomes; distribution
3. probability; return
4. standard deviation
5. coefficient of variation
6. risk averse
7. diversification
8. risk
9. positively
10. zero

11. diversifiable; market
12. beta
13. 2.0; half
14. weighted average
15. required
16. risk-free
17. beta coefficient
18. risk-free; risk premium
19. real risk-free; inflation
20. slope

21. b. The Y-axis intercept of the SML is k_{RF}, which is the required rate of return of a security with a beta of zero.

22. b. A zero beta stock could be made riskless if it were combined with enough other zero beta stocks, but it would still have company-specific risk and be risky when held in isolation.

23. a. By definition, if a stock has a beta of 1.0 it moves exactly with the market. In other words, if the market moves up by 7 percent, the stock will also move up by 7 percent, while if the market falls by 7 percent, the stock will fall by 7 percent.

24. b. Market risk is measured by the beta coefficient. The beta for the portfolio would be a weighted average of the betas of the stocks, so b_p would also be 1.0. Thus, the market risk for the portfolio would be the same as the market risk of the stocks in the portfolio.

25. a. Note that with a 200-stock portfolio, the actual returns would all be on or close to the regression line. However, when the portfolio (and the market) returns are quite high, some individual stocks would have higher returns than the portfolio, and some would have much lower returns. Thus, the range of returns, and the standard deviation, would be higher for the individual stocks.

26. b. RP_M, which is equal to $k_M - k_{RF}$, would rise, leading to an increase in k_M.

27. b. The required rate of return for a stock with $b = 0.5$ would increase less than for a stock with $b = 2.0$.

28. b. If the expected rate of inflation increased, the SML would shift parallel due to an increase in k_{RF}. Thus, the effect on the required rates of return for both the b = 0.5 and b = 2.0 stocks would be the same.

29. c. The best measure of risk is the beta coefficient, which is a measure of the extent to which the returns on a given stock move with the stock market.

30. c. The beta of the portfolio is a weighted average of the individual securities' betas, so it could not be less than the betas of all of the stocks. (See Self-Test Problem 6.)

31. a. The increase in inflation would cause the SML to shift up, and investors becoming more risk averse would cause the slope to increase. (This can be demonstrated by graphing the SML lines on the same graph in Self-Test Problems 2 through 5.)

32. e. Statement b is false because the slope of the SML is $k_M - k_{RF}$. Statement d is false because as investors become less risk averse the slope of the SML decreases. Statement a is correct because the financial manager has no control over k_M or k_{RF}. ($k_M - k_{RF}$ = slope and k_{RF} = intercept of the SML.) Statement c is correct because the slope of the regression line is beta and beta would be negative; thus, the required return would be less than the risk-free rate.

33. d. Statement a is false. The yield curve determines the value of k_{RF}; however, SML = k_{RF} + $(k_M - k_{RF})$b. The average return on the market will always be greater than the risk-free rate; thus, the SML will always be upward sloping. Statement b is false because RP_M is equal to $k_M - k_{RF}$. k_{RF} is equal to the risk-free rate, not the rate on an average company's bonds. Statement c is false. A decrease in an investor's aversion to risk would indicate a downward sloping yield curve. A decrease in risk aversion and an increase in inflation would cause the SML slope to decrease and to shift upward simultaneously.

34. e. All the statements are false. For equilibrium to exist, the expected return must equal the required return.

35. b. Statement b is correct because the stock with the higher standard deviation might not be highly correlated with most other stocks, hence have a relatively low beta, and thus not be very risky if held in a well-diversified portfolio. The other statements are simply false.

ANSWERS TO SELF-TEST PROBLEMS

1. e. $\hat{k}_A = 0.1(-15\%) + 0.2(0\%) + 0.4(5\%) + 0.2(10\%) + 0.1(25\%) = 5.0\%.$

   Variance $= 0.1(-0.15 - 0.05)^2 + 0.2(0.0 - 0.05)^2 + 0.4(0.05 - 0.05)^2$
   $\qquad\qquad + 0.2(0.10 - 0.05)^2 + 0.1(0.25 - 0.05)^2$
   $\qquad = 0.009.$
   Standard deviation $= \sqrt{0.009} = 0.0949 \approx 9.5\%.$

2. d. $k_X = k_{RF} + (k_M - k_{RF})b_X = 5\% + (11\% - 5\%)1.3 = 12.8\%.$

3. c. $k_X = k_{RF} + (k_M - k_{RF})b_X = 7\% + (13\% - 7\%)1.3 = 14.8\%.$

   A change in the inflation premium does *not* change the market risk premium ($k_M - k_{RF}$) since both k_M and k_{RF} are affected.

4. b. $k_X = k_{RF} + (k_M - k_{RF})b_X = 5\% + (14\% - 5\%)1.3 = 16.7\%.$

5. a. $k_X = k_{RF} + (k_M - k_{RF})b_X = 7\% + (16\% - 7\%)1.3 = 18.7\%.$

6. c. The calculation of the portfolio's beta is as follows:

   $b_p = (1/3)(0.5) + (1/3)(1.0) + (1/3)(1.5) = 1.0.$

7. d. $b_p = \sum_{i=1}^{5} w_i b_i$

   $= \dfrac{\$130}{\$450}(0.4) + \dfrac{\$110}{\$450}(1.5) + \dfrac{\$70}{\$450}(3.0) + \dfrac{\$90}{\$450}(2.0) + \dfrac{\$50}{\$450}(1.0) = 1.46.$

8. a. $k_p = k_{RF} + (k_M - k_{RF})b_p = 12\% + (6\%)1.46 = 20.76\%.$

9. c. We know $b_A = 1.20$, $b_B = 0.60$; $k_M = 12\%$, and $k_{RF} = 7\%.$
   $k_i = k_{RF} + (k_M - k_{RF})b_i = 7\% + (12\% - 7\%)b_i.$
   $k_A = 7\% + 5\%(1.20) = 13.0\%.$
   $k_B = 7\% + 5\%(0.60) = 10.0\%.$
   $k_A - k_B = 13\% - 10\% = 3\%.$

10. e. First find the beta of the remaining 9 stocks:

$1.8 = 0.9(b_R) + 0.1(b_A)$
$1.8 = 0.9(b_R) + 0.1(2.0)$
$1.8 = 0.9(b_R) + 0.2$
$1.6 = 0.9(b_R)$
$b_R = 1.78$.

Now find the beta of the new stock that produces $b_p = 1.7$.

$1.7 = 0.9(1.78) + 0.1(b_N)$
$1.7 = 1.6 + 0.1(b_N)$
$0.1 = 0.1(b_N)$
$b_N = 1.0$.

11. c. Determine the weight each stock represents in the portfolio:

Stock	Investment	w_i	Beta	$w_i \times$ Beta
A	\$ 400,000	0.10	1.2	0.1200
B	600,000	0.15	-0.4	-0.0600
C	1,000,000	0.25	1.5	0.3750
D	2,000,000	0.50	0.8	0.4000
				$b_p = \underline{0.8350}$ = Portfolio beta

Write out the SML equation, and substitute known values including the portfolio beta. Solve for the required portfolio return.

$k_p = k_{RF} + (k_M - k_{RF})b_p = 6\% + (12\% - 6\%)0.8350$
$\quad = 6\% + 5.01\% = 11.01\%$.

12. **b.** Use the given probability distribution of returns to calculate the expected value, variance, standard deviation, and coefficient of variation.

P_i	k_i	P_ik_i	k_i	$\hat{k}$		$(k_i - \hat{k})$	$(k_i - \hat{k})^2$	$P(k_i - \hat{k})^2$
$0.4 \times$	$\$30$	$= \$12.0$	$\$30$	$- \$22.5$	$=$	$\$ 7.5$	$\$ \quad 56.25$	$\$ \quad 22.500$
$0.5 \times$	25	$= 12.5$	25	$- 22.5$	$=$	2.5	6.25	3.125
$0.1 \times$	-20	$= \underline{-2.0}$	-20	$- 22.5$	$=$	-42.5	$1,806.25$	$\underline{180.625}$
		$\hat{k} = \underline{\$22.5}$					$\sigma^2 = \text{Variance} = \underline{\$206.250}$	

The standard deviation (σ) of $\hat{k}$ is $\sqrt{\$206.25}$ = $\$14.3614$.
Use the standard deviation and the expected return to calculate the coefficient of variation:
$\$14.3614/\$22.5 = 0.6383$.

13. **a.** Use the SML equation, substitute in the known values, and solve for beta.

$$k_{RF} = 8\%; \quad k_M = 13\%; \quad k_j = 15\%.$$
$$k_j = k_{RF} + (k_M - k_{RF})b_j$$
$$15\% = 8\% + (13\% - 8\%)b_j$$
$$7\% = (5\%)b_j$$
$$b_j = 1.4.$$

CHAPTER 5

RISK AND RETURN:
EXTENSIONS

OVERVIEW

In Chapter 4 we presented the key elements of risk and return analysis. There we saw that much of the risk inherent in a stock can be eliminated by diversification, so rational investors should hold portfolios of stocks rather than single stocks. We also introduced the Capital Asset Pricing Model (CAPM), which links risk and required rates of return, using a stock's beta coefficient as the relevant measure of risk.

In this chapter, we extend the Chapter 4 material by presenting an in-depth treatment of portfolio concepts and the CAPM. We continue the discussion of risk and return by adding a risk-free asset to the set of investment opportunities. This leads all investors to hold the same well-diversified portfolio of risky assets, and then to account for differing degrees of risk aversion by combining the risky portfolio in different proportions with the risk-free asset. Additionally, we show how betas are actually calculated, and we discuss an alternative view of the risk/return relationship, the Arbitrage Pricing Theory (APT).

OUTLINE

The riskiness of a portfolio is measured by the standard deviation of its return distribution. This equation is exactly the same as the one for the standard deviation of a single asset, except that here the asset is a portfolio of assets.

$$\text{Portfolio standard deviation} = \sigma_p = \sqrt{\sum_{i=1}^{n} (k_{pi} - \hat{k}_p)^2 P_i}.$$

■ Under the assumption that the distributions of returns on the individual securities are normal, the following equation can be used to determine the riskiness of a two-asset portfolio:

$$\text{Portfolio SD} = \sigma_p = \sqrt{x^2 \sigma_A^2 + (1 - x)^2 \sigma_B^2 + 2x(1 - x) r_{AB} \sigma_A \sigma_B}.$$

Two key concepts in portfolio analysis are covariance and the correlation coefficient.

■ Covariance is a measure of the general movement relationship between two variables. It combines the variance or volatility of a stock's returns with the tendency of those returns to move up or down at the same time other stocks move up or down. The following equation defines the covariance (Cov) between two variables such as Stocks A and B:

$$\text{Covariance} = \text{Cov(AB)} = \sum_{i=1}^{n} (k_{Ai} - \hat{k}_A)(k_{Bi} - \hat{k}_B) P_i .$$

■ The correlation coefficient also measures the degree of co-movement between two stocks, but its values are limited to the range from -1.0 (perfect negative correlation) to +1.0 (perfect positive correlation). The relationship between covariance and the correlation coefficient can be expressed as

$$\text{Correlation coefficient(AB)} = r_{AB} = \frac{\text{Cov(AB)}}{\sigma_A \sigma_B} .$$

□ The sign of the correlation coefficient is the same as the sign of the covariance, so a positive sign means that the variables move together, a negative sign indicates that they move in opposite directions, and if r is close to zero, they move independently of one another.

An efficient portfolio provides the highest expected return for any degree of risk, or the lowest degree of risk for any expected return.

■ While the riskiness of a multi-asset portfolio usually decreases as the number of stocks increase, the portfolio's risk depends on the degree of correlation among the stocks.

■ In general, the average correlation between two stocks is +0.5 to +0.7, and hence holding stocks in portfolios will reduce, but not eliminate, risk.

■ The *attainable*, or *feasible*, set of portfolios represents all portfolios that can be constructed from a given set of stocks.

The optimal portfolio is found by determining the efficient set of portfolios and then choosing from the efficient set the single portfolio that is best for the individual investor.

■ The efficient set of portfolios is also called the *efficient frontier*.
□ Portfolios to the left of the efficient set are not possible because they lie outside the attainable set.

☐ Portfolios to the right of the boundary line (interior portfolios) are inefficient because some other portfolio would provide either a higher return with the same degree of risk or a lower risk for the same rate of return.

■ An *indifference curve* (or risk/return trade-off function) reflects an individual investor's attitude towards risk. The optimal portfolio for each investor is found at the tangency point between the efficient set of portfolios and one of the investor's indifference curves. This tangency point marks the highest level of satisfaction the investor can attain.

The Capital Asset Pricing Model (CAPM) specifies the relationship between risk and required rates of return on assets when they are held in well-diversified portfolios.

■ As in all financial theories, a number of assumptions were made in the development of the CAPM. Theoretical extensions in finance literature have relaxed some of the assumptions, and in general these extensions have led to conclusions that are reasonably consistent with the basic theory. However, even the extensions contain assumptions which are both strong and unrealistic, so the validity of the model can only be established through empirical tests.

The Capital Market Line (CML) specifies a linear relationship between expected return and risk for any efficient portfolio.

■ The equation of the CML may be expressed as follows:

$$\hat{k}_p = k_{RF} + \left(\frac{\hat{k}_M - k_{RF}}{\sigma_M} \right) \sigma_p.$$

Here $\hat{k}_p$ is the expected (and in equilibrium required) rate of return on an efficient portfolio, k_{RF} is the rate of interest on risk-free securities, $\hat{k}_M$ is the return on the market portfolio, σ_M is the standard deviation of the market portfolio, and σ_p is the standard deviation of the efficient portfolio in question.

■ In words, the expected rate of return on any efficient portfolio (that is, any portfolio on the CML) is equal to the riskless rate plus a risk premium, and the risk premium is equal to $(\hat{k}_M - k_{RF})/\sigma_M$ multiplied by the portfolio's standard deviation.

■ An efficient portfolio is one that is well diversified, so unlike individual stocks, all the riskiness of an efficient portfolio is measured by its standard deviation σ_p.

The relevant measure of risk for use in the Security Market Line (SML) equation is the stock's beta coefficient, which measures the volatility of a stock relative to that of a portfolio containing all stocks.

■ Beta is estimated by plotting historical returns on a particular stock versus returns on a market index. The slope of the regression line, or *characteristic line*, is the stock's beta coefficient. The statistical equation for beta is:

$$b_i = \frac{Cov(\bar{k}_i, \bar{k}_M)}{\sigma_M^2} = \frac{r_{iM}\sigma_i\sigma_M}{\sigma_M^2} = r_{iM}\left(\frac{\sigma_i}{\sigma_M}\right),$$

where,

b_i = the slope, or beta coefficient, for Stock i.

$\bar{k}_i$ = the historical (realized) rate of return on Stock i.

$\bar{k}_M$ = the historical (realized) rate of return on the market.

r_{iM} = the correlation between Stock i and the market.

σ_i = the standard deviation of Stock i.

σ_M = the standard deviation of the market.

☐ We assume that the historical relationship between Stock i and the market as a whole will continue into the future.

☐ Besides general market movements, each firm also faces events that are both peculiar to it and independent of the general economic climate. This component of total risk is the stock's *diversifiable*, or *company-specific*, *risk*, and rational investors will eliminate its effects by holding diversified portfolios of stocks.

☐ An individual stock tends to move with the market as economic conditions change. This component of total risk is the stock's *market*, or *non-diversifiable*, risk. Even well-diversified portfolios contain some market risk.

☐ Total risk equals market risk plus diversifiable risk.

$$\frac{\text{Total}}{\text{risk}} = \frac{\text{Market}}{\text{risk}} + \frac{\text{Diversifiable}}{\text{risk}}$$

$$\sigma_i^2 = b_i^2\sigma_M^2 + \sigma_{e_i}^2.$$

☐ If the stock market never fluctuated, then stocks would have no market risk.

□ Beta is the measure of relative market risk, but the stock's actual risk depends on both its beta (market risk), and on the volatility of the market.

□ The diversifiable risk can and should be eliminated by diversification, so the relevant risk is market risk, not total risk.

□ A stock's risk premium, $(k_M - k_{RF})b_i$, depends only on its market risk, not its total risk.

Since the CAPM depends on some unrealistic assumptions, it must be tested empirically to determine if it gives accurate estimates of k_i.

■ Betas are generally calculated for some past period, and the assumption is made that the relative volatility of a stock will remain constant in the future. However, conditions may change and alter a stock's future volatility, which is the item of real concern to investors.

■ The CAPM should use expected (future) data, yet only historical data are generally available.

■ Studies indicate that the CAPM is a better concept for structuring investment portfolios than it is for purposes of estimating the cost of capital for individual securities.

■ Studies of the CAPM based on the slope of the SML have generally showed a significant positive relationship between realized returns and systematic risk and that the relationship between risk and return appears to be linear.

■ It is appropriate to think about many financial problems in a CAPM framework. However, it is equally important to recognize the limitations of the CAPM when using it in practice.

The CAPM assumes that required rates of return depend on only one risk factor, the stock's beta coefficient, but required returns may be a function of several risk factors. An approach called the Arbitrage Pricing Theory (APT) can include any number of risk factors.

$$\bar{k}_i = \hat{k}_i + (\bar{F}_1 - \hat{F}_1)b_{i1} + \ldots + (\bar{F}_j - \hat{F}_j)b_{ij} + e_i,$$

where,

$\bar{k}_i$ = the realized return on Stock i.

$\hat{k}_i$ = the expected rate of return on Stock i.

$\bar{F}_j$ = the realized value of economic Factor j.

$\hat{F}_j$ = the expected value of Factor j.

b_{ij} = the sensitivity of Stock i to economic Factor j.

e_i = the effect of unique events on the realized return of Stock i.

■ This equation shows that the realized return on any stock is equal to the stock's expected return plus increases or decreases which depend on (1) unexpected changes in fundamental economic factors, (2) the sensitivity of the stock to these changes, plus (3) a random term which reflects changes unique to the firm or industry.

■ Theoretically, one could construct a portfolio such that (1) the portfolio was riskless and (2) the net investment was zero. Such a zero investment portfolio would have to have a zero expected return, or else prices of the underlying assets would change until the portfolio's expected return was zero.

■ The end result is the APT:

$$\hat{k}_i = k_i = k_{RF} + (\lambda_1 - k_{RF})b_{i1} + \ldots + (\lambda_j - k_{RF})b_{ij},$$

where λ_j is the required rate of return on a portfolio that is sensitive only to the *j*th economic factor ($b_j = 1.0$) and has zero sensitivity to all other factors.

■ The primary advantage of the APT is that it permits several economic factors to influence individual stock returns, whereas the CAPM assumes that the impact of all factors, except those unique to the firm, can be captured in one measure, the volatility of the stock with respect to the market portfolio. The APT also requires fewer assumptions than the CAPM and hence is a more general theory.

■ However, the APT does not identify the relevant factors, nor does it even tell us how many factors should appear in the model. The APT is in an early stage of development, and there are still many unanswered questions.

Appendix 5A illustrates risk/return concepts for continuous probability distributions.

■ A *uniform distribution* is a continuous distribution in which each possible outcome has the same probability of occurrence as any other outcome.

■ A *triangular distribution* is a continuous distribution that has a clustering of values around the most likely outcome, and the probability of occurrence declines in each direction from the most likely outcome.

■ The most commonly used continuous distribution is the *normal distribution*, which is symmetric about the expected value and its tails extend out to plus and minus infinity.

SELF-TEST QUESTIONS

Definitional

1. _____ is a measure of the general movement relationship between two variables, while the _____ _____ also measures the degree of co-movement between two stocks but its values are limited from -1.0 to +1.0.

2. A(n) _____ _____ is that portfolio which provides the highest expected return for any given degree of risk, or the lowest degree of risk for any expected return.

3. The _____, or _____, set of portfolios represents all portfolios that can be constructed from a given set of stocks.

4. The _____ _____ is found by determining the efficient set of portfolios and then choosing from the efficient set the single portfolio that is best for the individual investor.

5. The efficient set of portfolios is also called the _____ _____.

6. A(n) _____ _____ (or risk/return trade-off function) reflects an individual investor's attitude towards risk.

7. The _____ _____ _____ _____ specifies the relationship between risk and required rates of return on assets when they are held in well-diversified portfolios.

8. The _____ _____ _____ specifies a linear relationship between expected return and risk for any efficient portfolio.

9. The relevant measure of risk for use in the Security Market Line (SML) equation is the stock's
    _____ _____, which measures the volatility of a stock relative to that of a
    portfolio containing all stocks.

10. Beta is estimated by plotting historical returns on a particular stock versus returns on a market
    index. The slope of the regression line, or _____ _____, is the stock's beta
    coefficient.

11. Besides general market movements, each firm also faces events that are both peculiar to it and
    independent of the general economic climate. This component of total risk is the stock's
    _____, or _____-_____, risk, and rational investors will eliminate
    its effects by holding diversified portfolios of stocks.

12. The relevant risk is _____ risk, not total risk.

13. Studies indicate that the CAPM is a better concept for structuring _____
    _____ than it is for purposes of estimating the cost of capital for individual
    _____.

14. The _____ _____ _____ uses several risk factors for determining the
    required return on a stock.

15. The most commonly used continuous distribution is the _____ _____, which
    is symmetric about the expected value and its tails extend out to plus and minus infinity.

Conceptual

16. The standard deviation of a portfolio is not the weighted average of the standard deviations of
    the individual stocks in the portfolio.

    a. True   **b.** False

17. If the correlation coefficient between two stocks is +1.0, risk can be completely diversified
    away.

    a. True   **b.** False

18. Total risk is relevant only for assets held in isolation.

    a. True   **b.** False

19. The Arbitrage Pricing Theory identifies the relevant factors for determining the required return beforehand.

    a. True   **b.** False

20. Which of the following statements is most *correct*?

  a. It is difficult to interpret the magnitude of the correlation coefficient, so a related statistic, the covariance, is often used to measure the degree of co-movement between two variables.

  b. The sign of the correlation coefficient is the same as the sign of the covariance, so a positive sign means that the variables move together, a negative sign indicates that they move in opposite directions, and if the correlation coefficient is close to zero, they move independently of one another.

  c. Attainable portfolios are defined as those portfolios which provide the highest expected return for any degree of risk, or the lowest degree of risk for any expected return.

  d. The efficient set of portfolios is also called the efficient frontier.

  e. Statements b and d are both correct.

21. Which of the following statements is most *correct*?

  a. The Capital Market Line (CML) specifies a curvilinear relationship between expected return and risk, whereas the Security Market Line (SML) specifies a linear relationship between expected return and risk.

  b. An efficient portfolio is one that is well diversified, so like individual stocks, all the riskiness of an efficient portfolio is measured by its standard deviation, σ_p.

  c. A stock's beta coefficient is the y-intercept of its characteristic line.

  d. Empirical tests of the stability of beta coefficients have indicated that the betas of individual stocks are stable, hence that past betas for individual securities are good estimators of their future risk, while betas of portfolios of ten or more randomly selected stocks are not stable, hence that past portfolio betas are not good estimators of future portfolio volatility.

  e. All of the above statements are false.

SELF-TEST PROBLEMS

1. You are evaluating two potential investment opportunities: Stocks A and B. The expected rate of return on Stock A is 15.8% and its standard deviation is 2.8%. Stock B's expected rate of return is 20.5% with a standard deviation of 3.5%. What is the coefficient of variation (CV) for Stocks A and B, respectively?

    a. 0.12; 0.12   **b.** 0.18; 0.12   **c.** 0.18; 0.17   **d.** 0.25; 0.17   **e.** 0.25; 0.25

2. Refer to Self-Test Problem 1. Assume that Stocks A and B have a correlation coefficient of 0.65. What is the covariance between Stocks A and B?

    a. 3.89   **b.** 4.35   **c.** 5.12   **d.** 6.37   **e.** 7.19

3. Refer to Self-Test Problem 1. Assume that Stocks A and B have a covariance of -5.4. What is the correlation coefficient between Stocks A and B?

    a. -0.55   **b.** -0.70   **c.** -0.85   **d.** -0.92   **e.** -1.00

4. Given the information below, calculate the betas for Stocks A and B.

Year	Stock A	Stock B	Market
1	-5%	10%	-10%
2	10	20	10
3	25	30	30

    (Hint: Think rise over run.)

    a. 1.0; 0.5   **b.** 0.75; 0.5   **c.** 0.75; 1.0   **d.** 0.5; 0.5   **e.** 0.75; 0.25

(The following data apply to the next two problems.)

You are given the following information:

Year	Stock N	Market
1	-5%	10%
2	-8	15
3	7	-10

The risk-free rate is equal to 7 percent, and the market required return is equal to 10 percent.

5. What is Stock N's beta coefficient?

   a. 1.00 **b.** -0.50 **c.** 0.60 **d.** -0.75 **e.** -0.60

6. What is Stock N's required rate of return?

   a. 6.40% **b.** 5.20% **c.** 8.80% **d.** 5.90% **e.** 7.00%

7. Stock Y and the Market had the following rates of return during the last 4 years. What is Stock Y's beta? (Hint: You will need a financial calculator to calculate the beta coefficient.)

	Y	Market
1993	10.0%	10.0%
1994	16.0	13.5
1995	-7.5	-4.0
1996	0.0	5.5

   a. 1.25 **b.** 0.75 **c.** 1.00 **d.** 1.34 **e.** 1.57

8. Stock Y, Stock Z, and the Market had the following rates of return during the last 4 years:

	Y	Z	Market
1993	10.0%	10.0%	10.0%
1994	16.0	11.5	13.5
1995	-7.5	1.0	-4.0
1996	0.0	6.0	5.5

The expected future return on the market is 15 percent, the real risk-free rate is 3.75 percent, and the expected inflation rate is a constant 5 percent. If the market risk premium rises by 3 percentage points, what will be the change in the required rate of return of the riskier stock?

a. 4.01%   **b.** 3.67%   **c.** 4.88%   **d.** 3.23%   **e.** 4.66%

ANSWERS TO SELF-TEST QUESTIONS

1. Covariance; correlation coefficient
2. efficient portfolio
3. attainable; feasible
4. optimal portfolio
5. efficient frontier
6. indifference curve
7. Capital Asset Pricing Model
8. Capital Market Line

9. beta coefficient
10. characteristic line
11. diversifiable; company-specific
12. market
13. investment portfolios; securities
14. Arbitrage Pricing Theory
15. normal distribution

16. a. The standard deviation of a portfolio depends on the correlations among the stocks as well as their individual standard deviations. The calculation for the portfolio standard deviation is:

$$\sigma_p = \sqrt{\sum_{i=1}^{n} (k_{pi} - \hat{k}_p)^2 P_i}.$$

17. b. A correlation coefficient of -1.0 is required to combine two stocks into a riskless portfolio.

18. a. When assets are combined into portfolios, then the relevant risk is an asset's market risk, which is the contribution of the asset to the riskiness of the portfolio.

19. b. The APT does not identify the relevant factors beforehand, nor does it even tell how many factors should appear in the model.

20. e. Statement a is false. It is difficult to interpret the magnitude of the covariance, so the correlation coefficient is used to measure co-movement between two variables. Statement c is false; this statement is true only for efficient portfolios. Both statement b and d are true, so statement e is the correct choice.

21. e. Statement a is false. The CML specifies the relationship between risk and return for efficient portfolios, while the SML specifies the relationship between risk and return for individual securities. Statement b is false. The standard deviation of an individual stock should not be used to measure the stock's riskiness because some of its risk as reflected in the standard deviation can be eliminated by diversification. Statement c is false; beta is the slope of the characteristic line. Statement d is false; just the reverse is true. Betas of portfolios of 10 or more randomly selected stocks have been shown to be stable, while the betas of individual securities have been shown to be unstable. Consequently, statement e is the correct choice.

SOLUTIONS TO SELF-TEST PROBLEMS

1. c. Stock A: $CV = 2.8\%/15.8\% = 0.18$. Stock B: $CV = 3.5\%/20.5\% = 0.17$.

   Since the CV for Project A is higher, it has more risk per unit of expected return.

2. d. $Cov(AB) = 0.65 (2.8) (3.5) = 6.37$.

3. a. $r_{AB} = -5.4/[(2.8)(3.5)] = -0.55$.

4. b. Stock A: $b_A = Rise/Run = [10 - (-5)]/[10 - (-10)] = 15/20 = 0.75$.

   Stock B: $b_B = Rise/Run = [20 - 10]/[10 - (-10)] = 10/20 = 0.50$.

   This problem can also be worked using most financial calculators having statistical functions.

5. e. $b_N = Rise/Run = [-8 - (-5)]/(15 - 10) = -3/5 = -0.60$.

   Again, this problem can also be worked using most financial calculators having statistical functions.

6. b. $k_N = 7\% + (10\% - 7\%)(-0.60) = 7\% + (-1.80\%) = 5.20\%$.

7. d.   Use the regression feature of the calculator. Enter data for the market and Stock Y, and then find $Beta_Y = 1.3374$ rounded to 1.34.

8. a.   We know $k_M = 15\%$; $k^* = 3.75\%$; $IP = 5\%$.

Original $RP_M = k_M - k_{RF} = 15\% - (3.75\% + 5\%) = 6.25\%$.

RP_M increases by 3%, to 9.25%.

Find the change in $k = \Delta k$ for the riskier stock.

First, find the betas for the two stocks. Enter data in the regression register, then find $b_Y = 1.3374$ and $b_Z = 0.6161$.

Y is the riskier stock. Originally, its required return was $k_Y = 8.75\% + 6.25\%(1.3374) = 17.11\%$. When RP_M increases by 3 percent, $k_Y = 8.75\% + (6.25\% + 3\%)(1.3374) = 21.12\%$. Difference $= 21.12\% - 17.11\% = 4.01\%$.

CHAPTER 6

DISCOUNTED CASH FLOW ANALYSIS

OVERVIEW

A dollar in the hand today is worth more than a dollar to be received in the future because, if you had it now, you could invest that dollar and earn interest. Of all the techniques used in finance, none is more important than the concept of discounted cash flow (DCF) analysis. Future value and present value techniques can be applied to a single cash flow (lump sum), ordinary annuities, annuities due, and uneven cash flow streams. Future and present values can be calculated using interest factor tables, a regular calculator, or a calculator with financial functions. When compounding occurs more frequently than once a year, the effective rate of interest is greater than the quoted rate.

OUTLINE

The time line is one of the most important tools in time value of money calculations. Time lines help to visualize what is happening in a particular problem. Cash flows are placed directly below the tick marks, and interest rates are shown directly above the time line; unknown cash flows are indicated by question marks. Thus, to find the future value of $100 after 5 years at 5 percent interest, the following time line can be set up:

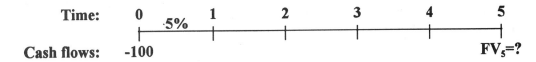

Finding the future value (FV), or compounding, is the process of going from today's values (or present values) to future amounts (or future values). It can be calculated as

$$FV_n = PV(1 + i)^n,$$

where PV = present value, or beginning amount; i = interest rate per year; and n = number of periods involved in the analysis. This equation can be solved in one of three ways: numerically, with interest tables, or with a financial calculator. For calculations, assume the following data that were presented in the time line above: present value (PV) = $100, interest rate (i) = 5%, and number of years (n) = 5.

- To solve numerically, use a regular calculator to find 1 + i = 1.05 raised to the fifth power, which equals 1.2763. Multiply this figure by PV = $100 to get the final answer of FV_5 = $127.63.

- To solve with interest tables, look at Table A-3 at the end of your textbook for future value interest factors. Look down the first column to Period 5, then look across that row to the 5% column for the number 1.2763. Multiplying by PV = $100 results in FV_5 = $127.63.

- With a financial calculator, the future value can be found by using the time value of money input keys, where N = number of periods, I = interest rate per period, PV = present value, PMT = payment, and FV = future value. By entering N = 5, I = 5, PV = -100, and PMT = 0, and then pressing the FV key, the answer 127.63 is displayed.
  □ Some financial calculators require that all cash flows be designated as either inflows or outflows, thus an outflow must be entered as a negative number (for example, PV = -100 instead of PV = 100).
  □ Some calculators require you to press a "Compute" key before pressing the FV key.

- Note that small rounding differences will often occur among the various solution methods.

- A graph of the compounding process shows how any sum grows over time at various interest rates. The greater the rate of interest, the faster is the rate of growth.

Finding present values is called discounting, and it is simply the reverse of compounding. In general, the present value of a cash flow due n years in the future is the amount which, if it were on hand today, would grow to equal the future amount. By solving for PV in the future value equation, the present value, or discounting, equation can be developed and written in several forms:

$$PV = \frac{FV_n}{(1 + i)^n} = FV_n\left(\frac{1}{1 + i}\right)^n = FV_n(PVIF_{i,n}).$$

- To solve for the present value of $127.63 discounted back 5 years at a 5% opportunity cost rate, one can utilize any of the three solution methods:
  □ Numerical solution: Divide $127.63 by 1.05 five times to get PV = $100.

- ☐ Tabular solution: Refer to Table A-1 in Appendix A of the text for the present value interest factors ($PVIF_{i,n}$). The value of $PVIF_{i,n}$ for i = 5% and n = 5 is 0.7835. Multiply this number by $127.63 to get PV = $100.
- ☐ Financial calculator solution: Enter N = 5, I = 5, PMT = 0, and FV = 127.63, and then press the PV key to get PV = -100.

■ A graph of the discounting process shows how the present value of any sum to be received in the future diminishes as the years to receipt increases. At relatively high interest rates, funds due in the future are worth very little today, and even at a relatively low discount rate, the present value of a sum due in the very distant future is quite small.

There are four variables in the time value of money equations: PV, FV, i, and n. If three of the four variables are known, you can find the value of the fourth.

■ If we are given PV, FV, and n, we can determine i by substituting the known values into either the present value or future value equations, and then solving for i. Thus, if you can buy a security at a price of $78.35 which will pay you $100 after 5 years, what is the interest rate earned on the investment?
- ☐ Numerical solution: Use a trial and error process to reach the 5% value for i. This is a tedious and inefficient process.
- ☐ Tabular solution: Find the interest rate in Table A-3 of the text that corresponds to the future value interest factor of 1.2763 (calculated by dividing $100 by $78.35).
- ☐ Financial calculator solution: Enter N = 5, PV = -78.35, PMT = 0, and FV = 100, then press the I key, and I = 5 is displayed.

■ Likewise, if we are given PV, FV, and i, we can determine n by substituting the known values into either the present value or future value equations, and then solving for n. Thus, if you can buy a security with a 5 percent interest rate at a price of $78.35 today, how long will it take for your investment to return $100?
- ☐ Numerical solution: Use a trial and error process to reach the value of 5 for n. This is a tedious and inefficient process.
- ☐ Tabular solution: Find the value of n in Table A-3 of the text that corresponds to the future value interest factor of 1.2763 (found by dividing $100 by $78.35).
- ☐ Financial calculator solution: Enter I = 5, PV = -78.35, PMT = 0, and FV = 100, then press the N key, and N = 5 is displayed.

An annuity is a series of equal payments at fixed intervals for a specified number of periods. If the payments occur at the end of each period, as they typically do, the annuity is an ordinary

(or deferred) annuity. If the payments occur at the beginning of each period, it is called an annuity due.

- ■ The future value of an annuity is the total amount one would have at the end of the annuity period if each payment were invested at a given interest rate and held to the end of the annuity period.
  - ☐ Defining FVA_n as the compound sum of an ordinary annuity of n years, and PMT as the periodic payment, we can write

$$FVA_n = PMT \sum_{t=1}^{n} (1 + i)^{n-t} = PMT(FVIFA_{i,n}).$$

  - ☐ $FVIFA_{i,n}$ is the future value interest factor for an ordinary annuity. FVIFAs may be found in Table A-4 of the text.
  - ☐ For example, the future value of a 3-year, 5 percent ordinary annuity of $100 per year would be $100(3.1525) = $315.25.
  - ☐ The same calculation can be made using the financial function keys of a calculator. Enter N = 3, I = 5, PV = 0, and PMT = -100. Then press the FV key, and 315.25 is displayed.
  - ☐ For an annuity due, each payment is compounded for one additional period, so the future value of the entire annuity is equal to the future value of an ordinary annuity compounded for one additional period. Thus:

$$FVA_n \text{ (Annuity due)} = PMT(FVIFA_{i,n})(1 + i).$$

  - ☐ For example, the future value of a 3-year, 5 percent annuity due of $100 per year is $100(3.1525)(1.05) = $331.01.
  - ☐ Most financial calculators have a switch, or key, marked "DUE" or "BEG" that permits you to switch from end-of-period payments (an ordinary annuity) to beginning-of-period payments (an annuity due). Switch your calculator to "BEG" mode, and calculate as for an ordinary annuity. Do not forget to switch your calculator back to "END" mode when you are finished.

- ■ The present value of an annuity is the single (lump sum) payment today that would be equivalent to the annuity payments spread over the annuity period. It is the amount today that would permit withdrawals of an equal amount (PMT) at the end (or beginning for an annuity due) of each period for n periods.
  - ☐ Defining PVA_n as the present value of an ordinary annuity of n years and PMT as the periodic payment, we can write

$$PVA_n = PMT \sum_{t=1}^{n} \left(\frac{1}{1 + i} \right)^t = PMT(PVIFA_{i,n}).$$

  - ☐ $PVIFA_{i,n}$ is the present value interest factor for an ordinary annuity. PVIFAs may be found in Table A-2 at the back of the text.

- For example, an annuity of $100 per year for 3 years at 5 percent would have a present value of $100(2.7232) = $272.32.
- Using a financial calculator, enter N = 3, I = 5, PMT = -100, and FV = 0, and then press the PV key, for an answer of $272.32.
- The present value for an annuity due is

$$PVA_n \text{ (Annuity due)} = PMT(PVIFA_{i,n})(1 + i).$$

- For example, the present value of a 3-year, 5 percent annuity due of $100 is $100(2.7232)(1.05) = $285.94.
- Using a financial calculator, switch to the "BEG" mode, and then enter N = 3, I = 5, PMT = -100, and FV = 0, and then press PV to get the answer, $285.94. Again, do not forget to switch your calculator back to "END" mode when you are finished.

An annuity that goes on indefinitely is called a perpetuity. The payments of a perpetuity constitute an infinite series.

- The present value of a perpetuity is:

$$PV \text{ (Perpetuity)} = \text{Payment/Interest rate} = PMT/i.$$

- For example, if the interest rate were 12 percent, a perpetuity of $1,000 a year would have a present value of $1,000/0.12 = $8,333.33.

Many financial decisions require the analysis of uneven, or nonconstant, cash flows rather than a stream of fixed payments such as an annuity.

- The present value of an uneven stream of income is the sum of the PVs of the individual cash flow components. Similarly, the future value of an uneven stream of income is the sum of the FVs of the individual cash flow components.
  - With a financial calculator, enter each cash flow (beginning with the t=0 cash flow) into the cash flow register, CF_j, enter the appropriate interest rate, and then press the NPV key to obtain the PV of the cash flow stream.
  - Some calculators have a net future value (NFV) key which allows you to obtain the FV of an uneven cash flow stream. However, the cash flow stream's net present value can be used to find its net future value: $NFV = NPV(1 + i)^n$.

- If one knows the relevant cash flows, the effective interest rate can be calculated efficiently with a financial calculator. Enter each cash flow (beginning with the t=0 cash flow) into the cash flow register, CF_j, and then press the IRR key to obtain the interest rate of an uneven cash flow stream.

Semiannual, quarterly, and other compounding periods more frequent than on an annual basis are often used in financial transactions. Compounding on a nonannual basis requires an adjustment to both the compounding and discounting procedures discussed previously.

■ The *effective annual rate* is the rate that would have produced the final compound value under annual compounding. The effective annual percentage rate is given by the following formula:

$$\text{Effective annual rate (EAR or EFF\%)} = (1 + i_{Nom}/m)^m - 1.0,$$

where i_{Nom} is the nominal, or quoted, annual rate and m is the number of compounding periods per year. The EAR is useful in comparing securities with different compounding periods.

■ For example, to find the effective annual rate if the nominal rate is 6 percent and semiannual compounding is used, we have:

$$\text{EAR} = (1 + 0.06/2)^2 - 1.0 = 6.09\%.$$

■ For annual compounding use the formula to find the future value of a single payment (lump sum):

$$FV_n = PV(1 + i)^n.$$

When compounding occurs more frequently than once a year, use this formula:

$$FV_n = PV(1 + i_{Nom}/m)^{mn}.$$

Here m is the number of times per year compounding occurs, and n is the number of years.

■ The amount to which $1,000 will grow after 5 years if quarterly compounding is applied to a nominal 8 percent interest rate is found as follows:

$$FV_n = \$1,000(1 + 0.08/4)^{(4 \times 5)} = \$1,000(1.02)^{20} = \$1,485.95.$$

☐ Tabular solution: Divide the interest rate by 4, so i = 8%/4 = 2%, and multiply the number of years by 4, so n = 5 × 4 = 20. Look down the first column of Table A-3 to Period 20 and then across to the 2% column to find $FVIF_{2\%,20}$ = 1.4859. FV = 1.4859 × $1,000 = $1,485.90.

☐ Financial calculator solution: Enter N = 20, I = 2, PV = -1000, and PMT = 0, and then press the FV key to find FV = $1,485.95.

■ The present value of a 5-year future investment equal to $1,485.95, with an 8 percent nominal interest rate, compounded quarterly, is found as follows:

$$\$1,485.95 = PV(1 + 0.08/4)^{(4 \times 5)}$$

$$PV = \frac{\$1,485.95}{(1.02)^{20}} = \$1,000.$$

- ☐ Tabular solution: Use Table A-1, look down to Period 20 and then across to the 2% column to find $PVIF_{2\%,20} = 0.6730$. $PV = \$1,485.95 \times 0.6730 = \$1,000.04$.
- ☐ Financial calculator solution: Enter N = 20, I = 2, PMT = 0, and FV = 1485.95, and then press the PV key to find PV = -$1,000.00.

■ In general, nonannual compounding can be handled one of two ways.
- ☐ State everything on a periodic rather than on an annual basis. For example, n = 6 periods rather than n = 3 years and i = 3% instead of i = 6% with semiannual compounding.
- ☐ Find the effective annual rate (EAR) with the equation below and then use the EAR as the rate over the given number of years.

$$EAR = \left(1 + \frac{i_{Nom}}{m} \right)^m - 1.0.$$

Fractional time periods are used when payments occur within periods, instead of at either the beginning or the end of periods. Solving these problems requires using the fraction of the time period for n, number of periods, and then solving either numerically or with a financial calculator. (Some older calculators will produce incorrect answers because of their internal "solution" programs.)

An important application of compound interest involves amortized loans, which are paid off in equal installments over time.

■ The amount of each payment, PMT, is found as follows: PV of the annuity = $PMT(PVIFA_{i,n})$, so PMT = PV of the annuity/$PVIFA_{i,n}$.

■ With a financial calculator, enter N (number of years), I (interest rate), PV (amount borrowed), and FV = 0, and then press the PMT key to find the periodic payment.

■ Each payment consists partly of interest and partly of the repayment of principal. This breakdown is often developed in a loan amortization schedule.
- ☐ The interest component is largest in the first period, and it declines over the life of the loan.
- ☐ The repayment of principal is smallest in the first period, and it increases thereafter.

Appendix 6A discusses the formulas necessary for continuous compounding and discounting. The equation for continuous compounding is $FV_n = PV(e^{in})$ where e is the approximate value 2.7183...; the equation for continuous discounting is $PV = FV_n(e^{-in})$.

SELF-TEST QUESTIONS

Definitional

1. The beginning value of an account or investment in a project is known as its _____ _____.

2. Using a savings account as an example, the difference between the account's present value and its future value at the end of the period is due to _____ earned during the period.

3. The equation $FV_n = PV(1 + i)^n$ determines the future value of a sum at the end of n periods. The factor $(1 + i)^n$ is known as the _____ _____ _____ _____.

4. The process of finding present values is often referred to as _____ and is the reverse of the _____ process.

5. The $PVIF_{i,n}$ for a 5-year, 5 percent investment is 0.7835. This value is the _____ of the $FVIF_{i,n}$ for 5 years at 5 percent.

6. For a given number of time periods, the $PVIF_{i,n}$ will decline as the _____ _____ increases.

7. A series of payments of a constant amount for a specified number of periods is a(n) _____. If the payments occur at the end of each period it is a(n) _____ annuity, while if the payments occur at the beginning of each period it is an annuity _____.

8. The present value of an uneven stream of future payments is the _____ of the PVs of the individual payments.

9. Since different types of investments use different compounding periods, it is important to distinguish between the quoted, or _____, rate and the _____ annual interest rate.

10. To use the interest factor tables when compounding occurs more than once a year, divide the _____ _____ by the number of times compounding occurs and multiply the years by the number of _____ _____ per year.

Conceptual

11. If a bank uses quarterly compounding for savings accounts, the nominal rate will be greater than the effective annual rate (EAR).

   a. True   **b.** False

12. If money has time value (that is, i > 0), the future value of some amount of money will always be more than the amount invested. The present value of some amount to be received in the future is always less than the amount to be received.

   a. True   **b.** False

13. You have determined the profitability of a planned project by finding the present value of all the cash flows from that project. Which of the following would cause the project to look less appealing, that is, have a lower present value?

   a. The discount rate decreases.
   b. The cash flows are extended over a longer period of time.
   c. The discount rate increases.
   d. Statements b and c are both correct.
   e. Statements a and b are both correct.

14. As the discount rate increases without limit, the present value of a future cash inflow

   a. Gets larger without limit.
   b. Stays unchanged.
   c. Approaches zero.
   d. Gets smaller without limit; that is, approaches minus infinity.
   e. Goes to e^{in}.

15. Which of the following statements is most *correct*?

    a. For all positive values of i and n, $FVIF_{i,n} \geq 1.0$ and $PVIFA_{i,n} \geq n$.

    b. You may use the PVIF tables to find the present value of an uneven series of payments. However, the PVIFA tables can never be of use, even if some of the payments constitute an annuity (for example, $100 each year for Years 3, 4, 5, and 6), because the entire series does not constitute an annuity.

    c. If a bank uses quarterly compounding for savings accounts, the nominal rate will be greater than the effective annual rate.

    d. The present value of a future sum decreases as either the nominal interest rate or the number of discounting periods per year increases.

    e. All of the above statements are false.

16. Which of the following statements is most *correct*?

    a. Except in situations where compounding occurs annually, the periodic interest rate exceeds the nominal interest rate.

    b. The effective annual rate always exceeds the nominal rate, no matter how few or many compounding periods occur each year.

    c. If compounding occurs more frequently than once a year, and if payments are made at times other than at the end of compounding periods, it is impossible to determine present or future values, even with a financial calculator. The reason is that under these conditions, the basic assumptions of discounted cash flow analysis are not met.

    d. Assume that compounding occurs quarterly, that the nominal interest rate is 8 percent, and that you need to find the present value of $1,000 due 10 months from today. You could get the correct answer by discounting the $1,000 at 8.2432 percent for 10/12ths of a year.

    e. Statements a, b, c, and d are all false.

SELF-TEST PROBLEMS

(Note: In working these problems, you may get an answer which differs from ours by a few cents due to differences in rounding. This should not concern you; just pick the closest answer.)

1. Assume that you purchase a 6-year, 8 percent savings certificate for $1,000. If interest is compounded annually, what will be the value of the certificate when it matures?

    a. $630.17   **b.** $1,469.33   **c.** $1,677.10   **d.** $1,586.90   **e.** $1,766.33

2. A savings certificate similar to the one in the previous problem is available with the exception that interest is compounded semiannually. What is the difference between the ending value of the savings certificate compounded semiannually and the one compounded annually?

    a. The semiannual is worth $14.10 more than the annual.
    b. The semiannual is worth $14.10 less than the annual.
    c. The semiannual is worth $21.54 more than the annual.
    d. The semiannual is worth $21.54 less than the annual.
    e. The semiannual is worth the same as the annual.

3. A friend promises to pay you $600 two years from now if you loan him $500 today. What annual interest rate is your friend offering?

    a. 7.5%   **b.** 8.5%   **c.** 9.5%   **d.** 10.5%   **e.** 11.5%

4. At an inflation rate of 9 percent, the purchasing power of $1 would be cut in half in just over 8 years (some calculators round to 9 years). How long, to the nearest year, would it take for the purchasing power of $1 to be cut in half if the inflation rate were only 4 percent?

    a. 12 years   **b.** 15 years   **c.** 18 years   **d.** 20 years   **e.** 23 years

5. You are offered an investment opportunity with the "guarantee" that your investment will double in 5 years. Assuming annual compounding, what annual rate of return would this investment provide?

    a. 40.00%   **b.** 100.00%   **c.** 14.87%   **d.** 20.00%   **e.** 18.74%

6. You decide to begin saving toward the purchase of a new car in 5 years. If you put $1,000 at the end of each of the next 5 years in a savings account paying 6 percent compounded annually, how much will you accumulate after 5 years?

    a. $6,691.13   **b.** $5,637.10   **c.** $1,338.23   **d.** $5,975.33   **e.** $5,732.00

7. Refer to Self-Test Problem 6. What would be the ending amount if the payments were made at the beginning of each year?

    a. $6,691.13   **b.** $5,637.10   **c.** $1,338.23   **d.** $5,975.33   **e.** $5,732.00

8. Refer to Self-Test Problem 6. What would be the ending amount if $500 payments were made at the end of each 6-month period for 5 years and the account paid 6 percent compounded semiannually?

    a. $6,691.13   **b.** $5,637.10   **c.** $1,338.23   **d.** $5,975.33   **e.** $5,732.00

9. Calculate the present value of $1,000 to be received at the end of 8 years. Assume an interest rate of 7 percent.

    a. $582.00   **b.** $1,718.19   **c.** $531.82   **d.** $5,971.30   **e.** $649.37

10. How much would you be willing to pay today for an investment that would return $800 each year at the end of each of the next 6 years? Assume a discount rate of 5 percent.

    a. $5,441.53   **b.** $4,800.00   **c.** $3,369.89   **d.** $4,060.56   **e.** $4,632.37

11. You have applied for a mortgage of $60,000 to finance the purchase of a new home. The bank will require you to make annual payments of $7,047.55 at the end of each of the next 20 years. Determine the interest rate in effect on this mortgage.

    a. 8.0%   **b.** 9.8%   **c.** 10.0%   **d.** 51.0%   **e.** 11.2%

12. If you would like to accumulate $7,500 over the next 5 years, how much must you deposit each six months, starting six months from now, given a 6 percent interest rate and semiannual compounding?

    a. $1,330.47   **b.** $879.23   **c.** $654.22   **d.** $569.00   **e.** $732.67

13. A company is offering bonds which pay $100 per year indefinitely. If you require a 12 percent return on these bonds—that is, the discount rate is 12 percent—what is the value of each bond?

   a. $1,000.00   b. $962.00   c. $904.67   d. $866.67   e. $833.33

14. What is the present value (t = 0) of the following cash flows if the discount rate is 12 percent?

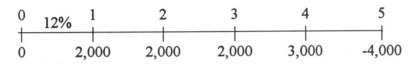

   a. $4,782.43   b. $4,440.50   c. $4,221.79   d. $4,041.23   e. $3,997.98

15. What is the effective annual percentage rate (EAR) of 12 percent compounded monthly?

   a. 12.00%   b. 12.55%   c. 12.68%   d. 12.75%   e. 13.00%

16. Martha Mills, manager of Plaza Gold Emporium, wants to sell on credit, giving customers 3 months in which to pay. However, Martha will have to borrow from her bank to carry the accounts payable. The bank will charge a nominal 16 percent, but with monthly compounding. Martha wants to quote a nominal rate to her customers (all of whom are expected to pay on time at the end of 3 months) *which will exactly cover her financing costs.* What nominal annual rate should she quote to her credit customers? (Note: Interest factor tables cannot be used to solve this problem.)

   a. 15.44%   b. 15.77%   c. 17.11%   d. 16.21%   e. 16.88%

17. Self-Test Problem 11 refers to a 20-year mortgage of $60,000. This is an amortized loan. How much principal will be repaid in the second year?

   a. $1,152.30   b. $1,725.70   c. $5,895.25   d. $7,047.55   e. $1,047.55

18. You have $1,000 invested in an account which pays 16 percent compounded annually. A commission agent (called a "finder") can locate for you an equally safe deposit which will pay 16 percent, compounded quarterly, for 2 years. What is the maximum amount you should be willing to pay him now as a fee for locating the new account?

   a. $10.92   b. $13.78   c. $16.14   d. $16.81   e. $21.13

19. The present value (t = 0) of the following cash flow stream is $11,958.20 when discounted at 12 percent annually. What is the value of the missing t = 2 cash flow?

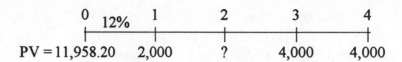

$$PV = 11,958.20 \quad 2,000 \quad ? \quad 4,000 \quad 4,000$$

   a. $4,000.00   **b.** $4,500.00   **c.** $5,000.00   **d.** $5,500.00   **e.** $6,000.00

20. Today is your birthday, and you decide to start saving for your college education. You will begin college on your 18th birthday and will need $4,000 per year at the *end* of each of the following 4 years. You will make a deposit 1 year from today in an account paying 12 percent annually and continue to make an identical deposit each year up to and including the year you begin college. If a deposit amount of $2,542.05 will allow you to reach your goal, what birthday are you celebrating today?

   a. 13   **b.** 14   **c.** 15   **d.** 16   **e.** 17

21. Assume that your aunt sold her house on December 31 and that she took a mortgage in the amount of $10,000 as part of the payment. The mortgage has a stated (or nominal) interest rate of 10 percent, but it calls for payments every 6 months, beginning on June 30, and the mortgage is to be amortized over 10 years. Now, one year later, your aunt must file Schedule B of her tax return with the IRS, informing them of the interest that was included in the two payments made during the year. (This interest will be income to your aunt and a deduction to the buyer of the house.) What is the total amount of interest that was paid during the first year?

   a. $1,604.86   **b.** $619.98   **c.** $984.88   **d.** $1,205.76   **e.** $750.02

22. Assume that you inherited some money. A friend of yours is working as an unpaid intern at a local brokerage firm, and her boss is selling some securities which call for four payments, $50 at the end of each of the next 3 years, plus a payment of $1,050 at the end of Year 4. Your friend says she can get you some of these securities at a cost of $900 each. Your money is now invested in a bank that pays an 8 percent nominal (quoted) interest rate, but with quarterly compounding. You regard the securities as being just as safe, and as liquid, as your bank deposit, so your required effective annual rate of return on the securities is the same as that on your bank deposit. You must calculate the value of the securities to decide whether they are a good investment. What is their present value to you? (Note: Interest factor tables cannot be used to solve this problem.)

    a. $957.75   **b.** $888.66   **c.** $923.44   **d.** $1,015.25   **e.** $893.26

23. Your company is planning to borrow $1,000,000 on a 5-year, 15 percent, annual payment, fully amortized term loan. What fraction of the payment made at the end of the second year will represent repayment of principal?

    a. 57.18%   **b.** 42.82%   **c.** 50.28%   **d.** 49.72%   **e.** 60.27%

24. Your firm can borrow from its bank for one month. The loan will have to be "rolled over" at the end of the month, but you are sure the rollover will be allowed. The nominal interest rate is 14 percent, but interest will have to be paid at the end of each month, so the bank interest rate is 14 percent, monthly compounding. Alternatively, your firm can borrow from an insurance company at a nominal rate which would involve quarterly compounding. What nominal quarterly rate would be equivalent to the rate charged by the bank? (Note: Interest factor tables cannot be used to solve this problem.)

    a. 12.44%   **b.** 14.16%   **c.** 13.55%   **d.** 13.12%   **e.** 12.88%

25. Assume that you have $15,000 in a bank account that pays 5 percent annual interest. You plan to go back to school for a combination MBA/law degree 5 years from today. It will take you an additional 5 years to complete your graduate studies. You figure you will need a fixed income of $25,000 in today's dollars; that is, you will need $25,000 of today's dollars during your first year and each subsequent year. (*Thus, your real income will decline while you are in school.*) You will withdraw funds for your annual expenses at the beginning of each year. Inflation is expected to occur at the rate of 3 percent per year. How much must you save during each of the next 5 years in order to achieve your goal? The first increment of savings will be deposited one year from today.

    a. $20,241.66   **b.** $19,224.55   **c.** $18,792.11   **d.** $19,559.42   **e.** $20,378.82

26. You plan to buy a new HDTV. The dealer offers to sell you the set on credit. You will have 3 months in which to pay, but the dealer says you will be charged a 15 percent interest rate; that is, the nominal rate is 15 percent, quarterly compounding. As an alternative to buying on credit, you can borrow the funds from your bank, but the bank will make you pay interest each month. At what nominal bank interest rate should you be indifferent between the two types of credit?

    a. 13.7643%   **b.** 14.2107%   **c.** 14.8163%   **d.** 15.5397%   **e.** 15.3984%

27. Assume that your father is now 50 years old, that he plans to retire in 10 years, and that he expects to live for 25 years after he retires, that is, until he is 85. He wants a fixed retirement income that has the same purchasing power at the time he retires as $60,000 has today (he realizes that the real value of his retirement income will decline year-by-year after he retires). His retirement income will begin the day he retires, 10 years from today, and he will then get 24 additional annual payments. Inflation is expected to be 5 percent per year from today forward; he currently has $150,000 saved up; and he expects to earn a return on his savings of 7 percent per year, annual compounding. To the nearest dollar, how much must he save during each of the next 10 years (with deposits being made at the end of each year) to meet his retirement goal?

    a. $66,847.95   **b.** $77,201.21   **c.** $54,332.88   **d.** $41,987.33   **e.** $62,191.25

Appendix 6A

A-1. If you receive $30,000 today and can invest it at a 4 percent annual rate compounded continuously, then what will its future value be in 10 years?

    a. $31,224.32   **b.** $38,327   **c.** $40,765   **d.** $44,754.74   **e.** $42,121

A-2. What is the present value of $125,000 due in 15 years, if the appropriate continuous discount rate is 6 percent?

    a. $44,754.74   **b.** $50,821.21   **c.** $38,327   **d.** $42,121   **e.** $40,765

ANSWERS TO SELF-TEST QUESTIONS

1. present value
2. interest
3. future value interest factor
4. discounting; compounding
5. reciprocal

6. interest rate
7. annuity; ordinary; due
8. sum
9. nominal; effective
10. nominal rate; compounding periods

11. b. The EAR is always greater than or equal to the nominal rate.

12. a. Both these statements are correct.

13. d. The slower the cash flows come in and the higher the interest rate, the lower the present value.

14. c. As the discount rate increases, the present value of a future sum decreases and eventually approaches zero.

15. d. As a future sum is discounted over more and more periods, the present value will get smaller and smaller. Likewise, as the discount rate increases, the present value of a future sum decreases and eventually approaches zero.

16. d. 8.2432 percent is the EAR corresponding to a nominal rate of 8 percent with quarterly compounding, and we would discount back for 10/12 of a year at the EAR to obtain the present value. Statement a is false because the periodic interest rate is equal to the nominal rate divided by the number of compounding periods, so it will be equal to or smaller than the nominal rate. Statement b is false because the EAR will equal the nominal rate if there is one compounding period per year (annual compounding). Statement c is false because we can determine present or future values under the stated conditions.

SOLUTIONS TO SELF-TEST PROBLEMS

1. d.

```
    0  8%  1    2    3    4    5    6
    |--+--+----+----+----+----+----+
   -1,000                      FV₆=?
```

$$FV_n = PV(FVIF_{i,n}) = \$1,000(FVIF_{8\%,6}) = \$1,000(1.5869) = \$1,586.90.$$

With a financial calculator, input $N = 6$, $I = 8$, $PV = -1000$, $PMT = 0$, and solve for $FV = \$1,586.87$.

2. a.

```
    0         1         2         3         4         5         6   Years
    0   1     2    3     4   5     6   7     8   9    10   11    12  Periods
    |-4%-+----+----+----+----+----+----+----+----+----+----+----+
  -1,000                                                     FV=?
```

$$FVIF_{i,n} = FVIF_{4\%,12} = 1.6010.$$

Thus, $FV_n = \$1,000(1.6010) = \$1,601.00$. The difference, $\$1,601.00 - \$1,586.90 = \$14.10$, is the additional interest.

With a financial calculator, input $N = 12$, $I = 4$, $PV = -1000$, and $PMT = 0$, and then solve for $FV = \$1,601.03$. The difference, $\$1,601.03 - \$1,586.87 = \$14.16$.

3. c.

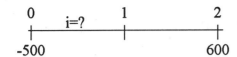

$$FV_2 = PV(FVIF_{i,2})$$
$$\$600 = \$500(FVIF_{i,2})$$
$$FVIF_{i,2} = 1.2000.$$

Looking across the Period 2 row in Table A-3, we see $FVIF_{9\%,2} = 1.1881$ and $FVIF_{10\%,2} = 1.2100$. Therefore, the annual interest rate is between 9% and 10%.

With a financial calculator, input N = 2, PV = -500, PMT = 0, FV = 600, and solve for I = 9.54%.

4. c.

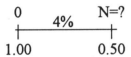

With a financial calculator, input I = 4, PV = -1.00, PMT = 0, and FV = 0.50. Solve for N = 17.67 ≈ 18 years.

5. c.

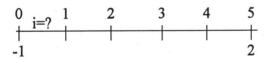

Assume any value for the present value and double it:

$$FV_5 = PV(FVIF_{i,5})$$
$$\$2 = \$1(FVIF_{i,5})$$
$$FVIF_{i,5} = 2.0000.$$

Looking across the Period 5 row in Table A-3, we see that 2.0000 occurs between 14% and 15%.

With a financial calculator, input N = 5, PV = -1, PMT = 0, FV = 2, and solve for I = 14.87%.

6. b.

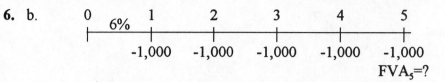

$FVA_5 = PMT(FVIFA_{6\%,5}) = \$1,000(5.6371) = \$5,637.10.$

With a financial calculator, input N = 5, I = 6, PV = 0, PMT = -1000, and solve for FV = $5,637.09.

7. d.

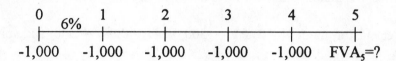

$FVA_5(\text{Annuity due}) = PMT(FVIFA_{6\%,5})(1 + i) = \$1,000(5.6371)(1.06) = \$5,975.33.$

With a financial calculator, switch to "BEG" mode, then input N = 5, I = 6, PV = 0, PMT = -1000, and solve for FV = $5,975.32. Be sure to switch back to "END" mode.

8. e.

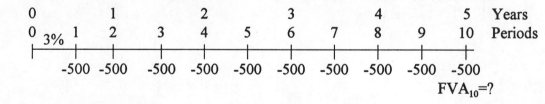

$FVA_{10} = PMT(FVIFA_{3\%,10}) = \$500(11.464) = \$5,732.00.$

With a financial calculator, input N = 10, I = 3, PV = 0, PMT = -500, and solve for FV = $5,731.94.

(Note: In order to use the annuity tables, the compounding period and payment period *must be the same*; in this case, both are semiannual. If this is not the case, each cash flow must be treated individually.)

9. a.

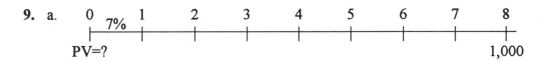

$$PV = FV_8(PVIF_{7\%,8}) = \$1{,}000(0.5820) = \$582.00.$$

With a financial calculator, input N = 8, I = 7, PMT = 0, FV = 1000, and solve for PV = -$582.01.

(Note: Annual compounding is assumed if not otherwise specified.)

10. d.

```
 0   5%   1     2     3     4     5     6
 |---------|-----|-----|-----|-----|-----|
PVA=?    800   800   800   800   800   800
```

$$PVA_6 = PMT(PVIFA_{5\%,6}) = \$800(5.0757) = \$4{,}060.56.$$

With a financial calculator, input N = 6, I = 5, PMT = 800, FV = 0, and solve for PV = -$4,060.55.

11. c.

```
   0    i=?   1         2         3              20
   |----------|---------|---------|-----...-------|
60,000   -7,047.55  -7,047.55  -7,047.55       -7,047.55
```

The amount of the mortgage ($60,000) is the present value of a 20-year ordinary annuity with payments of $7,047.55. Therefore,

$$
\begin{aligned}
PVA_{20} &= PMT(PVIFA_{i,20}) \\
\$60{,}000 &= \$7{,}047.55(PVIFA_{i,20}) \\
PVIFA_{i,20} &= 8.5136 \\
i &= 10.00\% \text{ exactly.}
\end{aligned}
$$

With a financial calculator, input N = 20, PV = 60000, PMT = -7047.55, FV = 0, and solve for I = 10.00%.

12. c.

	0		1		2		3		4		5	Years
0 3%	1	2	3	4	5	6	7	8	9	10		Periods

-PMT -PMT -PMT -PMT -PMT -PMT -PMT -PMT -PMT -PMT

7,500

$$FVA_{10} = PMT(FVIFA_{3\%,10})$$
$$\$7,500 = PMT(11.464)$$
$$PMT = \$654.22.$$

With a financial calculator, input N = 10, I = 3, PV = 0, FV = 7500, and solve for PMT = -\$654.23.

13. e. $PV = PMT/i = \$100/0.12 = \$833.33.$

14. b. $PV = \$2,000(PVIFA_{12\%,3}) + \$3,000(PVIF_{12\%,4}) - \$4,000(PVIF_{12\%,5})$
$$= \$2,000(2.4018) + \$3,000(0.6355) - \$4,000(0.5674)$$
$$= \$4,440.50.$$

With a financial calculator, using the cash flow register, CF_j, input 0; 2000; 2000; 2000; 3000; and -4000. Enter I = 12 and solve for NPV = \$4,440.51.

15. c. $EAR = (1 + i_{Nom}/m)^m - 1.0$
$$= (1 + 0.12/12)^{12} - 1.0$$
$$= (1.01)^{12} - 1.0$$
$$= 1.1268 - 1.0$$
$$= 0.1268 = 12.68\%.$$

16. d. Here we want to have the same effective annual rate on the credit extended as on the bank loan that will be used to finance the credit extension.

First, we must find the EAR = EFF% on the bank loan. Enter on your calculator P/YR = 12, NOM% = 16, and press EFF% to get EAR = 17.23%.

Now recognize that giving 3 months of credit is equivalent to quarterly compounding; interest is earned at the end of the quarter, so it is available to earn interest during the next quarter. Therefore, enter on your calculator P/YR = 4, EFF% = EAR = 17.23%, and press NOM% to find the nominal rate of 16.21%. Therefore, if Martha charges a 16.21% nominal rate and gives credit for 3 months, she will cover the cost of her bank loan.

Alternative solution: First, we need to find the effective annual rate charged by the bank:

$$\begin{aligned}
\text{EAR} &= (1 + i_{Nom}/m)^m - 1 \\
&= (1 + 0.16/12)^{12} - 1 \\
&= (1.0133)^{12} - 1 = 17.23\%.
\end{aligned}$$

Now, we can find the nominal rate Martha must quote her customers so that her financing costs are exactly covered:

$$\begin{aligned}
17.23\% &= (1 + i_{Nom}/4)^4 - 1 \\
1.1723 &= (1 + i_{Nom}/4)^4 \\
1.0405 &= 1 + i_{Nom}/4 \\
0.0405 &= i_{Nom}/4 \\
i_{Nom} &= 16.22\%.
\end{aligned}$$

17. a.

Year	Payment	Interest	Repayment on Principal	Remaining Principal Balance
1	$7,047.55	$6,000.00	$1,047.55	$58,952.45
2	7,047.55	5,895.25	1,152.30	57,800.15

18. d. Currently: $FV_n = \$1,000(FVIF_{16\%,2}) = \$1,000(1.3456) = \$1,345.60$.

With a financial calculator, input $N = 2$, $I = 16$, $PV = -1000$, $PMT = 0$, and solve for $FV = \$1,345.60$.

New account: $FV_n = \$1,000(1 + i_{Nom}/m)^{mn} = \$1,000(1.3686) = \$1,368.60$.

With a financial calculator, input $N = 8$, $I = 4$, $PV = -1000$, $PMT = 0$, and solve for $FV = \$1,368.57$.

Thus, the new account will be worth $\$1,368.60 - \$1,345.60 = \$23.00$ more after 2 years. (With a financial calculator, the new account will be worth $\$22.97$ more after 2 years.)

PV of difference $= \$23(PVIF_{4\%,8}) = \$23(0.7307) = \$16.81$. With a financial calculator, input $N = 8$, $I = 4$, $PMT = 0$, $FV = 22.97$, and solve for $PV = -\$16.78$.

Therefore, the most you should be willing to pay the finder for locating the new account is $\$16.81$.

19. e. $\$11,958.20 = \$2,000(PVIF_{12\%,1}) + CF_2(PVIF_{12\%,2}) + \$4,000(PVIF_{12\%,3}) + \$4,000(PVIF_{12\%,4})$
$\$11,958.20 = \$2,000(0.8929) + CF_2(0.7972) + \$4,000(0.7118) + \$4,000(0.6355)$
$\$11,958.20 = \$7,175.00 + 0.7972CF_2$
$0.7972CF_2 = \$4,783.20$
$CF_2 = \$6,000.00$.

With a financial calculator, input the cash flows in the cash flow register, using 0 as the value for the unknown cash flow, input $I = 12$, and then press the NPV key to solve for the present value of the unknown cash flow, $\$4,783.29$. This value should be compounded by $(1.12)^2$, so that $\$4,783.29(1.2544) = \$6,000.16$.

20. b. First, how much must you accumulate on your 18th birthday?

$$PVA_n = \$4,000(PVIFA_{12\%,4}) = \$4,000(3.0373) = \$12,149.20.$$

Present birthday = ?

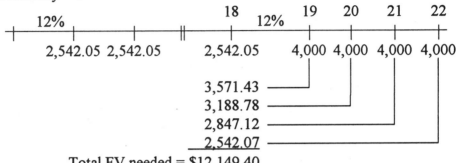

Total FV needed = $\underline{\$12,149.40}$

Using a financial calculator (with the calculator set for an ordinary annuity), enter N = 4, I = 12, PMT = 4000, FV = 0, and solve for PV = -$12,149.40. This is the amount (or lump sum) that must be present in your bank account on your 18th birthday in order for you to be able to withdraw $4,000 at the end of each year for the next 4 years.

Now, how many payments must you make to accumulate $12,149.20?

$$FVA_n = \$12,149.20 = \$2,542.05(FVIFA_{12\%,n}).$$
$$FVIFA_{12\%,n} = 4.7793$$
$$n = 4, \text{ from Table A-4 in text.}$$

Using a financial calculator, enter I = 12, PV = 0, PMT = -2542.05, FV = 12149.40, and solve for N = 4. Therefore, if you make payments at 18, 17, 16, and 15, you are now 14.

21. c. This can be done with a calculator by specifying an interest rate of 5 percent per period for 20 periods with 1 payment per period, or 10 percent interest, 20 periods, 2 payments per year. Either way, we get the payment each 6 months:

$N = 10 \times 2 = 20$.
$I = 10/2 = 5$.
$PV = -10000$.
$FV = 0$.
$PMT = \$802.43$.
Set up an amortization table:

Period	Beginning Balance	Payment	Interest	Payment of Principal	Ending Balance
1	$10,000.00	$802.43	$500.00	$302.43	$9,697.57
2	9,697.57	802.43	484.88		
			$984.88		

You can really just work the problem with a financial calculator using the amortization function. Find the interest in each 6-month period, sum them, and you have the answer. Even simpler, with some calculators such as the HP 17B, just input 2 for periods and press INT to get the interest during the first year, $984.88.

22. e.

Discount rate: Effective annual rate on bank deposit:

$$EAR = (1 + 0.08/4)^4 - 1 = 8.24\%.$$

Input the cash flows in the cash flow register, input I = 8.24, and solve for NPV = $893.26. Or, get PV = -$893.26 by inputting N = 4, I = 8.24, PMT = 50, and FV = 1000. Alternatively, each cash flow could be discounted to t = 0 and summed.

```
       0   8.24%  1       2       3       4
       +----------+-------+-------+-------+
     PV=?       50      50      50    1,050
     46.19 ——┘
     42.68 ————————┘
     39.43 ————————————————┘
     764.96 ————————————————————————┘
PV = 893.26
```

$$PV = \frac{\$50}{1.0824} + \frac{\$50}{(1.0824)^2} + \frac{\$50}{(1.0824)^3} + \frac{\$1,050}{(1.0824)^4} = \$893.26.$$

23. a. Input N = 5, I = 15, PV = -1000000, and FV = 0 to solve for PMT = $298,315.55.

Year	Beginning Balance	Payment	Interest	Payment of Principal	Ending Balance
1	$1,000,000.00	$298,315.55	$150,000.00	$148,315.55	$851,684.45
2	851,684.45	298,315.55	127,752.67	170,562.88	681,121.57

The fraction that is principal is $170,562.88/$298,315.55 = 57.18%.

24. b. Start with a time line to picture the situation:

Bank: 14% nominal; EAR = 14.93%.

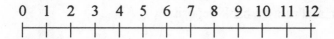

Insurance company: EAR = 14.93%; Nominal = 14.16%.

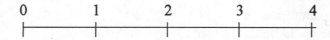

Here we must find the EAR on the bank loan and then find the quarterly nominal rate for that EAR. The bank loan amounts to a nominal 14 percent, monthly compounding.

Using the interest conversion feature of the calculator, or the EAR formula, we must find the EAR on the bank loan. Enter P/YR = 12 and NOM% = 14, and then press the EFF% key to find EAR bank loan = 14.93%.

Now, we can find the nominal rate with quarterly compounding that also has an EAR of 14.93 percent. Enter P/YR = 4 and EFF% = 14.93, and then press the NOM% key to get 14.16%. If the insurance company quotes a nominal rate of 14.16%, with quarterly compounding, then the bank and insurance company loans would be equivalent in the sense that they both have the same effective annual rate, 14.93%.

Alternative solution:

$$EAR = (1 + i_{Nom}/12)^{12} - 1$$
$$= (1 + 0.14/12)^{12} - 1$$
$$= 14.93\%.$$

$$14.93\% = (1 + i_{Nom}/4)^4 - 1$$
$$1.1493 = (1 + i_{Nom}/4)^4$$
$$1.0354 = 1 + i_{Nom}/4$$
$$0.0354 = i_{Nom}/4$$
$$i_{Nom} = 14.16\%.$$

25. e. Inflation = 3%

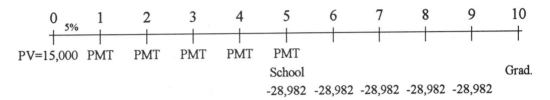

Fixed income = $25,000(1.03)^5 = $28,981.85.

1. Find the FV of $25,000 compounded for 5 years at 3 percent; that FV, $28,981.85, is the amount you will need each year while you are in school. (Note: Your real income will decline.)

2. You must have enough in 5 years to make the $28,981.85 payments to yourself. These payments will begin as soon as you start school, so we are dealing with a 5-year, 5 percent interest rate, *annuity due*. Set the calculator to "BEG" mode, because we are dealing with an annuity due, and then enter N = 5, I = 5, PMT = -28981.85, and FV = 0. Then press the PV key to find the PV, $131,750.06. This is the amount you must have in your account 5 years from today. (Do not forget to switch the calculator back to "END" mode.)

3. You now have $15,000. It will grow at 5 percent to $19,144.22 after 5 years. Enter N = 5, I = 5, PV = -15000, and PMT = 0 to solve for FV = 19,144.22. You can subtract this amount to determine the FV of the amount you must save: $131,750.06 – $19,144.22 = $112,605.84.

4. Therefore, you must accumulate an additional $112,605.84 by saving PMT per year for 5 years, with the first PMT being deposited at the end of this year and earning a 5 percent interest rate. Now we have an ordinary annuity, so be sure you returned your calculator to "END" mode. Enter N = 5, I = 5, PV = 0, FV = 112605.84, and then press PMT to find the required payments, -$20,378.82.

Alternative solution (using interest factor tables):

1. Find the FV of $25,000 compounded for 5 years at 3 percent:

    $$FV_5 = \$25,000(FVIF_{3\%,5}) = \$25,000(1.1593) = \$28,982.50.$$

    This is the amount you will need each year while you're in school. (Note: Your real income will decline.)

2. You must have enough in 5 years to make the $28,982.50 payments to yourself. These payments will begin as soon as you start school, so we are dealing with a 5-year, 5 percent interest rate, *annuity due*.

    $$\begin{aligned} PVA_5 \text{ (Annuity due)} &= PMT(PVIFA_{5\%,5})(1.05) \\ &= \$28,982.50(4.3295)(1.05) = \$131,753.72. \end{aligned}$$

    This is the amount you must have in your account 5 years from today.

3. You now have $15,000. It will grow at 5 percent for 5 years.

    $$FV_5 = \$15,000(FVIF_{5\%,5}) = \$15,000(1.2763) = \$19,144.50.$$

    You can subtract this amount to determine the FV of the amount you must save: $131,753.72 – $19,144.50 = $112,609.22.

4. Therefore, you must accumulate an additional $112,609.22 by saving PMT per year for 5 years, with the first PMT being deposited at the end of this year and earning a 5 percent interest rate. Now we have an ordinary annuity:

    $$\begin{aligned} FVA_5 &= PMT(FVIFA_{5\%,5}) \\ \$112,609.22 &= PMT(5.5256) \\ PMT &= \$20,379.55. \end{aligned}$$

26. c. Find the EAR on the TV dealer's credit. Use the interest conversion feature of your calculator. First, though, note that if you are charged a 15 percent nominal rate, you will have to pay interest of 15%/4 = 3.75% after 3 months. The dealer then has the use of the interest, so he can earn 3.75 percent on it for the next three months, and so forth. Thus, we are dealing with quarterly compounding. The nominal rate is 15 percent, quarterly compounding.

Enter NOM% = 15, P/YR = 4, and then press EFF% to get EAR = 15.8650%.

You should be indifferent between the dealer credit and the bank loan if the bank loan has an EAR of 15.8650 percent. The bank is using monthly compounding, or 12 periods per year. To find the nominal rate at which you should be indifferent, enter P/YR = 12, EFF% = 15.8650, and then press NOM% to get NOM% = 14.8163%.

Conclusion: A loan that has a 14.8163 percent nominal rate with monthly compounding is equivalent to a 15 percent nominal rate loan with quarterly compounding. Both have an EAR of 15.8650 percent.

Alternative solution:

$$EAR = (1 + i_{Nom}/4)^4 - 1 = (1 + 0.15/4)^4 - 1 = (1.0375)^4 - 1 = 15.8650\%.$$
$$15.8650\% = (1 + i_{Nom}/12)^{12} - 1$$
$$1.15865 = (1 + i_{Nom}/12)^{12}$$
$$1.012347 = 1 + i_{Nom}/12$$
$$i_{Nom} = 14.8163\%.$$

27. a. Information given:

1. Will save for 10 years, then receive payments for 25 years.

2. Wants payments of $60,000 per year in today's dollars for first payment only. Real income will decline. Inflation will be 5 percent. Therefore, to find the inflated fixed payments, we have this time line:

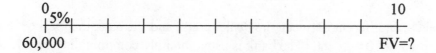

Enter N = 10, I = 5, PV = -60000, PMT = 0, and press FV to get FV = $97,733.68.

3. He now has $150,000 in an account which pays 7 percent, annual compounding. We need to find the FV of the $150,000 after 10 years. Enter N = 10, I = 7, PV = -150000, PMT = 0, and press FV to get FV = $295,072.70.

4. He wants to withdraw, or have payments of, $97,733.68 per year for 25 years, with the first payment made at the beginning of the first retirement year. So, we have a 25-year annuity due with PMT = $97,733.68, at an interest rate of 7 percent. (The interest rate is 7 percent annually, so no adjustment is required.) Set the calculator to "BEG" mode, then enter N = 25, I = 7, PMT = -97733.68, FV = 0, and press PV to get PV = $1,218,673.90. This amount must be on hand to make the 25 payments.

5. Since the original $150,000, which grows to $295,072.70, will be available, he must save enough to accumulate $1,218,673.90 - $295,072.70 = $923,601.20.

6. The $923,601.20 is the FV of a 10-year ordinary annuity. The payments will be deposited in the bank and earn 7 percent interest. Therefore, set the calculator to "END" mode and enter N = 10, I = 7, PV = 0, FV = 923601.20, and press PMT to find PMT = -$66,847.95.

Alternative solution (using interest factor tables):

Information given:

1. Will save for 10 years, then receive payments for 25 years.

2. Wants payments of $60,000 per year in today's dollars for *first payment only*. Real income will decline. Inflation will be 5 percent. Therefore, to find the inflated fixed payment use the following equation:

$$FV_{10} = PV(FVIF_{5\%,10}) = \$60,000(1.6289) = \$97,734.00.$$

3. He now has $150,000 in an account which pays 7 percent, annual compounding. We need to find the FV of the $150,000 after 10 years:

$$FV_{10} = PV(FVIF_{7\%,10}) = \$150,000(1.9672) = \$295,080.$$

4. He wants to withdraw, or have payments of, $97,734.00 per year for 25 years, with the first payment made at the beginning of the first retirement year. So, we have a 25-year *annuity due* with payments of $97,734.00, at an interest rate of 7 percent annually.

$$\begin{aligned} PVA_{25} \text{ (Annuity due)} &= \$97,734.00(PVIFA_{7\%,25})(1.07) \\ &= \$97,734.00(11.6536)(1.07) \\ &= \$1,218,679.65. \end{aligned}$$

This amount must be on hand to make the 25 payments.

5. Since the original $150,000, which grows to $295,080, will be available, he must save enough to accumulate $1,218,679.65 – $295,080.00 = $923,599.65.

6. The $923,599.65 is the FV of a 10-year ordinary annuity. The payments will be deposited in the bank and earn 7 percent interest. Therefore, use the following equation to calculate the yearly payments:

$$\begin{aligned} FVA_{10} &= PMT(FVIFA_{7\%,10}) \\ \$923,599.65 &= PMT(13.816) \\ PMT &= \$66,850.00. \end{aligned}$$

Appendix 6A

A-1. d. $FV_n = PV\,e^{in}$
$FV_{10} = \$30,000\,e^{0.04(10)}$
$= \$30,000\,e^{0.4}$
$= \$44,754.74.$

A-2. b. $PV = FV_n\,e^{-in} = \$125,000\,e^{-0.90} = \$50,821.21.$

CHAPTER 7

VALUATION MODELS

OVERVIEW

This chapter uses the discounted cash flow (DCF) concept to determine the values of bonds and stocks. The value of any financial asset is the present value of the cash flows expected from that asset. Therefore, once the cash flows have been estimated, and a discount rate determined, the value of the financial asset can be calculated. A bond is valued as the present value of the stream of interest payments (an annuity) plus the present value of the par value which is received by the investor on the bond's maturity date. Depending on the relationship between the current interest rate and the bond's coupon rate, a bond can sell at its par value, at

a discount, or at a premium. The total rate of return on a bond is comprised of two components: an interest yield and a capital gains yield.

The value of a share of preferred stock which is expected to pay a constant dividend forever is found as the dividend divided by the required rate of return. A common stock is valued as the present value of the expected future dividend stream. The total rate of return on a stock is comprised of a dividend yield plus a capital gains yield. For both stocks and bonds, the total expected return must equal the average investor's required rate of return.

OUTLINE

Securities are pieces of paper that represent claims against assets such as land, plant and equipment, commodities, or other securities. There are two basic types of securities: direct claim securities and indirect claim securities.

- *Direct claim securities* have claims against the cash flows produced by real assets; hence, their values are tied directly to those real assets. Examples of direct claim securities include bonds and stocks.
  - ☐ Stocks, bonds, and most other direct claim securities are valued using discounted cash flow techniques.
  - ☐ Direct claim securities can be broken down into three primary classes: debt, preferred stock, and common stock.

■ *Indirect claim, or derivative, securities* are those whose values are derived from some other security, asset, or index. Examples of indirect claim securities include options and futures.

   □ Options, futures, and other derivatives have values which are based on a set of factors which include the current price of the underlying asset, the price at which the asset can be purchased by exercising the option, the length of time before the option expires, and the expected variability of the underlying security.

The general valuation model of direct claim securities can be formalized as follows:

$$V = \frac{CF_1}{(1 + k_1)} + \frac{CF_2}{(1 + k_2)} + ... + \frac{CF_n}{(1 + k_n)^n}$$

$$= \sum_{t=1}^{n} \frac{CF_t}{(1 + k_1)^t}.$$

■ Here V is the current value of the asset; CF_t is the expected cash flow at Time t; k_t is the required rate of return for each period's cash flow; and n is the number of periods over which cash flows are expected to be generated.

■ This basic valuation model can be applied to physical assets as well as to direct claim securities.

Capital is raised in two primary forms—debt and equity. As the principal type of long-term debt, a bond is a long-term promissory note issued by a business or governmental unit.

■ The *par value* is the stated face value of a bond, usually $1,000. This is the amount of money that the firm borrows and promises to repay at some future date.

■ The *coupon interest payment* is the dollar amount that is paid yearly to a bondholder by the issuer for use of the $1,000 loan. This payment is a fixed amount, established at the time the bond is issued. The *coupon interest rate* is obtained by dividing the coupon payment by the par value of the bond.

■ The *maturity date* is the date on which the par value must be repaid. Most bonds have original maturities of from 10 to 40 years, but any maturity is legally permissible.

■ Most bonds have a *call provision*, whereby the issuer may pay off the bonds prior to maturity.

■ A *new issue* is the term applied to a bond that has just been issued. At the time of issue, the coupon payment is generally set at a level that will force the market price of the bond to equal its par value. Once the bond has been on the market for a while, it is classified as an outstanding bond, or a *seasoned issue*. Prices of outstanding bonds vary widely from par.

Using these definitions, a basic bond valuation model can be constructed.

■ A bond represents an annuity plus a lump sum, and its value is found as the present value of this payment stream:

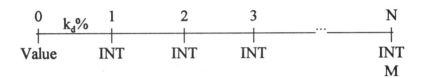

$$\text{Bond value} = V_B = \sum_{t=1}^{N} \frac{\text{INT}}{(1 + k_d)^t} + \frac{M}{(1 + k_d)^N}$$
$$= \text{INT}(\text{PVIFA}_{k_d,N}) + M(\text{PVIF}_{k_d,N})$$

where INT = dollars of interest paid each year, M = par, or maturity, value, which is typically $1,000, k_d = rate of interest on the bond, and N = number of years until the bond matures.

■ For example, consider a 15-year, $1,000 bond paying $150 annually, when the appropriate interest rate, k_d, is 15 percent. Utilizing the PVIFA and PVIF tables in the text, we find:

$$V_B = \$150(5.8474) + \$1,000(0.1229)$$
$$= \$877.11 + \$122.90$$
$$= \$1,000.01 \approx \$1,000.$$

Using a financial calculator, enter N = 15, k_d = I = 15, PMT = 150, and FV = 1000, and then press the PV key to find the value of the bond, $1,000.

■ Bond prices and interest rates are inversely related; that is, they tend to move in the opposite direction from one another.
  □ A bond will sell at par when its coupon interest rate is equal to the going rate of interest, k_d, as in the example above.
  □ When the going rate of interest is above the coupon rate, the bond will sell at a "discount" below its par value.

☐ If current interest rates are below the coupon rate, the bond will sell at a "premium" above its par value.

☐ The discount is equal to the present value of the amount of interest payment one sacrifices to buy a low-coupon old bond rather than a high-coupon new bond. The premium is equal to the present value of the additional interest payment one receives by buying a high-coupon old bond rather than a low-coupon new bond. The exact amount can be obtained by using the formula:

$$\text{Discount or premium} = \sum_{t=1}^{N} \frac{\text{Interest payment on the old bond} - \text{Interest payment on the new bond}}{(1 + k_d)^t}.$$

☐ Here N = years to maturity on the old bond and k_d = current rate of interest on a new bond.

■ The rate of interest earned on a bond if it is held until redeemed by the issuer is known as the *yield to maturity (YTM)*; it is the bond's expected rate of return. The YTM for a bond that sells at par consists entirely of an interest yield, but if the bond sells at a price other than its par value, the YTM consists of an interest yield plus a positive or negative capital gains yield.

■ If current interest rates are well below an outstanding bond's coupon rate, then a *callable bond* is likely to be called, and investors should estimate the expected rate of return on the bond as the *yield to call (YTC)* rather than as the yield to maturity. To calculate the YTC, solve this equation for k_d:

$$\text{Price of bond} = \sum_{t=1}^{N} \frac{\text{INT}}{(1 + k_d)^t} + \frac{\text{Call price}}{(1 + k_d)^N}.$$

■ The bond valuation model must be adjusted when interest is paid semiannually:

$$V_B = \sum_{t=1}^{2N} \frac{\text{INT}/2}{(1 + k_d/2)^t} + \frac{M}{(1 + k_d/2)^{2N}}$$

$$= (\text{INT}/2)(\text{PVIFA}_{k_d/2,2N}) + M(\text{PVIF}_{k_d/2,2N}).$$

■ Interest rates fluctuate over time, and people or firms who invest in bonds are exposed to two types of risk. These two types of risk are *interest rate risk* and *reinvestment rate risk*. The longer the maturity of the bond, the greater the exposure to *interest rate risk*. However, the shorter the maturity of the bond, the greater the exposure to *reinvestment rate risk*.

- ☐ Price sensitivity is also affected by a bond's coupon. The lower the coupon, the larger the maturity value will be relative to the stream of interest payments. In addition, distant cash flows are more seriously affected by changes in interest rates. Therefore, a zero coupon bond with a 10-year maturity will have more price sensitivity to changing rates than will a 10-year, 10 percent coupon bond.

- ■ Corporate bonds are traded primarily in the over-the-counter market, and most bonds are owned by and traded among the large financial institutions.

Preferred stock is a hybrid—it is similar to bonds in some respects and to common stock in other respects.

- ■ Preferred dividends are similar to interest payments on bonds in that they are fixed in amount and generally must be paid before common stock dividends can be paid.

- ■ Most preferred stocks entitle their owners to regular fixed dividend payments. If the payments last forever, the issue is a perpetuity whose value, V_{ps}, is found as follows:

$$V_{ps} = \frac{D_{ps}}{k_{ps}}.$$

Here D_{ps} is the dividend to be received in each year and k_{ps} is the required rate of return on the preferred stock.

Common stocks are also valued by finding the present value of the expected future cash flow stream.

- ■ Common stock represents an ownership interest in a corporation.

- ■ People typically buy common stock expecting to earn *dividends* plus a *capital gain* when they sell their shares at the end of some holding period. The capital gain may or may not be realized, but most people expect a gain or else they would not buy stocks.

- ■ The expected dividend yield on a stock during the coming year is equal to the expected dividend, D_1, divided by the current stock price, P_0. $(\hat{P}_1 - P_0)/P_0$ is the expected capital gains yield. The expected dividend yield plus the expected capital gains yield equals the expected total return.

■ The value of the stock today is calculated as the present value of an infinite stream of dividends. For any investor, cash flows consist of dividends plus the expected future sales price of the stock. This sales price, however, depends on dividends expected by future investors:

$$\text{Value of stock} = \hat{P}_0 = \text{PV of expected dividends}$$

$$= \frac{D_1}{(1 + k_s)^1} + \frac{D_2}{(1 + k_s)^2} + \cdots + \frac{D_\infty}{(1 + k_s)^\infty}$$

$$= \sum_{t=1}^{\infty} \frac{D_t}{(1 + k_s)^t}.$$

Here k_s is the discount rate used to find the present value of the dividends.

■ Dividends are not expected to remain constant in the future, and dividends are harder to predict than bond interest payments. Thus, stock valuation is a more complex task than bond valuation.

■ If expected dividend growth is zero ($g = 0$), the value of the stock is found as follows: $\hat{P}_0 = D/k_s$. Since a zero growth stock is expected to pay a constant dividend, it can be thought of as a perpetuity. The expected rate of return is simply the dividend yield: $\hat{k}_s = D/P_0$.

■ For many companies, earnings and dividends are expected to grow at some normal, or constant, rate. Dividends in any future Year t may be forecasted as $D_t = D_0(1 + g)^t$, where D_0 is the last dividend paid and g is the expected rate of growth. For a company which last paid a \$2.00 dividend and which has an expected 6 percent constant growth rate, the estimated dividend one year from now would be $D_1 = \$2.00(1.06) = \$2.12$; D_2 would be $\$2.00(1.06)^2 = \$2.25$, and the estimated dividend 4 years hence would be $D_t = D_0(1 + g)^t = \$2.00(1.06)^4 = \$2.525$. Using this method of estimating future dividends, the current price, P_0, is determined as follows:

$$\hat{P}_0 = \frac{D_0(1 + g)}{k_s - g} = \frac{D_1}{k_s - g}.$$

This equation for valuing a constant growth stock is often called the Gordon Model, after Myron J. Gordon, who developed it. A necessary condition of this equation is that k_s be greater than g; otherwise, the results will be meaningless.

■ For all stocks, the total expected return is composed of an expected dividend yield plus an expected capital gains yield. For a constant growth stock, the formula for the total expected return can be written as:

$$\hat{k}_s = \frac{D_1}{P_0} + g.$$

■ Firms typically go through periods of nonconstant growth, after which time their growth rate settles to a rate close to that of the economy as a whole. The value of such a firm is equal to the present value of its expected future dividends. To find the value of such a stock, we proceed in three steps:

  □ Find the present value of the dividends during the period of nonconstant growth.
  □ Find the price of the stock at the end of the nonconstant growth period, at which point it has become a constant growth stock, and discount this price back to the present.
  □ Add these two components to find the present value of the stock.

■ A firm whose growth rate changes over some fairly long period of time before reaching a constant growth situation evaluates its stock price using the following equation:

$$P_0 = \frac{D_0(1 + g_1)}{(1 + k_s)^1} + \frac{D_1(1 + g_2)}{(1 + k_s)^2} + \ldots + \frac{D_{m-1}(1 + g_m)}{(1 + k_s)^m} + \left(\frac{D_m(1 + g_n)}{k_s - g_n} \right) \left(\frac{1}{1 + k_s} \right)^m.$$

The relationship between a stock's required and expected rates of return determines the equilibrium price level where buying and selling pressures will just offset each other.

■ If the expected rate of return is less than the required rate, investors will desire to sell the stock; there will also be a tendency for the price to decline.

■ When the expected rate of return is greater than the required rate, investors will try to purchase shares of the stock; this will drive the price upward.

■ Only at the equilibrium price, where the expected and required rates are equal, will the stock be stable.

■ Equilibrium will generally exist for a given stock because security prices adjust rapidly to new developments.

■ Changes in the equilibrium price can be brought about (1) by a change in risk aversion, (2) by a change in the risk-free rate, (3) by a change in the stock's beta coefficient, or (4) by a change in the stock's expected rate of growth.

- The *Efficient Markets Hypothesis (EMH)* holds that stocks are always in equilibrium and that it is impossible for an investor to consistently "beat the market."
  - The *weak-form* of the EMH states that all information contained in past price movements is fully reflected in current market prices. If this were true, then information about recent trends in stock prices would be of no use in selecting stocks.
  - The *semistrong-form* of the EMH states that current market prices reflect all *publicly available* information. If this is true, no abnormal returns can be gained by analyzing stocks.
  - The *strong-form* of the EMH states that current market prices reflect all pertinent information, whether publicly available or privately held (inside information). If this form holds, even insiders would find it impossible to earn abnormal returns in the stock market.

Anyone who has ever invested in the stock market knows that there can be, and generally are, large differences between expected and realized prices and returns.

- Investors always expect positive returns from stock investments or else they would not buy them. However, in some years negative returns are actually earned.

- Even in bad years, some individual stocks do well, and the "name of the game" in security analysis is to pick the winners. Financial managers are trying to take those actions that will help put their companies in the winner's column.

Are stock prices actually determined as described in the chapter, by forecasting future dividends, finding the PV of those dividends, and then setting the price equal to the PV of the dividends? Individual investors do not necessarily operate as the chapter suggests—most actually rely on analysts' recommendations. However, security analysts do evaluate stocks as indicated in this chapter, so it is fair to say that most stocks' prices are at most times determined as indicated in the chapter.

SELF-TEST QUESTIONS

Definitional

1. _____ _____ _____ have claims against the cash flows produced by real assets.

2. _____ _____ _____ are those whose values are derived from some other security, asset, or index.

3. A(n) _____ is a long-term promissory note issued by a business firm or governmental unit.

4. The stated face value of a bond is referred to as its _____ value and is usually set at $_____.

5. The "coupon interest rate" on a bond is determined by dividing the _____ _____ by the _____ _____ of the bond.

6. The date at which the par value of a bond is repaid to each bondholder is known as the _____ _____.

7. A bond with annual coupon payments represents an annuity of INT dollars per year for N years, plus a lump sum of M dollars at the end of N years, and its value, V_B, is the _____ _____ of this payment stream.

8. At the time a bond is issued, the coupon interest rate is generally set at a level that will cause the _____ _____ and the _____ _____ of the bond to be approximately equal.

9. Market interest rates and bond prices move in _____ directions from one another.

10. The rate of interest earned by purchasing a bond and holding it until maturity is known as the bond's _____ _____ _____.

11. To adjust the bond valuation formula for semiannual coupon payments, the _____ _____ and _____ _____ must be divided by 2, and the number of _____ must be multiplied by 2.

12. Like other financial assets, the value of common stock is the _____ value of a future stream of income.

13. The income stream expected from a common stock consists of a(n) _____ yield and a(n) _____ _____ yield.

14. If the future growth rate of dividends is expected to be _____, the rate of return is simply the _____ yield.

15. Investors always expect a(n) _____ return on stock investments, but in some years _____ returns may actually be earned.

16. Once a bond has been on the market for a while, it is classified as an outstanding bond, or a
    _____ _____.

17. If current interest rates are well below an outstanding bond's coupon rate, then investors should
    estimate the expected rate of return on the bond as the _____ ____ _____ rather than as
    the _____ _____ _____.

18. The longer the maturity of a bond, the greater the exposure to _____ _____ risk;
    however, the shorter the maturity of the bond, the greater the exposure to _____
    _____ risk.

19. The _____ _____ _____ holds that stocks are always in equilibrium
    and that it is impossible for an investor to consistently "beat the market."

20. The _____-_____ of the EMH states that current market prices reflect all pertinent
    information, whether publicly available or privately held.

Conceptual

21. Changes in economic conditions cause interest rates and bond prices to vary over time.

    a. True   **b.** False

22. If the appropriate rate of interest on a bond is greater than its coupon rate, the market value of
    that bond will be above par value.

    a. True   **b.** False

23. A 20-year, annual coupon bond with one year left to maturity has the same interest rate risk as
    a 10-year, annual coupon bond with one year left to maturity. Both bonds are of equal risk,
    have the same coupon rate, and the prices of the two bonds are equal.

    a. True   **b.** False

24. According to the valuation model developed in this chapter, the value that an investor assigns
    to a share of stock is independent of the length of time the investor plans to hold the stock.

    a. True   **b.** False

25. Which of the following assumptions would cause the constant growth stock valuation model to be invalid? The constant growth model is given below:

$$\hat{P}_0 = \frac{D_0(1 + g)}{k_s - g}.$$

a. The growth rate is negative.
b. The growth rate is zero.
c. The growth rate is less than the required rate of return.
d. The required rate of return is above 30 percent.
e. None of the above assumptions would invalidate the model.

26. Which of the following statements is *false*? In all of the statements, assume that "other things are held constant."

a. Price sensitivity—that is, the change in price due to a given change in the required rate of return—increases as a bond's maturity increases.
b. For a given bond of any maturity, a given percentage point increase in the going interest rate (k_d) causes a *larger* dollar capital loss than the capital gain stemming from an identical decrease in the interest rate.
c. For any given maturity, a given percentage point increase in the interest rate causes a *smaller* dollar capital loss than the capital gain stemming from an identical decrease in the interest rate.
d. From a borrower's point of view, interest paid on bonds is tax deductible.
e. A 20-year zero-coupon bond has less reinvestment rate risk than a 20-year coupon bond.

27. Which of the following statements is most *correct*?

   a. Ignoring interest accrued between payment dates, if the required rate of return on a bond is less than its coupon interest rate, and k_d remains below the coupon rate until maturity, then the market value of that bond will be below its par value until the bond matures, at which time its market value will equal its par value.

   b. Assuming equal coupon rates, a 20-year original maturity bond with one year left to maturity has more interest rate risk than a 10-year original maturity bond with one year left to maturity.

   c. Regardless of the size of the coupon payment, the price of a bond moves in the same direction as interest rates; for example, if interest rates rise, bond prices also rise.

   d. For bonds, price sensitivity to a given change in interest rates generally increases as years remaining to maturity increases.

   e. Because short-term interest rates are much more volatile than long-term rates, you would, in the real world, be subject to more interest rate risk if you purchased a 30-*day* bond than if you bought a 30-*year* bond.

28. Which of the following statements is most *correct*?

   a. If two firms have the same expected D_1 and the same expected growth rate, their stocks must sell at the same current price, or else the market will not be in equilibrium.

   b. Interest rate risk and reinvestment rate risk tend to move in the same direction; that is, if a bond provides a lot of protection against interest rate risk, then it probably also provides a lot of protection against reinvestment rate risk.

   c. The existence of a positive maturity risk premium is an indication that investors, in general, regard interest rate risk as being more important than reinvestment rate risk.

   d. The constant growth stock valuation model requires that k be greater than g, that g be constant for all future years, and that g be equal to or greater than zero.

   e. All of the above statements are false.

29. Assume that a company's dividends are expected to grow at a rate of 25 percent per year for 5 years and then to slow down and to grow at a constant rate of 5 percent thereafter. The required (and expected) total return, k_s, is expected to remain constant at 12 percent. Which of the following statements is most *correct*?

    a. The dividend yield will be higher in the early years and then will decline as the annual capital gains yield gets larger and larger, other things held constant.

    b. Right now, it would be easier (require fewer calculations) to find the dividend yield expected in Year 7 than the dividend yield expected in Year 3.

    c. The stock price will grow each year at the same rate as the dividends.

    d. The stock price will grow at a different rate each year during the first 5 years, but its average growth rate over this period will be the same as the average growth rate in dividends; that is, the average stock price growth rate will be $(25 + 5)/2$.

    e. Statements a, b, c, and d are all false.

30. Which of the following statements is most *correct*?

    a. Bonds C and Z both have a $1,000 par value and 10 years to maturity. They have the same risk of default, and they both have an effective annual rate of EAR = 8%. If Bond C has a 15 percent annual coupon and Bond Z a zero coupon (paying just $1,000 at maturity), then Bond Z will be exposed to more *interest rate risk*, which is defined as the *percentage loss of value in response to a given increase in the going interest rate*.

    b. If the words "interest rate risk" were replaced by the words "reinvestment rate risk" in Statement a, then the statement would be true.

    c. The interest rate paid by the state of Florida on its debt would be lower, other things held constant, if interest on the debt was not exempt from federal income taxes.

    d. Given the conditions in Statement a, we can be sure that Bond Z would have the higher price.

    e. Statements a, b, c, and d are all false.

31. Which of the following statements is most *correct*?

    a. According to the text, the constant growth stock valuation model is especially useful in situations where g is greater than 15 percent and k_s is 10 percent or less.
    b. According to the text, the constant growth model can be used as one part of the process of finding the value of a stock which is expected to experience a very rapid rate of growth for a few years and then to grow at a constant ("normal") rate.
    c. According to the text, the constant growth model cannot be used unless g is greater than zero.
    d. According to the text, the constant growth model cannot be used unless the constant g is greater than k.
    e. Statements a, b, c, and d are all true.

32. If a company's bonds are selling at a *discount*, then:

    a. The YTM is the return investors probably expect to earn.
    b. The YTC is probably the expected return.
    c. Either a or b could be correct, depending on the yield curve.
    d. The current yield will exceed the expected rate of return.
    e. The after-tax cost of debt to the company will have to be less than the coupon rate on the bonds.

SELF-TEST PROBLEMS

1. Delta Corporation has a bond issue outstanding with an annual coupon rate of 7 percent and 4 years remaining until maturity. The par value of the bond is $1,000. Determine the current value of the bond if present market conditions justify a 14 percent required rate of return. The bond pays interest annually.

    a. $1,126.42   b. $1,000.00   c. $796.06   d. $791.00   e. $536.42

2. Refer to Self-Test Problem 1. Suppose the bond had a semiannual coupon. Now what would be its current value?

    a. $1,126.42   b. $1,000.00   c. $796.06   d. $791.00   e. $536.42

3. Refer to Self-Test Problem 1. Assume an annual coupon but 20 years remaining to maturity. What is the current value under these conditions?

   a. $1,126.42 **b.** $1,000.00 **c.** $796.06 **d.** $791.00 **e.** $536.42

4. Acme Products has a bond issue outstanding with 8 years remaining to maturity, a coupon rate of 10 percent with interest paid annually, and a par value of $1,000. If the current market price of the bond issue is $814.45, what is the yield to maturity, k_d?

   a. 12% **b.** 13% **c.** 14% **d.** 15% **e.** 16%

5. Stability Inc. has maintained a dividend rate of $4 per share for many years. The same rate is expected to be paid in future years. If investors require a 12 percent rate of return on similar investments, determine the present value of the company's stock.

   a. $15.00 **b.** $30.00 **c.** $33.33 **d.** $35.00 **e.** $40.00

6. Your sister-in-law, a stockbroker at Invest Inc., is trying to sell you a stock with a current market price of $25. The stock's last dividend (D_0) was $2.00, and earnings and dividends are expected to increase at a constant growth rate of 10 percent. Your required return on this stock is 20 percent. From a strict valuation standpoint, you should:

   a. Buy the stock; it is fairly valued.
   b. Buy the stock; it is undervalued by $3.00.
   c. Buy the stock; it is undervalued by $2.00.
   d. Not buy the stock; it is overvalued by $2.00.
   e. Not buy the stock; it is overvalued by $3.00.

7. Lucas Laboratories' last dividend was $1.50. Its current equilibrium stock price is $15.75, and its expected growth rate is a constant 5 percent. If the stockholders' required rate of return is 15 percent, what is the expected dividend yield and expected capital gains yield for the coming year?

   a. 0%; 15% **b.** 5%; 10% **c.** 10%; 5% **d.** 15%; 0% **e.** 15%; 15%

8. The Canning Company has been hard hit by increased competition. Analysts predict that earnings (and dividends) will decline at a rate of 5 percent annually into the foreseeable future. If Canning's last dividend (D_0) was $2.00, and investors' required rate of return is 15 percent, what will be Canning's stock price *in 3 years*?

   a. $8.15   **b.** $9.50   **c.** $10.00   **d.** $10.42   **e.** $10.96

   (The following data relate to Self-Test Problems 9 through 11.)

   The Club Auto Parts Company has just recently been organized. It is expected to experience no growth for the next 2 years as it identifies its market and acquires its inventory. However, Club will grow at an annual rate of 5 percent in the third year and, beginning with the fourth year, should attain a 10 percent growth rate which it will sustain thereafter. The first dividend (D_1) to be paid at the end of the first year is expected to be $0.50 per share. Investors require a 15 percent rate of return on Club's stock.

9. What is the current equilibrium stock price?

   a. $5.00   **b.** $8.75   **c.** $9.57   **d.** $12.43   **e.** $15.00

10. What will Club's stock price be at the end of the first year (P_1)?

    a. $5.00   **b.** $8.76   **c.** $9.56   **d.** $12.43   **e.** $15.00

11. What dividend yield and capital gains yield should an investor in Club expect for the first year?

    a. 7.5%; 7.5%   **b.** 4.7%; 10.3%   **c.** 5.7%; 9.3%   **d.** 10.5%; 4.5%   **e.** 11.5%; 3.5%

12. You have just been offered a bond for $863.73. The coupon rate is 8 percent, payable annually, and interest rates on new issues with the same degree of risk are 10 percent. You want to know how many more interest payments you will receive, but the party selling the bond cannot remember. If the par value is $1,000, how many interest payments remain?

    a. 10   **b.** 11   **c.** 12   **d.** 13   **e.** 14

13. Johnson Corporation's stock is currently selling at $45.83 per share. The last dividend paid (D_0) was $2.50. Johnson is a constant growth firm. If investors require a return of 16 percent on Johnson's stock, what do they think Johnson's growth rate will be?

    a. 6%   **b.** 7%   **c.** 8%   **d.** 9%   **e.** 10%

14. Assume that the average firm in your company's industry is expected to grow at a constant rate of 7 percent and its dividend yield is 8 percent. Your company is about as risky as the average firm in the industry, but it has just successfully completed some R&D work which leads you to expect that its earnings and dividends will grow at a rate of 40 percent [$D_1 = D_0(1 + g) = D_0(1.40)$] this year and 20 percent the following year, after which growth should match the 7 percent industry average rate. The last dividend paid (D_0) was $1. What is the value per share of your firm's stock?

    a. $22.47   **b.** $24.15   **c.** $21.00   **d.** $19.48   **e.** $22.00

15. Assume that as investment manager of Maine Electric Company's pension plan (which is exempt from income taxes), you must choose between Exxon bonds and GM preferred stock. The bonds have a $1,000 par value; they mature in 20 years; they pay $35 each 6 months; they are callable at Exxon's option at a price of $1,150 after 5 years (ten 6-month periods); and they sell at a price of $815.98 per bond. The preferred stock is a perpetuity; it pays a dividend of $1.50 each quarter, and it sells for $75 per share. Assume interest rates do not change. What is the most likely effective annual rate of return (EAR) on the *higher* yielding security? (Hint: You will need a financial calculator to work this problem.)

    a. 9.20%   **b.** 8.24%   **c.** 9.00%   **d.** 8.00%   **e.** 8.50%

16. Bird Corporation's 12 percent coupon rate, semiannual payment, $1,000 par value bonds which mature in 20 years are callable at a price of $1,100 five years from now. The bonds sell at a price of $1,300, and the yield curve is flat. Assuming that interest rates in the economy are expected to remain at their current level, what is the best estimate of Bird's *nominal* interest rate on the new bonds? (Hint: You will need a financial calculator to work this problem.)

    a. 8.46%   **b.** 6.16%   **c.** 9.28%   **d.** 6.58%   **e.** 8.76%

17. Chadmark Corporation is expanding rapidly, and it currently needs to retain all of its earnings, hence it does not pay any dividends. However, investors expect Chadmark to begin paying dividends, with the first dividend of $0.75 coming 2 years from today. The dividend should grow rapidly, at a rate of 40 percent per year, during Years 3 and 4. After Year 4, the company should grow at a constant rate of 10 percent per year. If the required return on the stock is 16 percent, what is the value of the stock today?

    a. $16.93   **b.** $17.54   **c.** $15.78   **d.** $18.87   **e.** $16.05

18. The Graf Company needs to finance some new R&D programs, so it will sell new bonds for this purpose. Graf's currently outstanding bonds have a $1,000 par value, a 10 percent coupon rate, and pay interest semiannually. The outstanding bonds have 25 years remaining to maturity, are callable after 5 years at a price of $1,090, and currently sell at a price of $700. The yield curve is expected to remain flat. On the basis of these data, what is the best estimate of Graf's *nominal* interest rate on the new bonds it plans to sell? (Hint: You will need a financial calculator to work this problem.)

    a. 21.10%   **b.** 14.48%   **c.** 15.67%   **d.** 16.25%   **e.** 18.29%

19. Suppose Hadden Inc. is negotiating with an insurance company to sell a bond issue. Each bond has a par value of $1,000, it would pay 10 percent per year in quarterly payments of $25 per quarter for 10 years, and then it would pay 12 percent per year ($30 per quarter) for the next 10 years (Years 11-20). The $1,000 principal would be returned at the end of 20 years. The insurance company's alternative investment is in a 20-year mortgage which has a nominal rate of 14 percent and which provides monthly payments. If the mortgage and the bond issue are equally risky, how much should the insurance company be willing to pay Hadden for each bond? (Hint: You will need a financial calculator to work this problem.)

    a. $750.78   **b.** $781.50   **c.** $804.65   **d.** $710.49   **e.** $840.97

20. Some investors expect Endicott Industries to have an irregular dividend pattern for several years, and then to grow at a constant rate. Suppose Endicott has $D_0 = \$2.00$; no growth is expected for 2 years ($g_1 = 0$); then the expected growth rate is 8 percent for 2 years; and finally the growth rate is expected to be constant at 15 percent thereafter. If the required return is 20 percent, what will be the value of the stock?

    a. $28.53   **b.** $25.14   **c.** $31.31   **d.** $21.24   **e.** $23.84

ANSWERS TO SELF-TEST QUESTIONS

1. Direct claim securities
2. Indirect claim securities
3. bond
4. par; 1,000
5. coupon payment; par value
6. maturity date
7. present value
8. market price; par value
9. opposite
10. yield to maturity
11. coupon payment; interest rate; years
12. present
13. dividend; capital gains
14. zero; dividend
15. positive; negative
16. seasoned issue
17. yield to call; yield to maturity
18. interest rate; reinvestment rate
19. Efficient Markets Hypothesis
20. strong-form

21. a. For example, if inflation increases, the interest rate (or required return) will increase, resulting in a decline in bond price.

22. b. It will sell at a discount, below its par value.

23. a. Both bonds are valued as 1-year bonds regardless of their original issue dates, and since they are of equal risk and have the same coupon rate, their prices must be equal.

24. a. The model considers all future dividends. This produces a current value which is appropriate for all investors independent of their expected holding period.

25. e. The model would be invalid, however, if the growth rate *exceeded* the required rate of return.

26. b. Statements a, d, and e are all true. To determine which of the remaining statements is false, it is best to use an example. Assume you have a 10-year, 10 percent annual coupon bond which sold at par. If interest rates increase to 13 percent, the value of the bond decreases to $837.21, while if interest rates decrease to 7 percent, the value of the bond increases to $1,210.71. Thus, the capital gain is greater than the capital loss and statement b is false.

27. d.   Statement a is false because the bond would have a premium and thus sell above par value. Statement b is false because both bonds would have the same interest rate risk because they both have one year left to maturity. Statement c is false because the price of a bond moves in the opposite direction as interest rates. Statement e is false because the 30-year bond would have more interest rate risk than the 30-day bond. Statement d is correct. As years to maturity increases for a bond, the number of discount periods used in finding the current bond value also increases. Therefore, bonds with longer maturities will have more price sensitivity to a given change in interest rates.

28. c.   Statement a is false. $\hat{P}_0 = D_1/(k_s - g)$. Thus, if the two stocks had different required rates of return, their prices would be different. Statement b is false because interest rate risk and reinvestment rate risk move in the opposite direction. Statement c is correct. The maturity risk premium (MRP) compensates investors for interest rate risk. As a given security's maturity increases, the MRP also increases. If reinvestment rate risk was regarded as more important, then short-term securities would have a higher required yield than long-term securities. However, this is not true because of the existence of a positive MRP. Statement d is false because g may be negative in the constant growth stock valuation model, but it cannot be greater than k_s, the required return.

29. b.   Statement b is correct. We know that after Year 5, the stock will have a constant growth rate, and the capital gains yield will be equal to that growth rate. We also know that the total return is expected to be constant. Therefore, we could find the expected dividend yield in Year 7 simply by subtracting the growth rate from the total return: yield = 12% – 5% = 7% in Year 7.

The other statements are all false. This could be confirmed by thinking about how the dividend growth rate starts high, ends up at the constant growth rate, and must lie between these two rates and be declining between Years 1 and 5. The average growth rate in dividends during Years 1 through 5 will be (25 + 5)/2 = 15%, which is above k_s = 12%, so statements c and d must be false.

30. a. Statement a is correct. Bond C has a high coupon (hence its name), so bondholders get cash flows right away. Bond Z has a zero coupon, so its holders will get no cash flows until the bond matures. Since all of the cash flows on Z come at the end, a given increase in the interest rate will cause this bond's value to fall sharply relative to the decline in value of the coupon bond.

You could also use the data in the problem to find the value of the two bonds at two different interest rates, and then calculate the percentage change. For example, at $k_d = 15\%$, $V_C = \$1,000$ and $V_Z = \$247.18$. At $k_d = 20\%$, $V_C = \$790.38$ and $V_Z = \$161.51$. Therefore, Bond Z declines in value by 34.66%, while Bond C declines by only 20.96 percent. Note that Bond Z is exposed to *less* reinvestment rate risk than Bond C.

31. b. Statement b is correct. In the case of a nonconstant growth stock which is expected to grow at a constant rate after Year N, we would find the value of D_{N+1} and use it in the constant growth model to find P_N. The other statements are all false. Note that the constant growth model can be used for $g = 0$ or $g < 0$.

32. a. When bonds sell at a discount, the going interest rate (k_d) is above the coupon rate. If a company called the old discount bonds and replaced them with new bonds, the new coupon would be above the old coupon. This would increase a firm's interest cost, hence the company would not call the discount bonds. Therefore, the YTM would be the expected rate of return. The shape of the yield curve would have no effect in the situation described in this question, but if the bonds had been selling at premium, making the YTC the relevant yield, then the yield curve in a sense would have an effect. The YTC would be below the cost if the company were to sell new long-term bonds, if the yield curve were steeply upward sloping. Statement d is false because the expected rate of return would include a current yield component and a capital gains component (because the bond's price will rise from its current discounted price to par as maturity approaches). Therefore, the current yield will *not* exceed the expected rate of return. The after-tax cost of debt is the expected rate adjusted for taxes, $k_d(1 - T)$. Because the bonds are selling at a discount, the coupon rate could be quite low, even zero, so we know that statement e is false. Therefore, statement a is correct.

SOLUTIONS TO SELF-TEST PROBLEMS

1. c. $V_B = INT(PVIFA_{k_d,N}) + M(PVIF_{k_d,N})$
   $= \$70(PVIFA_{14\%,4}) + \$1,000(PVIF_{14\%,4})$
   $= \$70(2.9137) + \$1,000(0.5921) = \$796.06.$

Calculator solution: Input N = 4, I = 14, PMT = 70, FV = 1000, and solve for PV = −$796.04.

2. d. $V_B = (INT/2)(PVIFA_{k_d/2,2N}) + M(PVIF_{k_d/2,2N})$
   $= \$35(PVIFA_{7\%,8}) + \$1,000(PVIF_{7\%,8})$
   $= \$35(5.9713) + \$1,000(0.5820) = \$791.00.$

Calculator solution: Input N = 8, I = 7, PMT = 35, FV = 1000, and solve for PV = −$791.00.

3. e. $V_B = INT(PVIFA_{k_d,N}) + M(PVIF_{k_d,N})$
   $= \$70(PVIFA_{14\%,20}) + \$1,000(PVIF_{14\%,20})$
   $= \$70(6.6231) + \$1,000(0.0728) = \$536.42.$

Calculator solution: Input N = 20, I = 14, PMT = 70, FV = 1000, and solve for PV = −$536.38.

4. c. $V_B = INT(PVIFA_{k_d,N}) + M(PVIF_{k_d,N})$
   $\$814.45 = \$100(PVIFA_{k_d,8}) + \$1,000(PVIF_{k_d,8}).$

Now use trial and error techniques. Try $I = k_d = 12\%$:

$\$814.45 = \$100(4.9676) + \$1,000(0.4039) = \$900.66.$

Since $\$814.45 \neq \$900.66$, the yield to maturity is not 12 percent. The calculated value is too large. Therefore, increase the value of I to 14 percent to lower the calculated value: $\$814.45 = \$100(4.6389) + \$1,000(0.3506) = \$814.49$. This is close enough to conclude that k_d = yield to maturity = 14%.

Calculator solution: Input N = 8, PV = -814.45, PMT = 100, FV = 1000, and solve for I = k_d = 14.00%.

5. c. This is a zero-growth stock, or perpetuity: $\hat{P}_0 = D/k_s = \$4.00/0.12 = \$33.33$.

6. e. $\hat{P}_0 = \dfrac{D_0(1 + g)}{k_s - g} = \dfrac{\$2.00(1.10)}{0.20 - 0.10} = \$22.00$.

Since the stock is currently selling for $25.00, the stock is not in equilibrium and is overvalued by $3.00.

7. c. $\dfrac{\text{Dividend}}{\text{yield}} = \dfrac{D_1}{P_0} = \dfrac{D_0(1 + g)}{P_0} = \dfrac{\$1.50(1.05)}{\$15.75} = 0.10 = 10\%$.

$\dfrac{\text{Capital}}{\text{gains yield}} = \dfrac{\hat{P}_1 - P_0}{P_0} = \dfrac{P_0(1 + g) - P_0}{P_0} = \dfrac{\$16.54 - \$15.75}{\$15.75} = g = 5\%$.

For a constant growth stock, the capital gains yield is equal to g.

8. a. $\hat{P}_0 = \dfrac{D_0(1 + g)}{k_s - g} = \dfrac{\$2.00(0.95)}{0.15 - (-0.05)} = \dfrac{\$1.90}{0.20} = \$9.50$.

$\hat{P}_3 = \hat{P}_0(1 + g)^3 = \$9.50(0.95)^3 = \$9.50(0.8574) = \$8.15$.

The Gordon model can also be used:

$\hat{P}_3 = \dfrac{D_4}{k_s - g} = \dfrac{D_0(1 + g)^4}{0.15 - (-0.05)} = \dfrac{\$2.00(0.95)^4}{0.20} = \dfrac{\$2.00(0.8145)}{0.20} = \$8.15$.

9. b. To calculate the current value of a nonconstant growth stock, follow these steps:

1. Determine the expected stream of dividends during the nonconstant growth period. Also, calculate the expected dividend at the end of the first year of constant growth that will be used later to calculate stock price.

$D_1 = \$0.50.$
$D_2 = D_1(1 + g) = \$0.50(1 + 0.0) = \$0.50.$
$D_3 = D_2(1 + g) = \$0.50(1.05) = \$0.525.$
$D_4 = D_3(1 + g) = \$0.525(1.10) = \$0.5775.$

2. Discount the expected dividends during the nonconstant growth period at the investor's required rate of return to find their present value.

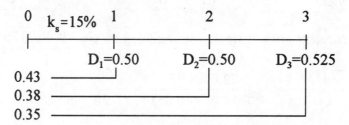

3. Calculate the expected stock price at the end of the final year of nonconstant growth. This occurs at the end of Year 3. Use the Gordon model for this calculation.

$$\hat{P}_3 = \frac{D_4}{k_s - g} = \frac{\$0.5775}{0.15 - 0.10} = \$11.55.$$

Then discount this stock price back 3 periods at the investor's required rate of return to find its present value.

$$PV = \$11.55(PVIF_{15\%,3}) = \$11.55(0.6575) = \$7.59.$$

4. Add the present value of the stock price expected at the end of Year 3 plus the dividends expected in Years 1, 2, and 3 to find the present value of the stock, P_0.

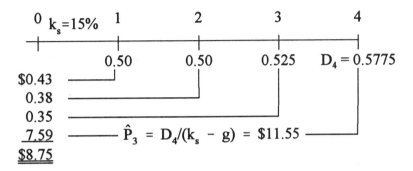

Alternatively, input 0, 0.5, 0.5, 12.075 (0.525 + 11.55) into the cash flow register, input I = 15, and then solve for NPV = $8.75.

10. c. To calculate the expected stock price at the end of Year 1, $\hat{P}_1$, follow the same procedure you did to find the value of the nonconstant growth stock in Self-Test Problem 9. However, discount values to Year 1 instead of Year 0. Also, remember that the dividend in Year 1, D_1, is not included in the valuation because it has already been paid and therefore adds nothing to the wealth of the investor buying the stock at the end of Year 1.

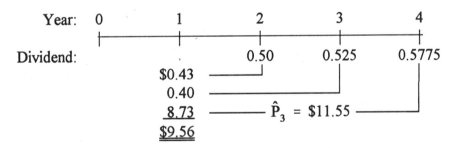

Alternatively, input 0, 0.5, 12.075 (0.525 + 11.55) into the cash flow register, input I = 15, and then solve for NPV = $9.57.

11. c. $\dfrac{\text{Dividend}}{\text{yield}} = \dfrac{D_1}{P_0} = \dfrac{\$0.50}{\$8.75} = 5.7\%.$

$\dfrac{\text{Capital}}{\text{gains yield}} = \dfrac{\hat{P}_1 - P_0}{P_0} = \dfrac{\$9.56 - \$8.75}{\$8.75} = 9.3\%.$

The Total yield = Dividend yield + Capital gains yield = 5.7% + 9.3% = 15%. The total yield must equal the required rate of return. Also, the capital gains yield is not equal to the growth rate during the nonconstant growth phase of a nonconstant growth stock. Finally, the dividend and capital gains yields are not constant until the constant growth state is reached.

12. c. $V_B = INT(PVIFA_{k_d,N}) + M(PVIF_{k_d,N})$
$\$863.73 = \$80(PVIFA_{10\%,N}) + \$1,000(PVIF_{10\%,N})$

Now use trial and error to find the value of N for which the equality holds. For N = 12, $80(6.8137) + $1,000(0.3186) = $863.70. Or using a financial calculator, input I = 10, PV = -863.73, PMT = 80, FV = 1000, and solve for N = 12.

13. e. $P_0 = \dfrac{D_0(1 + g)}{k_s - g}$

$\$45.83 = \dfrac{\$2.50(1 + g)}{0.16 - g}$

$\$7.33 - \$45.83g = \$2.50 + \$2.50g$

$\$48.33g = \$4.83$

$g = 0.0999 \approx 10\%.$

14. d. $D_0 = \$1.00$; $k_s = 8\% + 7\% = 15\%$; $g_1 = 40\%$; $g_2 = 20\%$; $g_n = 7\%$.

$$*\hat{P}_2 = \frac{\$1.7976}{0.15 - 0.07} = \$22.47.$$

15. a. Exxon bonds: Price = \$815.98, Maturity = 20 years, PMT = \$35/6 months, and they are callable at \$1,150 after 10 periods (5 years).

Will the bond's YTM or YTC be applicable? The bond is selling at a discount, so $k_d >$ Coupon interest rate. Therefore, the bond is not likely to be called, so calculate the YTM.

Input N = 40, PV = -815.98, PMT = 35, FV = 1000, and solve for I = $k_d/2$ = 4.5%. EAR = $(1.045)^2 - 1 = 9.2\%$.

Preferred: D = \$1.50/quarter and P_0 = \$75.

k_{ps} = \$1.50/\$75 = 2% = periodic rate. EAR = $(1.02)^4 - 1 = 8.24\%$.

Thus, the Exxon bonds provide the higher effective annual rate of return.

16. d. The bond is selling at a large premium, which means that its coupon rate is much higher than the going rate of interest. Therefore, the bond is likely to be called—it is more likely to be called than to remain outstanding until it matures. Thus, it will probably provide a return equal to the YTC rather than the YTM. So, there is no point in calculating the YTM; just calculate the YTC. Enter these values: N = 10, PV = -1300, PMT = 60, and FV = 1100. The periodic rate is 3.29 percent, so the nominal YTC is 2(3.29%) = 6.58%. This would be close to the going rate, and it is about what Bird would have to pay on new bonds.

17. a. To calculate Chadmark's current stock price, follow the following steps: (1) Determine the expected stream of dividends during the nonconstant growth period. You will need to calculate the expected dividend at the end of Year 5, which is the first year of constant growth. This dividend will be used in the next step to calculate the stock price. (2) Calculate the expected stock price at the end of the final year of nonconstant growth. This occurs at the end of Year 4. Use the Gordon model for this calculation. (3) Add the value obtained in Step 2 to the dividend expected in Year 4. (4) Put the values obtained in the prior steps on a time line and discount them at the required rate of return to find the present value of Chadmark's stock. These steps are shown below.

$D_0 = \$0$; $D_1 = \$0$; $D_2 = \$0.75$; $D_3 = \$0.75(1.4) = \$1.05$; $D_4 = \$0.75(1.4)^2 = \$1.47$; $D_5 = \$0.75(1.4)^2(1.10) = \$1.617$.

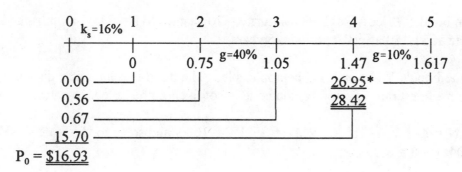

$*\hat{P}_4 = \$1.617/(0.16 - 0.10) = \$26.95$.

$CF_0 = 0$; $CF_1 = 0$; $CF_2 = 0.75$; $CF_3 = 1.05$; $CF_4 = 28.42$.

Alternatively, using a financial calculator you could input the cash flows as shown above into the cash flow register, input I = 16, and press NPV to obtain the stock's value today of $16.93.

18. b. Investors would expect to earn either the YTM or the YTC, and the expected return on the old bonds is the cost Graf would have to pay in order to sell new bonds.

YTM: Enter N = 2(25) = 50; PV = -700; PMT = 100/2 = 50; and FV = 1000. Press I to get I = k_d/2 = 7.24%. Multiply 7.24%(2) = 14.48% to get the YTM.

YTC: Enter N = 2(5) = 10, PV = -700, PMT = 50, FV = 1090, and then press I to get I = 10.55%. Multiply by 2 to get YTC = 21.10%.

Would investors expect the company to call the bonds? Graf currently pays 10 percent on its debt (the coupon rate). New debt would cost at least 14.48 percent. Because k_d > 10% coupon rate, it would be stupid for the company to call, so investors would not expect a call. Therefore, they would expect to earn 14.48 percent on the bonds. This is k_d, so 14.48 percent is the rate Graf would probably have to pay on new bonds.

19. a. Time line:

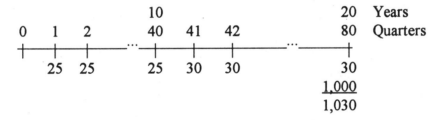

1. You could enter the time line values into the cash flow register, but one element is missing: the interest rate. Once we have the interest rate, we could press the NPV key to get the value of the bond.

2. We need a *periodic* interest rate, and it needs to be a quarterly rate, found as the annual nominal rate divided by 4: $k_{PER} = k_{NOM}$/4. So, we need to find k_{NOM} so that we can find k_{PER}.

3. The insurance company will insist on earning at least the same effective annual rate on the bond issue as it can earn on the mortgage. The mortgage pays 14 percent monthly, which is equivalent to an EAR = 14.93%. Using a financial calculator, enter NOM% = 14, P/YR = 12, and press EFF% to obtain 14.93%. So, the bond issue will have to have a k_{NOM}, with quarterly payments, which translates into an EAR of 14.93 percent.

4. EAR = 14.93% is equivalent to a quarterly nominal rate of 14.16 percent; that is, a nominal rate of 14.16 percent with quarterly compounding has an EAR of 14.93 percent. You can find this by entering EFF% = 14.93, P/YR = 4, and pressing the NOM% key to get NOM% = 14.16%. If this nominal rate is set on the bond issue, the insurance company will earn the same effective rate as it can get on the mortgage.

5. The periodic rate for a 14.16 percent nominal rate, with quarterly compounding, is 14.16%/4 = 3.54%. This 3.54% is the rate to use in the time line calculations.

With an HP 10B calculator, enter the following data:

$CF_0 = 0$, $CF_j = 25$; $N_j = 40$; $CF_j = 30$; $N_j = 39$; $CF_j = 1030$; I = 3.54.
Solve for NPV = $750.78 = Value of each bond.

With an HP 17B calculator, enter the following data:
Flow(0) = 0 Input; Flow(1) = 25 Input; # Times = 40 Input; Flow(2) = 30 Input; # Times = 39 Input; Flow(3) = 1030 Input; # Times = 1 Input; Exit, Calc; I = 3.54; NPV = $750.78 = Value of each bond.

If each bond is priced at $750.78, the insurance company will earn the same effective rate of return as on the mortgage.

20. c. First, set up the time line as follows. Note that D_5 is used to find $\hat{P}_4$, which is treated as part of the cash flow at t = 4:

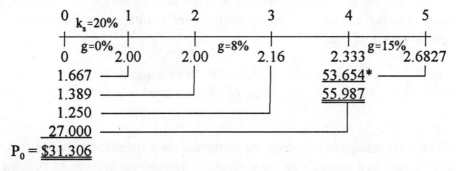

$*\hat{P}_4 = \$2.6827/(0.20 - 0.15) = \$53.654.$

Enter the time line values into the cash flow register, with I = 20, to find NPV = $31.31. Be sure to enter $CF_0 = 0$. Note that P_4 is the PV, at t = 4, of dividends from t = 5 to infinity; that is, the PV of the dividends after the stock is expected to become a constant growth stock.

CHAPTER 8

THE COST OF
CAPITAL

OVERVIEW

A firm's cost of capital is critically important for three reasons: (1) Maximizing the value of a firm requires that the costs of all inputs, including capital, be minimized, and to minimize the cost of capital, we must be able to estimate it. (2) Capital budgeting decisions require an estimate of the cost of capital. (3) Many other types of decisions, including those related to public utility regulation, leasing, bond refunding, and working capital, require estimates of capital costs. In this chapter, we discuss the actual process of estimating a firm's overall, or weighted average, cost of capital. Then, in Chapter 11, we discuss the adjustment process used to estimate divisional and project costs of capital.

OUTLINE

The appropriate cost of capital for most decisions is a weighted average of the various capital components.

- Capital represents the funds used to finance the firm's assets and operations. Capital components are items on the right-hand side of the balance sheet such as debt, preferred stock, common stock, and retained earnings.

- The first decision that must be made is what capital components to include in the *weighted average cost of capital* estimate.
  - ☐ Accounts payable and accruals are generally excluded from the cost of capital estimate because (1) they represent "free" capital, (2) they are not very controllable by management, and (3) they are subtracted from the amount that otherwise would be required to finance the project in the capital budgeting process.
  - ☐ Short-term interest-bearing debt (notes payable) is included only if the debt is part of the firm's permanent financing mix.
  - ☐ Long-term debt, preferred stock, and common stock are generally included in the firm's weighted average cost of capital estimate.

■ The next decision involves the nature of the component costs to be estimated.
   □ The cost of capital must be developed on an after-tax basis, because after-tax cash flows are the most relevant to investment decisions.
   □ The relevant component costs are the marginal costs of new funds, and not the historical costs of funds raised in the past.

The relevant cost of debt is the after-tax cost of new debt.

■ The cost of debt can be adjusted to reflect flotation costs, but since these are typically small on debt issues, most managers neglect flotation costs in their estimates.
■ The component cost of debt is the after-tax cost of debt, $k_d(1 - T)$.
   □ The tax deductibility of interest payments reduces the cost of debt to the firm. In effect, the federal government pays part of the interest charges.
   □ k_d is the interest rate on new debt. The interest rate paid on debt in the past (the embedded rate) is not relevant to today's capital costs.
   □ Although the effective annual cost rate of debt could be calculated, it is normally best to use the nominal rate.
   □ Note that firms cannot be sure of the exact future benefit of the tax deduction on interest payments because taxable income and statutory tax rates change over time.
   □ Assume that Firm A has $k_d = 12\%$ and $T = 40\%$. Then its component cost of debt = $k_d(1 - T)$ = $12\%(1 - 0.4) = 12\%(0.6) = 7.2\%$.

A number of firms use preferred stock as part of their permanent financing mix. Preferred stock may be perpetual, or it may have sinking fund or mandatory redemption provisions.

■ The component cost of perpetual preferred stock, k_{ps}, is the required dividend, D_{ps}, divided by the issuance price net of flotation costs, P_n, or $k_{ps} = D_{ps}/P_n$.
   □ Note that no tax adjustment is made since preferred stock dividends are paid from after-tax earnings.
   □ If Firm A's new preferred stock requires a dividend of $12 to sell at $100, and if flotation costs were 5 percent, then $k_{ps} = D_p/P_n = \$12/\$95 = 12.6\%$.

■ The cost of preferred stock that is not perpetual must be estimated using bond valuation techniques.

A firm can raise common equity capital in two ways: (1) by retaining earnings and (2) by issuing new common stock.

■ The cost of equity, k_s, obtained by retaining earnings is the rate of return stockholders require on the firm's common stock. Three approaches are used to estimate k_s.

■ The Capital Asset Pricing Model (CAPM) is one approach used to estimate k_s.
   □ Estimate the riskless rate, k_{RF}. The preferred proxy for k_{RF} is the rate on long-term Treasury bonds.
   □ The stock's beta coefficient, b, is used as the measure of risk.
   □ Estimate the required rate of return on the market, or an "average" stock, k_M.
   □ Estimate the required rate of return on the firm's stock using the SML.
   □ If $k_{RF} = 10\%$, $k_M = 15\%$, and the beta of Firm A is 1.3, then

   $$k_s = k_{RF} + (k_M - k_{RF})b = 10\% + (5\%)1.3 = 16.5\%.$$

   □ The market risk premium $= RP_M = (k_M - k_{RF})$ can be estimated by analyzing (1) *ex post* (historical) returns or (2) *ex ante* (forward-looking) returns. Since risk premiums vary over time, current estimates of RP_M are better than historical estimates.
   □ Three commonly used types of betas are (1) *historical betas* which are based on a stock's characteristic line using historical data, (2) *adjusted betas* which account for expected future movement toward 1.0, and (3) *fundamental betas* which are constantly adjusted to reflect changes in a firm's operations and capital structure. Managers select the appropriate beta given the circumstances at that time.
   □ High and low estimates can be developed for the risk-free rate, beta, and market risk premium. In this situation, the CAPM method provides an estimation range for k_s rather than a point estimate.

■ The cost of retained earnings, k_s, may also be estimated by the discounted cash flow (DCF) approach. This approach is valid for all stocks, but the procedure is much easier for constant growth stocks:

   $$k_s = \hat{k}_s = D_1/P_0 + g.$$

   □ The DCF approach assumes that stocks are normally in equilibrium.
   □ The DCF approach can be applied to nonconstant growth stocks by using the nonconstant growth model.
   □ The expected growth rate may be based on (1) projections of past growth rates, (2) the retention growth model, or (3) analysts' forecasts.
   □ The retention growth model estimates growth by the equation $g = b(r)$. Here b = expected future retention ratio and r = expected future return on equity (ROE). This model assumes (1) that the retention ratio, b, will remain constant over time, (2) that the expected return on equity, r, will remain constant over time, (3) that the firm will not issue new common stock,

or that any new stock issued will be priced at book value, and (4) that the aggregate risk of future projects will be the same as for the firm's current projects.

☐ If Firm A last paid $4.00 in annual dividends, which are expected to grow at a constant 10 percent per year, and Firm A's stock is currently selling for $73.33 per share, then

$$k_s = \hat{k}_s = \frac{\$4.00\,(1.10)}{\$73.33} + 10\% = 6.0\% + 10\% = 16.0\%.$$

■ A simple but sometimes useful approach to estimate k_s, the bond-yield-plus-risk-premium approach, adds a risk premium to the firm's own before-tax cost of long-term debt:

$$k_s = \text{Company's own bond yield} + \text{Risk premium}.$$

☐ Corporate treasurers can easily estimate the firm's bond yield to maturity (before-tax cost of debt), so the real problem occurs in estimating the risk premium. Risk premiums can be estimated using a market analysts' survey approach or by subtracting the yield on an average (A-rated) corporate long-term bond from the k_M estimate. The risk premium obtained will depend on the company and the state of the economy.

☐ If Firm A uses a risk premium of 5 percentage points to add to their own bond yield, and k_d is equal to 12 percent, then $k_s = 17\%$:

$$k_s = 12\% + 5\% = 17\%.$$

■ All three approaches are recommended for estimating the required rate of return on common stock. When different methods produce different results, judgment must be used in selecting the best estimate. In the case of Firm A, the estimates are reasonably consistent, so we could use the average of 16.5 percent as our estimate for the cost of retained earnings.

■ k_s represents an opportunity cost to the firm—by retaining earnings within the firm rather than paying them out as dividends, stockholders are deprived of the opportunity to invest the earnings in other assets of similar risk that provide a return of 16.5 percent.

The cost of new common stock, or external equity capital, k_e, is higher than the cost of retained earnings, k_s, because of flotation costs on new common stock.

■ To allow for flotation costs, F, we must adjust the DCF formula for the required rate of return on common stock as follows:

$$k_e = \hat{k}_e = \frac{D_1}{P_0(1 - F)} + g.$$

■ If Firm A incurred flotation costs of 10 percent in issuing new common shares, the cost of new stock, according to the DCF model, would be 16.7 percent:

$$k_e = \hat{k}_e = \frac{\$4.00(1.10)}{\$73.33(1 - 0.10)} + 10\% = 6.7\% + 10\% = 16.7\%.$$

■ The DCF cost of new common stock is 16.7 percent, while the DCF cost of retained earnings is 16.0 percent. Thus, the flotation premium is 16.7% - 16.0% = 0.7 percentage points.

■ This premium must be added to the final estimate of the cost of retained earnings (determined previously in this example to be an average of the three estimation methods) to obtain the estimate of the cost of new common stock:

$$k_e = k_s + \text{Flotation cost adjustment} = 16.5\% + 0.7\% = 17.2\%.$$

The costs of the individual capital components must be combined to estimate the weighted average cost of capital, WACC.

■ The formula for the weighted average cost of capital is

$$WACC = w_d k_d (1 - T) + w_{ps} k_{ps} + w_{ce}(k_s \text{ or } k_e).$$

■ *The WACC is the weighted average cost of each new dollar of capital raised at the margin,* and not the average cost of all dollars raised in the past nor the average cost of dollars the firm will raise during the year.

■ The weights, w_d, w_{ps}, and w_{ce}, are based on the firm's target market value capital structure and not on book values. Each firm has a target capital structure which minimizes its overall cost of capital, and hence maximizes stock price.

■ If the target capital structure for Firm A is 30 percent debt, 10 percent preferred stock, and 60 percent common equity, and its marginal tax rate is 40 percent, then the firm's weighted average cost of capital, using retained earnings as the common equity component, is 13.32 percent:

$$
\begin{aligned}
WACC &= w_d k_d (1 - T) + w_{ps} k_{ps} + w_{ce} k_s \\
&= 0.3(12\%)(0.6) + 0.1(12.6\%) + 0.6(16.5\%) \\
&= 2.16\% + 1.26\% + 9.90\% = 13.32\%.
\end{aligned}
$$

■ Firms raise capital in accordance with their target capital structures.

The marginal cost of capital is defined as the cost of raising another dollar of new capital. In general, the marginal cost of any factor of production, including capital, will eventually rise as more and more of the factor is used.

■ As companies raise larger and larger sums during a given time period, the component costs begin to rise. This causes an increase in the weighted average cost of each additional dollar of new capital.

■ Suppose that a firm needs $500,000 in new capital. Its capital structure is 60 percent common equity, 30 percent debt, and 10 percent preferred stock, and its marginal tax rate is 40 percent. The before-tax cost of debt is 14 percent, and the cost of preferred stock is 12.6 percent. The firm will need to raise 0.6($500,000) = $300,000 in common equity. It expects retained earnings for the year to be $100,000; therefore, it needs to sell $300,000 - $100,000 = $200,000 of new common stock. The cost of retained earnings is 16.0 percent, but the cost of new equity is 16.8 percent. The weighted average cost of capital, using retained earnings, is:

$$\text{WACC} = w_d k_d (1 - T) + w_{ps} k_{ps} + w_{ce} k_s$$
$$= 0.3(14\%)(0.6) + 0.1(12.6\%) + 0.6(16.0\%)$$
$$= 13.38\%,$$

while the weighted average cost of capital, using new equity, is:

$$\text{WACC} = w_d k_d (1 - T) + w_{ps} k_{ps} + w_{ce} k_s$$
$$= 0.3(14\%)(0.6) + 0.1(12.6\%) + 0.6(16.8\%)$$
$$= 13.86\%.$$

■ The point at which the marginal cost of capital increases is called a *break point*. The *retained earnings break point* is calculated as Retained earnings/Equity fraction. In this example, the break point is $100,000/0.6 = $166,667. That is, when $166,667 of new capital is raised, the firm will have used 0.6($166,667) = $100,000 of retained earnings. After that, more costly new common equity must be used.

■ The *marginal cost of capital (MCC) schedule* shows the relationship between the cost of each dollar raised and the total amount of capital raised during the year.

■ The optimal capital structure is the one that produces the lowest MCC schedule.

■ In general, a jump, or break, will occur in the MCC schedule any time the cost of one of the components rises. Firms generally have additional break points beyond that for retained earnings.

As more and more securities are issued during the year, the costs of debt, preferred stock, and new common stock will rise.

☐ The break point is determined by the following equation:

$$\text{Break point} = \frac{\text{Total amount of lower-cost capital of a given type}}{\text{Fraction of this type of capital in the optimal structure}}.$$

☐ If there are no break points, there will be one MCC. If there are n break points, there will be n + 1 different MCCs.

☐ Since break points beyond retained earnings are difficult to estimate, firms' WACCs typically have only one break point. If an extraordinarily large amount of new capital is required, the WACC using new equity is subjectively adjusted upward.

We have concentrated on retained earnings and new securities as the sources of capital. Actually, companies have other sources—depreciation and deferred taxes—which are often quite large.

■ Depreciation is a noncash expense; thus, for a profitable firm, depreciation cash flow is available for investment in fixed assets in addition to retained earnings.

☐ Depreciation cash flow can either be reinvested in the firm or returned to the capital suppliers. If returned, the cash flow would be used to repurchase common and preferred stock, as well as debt, so that the capital structure would not be altered. Thus, depreciation-generated funds have an opportunity cost equal to the firm's WACC prior to the retained earnings break point.

☐ Depreciation-generated funds push the retained earnings break point out to the right by an amount equal to the depreciation expense.

■ Deferred taxes arise when a firm uses accelerated (MACRS) depreciation for tax purposes and normal (straight line) depreciation for reporting purposes.

☐ Like depreciation, deferred taxes represent a noncash charge which provides a source of cash flow.

☐ Deferred tax cash flows also have an opportunity cost equal to the firm's WACC using retained earnings as the equity component, and they also push the retained earnings break point to the right.

■ Since the WACC is based strictly on the firm's target capital structure, cash flows from depreciation or deferred taxes are not included in the WACC estimate. However, these flows do affect the point at which the WACC increases.

An alternative approach to handling flotation costs is to ignore them when estimating the firm's WACC, but then, in the capital budgeting process, to allocate dollar flotation costs to the firm's new projects, hence increasing project costs rather than capital costs.

SELF-TEST QUESTIONS

Definitional

1. A firm should calculate its cost of capital as a(n) _____ _____ of the after-tax costs of the various capital components.

2. Capital components are items on the right-hand side of the balance sheet such as (1) _____, (2) _____ _____, and (3) _____ _____.

3. The cost of retained earnings is defined as the _____ _____ _____ stockholders require on the firm's common stock.

4. _____ approaches can be used to estimate the cost of retained earnings.

5. Assigning a cost to retained earnings is based on the _____ _____ principle.

6. The cost of external equity capital is higher than the cost of retained earnings because of _____ _____.

7. In using the Capital Asset Pricing Model (CAPM), the required rate of return on common stock is found as a function of the _____-_____ _____, the firm's _____ _____, and the required rate of return on an average _____.

8. The cost of retained earnings may also be found by adding a(n) _____ _____ to the interest rate on the firm's own _____-_____ _____.

9. The cost of retained earnings may also be estimated using the DCF method which assumes that markets are in equilibrium and the _____ rate of return (k_s) equals the _____ rate of return ($\hat{k}_s$).

10. Minimizing the firm's weighted average cost of capital will maximize the firm's _____ _____.

11. A plot of the WACC versus dollars of new capital raised is called the _____ _____ ____ _____ schedule.

12. Three commonly used betas are _____, _____, and _____ betas.

13. In estimating the WACC, the weights are based on the firm's target _____ _____ capital structure.

14. _____-_____ and _____ _____funds have a cost equal to the firm's lowest WACC.

Conceptual

15. The preferred proxy for k_{RF} in the CAPM cost of equity estimate is the rate on long-term Treasury bonds, because it relates more closely to common equity costs than does the rate of return on Treasury bills.

    a. True   **b.** False

16. If a firm obtains all of its common equity from retained earnings, its MCC schedule would be flat; that is there would be no break points.

    a. True   **b.** False

17. The component costs of capital are based on historical, or embedded, costs.

    a. True   **b.** False

18. The DCF method can only be used for constant growth stocks.

    a. True   **b.** False

19. Funds acquired by the firm through perpetual preferred stock have a cost to the firm equal to the preferred dividend divided by the price investors would pay for one share.

    a. True   **b.** False

20. If there are n break points in the MCC schedule, there will be n + 1 different MCCs.

    a. True   **b.** False

21. Which of the following statements *could* be true concerning the costs of debt and equity?

    a. The cost of debt for Firm A is greater than the cost of equity for Firm A.
    b. The cost of debt for Firm A is greater than the cost of equity for Firm B.
    c. The cost of retained earnings for Firm A is less than the external equity cost for Firm A.
    d. The cost of retained earnings for Firm A is less than the cost of debt for Firm A.
    e. Statements b and c could both be true.

22. Which of the following statements is most *correct*?

    a. If Congress raised the corporate tax rate, this would lower the effective cost of debt but probably would also reduce the amount of retained earnings available to corporations, so the effect on the marginal cost of capital is uncertain.
    b. For corporate investors, 70 percent of the dividends received on both common and preferred stocks is exempt from taxes. However, neither preferred nor common dividends is tax deductible by the issuing company. Therefore, the dividend exclusion has no effect on a company's cost of capital, so its WACC would probably not change at all if the dividend exclusion rule were rescinded by Congress.
    c. Normally, the MCC schedule is drawn with an upward slope, reflecting the fact that as more capital is raised, the cost of capital increases. However, if the firm uses a lot of short-term debt to finance short-term investments, then its MCC schedule could, according to the text, have a U shape.
    d. Each of the above statements is true.
    e. Each of the above statements is false.

23. Which of the following statements is most *correct*?

    a. Three procedures for determining the cost of retained earnings were discussed in the text: the CAPM, the DCF, and the WACC.

    b. One reason why new common stock has a higher cost than retained earnings is because, to raise capital by selling stock, the firm must attract new investors who are less sanguine (that is, less optimistic) about the firm's prospects. This requires that the price of the stock be reduced, and this price reduction is built into the flotation cost. Therefore, the steeper the demand curve for the stock, the greater the differential between the cost of new equity and the cost of retained earnings.

    c. Logically, one can think of a high dividend payout stock as being similar to a shorter-term bond and of a low payout stock as being similar to a longer-term bond because cash flows come in faster if the payout is higher. Because of this factor, the differential between the cost of retained earnings and the cost of new outside equity should normally be *greater* for a low payout stock, other things held constant.

    d. When calculating the WACC for a firm which will obtain equity both from retained earnings and by selling new stock, the cost of equity used in the WACC formula should normally be a weighted average of k_s and k_e; that is, the equity component will be $w_{ce}(k_s + k_e)$.

    e. Each of the above statements is false.

24. Which of the following statements is most *correct*?

    a. Holding other things constant, an increase in the corporate tax rate would generally increase the WACC for a company which uses no debt.

    b. Holding other things constant, an increase in the corporate tax rate would generally lower the WACC for a company which uses no debt.

    c. Other things held constant, changes in the corporate tax rate would generally have no effect on a company's WACC, regardless of its use of debt.

    d. According to the text, new retained earnings are generated from income after the payment of taxes, but new common stock issues do not require the payment of income taxes. Therefore, an increase in the corporate tax rate would have a greater impact on the cost of retained earnings (k_s) than on the cost of equity obtained by selling new stock (k_e).

    e. Statements a, b, c, and d are all false.

25. The first break point in the WACC:

   a. Always results from using up retained earnings.
   b. Always results from using up cheap debt.
   c. Depends jointly on the capital structure and the amount of each type of low-cost funds that are available.
   d. Assuming net income is held constant, the first break point is directly affected by the tax rate because the cost of debt is reduced due to the deductibility of interest.
   e. Statements c and d are both true.

SELF-TEST PROBLEMS

1. NBC's last dividend (D_0), which was paid yesterday, was $2.50. The firm has maintained a constant payout ratio of 50 percent during the past 7 years. Seven years ago its EPS was $1.50. The firm's beta coefficient is 1.2. The required return on an average stock is 13 percent, and the risk-free rate is 7 percent. NBC's A-rated bonds are yielding 10 percent, and its current stock price is $30. Which of the following values is the most reasonable estimate of NBC's cost of retained earnings, k_s?

   a. 10%   b. 12%   c. 14%   d. 20%   e. 26%

2. The director of capital budgeting for ICU Inc., manufacturers of playground equipment, is considering a plan to expand production facilities in order to meet an increase in demand. The firm's target capital structure calls for a debt/equity ratio of 0.8. ICU currently has a bond issue outstanding which will mature in 25 years, has a 7 percent annual coupon, and a par value of $1,000. The bonds are currently selling for $804. The firm has maintained a constant growth rate of 6 percent. ICU's next expected dividend is $2 and its current stock price is $40. Its tax rate is 40 percent. What is the firm's weighted average cost of capital? (Assume that there is no preferred stock outstanding and that any new debt will have a 25-year maturity.)

   a. 6.5%   b. 7.5%   c. 8.5%   d. 9.5%   e. 10.5%

3. Midterm Corporation's present capital structure, which is also its target capital structure, calls for 50 percent debt and 50 percent common equity. Midterm expects to retain $3 million of earnings next year. It can raise new debt at a before-tax cost of 8 percent. The cost of retained earnings is 12 percent, and Midterm can sell any amount of new common stock desired at a cost of new equity of 15 percent. The firm's marginal tax rate is 40 percent. Which of the following statements are correct?

   a. Midterm's WACC using retained earnings is 8.4 percent.
   b. Midterm's WACC using new common stock is 9.9 percent.
   c. Midterm's retained earnings break point is $6 million.
   d. All of the above statements are correct.
   e. All of the above statements are incorrect.

4. The management of Florida Phosphate Industries (FPI) is estimating the firm's WACC. FPI projects net income of $10,500, and its payout ratio is 40 percent. The company's earnings and dividends are growing at a constant rate of 5 percent; the last dividend, D_0, was $0.90; and the current equilibrium stock price is $8.59. FPI can raise debt at a 12 percent before-tax cost. If FPI issues new common stock, a 10 percent flotation cost will be incurred. FPI is at its optimal capital structure, which is 40 percent debt and 60 percent equity, and the firm's marginal tax rate is 40 percent. What is FPI's cost of equity when it uses retained earnings and what is the weighted average cost of capital when it uses new common stock?

   a. 16.0%; 13.2%   **d.** 11.0%; 12.5%
   b. 13.2%; 16.0%   **e.** 16.6%; 13.2%
   c. 12.5%; 11.0%

(The following data apply to the next six problems.)

The Richman Corporation's long-term debt currently yields 13 percent. It could sell preferred stock with a $10 annual dividend for $100, but flotation costs would be 5 percent. The firm's beta coefficient is 1.2, the risk-free rate is 10 percent, and the required rate of return on the market is 15 percent. Richman's next dividend is estimated to be $2.00, and it is growing at a constant 5 percent. The firm's stock is currently selling for $20.00. The firm's best estimate of the "over-own-bond" risk premium is 2.5 percentage points. Richman's target capital structure is 40 percent debt, 10 percent preferred stock, and 50 percent common stock. Richman expects $40,000 in retained earnings and must incur flotation costs of 10 percent on new common stock sales. Its tax rate is 40 percent.

5. What is the firm's after-tax cost of debt?

   a. 7.8%   **b.** 10.5%   **c.** 11.9%   **d.** 12.5%   **e.** 15.5%

6. What is Richman's cost of preferred stock?

   a. 7.8%   **b.** 10.5%   **c.** 11.9%   **d.** 12.5%   **e.** 15.5%

7. What is the firm's cost of retained earnings? (Use all three methods.)

   a. 11.9%   **b.** 12.5%   **c.** 15.5%   **d.** 16.6%   **e.** 15.0%

8. What is the firm's weighted average cost of capital using retained earnings as the equity component?

   a. 11.9%   **b.** 12.5%   **c.** 15.5%   **d.** 16.6%   **e.** 17.0%

9. What is Richman's weighted average cost of capital using new common stock as the equity component?

   a. 11.9%   **b.** 12.5%   **c.** 15.5%   **d.** 16.6%   **e.** 17.0%

10. Suppose the firm is forecasting $20,000 in depreciation-generated funds and an additional $5,000 in deferred taxes. What is the cost of these funds?

   a. 11.9%   **b.** 12.5%   **c.** 15.5%   **d.** 16.6%   **e.** 17.0%

11. A company's 7 percent coupon rate, semiannual payment, $1,000 par value bond which matures in 40 years sells at a price of $600. The company's federal-plus-state tax rate is 35 percent. What is the firm's component cost of debt for purposes of calculating the WACC? (Hint: Use a financial calculator and base your answer on the nominal rate, not the EAR.)

   a. 8.67%   **b.** 7.24%   **c.** 7.64%   **d.** 11.75%   **e.** 11.42%

ANSWERS TO SELF-TEST QUESTIONS

1. weighted average
2. debt; preferred stock; common equity
3. rate of return
4. Three
5. opportunity cost
6. flotation costs
7. risk-free rate (k_{RF}); beta coefficient (b); stock (k_M)

8. risk premium; long-term debt
9. required; expected
10. stock price
11. marginal cost of capital
12. historical; fundamental; adjusted
13. market value
14. Depreciation-generated; deferred tax

15. a. The rate on long-term Treasury bonds is more logically related to common equity costs.

16. b. The component cost of debt and/or preferred equity might increase, thus causing break points in the MCC schedule.

17. b. The costs reflect the costs of current borrowing, earnings retention, or stock sales.

18. b. The method can also be used for nonconstant growth stocks, but the procedure is more involved.

19. b. Flotation costs must be subtracted from the investor's cost to get the net issuance price.

20. a. This statement is correct.

21. e. If Firm A has significantly more risk than Firm B, Firm A's cost of debt could be greater than Firm B's cost of equity. Also, the cost of retained earnings is less than the cost of external equity because of flotation costs.

22. a. Statement a is correct. If Congress were to raise the tax rate, this would lower the cost of debt; however, a bigger chunk of the firm's earnings would go to Uncle Sam. The effect on the MCC would depend on which had the greater effect on the MCC. Statement b is false. Preferred stock generally has a lower cost than debt due to the dividend exclusion; however, if the dividend exclusion were omitted, preferred stock would have an increased cost. Statement c is false because short-term debt is not considered in the MCC schedule, except when it is used to finance long-term investments. The MCC schedule is usually drawn as a step function; however, at some point numerous break points would occur and the MCC would rise almost continuously beyond some level of new financing.

23. b. Statement a is false. The three methods for determining the cost of equity are DCF, CAPM, and bond-yield-plus-risk-premium. Statement b is correct. Statement c is false. The reason for the differential in the cost of retained earnings and the cost of new stock is discussed in statement b. Statement d is false. The MCC will contain a break where retained earnings are used up and new common stock is used, and there would be 2 different MCC's calculated—one using k_s and one using k_e.

24. e. Statement e is true because the other statements are all false. Recall that the component cost of debt for use in the WACC is $k_d(1 - T)$. Therefore, an increase in the tax rate would, other things held constant, decrease the WACC for a company which uses debt.

25. c. Look at the break point formula; it is obvious that the capital structure and the amount of low-cost funds of each type affect the break point. The tax rate affects the after-tax cost of debt, but it does not directly affect the break point, so statement d is incorrect. Therefore, statement c is the correct response.

SOLUTIONS TO SELF-TEST PROBLEMS

1. c. Use all three methods to estimate k_s.

(1) CAPM: $k_s = k_{RF} + (k_M - k_{RF})b = 7\% + (13\% - 7\%)1.2 = 14.2\%$.

(2) RP: k_s = Bond yield + Risk premium = 10% + Approximately 4% = 14%.

(3) DCF: $k_s = D_1/P_0 + g = [\$2.50(1 + g)]/\$30 + g$, where g can be estimated:

$$\$0.75 = \$2.50(PVIF_{k,7}); \quad PVIF_{k,7} = \$0.75/\$2.50 = 0.3000.$$

Thus k, which is the compound growth rate, g, is about 19 percent. Alternatively, with a financial calculator, input N = 7, PV = -0.75, PMT = 0, FV = 2.50, and solve for I = 18.8%. Therefore, $k_s = 0.099 + 0.188 = 28.7\%$.

NBC has apparently been experiencing supernormal growth during the past 7 years, and it is not reasonable to assume that this growth will continue. The first two methods yield a k_s of about 14 percent, which appears reasonable.

2. c. Cost of equity = k_s = \$2/\$40 + 0.06 = 0.11 = 11%.

Cost of debt = k_d = Yield to maturity on outstanding issue.

$$V_B = INT(PVIFA_{k_d, n}) + M(PVIF_{k_d, n})$$
$$\$804 = \$70(PVIFA_{k_d, 25}) + \$1,000(PVIF_{k_d, 25}).$$

Solving this gives k_d = 9%. Alternatively, using a financial calculator, input N = 25, PV = -804, PMT = 70, FV = 1000, and solve for I = 9%.

In determining the capital structure weights, note that debt/equity = 0.8 or, for example, 4/5. Therefore, debt/assets is

$$\frac{D}{A} = \frac{Debt}{Debt + Equity} = \frac{4}{4 + 5} = \frac{4}{9}$$

and equity/assets = 5/9. Hence, the weighted average cost of capital is

WACC = $(D/A)(k_d)(1 - T) + (E/A)k_s$
       = (4/9)(0.09)(1 - 0.4) + (5/9)(0.11)
       = 0.024 + 0.061 = 0.085 = 8.5%.

3. d. WACC = $w_d k_d(1 - T) + w_{ce}(k_s$ or $k_e)$

WACC (Retained earnings) = 0.5(8%)(0.6) + 0.5(12%) = 8.4%.

WACC (New common stock) = 0.5(8%)(0.6) + 0.5(15%) = 9.9%.

Now the retained earnings break point is \$3 million/0.5 = \$6 million. Thus, Midterm's overall cost of capital is 8.4 percent up to \$6 million of new capital and 9.9 percent for all new capital above \$6 million.

4. a. The cost of retained earnings is 16.0 percent:

$$k_s = \frac{D_0(1 + g)}{P_0} + g = \frac{\$0.90(1.05)}{\$8.59} + 0.05 = 0.160 = 16\%.$$

The cost of new common equity is 17.2 percent:

$$k_s = \frac{D_0(1 + g)}{P_0(1 - F)} + g = \frac{\$0.90(1.05)}{\$8.59(0.90)} + 0.05 = 17.2\%,$$

and the weighted average cost of capital using new common stock is 13.2 percent:

$$0.4(12\%)(0.6) + 0.6(17.2\%) = 13.2\%.$$

5. a. $k_d(1 - T) = 13\%(0.6) = 7.8\%.$

6. b. $k_{ps} = D_{ps}/P_n = \$10/\$95 = 10.5\%.$

7. c. CAPM: $k_s = k_{RF} + (k_M - k_{RF})b = 10\% + (15\% - 10\%)1.2 = 16.0\%.$

DCF: $k_s = \hat{k}_s = D_1/P_0 + g = \$2.00/\$20.00 + 5\% = 15.0\%.$

Bond-yield-plus-risk-premium: $13.0\% + 2.5\% = 15.5\%.$

Now judgment must be applied. Since all results are consistent, we could use a weighted average of the three methods, and conclude that $k_s = 15.5\%.$

8. a. WACC(RE) $= w_d k_d(1 - T) + w_{ps}k_{ps} + w_{cc}k_s$
$= 0.4(13\%)(0.6) + 0.1(10.5\%) + 0.5(15.5\%) = 11.9\%.$

9. b. $\text{WACC(New CS)} = w_d k_d (1 - T) + w_{ps} k_{ps} + w_{ce} k_e.$

But, we first have to estimate k_e:

$$k_e = \hat{k}_e = \frac{D_1}{P_0(1 - F)} + g = \frac{\$2.00}{\$20(0.9)} + 5\% = 16.1\%.$$

Flotation premium = $k_{e(DCF)} - k_{s(DCF)} = 16.1\% - 15.0\% = 1.1$ percentage points.

Now, add the flotation premium to the judgmental estimate of k_s:

$k_e = 15.5\% + 1.1\% = 16.6\%.$

Finally, use this cost in the calculation of WACC:

$\text{WACC(New CS)} = 0.4(13.0\%)(0.6) + 0.1(10.5\%) + 0.5(16.6\%) = 12.5\%.$

10. a. Depreciation-generated funds and cash flow from deferred taxes can be reinvested in the firm or returned to the capital suppliers (debtholders, preferred stockholders, and common stockholders). Thus, these funds have an opportunity cost equal to the firm's lowest cost of capital, or WACC (RE) = 11.9%.

11. c. Enter these values into a financial calculator: N = 80, PV = -600, PMT = 35, FV = 1000, and press I to get I = 5.8745% = periodic rate. The nominal rate is 5.8745%(2) = 11.75%, and the after-tax component cost of debt is 11.75%(0.65) = 7.64%.

CHAPTER 9

THE BASICS OF CAPITAL BUDGETING

OVERVIEW

In the preceding chapters, we discussed security valuation and the cost of capital. Now, we turn to investment decisions involving fixed assets, or *capital budgeting*. Capital budgeting is similar in principle to security valuation in that future cash flows are estimated, risks are appraised and reflected in a cost of capital discount rate, and all cash flows are evaluated on a present value basis.

The term *capital* refers to fixed assets used in operations, while a *budget* is a plan which details projected inflows and outflows during some future period. Thus, the *capital budget* is an outline of planned expenditures on fixed assets, and *capital budgeting* is the whole process of analyzing projects and deciding whether they should be included in the capital budget.

OUTLINE

A number of factors combine to make capital budgeting extremely important.

■ Because the results of capital budgeting decisions continue over an extended period, capital budgeting decisions have long-term consequences and the decision maker loses some flexibility.

■ Capital budgeting decisions define the makeup of the firm's assets and, hence, its basic character.

■ A firm's capital budgeting decisions define its strategic direction, because moves into new products, services, or markets must be preceded by capital expenditures.

■ Capital budgeting typically involves large expenditures and, thus, requires extensive planning both for funds acquisition and allocation.

■ Capital assets must be available when they are needed.

■ Capital budgeting projects are created by the firm. A firm's growth, and even its ability to remain competitive and to survive, depends upon a constant flow of ideas for new products, for ways to make existing products better, and for ways to produce at a lower cost.

■ Analyzing capital expenditure proposals has a cost, so firms classify projects into different categories to help differentiate the level of analysis required:
  ☐ Replacement: maintenance of business.
  ☐ Replacement: cost reduction.
  ☐ Expansion of existing products or markets.
  ☐ Expansion into new products or markets.
  ☐ Safety and/or environmental projects.
  ☐ Other miscellaneous projects. Mergers are essentially a type of capital budgeting expenditure.

■ The capital budgeting process involves the same procedures that are used in security valuation.
  ☐ The cost of the project must be determined.
  ☐ Cash flows from the project are estimated, including the value of the asset at a specified terminal date.
  ☐ The riskiness of these projected cash flows is estimated.
  ☐ Given the riskiness of the projected cash flows, management determines the appropriate cost of capital at which the project's cash flows are to be discounted.
  ☐ Cash flows are discounted to their present values.
  ☐ The present value of the benefits (the cash inflows) is compared to the present value of costs (the cash outflows). If the benefits exceed the costs, the project should be accepted since it will increase the value of the firm.

Estimating the cash flows associated with a project is the most important and most difficult step in capital budgeting analysis. This topic will be discussed in detail in Chapter 10. Once cash flow estimates have been made for various projects, different methods can be used to evaluate the proposals and to decide which ones should be accepted for inclusion in the capital budget. The six primary methods generally used are (1) payback, (2) accounting rate of return (ARR), (3) net present value (NPV), (4) internal rate of return (IRR), (5) modified IRR (MIRR), and (6) profitability index (PI).

■ The *payback period* is defined as the number of years required to recover the original investment in the project.
  ☐ Its major advantage is that it is easy to calculate and to understand.
  ☐ Its major disadvantages are: (1) It ignores cash flows beyond the payback period. This penalizes long-term projects which may be vital to the firm's long-term success. (2) It ignores

the time value of money by assigning equal weight to cash flows in each year during the payback period.

☐ The *discounted payback period*, which uses discounted cash flows to determine the payback period, does consider the time value of money.

☐ In spite of its disadvantages, payback continues to be used extensively in capital budgeting decision making. However, it is not used as a primary decision tool, but rather as an indicator of a project's liquidity and risk.

■ The *accounting rate of return (ARR)* method focuses on a project's contribution to the firm's net income rather than on its cash flow. In its most common form, the ARR is measured as the ratio of the project's average annual expected net income to its average investment. Note that this method ignores the time value of money and thus could lead to incorrect conclusions.

■ The *net present value (NPV)* method of evaluating investment proposals is a discounted cash flow (DCF) technique that accounts for the time value of all cash flows from a project.

☐ The NPV is defined as

$$NPV = \sum_{t=0}^{n} \frac{CF_t}{(1 + k)^t}.$$

Here CF_t is the expected net cash flow in Period t, and k is the project cost of capital. Project costs, or outflows, are treated as negative cash flows and cash inflows are treated as positive flows.

☐ If the NPV is positive, the project should be accepted; if negative, it should be rejected.

☐ If two projects are mutually exclusive (that is, only one can be accepted), the one with the higher NPV should be chosen, assuming that the NPV is positive. If both projects have negative NPVs, neither should be chosen.

☐ The NPV method is typically regarded by academicians as the best single method because it focuses on the contribution of the project to shareholder wealth. A positive NPV means that an excess return exists after the capital contributors have recovered their investments and earned their required rates of return, and this excess return accrues solely to the equity holders.

☐ There is a direct relationship between NPV and EVA. Over time positive NPVs should translate into positive EVAs, and to a positive MVA (the excess of the firm's market value over its book value.)

■ The *internal rate of return (IRR)* is defined as the discount rate that equates the present value of the expected future cash inflows to the present value of the project's expected costs.

☐ The equation for calculating the IRR is

$$NPV = \sum_{t=0}^{n} \frac{CF_t}{(1 + IRR)^t} = 0.$$

This is an equation with one unknown, IRR, and we can solve for the value of IRR that forces the equation to equal zero. The solution value is defined as the internal rate of return.

☐ The IRR formula is simply the NPV formula solved for the particular discount rate that causes the NPV to equal zero.

☐ The IRR can be found by trial and error, but most financial calculators and computers with financial analysis software can easily calculate IRRs and NPVs.

☐ Whereas the NPV measures the dollar profitability of a project, the IRR measures the percentage profitability of a project. In effect, the IRR is a project's expected rate of return.

☐ If the IRR is greater than the project cost of capital, then the project should be accepted; if the IRR is less than the cost of capital, it should be rejected.

☐ If two projects are mutually exclusive, the one with the higher IRR should be chosen, assuming that the IRR is greater than the cost of capital.

☐ Note that the IRR gives some indication of the "safety margin" of a project—a project with an IRR that is far above its cost of capital can tolerate cash flows well below those expected and still be profitable.

■ Another method that is used to evaluate projects is the *profitability index (PI)*, or the benefit/cost ratio as it is sometimes called.

☐ The profitability index is defined as

$$PI = \frac{PV\ benefits}{PV\ costs} = \frac{\sum_{t=0}^{n} \dfrac{CIF_t}{(1 + k)^t}}{\sum_{t=0}^{n} \dfrac{COF_t}{(1 + k)^t}}.$$

Here CIF_t represents the expected cash inflow in Period t, while COF_t represents the expected cash outflow, or cost, in Period t.

☐ A project is acceptable if its PI is greater than 1.0, and the higher the PI, the higher is the project's ranking.

☐ The PI measures a project's relative dollar profitability, or its "bang for the buck."

☐ Note that, like the IRR, a high PI indicates a high "margin of safety."

■ So far, we have discussed five possible decision methods and presented advantages and disadvantages of each method.

- ☐ The payback method and accounting rate of return method both have several faults and should not be used as the sole criteria in making capital budgeting decisions.
- ☐ The NPV, IRR, and PI methods all recognize time value, all consider the complete set of project cash flows, and all lead to the same accept/reject decision for independent projects. Thus, any of these methods can be used to choose among independent projects. However, NPV, IRR, and PI can give conflicting rankings for mutually exclusive projects.

The net present value profile, a plot of a project's NPV versus the corresponding discount rate, is a useful tool both in project analysis and in understanding the differences between the NPV and IRR methods.

- ■ The NPV profile crosses the Y axis at the undiscounted NPV, while the profile crosses the X axis at the IRR.

- ■ If two mutually exclusive projects have NPV profiles which intersect in the upper righthand quadrant, then there may be a conflict in rankings between the NPV and the IRR methods.
  - ☐ The intersection point of the profiles is the *crossover rate*. If the cost of capital is greater than the crossover rate there is never a conflict between NPV and IRR; however, if the cost of capital is less than the crossover rate there will be a conflict between NPV and IRR.

- ■ Conflicts can occur under two circumstances.
  - ☐ The projects differ in size (or scale); that is, one project costs $100,000 while a mutually exclusive project costs $1 million.
  - ☐ The projects differ in the timing of cash flows; that is, one project has larger cash flows in its early years, while the other has larger cash flows in its later years. Note that cash flow timing does not refer to project life, but rather to the relative sizes of the flows. Differences in project lives are discussed in Chapter 10.

- ■ The underlying cause of conflicts in project rankings lies in differing reinvestment rate assumptions.
  - ☐ The NPV method implicitly assumes that project cash flows are reinvested at the project's cost of capital.
  - ☐ The IRR method implicitly assumes that project cash flows are reinvested at the project's IRR.
  - ☐ The opportunity cost of a project's cash flows is the project's cost of capital. If a project's cash inflows were not available to the firm, and if the firm had good investment opportunities, then the funds would be obtained from the firm's capital suppliers, and the cost would be the overall cost of capital. Thus, the assumption of reinvestment at the cost of capital is the correct assumption, and NPV is superior to IRR.

■ There can also be ranking conflicts between the NPV and PI decision rules. All conflicts should be resolved in favor of the project with the highest NPV.

■ The conflicts between NPV and IRR, and between NPV and PI, only affect the decisions on mutually exclusive projects. All three methods lead to the same accept/reject decisions on independent projects. Thus, the IRR or PI methods can be used in place of the NPV method when evaluating independent projects. (We will use the IRR rule when we find the optimal capital budget.) However, when evaluating mutually exclusive projects, NPV should be used.

■ One other situation in which the IRR method may not be usable occurs when non-normal cash flows are involved. Non-normal cash flows can present unique difficulties when evaluated by the IRR method, especially the problem of *multiple IRRs*.
    □ A project has *normal* cash flows when one or more cash outflows are followed by a series of cash inflows.
    □ If a project calls for a large cash outflow either sometime during or at the end of its life, then it has *non-normal* cash flows.

Business executives often prefer to work with percentage rates of return, such as IRR, rather than dollar amounts of NPV. The modified IRR, or MIRR, overcomes many of the IRR's disadvantages.

■ The MIRR is defined as the discount rate which forces

$$PV \text{ costs} = PV \text{ terminal value,}$$

where terminal value (TV) is the future value of the inflows. Thus,

$$\text{Costs} = \frac{TV}{(1 + MIRR)^n} = \frac{\sum_{t=0}^{n} CIF_t(1 + k)^{n-t}}{(1 + MIRR)^n}.$$

■ The MIRR forces cash flow reinvestment at the cost of capital rather than the project's own IRR, making it a better indicator of a project's true profitability.

■ NPV and MIRR will lead to the same project selection decision if the two projects are of equal size. However, conflicts can still occur when projects differ in scale, and when this happens NPV should be used.

- MIRR also avoids the problem of multiple IRRs, which can arise when a project has *nonnormal* cash flows. NPV can be easily applied to such situations, and MIRR can also overcome the multiple IRR problem, because there is but one MIRR for any set of cash flows.

Firms often choose between mutually exclusive projects on the basis of the present value of future costs rather than on the basis of the projects' NPVs or MIRRs.

- If the mutually exclusive projects will generate the same revenues, then they can be evaluated on the basis of their costs.

- In this situation, each project's costs would be placed on a time line, and the project with the lower (or lowest) present value of costs should be selected.

We have presented six potential capital budgeting decision methods in this chapter, and each has its own set of advantages and disadvantages.

- Today, virtually all capital budgeting decisions of importance are analyzed by computer, and hence it is relatively easy to calculate the values for all six methods.

- In making the ultimate accept/reject decision, most sophisticated managers would consider all of the measures, because each measure provides a somewhat different piece of relevant information.

An important aspect of the capital budgeting process is the post-audit, which involves comparing actual results with those predicted by the project's sponsors and explaining why any differences occurred. The results of the post-audit help to improve forecasts, to increase efficiency of the firm's operations, and to identify abandonment/termination opportunities (if initial results indicate that a project is likely to be a loser rather than a winner).

SELF-TEST QUESTIONS

Definitional

1. A firm's _____ _____ outlines its planned expenditures on fixed assets.

2. The most difficult step in the analysis of capital expenditure proposals involves estimating future _____ _____.

3. The number of years required to recover the original investment in a project is known as the _____ _____.

4. The primary advantage of payback analysis is its _____.

5. One important weakness of payback analysis is the fact that _____ _____ beyond the payback period are ignored.

6. Payback is generally not used as a primary decision tool, but rather as an indicator of a project's _____ and _____.

7. The _____ _____ _____ _____ method focuses on a project's contribution to the firm's net income rather than on its cash flow.

8. The net present value (NPV) method of evaluating investment proposals is a _____ _____ _____ technique.

9. A capital investment proposal should be accepted if its NPV is _____.

10. If two projects are _____ _____, the one with the _____ positive NPV should be selected.

11. In the IRR approach, a discount rate is sought which forces the project's NPV to equal _____.

12. The profitability index is also called the _____/_____ ratio.

13. A net present value profile shows the relationship between a project's NPV and the _____ _____ used to calculate the NPV.

14. If an independent project's _____ is greater than the project's cost of capital, it should be accepted.

15. If a project's _____ _____ is greater than 1.0, it should be accepted.

16. If two mutually exclusive projects are being evaluated, and one project has a higher positive NPV while the other project has a higher IRR, the project with the higher _____ should be chosen.

17. The NPV method implicitly assumes reinvestment at the project's _____ _____ _____, while the IRR method implicitly assumes reinvestment at the _____ _____ _____ _____.

18. Conflicts between NPV and IRR can occur if projects differ in _____ or they differ in the _____ of cash flows.

19. The MIRR method assumes reinvestment at the _____ _____ _____, making it a better indicator of a project's profitability than the IRR method.

20. The internal rate of return (IRR) is that _____ rate which equates the present value of a project's _____ _____ with the present value of its cash outflows.

21. The process of comparing a project's actual results with its projected results is known as a(n) _____ - _____.

22. The objective of the post-audit is to improve _____, _____, and to identify _____ opportunities..

23. The MIRR is defined as the discount rate which forces the present value of costs to equal the present value of the _____ _____.

24. Conflicts between NPV and MIRR can still occur when projects differ in _____, and when this happens the _____ method should be used.

Conceptual

25. The NPV of a project with cash flows that accrue relatively slowly is *more sensitive* to changes in the discount rate than is the NPV of a project with cash flows that come in more rapidly.

    a. True   b. False

26. The NPV method is preferred over the IRR method because the NPV method's reinvestment rate assumption is better.

    a. True   b. False

27. When you find the yield to maturity on a bond, you are finding the bond's net present value (NPV).

    a. True   **b.** False

28. Other things held constant, a decrease in the cost of capital (discount rate) will cause an increase in a project's IRR.

    a. True   **b.** False

29. The IRR method can be used in place of the NPV method for all independent projects.

    a. True   **b.** False

30. The NPV and MIRR methods lead to the same decision for mutually exclusive projects regardless of the projects' relative sizes.

    a. True   **b.** False

31. Projects with nonnormal cash flows sometimes have multiple MIRRs.

    a. True   **b.** False

32. Projects A and B each have an initial cost of $5,000, followed by a series of positive cash inflows. Project A has total undiscounted cash inflows of $12,000, while B has total undiscounted inflows of $10,000. Further, at a discount rate of 10 percent, the two projects have identical NPVs. Which project's NPV will be *more sensitive* to changes in the discount rate? (Hint: Projects with steeper NPV profiles are more sensitive to discount rate changes.)

    a. Project A.
    b. Project B.
    c. Both projects are equally sensitive to changes in the discount rate since their NPVs are equal at all costs of capital.
    d. Neither project is sensitive to changes in the discount rate, since both have NPV profiles which are horizontal.
    e. The solution cannot be determined unless the timing of the cash flows is known.

33. Which of the following statements is most *correct*?

   a. The IRR of a project whose cash flows accrue relatively rapidly is more sensitive to changes in the discount rate than is the IRR of a project whose cash flows come in more slowly.
   b. There are many conditions under which a project can have more than one IRR. One such condition is where an otherwise normal project has a negative cash flow at the end of its life.
   c. The phenomenon called "multiple internal rates of return" arises when two or more mutually exclusive projects which have different lives are being compared.
   d. The modified IRR (MIRR) method has wide appeal to professors, but most business executives prefer the NPV method to either the regular or modified IRR.
   e. Each of the above statements is false.

34. Which of the following statements is most *correct*?

   a. If a project has an IRR greater than zero, then taking on the project will increase the value of the company's common stock because the project will make a positive contribution to net income.
   b. If a project has an NPV greater than zero, then taking on the project will increase the value of the firm's stock.
   c. Assume that you plot the NPV profiles of two mutually exclusive, normal projects and that the cost of capital is *greater* than the rate at which the profiles cross one another. In this case, the NPV and IRR methods will lead to contradictory rankings of the two projects.
   d. For independent (as opposed to mutually exclusive) normal projects, the NPV and IRR methods will generally lead to conflicting accept/reject decisions.
   e. Statements b, c, and d are all true.

35. Which of the following statements is most *correct*?

   a. Underlying the MIRR is the assumption that cash flows can be reinvested at the firm's cost of capital.
   b. Underlying the IRR is the assumption that cash flows can be reinvested at the firm's cost of capital.
   c. Underlying the NPV is the assumption that cash flows can be reinvested at the firm's cost of capital.
   d. The discounted payback method always leads to the same accept/reject decisions as the NPV method.
   e. Statements a and c are both correct.

SELF-TEST PROBLEMS

1. Your firm is considering a fast-food concession at the World's Fair. The cash flow pattern is somewhat unusual since you must build the stands, operate them for 2 years, and then tear the stands down and restore the sites to original condition. You estimate the net cash flows to be as follows:

Year	Expected Net Cash Flow
0	($800,000)
1	700,000
2	700,000
3	(400,000)

What is the approximate IRR of this venture?

a. 5%   **b.** 15%   **c.** 25%   **d.** 35%   **e.** 45%

(The following data apply to the next three problems.)

Toy Motors needs a new machine for production of its 1997 models. The financial vice president has appointed you to do the capital budgeting analysis. You have identified two different machines that are capable of performing the job. You have completed the cash flow analysis, and the expected net cash flows are as follows:

	Expected Net Cash Flow	
Year	Machine B	Machine O
0	($5,000)	($5,000)
1	2,085	0
2	2,085	0
3	2,085	0
4	2,085	9,677

2. What is the payback period (in years) for Machine B?

a. 1.0   **b.** 2.0   **c.** 2.4   **d.** 2.6   **e.** 3.0

3. The cost of capital is uncertain at this time, so you construct NPV profiles to assist in the final decision. The profiles for Machines B and O cross at what cost of capital?

   a. 6%   **b.** 10%   **c.** 18%   **d.** 24%
   e. They do not cross in the upper righthand quadrant.

4. If the cost of capital for both projects is 14 percent at the time the decision is made, which project would you choose?

   a. Project B; it has the higher positive NPV.
   b. Project O; it has the higher positive NPV.
   c. Neither; both have negative NPVs.
   d. Either; both have the same NPV.
   e. Project B; it has the higher IRR.

(The following data apply to the next six problems.)

The director of capital budgeting for Giant Inc. has identified two mutually exclusive projects, L and S, with the following expected net cash flows:

	Expected Net Cash Flow	
Year	Project L	Project S
0	($100)	($100)
1	10	70
2	60	50
3	80	20

Both projects have a cost of capital of 10 percent.

5. What is the payback period (in years) for Project S?

   a. 1.6   **b.** 1.8   **c.** 2.1   **d.** 2.5   **e.** 2.8

6. What is Project L's NPV?

   a. $50.00   **b.** $34.25   **c.** $22.64   **d.** $18.79   **e.** $10.06

7. What is Project S's PI?

   a. 0.96   **b.** 1.03   **c.** 1.12   **d.** 1.15   **e.** 1.20

8. What is Project L's IRR?

   a. 18.1%   **b.** 19.7%   **c.** 21.4%   **d.** 23.6%   **e.** 24.2%

9. What is Project L's MIRR?

   a. 15.3%   **b.** 16.5%   **c.** 16.9%   **d.** 17.1%   **e.** 17.4%

10. Plot the NPV profiles for the two projects. Where is the crossover point?

   a. 6.9%   **b.** 7.8%   **c.** 8.7%   **d.** 9.6%   **e.** 9.9%

11. Your company is considering two mutually exclusive projects, X and Y, whose costs and cash flows are shown below:

Year	Project X	Project Y
0	($2,000)	($2,000)
1	200	2,000
2	600	200
3	800	100
4	1,400	100

The projects are equally risky, and their cost of capital is 10 percent. You must make a recommendation, and you must base it on the modified IRR. What is the MIRR of the better project?

   a. 11.50%   **b.** 12.00%   **c.** 11.70%   **d.** 12.50%   **e.** 13.10%

12. A company is analyzing two mutually exclusive projects, S and L, whose cash flows are shown below:

Year	Project S	Project L
0	($2,000)	($2,000)
1	1,800	0
2	500	500
3	20	800
4	20	1,600

The company's cost of capital is 9 percent, and it can get an unlimited amount of capital at that cost. What is the regular IRR (not MIRR) of the better project? (Hint: Note that the better project may or may not be the one with the higher IRR.)

   a. 11.45%   **b.** 11.74%   **c.** 13.02%   **d.** 13.49%   **e.** 12.67%

13. The stock of Barkley Inc. and "the market" provided the following returns over the last 5 years:

Year	Barkley	Market
1992	(5)	(3)
1993	21	10
1994	9	4
1995	23	11
1996	31	15

Barkley finances only with retained earnings, and it uses the CAPM with a historical beta to determine its cost of equity. The risk-free rate is 7 percent, and the market risk premium is 5 percent. Barkley is considering a project which has a cost at t = 0 of $2,000 and which is expected to provide cash inflows of $1,000 per year for 3 years. What is the project's MIRR?

a. 23.46%   b. 18.25%   c. 22.92%   d. 20.95%   e. 21.82%

14. CDH Worldwide's stock returns versus the market were as follows, and the same relative volatility is expected in the future:

Year	CDH	Market
1993	12	15
1994	(6)	(3)
1995	25	19
1996	18	12

The T-bond rate is 6 percent; the market risk premium is 7 percent; CDH finances only with equity from retained earnings; and it uses the CAPM to estimate its cost of capital. Now CDH is considering two alternative trucks. Truck S has a cost of $12,000 and is expected to produce cash flows of $4,500 per year for 4 years. Truck L has a cost of $20,000 and is expected to produce cash flows of $7,500 per year for 4 years. By how much would CDH's value rise if it buys the better truck, and what is the MIRR of the better truck?

a. $803.35; 17.05%   d. $1,338.91; 16.06%
b. $1,338.91; 17.05%   e. $803.35; 14.41%
c. $1,896.47; 16.06%

15. Assume that your company has a cost of capital of 14 percent ad that it is analyzing the following project:

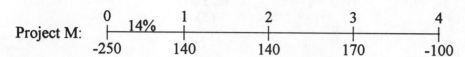

Project M:

0	14%	1	2	3	4
-250		140	140	170	-100

What are the project's IRR and MIRR?

a. 24.26%; 16.28%
b. 23.12%; 17.19%
c. 23.12%; 16.28%

d. 24.26%; 17.19%
e. None of the above

ANSWERS TO SELF-TEST QUESTIONS

1. capital budget
2. cash flows
3. payback period
4. simplicity
5. cash flows
6. liquidity; risk
7. accounting rate of return
8. discounted cash flow
9. positive
10. mutually exclusive; higher
11. zero
12. benefit; cost

13. discount rate
14. IRR
15. profitability index
16. NPV
17. cost of capital; internal rate of return
18. size (scale); timing
19. cost of capital
20. discount; cash inflows
21. post-audit
22. forecasts; operations; abandonment
23. terminal value
24. scale; NPV

25. a. The more the cash flows are spread over time, the greater is the effect of a change in discount rate. This is because the compounding process has a greater effect as the number of years increases.

26. a. Project cash flows are substitutes for outside capital. Thus, the opportunity cost of these flows is the firm's cost of capital, adjusted for risk. The NPV method uses this cost as the reinvestment rate, while the IRR method assumes reinvestment at the IRR.

27. b. The yield to maturity on a bond is the bond's IRR.

28. b. A project's IRR is independent of its cost of capital.

29. a. Both the NPV and IRR methods lead to the same accept/reject decisions for independent projects. Thus, the IRR method can be used as a proxy for the NPV method when choosing independent projects.

30. b. NPV and MIRR may not lead to the same decision when the projects differ in scale.

31. b. Multiple IRRs occur in projects with nonnormal cash flows, but there is only one MIRR for each project.

32. a. If we were to begin graphing the NPV profiles for each of these projects, we would know 2 of the points for each project. The Y intercepts for Projects A and B would be $7,000 and $5,000, respectively, and the crossover rate would be 10 percent. Thus, from this information we can conclude that Project A's NPV profile would have the steeper slope and would be more sensitive to changes in the discount rate.

33. b. Statement a is false because the IRR is independent of the discount rate. Statement b is true; the situation identified is that of a project with nonnormal cash flows, which has multiple IRRs. Statement c is false; multiple IRRs occur with projects having nonnormal cash flows, not with mutually exclusive projects with different lives. Statement d is false; business executives tend to prefer the IRR because it gives a measure of the project's safety margin.

34. b. Statement b is true, the other statements are all false. Note that IRR must be greater than the cost of capital; that conflicts arise if the cost of capital is to the left of the crossover rate; and that for some projects with nonnormal cash flows there are two IRRs, so NPV and IRR could lead to conflicting accept/reject decisions, depending on which IRR we examine.

35. e. Statement e is correct, because both a and c are true. The IRR assumes reinvestment at the IRR, and since the discounted payback ignores cash flows beyond the payback period, it could lead to rejections of projects with high late cash flows and hence NPV > 0.

SOLUTIONS TO SELF-TEST PROBLEMS

1. c. Unless you have a calculator that performs IRR calculations, the IRR must be obtained by trial and error or graphically. (The calculator solution is 25.48 percent.) Note that this project actually has multiple IRRs, with a second IRR at about -53 percent.

2. c. After Year 1, there is $5,000 - $2,085 = $2,915 remaining to pay back. After Year 2, only $2,915 - $2,085 = $830 is remaining. In Year 3, another $2,085 is collected. Assuming that the Year 3 cash flow occurs evenly over time, then payback occurs $830/$2,085 = 0.4 of the way through Year 3. Thus, the payback period is 2.4 years.

3. b. To solve graphically, construct the NPV profiles:

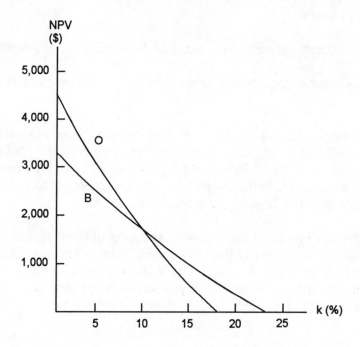

The Y intercept is the NPV when k = 0%. For B, 4($2,085) - $5,000 = $3,340. For O, $9,677 - $5,000 = $4,677. The X intercept is the discount rate when NPV = $0, or the IRR. For B, $5,000 = $2,085(PVIFA$_{IRR,4}$); IRR ≈ 24%. For O, $5,000 = $9,677(PVIF$_{IRR,4}$); IRR ≈ 18%. The graph is an approximation since we are only using two points to plot lines that are curvilinear. However, it shows that there is a crossover point and that it occurs somewhere in the vicinity of k = 10%. To find the exact value, create a Project D (for delta) which is the difference in the cash flows between the projects.

Year	B	O	Project D (B – O)
0	($5,000)	($5,000)	$ 0
1	2,085	0	2,085
2	2,085	0	2,085
3	2,085	0	2,085
4	2,085	9,677	(7,592)

The IRR of Project D, 10 percent, is the crossover point.

4. a. Refer to the NPV profiles. When $k = 14\%$, we are to the right of the crossover point and Project B has the higher NPV. You can verify this fact by calculating the NPVs. $NPV_B = \$1,075$ and $NPV_O = \$730$. Note that Project B also has the higher IRR. However, the NPV method should be used when evaluating mutually exclusive projects. Note that had the project cost of capital been 8 percent, then Project O would be chosen on the basis of the higher NPV.

5. a. After the first year, there is only $30 remaining to be repaid, and $50 is received in Year 2. Assuming an even cash flow throughout the year, the payback period is $1 + \$30/\$50 = 1.6$ years.

6. d. $NPV_L = -\$100 + \$10/1.10 + \$60/(1.10)^2 + \$80/(1.10)^3$
$= -\$100 + \$9.09 + \$49.59 + \$60.11 = \$18.79.$

7. e. The present value of the cash outflow is $\$100/1.00 = \$100$. The present value of the cash inflows is $\$70/1.10 + \$50/(1.10)^2 + \$20/(1.10)^3 = \$63.64 + \$41.32 + \$15.03 = \$119.99$. Thus, the profitability index is $\$119.99/\$100 = 1.20$.

8. a. We used a calculator to find $IRR_L = 18.1\%$.

9. b. $$\text{Costs} = \frac{TV}{(1 + MIRR)^n} = \frac{\sum\limits_{t=0}^{n} CIF_t(1 + k)^{n-t}}{(1 + MIRR)^n}.$$

$$\$100 = \frac{\$10(1.10)^2 + \$60(1.10)^1 + \$80(1.10)^0}{(1 + MIRR)^3}$$

$$= \frac{\$12.10 + \$66.00 + \$80.00}{(1 + MIRR)^3} = \frac{\$158.10}{(1 + MIRR)^3}$$

$MIRR_L = 16.50\%.$

10. c. The NPV profiles plot as follows:

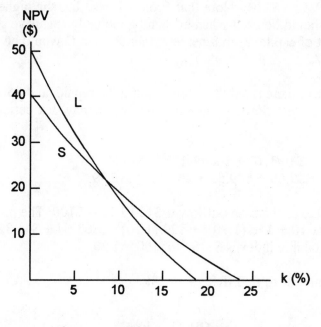

k	NPV_L	NPV_S
0%	$50	$40
5	33	29
10	19	20
15	7	12
20	(4)	5
25	(13)	(2)

Now to find the precise crossover point, determine the cash flows for Project D, which is the difference between the project's cash flows:

Year	Project L	S	Project D (L - S)
0	($100)	($100)	$ 0
1	10	70	(60)
2	60	50	10
3	80	20	60

The crossover point is the IRR of Project D, or 8.7 percent.

11. e. Project X:

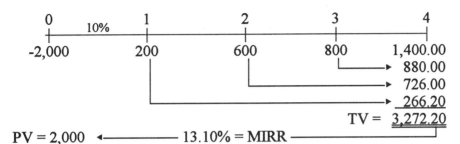

$$\$2,000 = \frac{\$3,272.20}{(1 + MIRR_X)^4}$$

Project Y:

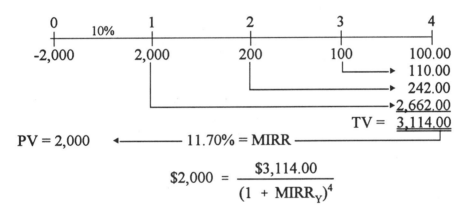

$$\$2,000 = \frac{\$3,114.00}{(1 + MIRR_Y)^4}$$

Project X has the higher MIRR; $MIRR_X = 13.10\%$.

Alternate step: You could calculate NPVs, see that X has the higher NPV, and just calculate $MIRR_X$. $NPV_X = \$234.96$ and $NPV_Y = \$126.90$.

12. b. Put the cash flows into the cash flow register, and then calculate NPV at 9% and IRR:

Project S: $NPV_S = \$101.83$; $IRR_S = 13.49\%$.

Project L: $NPV_L = \$172.07$; $IRR_L = 11.74\%$.

Because $NPV_L > NPV_S$, it is the better project. $IRR_L = 11.74\%$.

Alternatively, the PVIF table could be used to calculate the NPVs of both projects; however, calculating the IRR by trial and error would be tedious.

13. d. First, calculate the beta coefficient. Barkley's stock has been exactly twice as volatile as the market; thus, beta = 2.0. This can be calculated as $[21 - (-5)]/[10 - (-3)] = 26/13 = 2.0$. (Alternatively, you could use a calculator with statistical functions to determine the beta.)

Next, enter the known values in the CAPM equation to find the required rate of return, or the cost of equity capital. Since the company finances only with equity, this is the cost of capital:

$$CAPM = k_{RF} + (k_M - k_{RF})b = 7\% + (5\%)b = 7\% + 5\%(2.0) = 17\% = k_s.$$

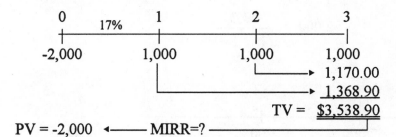

Find TV: N = 3; I = 17; PV = 0; PMT = -1000; FV = 3,538.90.

Find MIRR: N = 3; PV = -2000; PMT = 0; FV = 3538.90; I = MIRR = 20.95%.

14. b. First, we must find the cost of capital. Run a regression between the market and CDH stock returns to get beta = 1.31. Then apply the SML: $k_{CDH} = 6\% + 1.31(7) = 15.17\%$.

    (1) Now set up the time lines, insert the proper data into the cash flow register of the calculator, and find the NPV and IRRs for the trucks.

Truck S: NPV = $803.35; IRR = 18.45%.

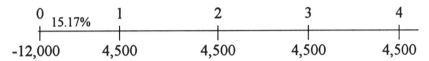

Truck L: NPV = $1,338.91; IRR = 18.45%.

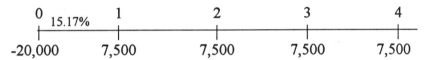

$NPV_L > NPV_S$, thus $Truck_L$ is the better truck.

    (2) To find Truck L's MIRR, compound its cash inflows at 15.17 percent to find the TV, then find the MIRR = I that causes PV of TV = $20,000:

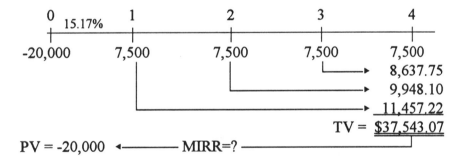

Find TV: Enter N = 4; I = 15.17; PV = 0; PMT = -7500; and solve for FV = $37,543.07.

Find MIRR: Enter N = 4; PV = -20000; PMT = 0; FV = 37543.07; and solve for I = MIRR = 17.05%.

It is interesting to note that both trucks have the same IRR and MIRR; however, the NPV rule should be used so Truck L is the better truck. This problem shows that the NPV method is superior when choosing among competing projects that differ in size.

15. d. IRR = 24.26%; MIRR = 17.19%.

To calculate the IRR, enter the given values into the cash flow register and press the IRR key to get IRR = 24.26%.

MIRR:

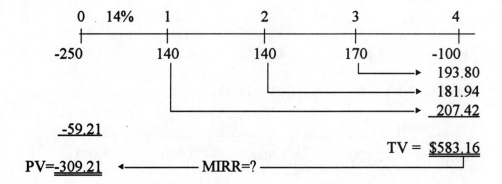

Enter N = 4, PV = -309.21, PMT = 0, FV = 583.16, and solve for MIRR = I = 17.19%.

Chapter 10

Project Cash Flow Analysis

Overview

The basic capital budgeting decision methods have already been covered in Chapter 9. Now, we examine some cash flow analysis issues, including (1) cash flow estimation, (2) replacement analysis, (3) cash flow estimation bias, (4) option values, (5) evaluation of mutually exclusive projects with unequal lives, (6) abandonment value, and (7) effects of inflation.

Outline

The most important step in project analysis is estimating the cash flows. The key concept in the process is to consider only incremental cash flows, which are defined as the difference between the firm's cash flows if the project were undertaken and the firm's cash flows without the project.

- Cash flow must be distinguished from accounting income.
  - Operating cash flow is, in general, a project's operating income plus depreciation.
  - Interest expense is not included in a project's operating cash flows, because capital costs are included in the project cost of capital, the discount rate.

- There are three aspects of cash flow estimation which often present special problems.
  - A *sunk cost* is an outlay that has already occurred or has been committed. Sunk costs are not incremental and hence should not be included in the analysis.
  - All relevant *opportunity costs* must be included in the analysis. For example, suppose Classic Video Rentals already owns a piece of land that is suitable to the outlet. If the firm were analyzing a project for that land, it must include the current net market value of the land as an opportunity cost. If the project were not undertaken, Classic Video would have the opportunity to sell the land. Note that the relevant opportunity cost is the current net market value, and not the price Classic Video paid to acquire the land.

☐ The analysis must include the effects of a proposed project on the firm's existing projects, or *externalities*. If the introduction of a new liquid detergent would reduce sales of a firm's existing line of powder detergents, then the reduction must be included in the analysis.

Tax effects can have a major impact on cash flows, and the improper treatment of taxes can have serious consequences. Therefore, it is critical that taxes be dealt with properly when a project's cash flows are being analyzed.

■ For tax purposes, an asset's depreciation expense is calculated using the *Modified Accelerated Cost Recovery System (MACRS)*.

☐ Assets are categorized into one of several MACRS class lives. Then, the depreciation expense in each year is found by multiplying the asset's depreciable basis by the appropriate allowance percentage. Here are the allowance percentages for personal property:

	MACRS Class			
Year	3-Year	5-Year	7-Year	10-Year
1	33%	20%	14%	10%
2	45	32	25	18
3	15	19	17	14
4	7	12	13	12
5		11	9	9
6		6	9	7
7			9	7
8			4	7
9				7
10				6
11				3

☐ Under MACRS, the assumption is generally made that property is placed in service in the middle of the first year. Then, the remaining half-year's depreciation is taken at the end. Thus, a 3-year class life asset is depreciated over 4 years, and so on.

☐ The *depreciable basis* is the price of the asset, plus any shipping and installation charges. Note that, under MACRS, the depreciable basis is *not* reduced by the asset's expected salvage value.

■ When a depreciable asset is sold, the actual sales price (the realized salvage value) minus the then-existing book value is multiplied by the tax rate to determine the applicable taxes. The net salvage value, salvage value minus the applicable taxes, is then added to after-tax operating income.

Normally, additional inventories are required to support a new project, and expanded sales also produce additional accounts receivable, both of which must be financed. However, accounts payable and accruals may also increase, and these increases would tend to offset the increases in inventories and receivables.

- The difference between the projected increase in current assets and the projected increase in current liabilities is the projected change in *net working capital*.

- If the change is positive, additional financing above that required for fixed assets is needed.

- Conversely, if the change is negative, then the project is generating a cash inflow from working capital changes.

- At the end of the project's life, the firm's total working capital requirements should revert to prior levels, so it will receive an end-of-project cash inflow (outflow) equal to the net investment (reduction) in working capital.

The cash flow analysis on an expansion, or new, project consists of three types of cash flows.

- Consider the cash flows which occur at the time the investment is made; we generally call this time t = 0, or Time 0. (For simplicity, we assume that all investment outflows occur at Time 0.)
  - ☐ Record the purchase price of the asset, plus any transportation and installation costs.
  - ☐ Show any changes in net working capital.
  - ☐ The net of these items is the project's Time 0 net investment outlay.

- Now consider the future cash flows from operations.
  - ☐ First, look at the effects of the new equipment on revenues and costs. An incremental increase in revenues would produce a cash inflow, while an incremental increase in costs would produce a cash outflow.
  - ☐ Then, the depreciation expense in each year must be calculated, and taxes applied.
  - ☐ The operating cash flows in each year can be structured like an income statement, but without interest expense. Here, the net operating cash flow equals Operating income + Depreciation.

- Next, consider the additional cash flows which are projected to occur at the end of the project's life.
  - ☐ The salvage value represents a cash inflow in the final year. However, any tax effects must also be included.

☐ Any net working capital change that occurred at Time 0 is offset now. For example, if the project had an increase in net working capital and hence an outflow at Time 0, an equal inflow would be recorded at the end of the project.

■ Finally, place all the cash flows for each year on a time line and sum to estimate the net cash flows. These are then used to determine the project's NPV, IRR, MIRR, and so on.

■ The analysis becomes slightly more involved if cash outflows (investment costs) occur over more than one year, but the principles remain the same.

Replacement analysis is somewhat more complicated than that for expansion projects, because there are additional cash flows involved.

■ The following additional cash flows must be considered at Time 0:
  ☐ The cash received from the sale of the old equipment is an inflow.
  ☐ However, the sale of the old machine will usually have tax effects. If the old equipment is sold below book value, there will be a tax savings; otherwise, taxes must be paid. The tax effect is equal to the loss or gain times the firm's marginal tax rate.

■ The calculation for cash flow from operations must also be modified.
  ☐ First, look at the effects of the new equipment on revenues and costs. An incremental increase in revenues would produce a cash inflow, while an incremental increase in costs would produce a cash outflow, just as before. But, the incremental flows must be based on the flows generated by the old asset. After combining the revenue and cost effects into a single incremental cash inflow, multiply by $(1 - T)$ to obtain the after-tax cash inflow.
  ☐ The depreciation expense on the new equipment must be compared with the depreciation expense on the old equipment to get the net change in depreciation. This amount is then multiplied by the tax rate to find the tax savings or loss from the change in depreciation.
  ☐ Any salvage value on the old machine, including tax effects, must be included as a cash outflow at the end of the old project's life. Accepting the new project causes the firm to forego the old machine's salvage value. Thus, it must be included as an opportunity cost. Of course, any salvage value on the new machine must also be included in the analysis.

■ The analysis here assumes that the replacement project has the same expected life as the remaining years of usage on the old machine. If this is not true, an adjustment must be made to account for differing project lives.

There is a good deal of evidence that suggests that capital budgeting cash flow forecasts are biased; that is, managers tend to be overly optimistic in their forecasts, and, as a result, revenues tend to be systematically overstated and costs tend to be understated.

- If bias exists, then the acceptance of a project with a zero estimated NPV will likely result in a realized loss and, hence, a decrease in shareholders' wealth.

- A first step to recognizing cash flow estimation bias, especially in projects which are highly profitable, is to ask this question: What is the underlying cause of this project's high profitability?
  - ☐ If the firm has some inherent advantage in the marketplace, such as patent protection or unique production or marketing expertise, then projects which utilize this advantage may truly be extraordinarily profitable.
  - ☐ However, in the long run, profitability will probably be eroded by competition, and hence project returns will be driven down to a normal level, which is equal to the firm's cost of capital.

- If management believes that cash flow estimation bias exists, and historical performance can be used as an indicator, then those managers' estimates should be adjusted, either by raising the cost of capital or by lowering the cash flow estimates.

Cash flow estimation bias can cause a project's profitability to be overstated, but failure to recognize a project's additional opportunities, or options, can cause the project's profitability to be understated.

- Real assets are not passive investments—managerial actions can influence their results.

- Any project that expands the set of opportunities facing a firm has positive option value, and any project that reduces the set of future opportunities has negative option value. A project's impact on the firm's opportunities, or the project's option value, may not be captured by conventional NPV analyses.

- Another type of option that can add value is the ability to *abandon*, or discontinue, the project, either to cut losses or because the operation is more valuable to some other party and can be sold for more than the present value of the remaining cash flows.

- Conventional NPV analysis can at times overstate the value of a project. This occurs because accepting a certain type of project today "kills off" future opportunities. In these instances, decision makers should insist on an NPV that is both positive and also large enough to offset the option value given up. Some companies set hurdle rates that are above the calculated cost of capital when evaluating projects that contain such *timing options*.

■ The true values of projects which include embedded options exceed those shown in a straightforward NPV calculation, while the NPVs of projects which limit future opportunities are overstated. Decision trees provide one method for formally dealing with options. Option pricing models can be used in certain situations.

■ As a result of embedded options, some projects have more or less value than is indicated by their NPVs, and this value should, at a minimum, be subjectively considered when making capital budgeting decisions.

If two mutually exclusive projects have unequal lives, the analysis must compare the projects over a common life.

■ The *replacement chain (common life)* approach extends one, or both, projects until an equal life is achieved.
   □ Suppose two mutually exclusive projects are being considered: Project A, with a 2-year life, and Project B, with a 3-year life.
   □ The projects would be extended to a common life of 6 years.
   □ Project A would have an adjusted NPV equal to the NPV_A plus the NPV_A discounted for 2 years at the project's cost of capital plus the NPV_A discounted for 4 years at the project's cost of capital.
   □ Project B would have an adjusted NPV equal to the NPV_B plus the NPV_B discounted for 3 years at the project's cost of capital.
   □ The project with the higher adjusted NPV would be chosen.

■ Another way to deal with unequal lives is the *equivalent annual annuity (EAA)* approach.
   □ Find each project's NPV over its original life.
   □ Divide the original NPV of each project by the PVIFA for the project's original life and cost of capital to find the equivalent annual annuity (EAA). Alternatively, on a financial calculator enter the project's original NPV = PV, n = life, k = i, and solve for PMT.
   □ The project with the higher EAA will have the higher NPV over any common life, as long as both projects have the same riskiness and, hence, the same project cost of capital.

■ As a general rule, the unequal life issue does not arise for independent projects. Also, common life techniques can only be applied when the shorter-life project is actually expected to be replicated.

■ A serious weakness of the analysis techniques discussed is that changing revenues and/or costs have not been considered. These complications are handled by building the new revenue/cost estimates directly into the cash flow estimates and then using the replacement chain approach.

Thus far, all the capital budgeting examples have been based on a well-defined economic life. However, in most situations, the economic life, or that life which maximizes the project's NPV, is not the same as the project's physical life. The concept of abandonment value recognizes that abandonment of a project before the end of its physical life can have a significant impact on the project's profitability and risk.

■ Two very different types of abandonment can occur:
  □ Sale by the original user of a still-valuable asset to some other party who can extract more value from the asset.
  □ Abandonment of an asset because the project is losing money.

■ Abandonment value should be considered during routine performance reviews of ongoing projects.

When inflation occurs, the analysis must either explicitly adjust for inflation or treat all variables in real terms.

■ Investors recognize that inflation erodes purchasing power; they demand an inflation premium in addition to the real required rate of return, and hence they consider expected inflation rates when setting required rates of return. Thus, a firm's market-determined overall cost of capital is a nominal rate.
  □ Inflation can be explicitly considered in capital budgeting analysis by expressing all cash flows in nominal terms (CF_t) and then using the nominal cost of capital (k_n):

$$NPV = \sum_{t=0}^{n} \frac{CF_t}{(1 + k_n)^t}.$$

  □ The same result can be obtained by expressing all cash flows in real terms (RCF_t) and then by using the real cost of capital (k_r):

$$NPV = \sum_{t=0}^{n} \frac{RCF_t}{(1 + k_r)^t}.$$

■ Occasionally, the procedures set forth above are violated; that is, real, or constant dollar, cash flows that are not adjusted for inflation are used with the nominal cost of capital. If this occurs, the calculated NPV will be biased downward.

■ In practice, it is best to express the cash flows in nominal dollars; that is, to include inflation effects in the cash flow estimates and then to discount by the nominal cost of capital. This procedure is preferred because it allows various cash flow components to be adjusted at differing inflation rates.

SELF-TEST QUESTIONS

Definitional

1. _____ cash flows are defined as the difference between the firm's cash flows if the project were undertaken and the firm's cash flows without the project.

2. An increase in net working capital would show up as a cash _____ at Time 0, and then again as a cash _____ at the end of the project's life.

3. A(n) _____ _____ is a cash outlay which has already occurred or has been committed.

4. _____ include the effects of a proposed project on the firm's existing projects.

5. In general, a project's operating cash flow in any year is equal to the project's _____ _____ plus its _____ expense.

6. In replacement analysis, two cash flows that occur at t = 0 that are not present in expansion projects are the price received from the sale of the _____ equipment and the _____ effects of the sale.

7. In replacement analysis, the depreciation tax savings or loss is based on the _____ in depreciation expense between the old and new asset.

8. If _____ exists, then the acceptance of a project with a zero estimated NPV will likely result in a realized loss and, hence, a decrease in shareholders' wealth.

9. Cash flow estimation bias can cause a project's profitability to be overstated, but failure to recognize a project's additional opportunities, or _____, can cause the project's profitability to be understated.

10. Another type of option that can add value to a project is the ability to _____, or discontinue, the project, either to cut losses or because the operation is more valuable to some other party and can be sold for more than the present value of the remaining cash flows.

11. If two projects are _____, the fact that they have unequal lives will not affect the analysis.

12. If two mutually exclusive projects have unequal lives, either the _____ _____ or _____ _____ _____ method may be used for the analysis.

13. In dealing with inflation in capital budgeting, cash flows and cost of capital must both be in _____ terms or both be in _____ terms.

14. If the cash flows are real, but the cost of capital is nominal, there will be a _____ bias to the calculated NPV.

Conceptual

15. In general, the value of land currently owned by a firm is irrelevant to a capital budgeting decision because the cost of that property is a sunk cost.

    a. True   **b.** False

16. McDonald's is planning to open a new location across from the student union. Annual revenues are expected to be $5 million. However, opening the new location will cause annual revenues to drop by $3 million at McDonald's existing stadium location. The relevant revenues for the capital budgeting analysis are $2 million per year.

    a. True   **b.** False

17. In a replacement decision, the salvage value of the old asset need not be considered since the current market value of the asset is included in the analysis.

    a. True   **b.** False

18. Abandoning a project before the end of its useful physical life may result in a higher NPV for the project.

   a. True   **b.** False

19. The equivalent annual annuity (EAA) for a project is determined by dividing the project's original NPV by

   a. The PVIF for the project's original life and cost of capital.
   b. The cost of the project.
   c. The cost of capital.
   d. The PVIFA for the project's original life and cost of capital.
   e. The number of years of the project's life.

20. Two corporations are formed. They are identical in all respects except for their methods of depreciation. Firm A uses MACRS depreciation, while Firm B uses the straight line method. Both plan to depreciate their assets for tax purposes over a 5-year life (6 calendar years), which is equal to the useful life, and both pay a 34 percent federal-plus-state tax rate. (Note: The half-year convention will apply, so the firm using the straight line method will take 10 percent depreciation in Year 1 and 10 percent in Year 6.) Which of the following statements is *false*?

   a. Firm A will generate higher cash flows from operations in the first year than B.
   b. Firm A will pay more federal corporate income taxes in the first year than B.
   c. If there is no change in tax rates over the 6-year period and if we disregard the time value of money, the total amount of funds generated from operations by these projects for each corporation will be the same over the 6 years.
   d. Firm B will pay the same amount of federal corporate income taxes, over the 6-year period, as A.
   e. Firm A could, if it chose to, use straight line depreciation for stockholder reporting even if it used MACRS for tax purposes.

21. A company owns a building, free and clear, which had a cost of $100,000. The building is currently unoccupied, but it can be sold at a net price of $50,000, after taxes. Now the company is thinking of using the building for a new project. Which of the following statements is most *correct*?

    a. The building is unoccupied, and its cost was incurred in the past, and hence, is a sunk cost. Therefore, no cost for the building should be charged to the new project.

    b. A cost should be charged to the new project, and that cost should be $100,000.

    c. A cost should be charged to the new project, and that cost should be $50,000.

    d. The cost charged to the building would vary depending on the expected profitability of the new project and hence on the new project's ability to help carry the corporation's overhead.

    e. A cost for the building should be charged to the new project only if the NPV on the new project without considering the building is less than zero.

22. Which of the following statements is most *correct*?

    a. Since capital budgeting involves fixed assets, current assets (also called "working capital") should never be reflected in a capital budgeting analysis.

    b. If Congress changed the tax law such that depreciation allowances were reduced in the early years of an asset's life and then were increased in later years, this would increase net income in the early years and lower it in the later years. Such a change would stimulate investment in the economy because, other things held constant, it would raise projects' NPVs and IRRs.

    c. Either the replacement chain approach or the equivalent annual annuity approach can be used to evaluate mutually exclusive, repeatable projects which have unequal lives.

    d. If expected inflation is ignored when cash flows are estimated, this will generally cause the calculated NPV, IRR, and MIRR to be overstated, and that could cause projects which should be rejected to be accepted.

    e. Statements c and d are both correct.

SELF-TEST PROBLEMS

(The following data apply to the next two problems.)

Buckeye Foundries builds railroad cars and then leases them to railroads and shippers. The company has some old boxcars which it plans to convert into specialized carriers. Its analysts foresee demand in two areas--cars to carry coal and cars to carry livestock. Each type of car will cost $50,000 per car to convert. Because of the greater weight they will carry, the coal cars will last only 10 years but will provide an after-tax cash flow of $9,500 per year. The livestock cars will last for 15 years, and their annual after-tax cash flow is estimated at $8,140. Buckeye's cost of capital is 10 percent. At the end of each car's original life, it can be rebuilt into "like new" condition at a cost expected to equal the original conversion cost. Also, since Buckeye has only a limited number of cars to convert, regard the two types of cars as being mutually exclusive.

1. Using the replacement chain method of evaluation, find the adjusted NPV for each alternative.

    a. $8,373; $11,913   d. $12,846; $11,913
    b. $8,373; $14,765   e. $12,846; $14,765
    c. $8,373; $16,212

2. Which alternative should be taken according to the equivalent annual annuity method?

    a. Livestock cars, since their EAA is $11,913, which is $3,540 greater than the coal cars' EAA.
    b. Either one, since their EAAs are equal.
    c. Livestock cars, since their EAA is $1,566, which is $203 greater than the coal cars' EAA.
    d. Coal cars, since their EAA is $8,373, which is $1,119 greater than the livestock cars' EAA.
    e. Coal cars, since their EAA is $1,363, which is $505 greater than the livestock cars' EAA.

3. The capital budgeting director of National Products Inc. is evaluating a new project that would decrease operating costs by $30,000 per year without affecting revenues. The project's cost is $50,000. The project will be depreciated using the MACRS method over its 3-year life. It will have a zero salvage value after 3 years. The marginal tax rate of National Products is 40 percent, and the project's cost of capital is 12 percent. What is the project's NPV?

    a. $7,068   b. $8,324   c. $9,432   d. $10,214   e. $12,387

4. Your firm has a marginal tax rate of 40 percent and a cost of capital of 14 percent. You are performing a capital budgeting analysis on a new project that will cost $500,000. The project is expected to have a useful life of 10 years, although its MACRS class life is only 5 years. The project is expected to increase the firm's net income by $61,257 per year and to have a salvage value of $35,000 at the end of 10 years. What is the project's NPV?

    a. $48,257   **b.** $81,359   **c.** $105,000   **d.** $132,451   **e.** $177,902

5. The Board of Directors of Midwest Brewing Inc. is considering the acquisition of a new still. The still is priced at $600,000 but would require $60,000 in transportation costs and $40,000 for installation. The still has a useful life of 10 years but will be depreciated over its 5-year MACRS life. It is expected to have a salvage value of $10,000 at the end of 10 years. The still would increase revenues by $120,000 per year and increase yearly operating costs by $20,000 per year. Additionally, the still would require a $30,000 increase in net working capital. The firm's marginal tax rate is 40 percent, and the project's cost of capital is 10 percent. What is the NPV of the still?

    a. $60,892   **b.** $18,430   **c.** -$35,821   **d.** -$130,961   **e.** -$203,450

(The following data apply to the next three problems.)

As the capital budgeting director of Union Mills Inc., you are analyzing the replacement of an automated loom system. The old system was purchased 5 years ago for $200,000; it has been depreciated to a zero book value; and it has 5 years of remaining life and a $50,000 salvage value. The market value of the old system is $100,000. The new system has a price of $300,000, plus an additional $50,000 in installation costs. The new system falls into the MACRS 5-year class, has a 5-year economic life, and a $100,000 salvage value. The new system will require a $40,000 increase in the spare parts inventory. The primary advantage of the new system is that it will decrease operating costs by $40,000 per year. Union Mills has a 12 percent cost of capital and a marginal tax rate of 40 percent.

6. What is the net cash investment at Year 0?

    a. $350,000   **b.** $340,000   **c.** $330,000   **d.** $40,000   **e.** $23,200

7. What is the annual net operating cash inflow in Year 1?

    a. $52,000   **b.** $40,000   **c.** $36,750   **d.** $33,350   **e.** $31,475

8. What is the net cash flow in the final year (Year 5)?

   a. $31,360   **b.** $40,000   **c.** $100,740   **d.** $117,800   **e.** $171,000

9. A firm is considering a project with a cost of $5,000 and operating cash flows of $2,000 for 3 years. The expected abandonment cash flows for Years 0, 1, 2, and 3 are $5,000, $3,500, $2,000, and $0, respectively. If the firm's cost of capital is 10 percent, what should the firm do?

   a. Do not accept the project.
   b. Abandon after Year 1; NPV is $0.
   c. Abandon after Year 2; NPV is $56.
   d. Abandon after Year 2; NPV is $124.
   e. Continue the project until the end of its 3-year physical life.

10. As financial vice president, you are evaluating a potential new project. The VP-manufacturing and VP-sales have provided the following real revenue, operating cost, and depreciation data, all stated in constant Year 0 dollars:

Year	Revenue	Cost	Depreciation
0	$ 0	$90,000	$ 0
1	40,000	10,000	30,000
2	40,000	10,000	30,000
3	40,000	10,000	30,000

    The cost of capital to the firm is 14 percent, including the current inflation premium. You estimate that the reported real costs will escalate by 10 percent per year over the project's life, starting at t = 0, while revenues will increase by only 5 percent per year. The firm's marginal tax rate is 40 percent. The $90,000 cost in Year 0 is the net after-tax cost of the project, while the $40,000 annual revenues and $10,000 annual costs are before tax. The project has no salvage value and does not require a change in net working capital. What is the project's NPV?

    a. $10,593   **b.** $3,297   **c.** -$5,586   **d.** -$17,689   **e.** -$20,351

11. Central City Electric is considering two alternative ways to meet demand: It can build a coal-fired plant (Project C) at a cost of $1,000 million. This plant would have a 20-year life and would provide after-tax net cash flows of $120 million per year over its life. Alternatively, the company can build a gas-fired plant (Project G) that would cost $400 million and would produce after-tax net cash flows of $68 million per year for 10 years, after which the plant would have to be replaced. The power will be needed for exactly 20 years; the cost of capital for either plant is 10 percent; and inflation and productivity gains are expected to offset one another so as to leave expected costs and cash flows constant over time. What is the NPV of the *better* project; that is, how much (in millions) will the *better* project add to Central City's total value?

    a. $17.83   **b.** $21.63   **c.** $20.03   **d.** $24.70   **e.** $19.57

12. Wild West Air is considering two alternative planes. Plane A has an expected life of 5 years, will cost $200, and will produce net cash flows of $60 per year. Plane B has a life of 10 years, will cost $245, and will produce net cash flows of $48 per year. Wild West plans to serve the route for 10 years. Inflation in operating costs, airplane costs, and fares is expected to be zero, and the company's cost of capital is 14 percent. Assume all costs are in millions. By how much (in millions) would the value of the company increase if it accepted the better project (plane)?

    a. $12.76   **b.** $9.78   **c.** $5.37   **d.** $6.65   **e.** $9.09

ANSWERS TO SELF-TEST QUESTIONS

1. Incremental
2. outflow; inflow
3. sunk cost
4. Externalities
5. operating income; depreciation
6. old; tax
7. difference
8. bias
9. options
10. abandon
11. independent
12. replacement chain; equivalent annual annuity
13. nominal; real
14. downward

15. b. The net value of land currently owned is an opportunity cost of the project. If the project is not undertaken, the land could be sold to realize its current market value less any taxes and expenses. Thus, project acceptance means foregoing this cash inflow.

16. a. Incremental revenues, which are relevant in a capital budgeting decision, must consider the effects on other parts of the firm.

17. b. In an incremental analysis, the cash flows assuming replacement are compared with the cash flows assuming the old asset is retained. If the old asset is retained, it will produce a salvage value cash flow which must be included, with tax effects, in the replacement analysis.

18. a. The NPV of a project may be maximized by abandoning at some point, thus making the economic life of the project shorter than the physical life.

19. d. The EAA is the annual constant cash flow which, over the project's original life, produces the project's original NPV. Thus, the divisor is the PVIFA.

20. b. Statement a is true; MACRS is an accelerated depreciation method, so Firm A will have a higher depreciation expense than Firm B. We are also given that both firms are identical, except for depreciation methods used. Net cash flow is equal to net income plus depreciation. In Year 1, Firm A's depreciation expense is twice as great as Firm B's; however, Firm A's lower net income is more than compensated for by the addition of depreciation (which is twice as high as Firm B's). Thus, in Year 1, Firm A's net cash flow is greater than Firm B's. Statement b is false; because Firm A's depreciation expense is larger, it's earnings before taxes will be lower, and thus it will pay less income taxes than Firm B. Finally, statements c, d, and e are all true.

21. c. Statement c is correct. The opportunity cost of the building should be assessed against the new project, and that cost is what the company could get for the building, $50,000. All of the other statements are incorrect.

22. c. Statement c is correct. Statement a is incorrect because the required investment in working capital is often reflected in capital budgeting decision analyses. Statement b is incorrect because higher early depreciation reduces taxes, increases cash flows, and thus leads to higher NPVs and IRRs. Statement d is incorrect because generally considering inflation will increase projected cash flows and thus increase the NPV.

ANSWERS TO SELF-TEST PROBLEMS

1. e. First, find each car's original NPV as follows:

$NPV_C = \$9,500(PVIFA_{10\%,10}) - \$50,000 = \$8,373.$

$NPV_L = \$8,140(PVIFA_{10\%,15}) - \$50,000 = \$11,913.$

Now look at the projects at a common life of 30 years:

Adjusted $NPV_C = \$8,373 + \$8,373(PVIF_{10\%,10}) + \$8,373(PVIF_{10\%,20}) = \$12,846.$

Adjusted $NPV_L = \$11,913 + \$11,913(PVIF_{10\%,15}) = \$14,765.$

2. c. The original NPVs were calculated above. Now:

$EAA_C = \$8,373/PVIFA_{10\%,10} = \$8,373/6.1446 = \$1,363.$

$EAA_L = \$11,913/PVIFA_{10\%,15} = \$11,913/7.6061 = \$1,566.$

The livestock car should be chosen since EAA_L is greater than EAA_C.

3. c. The only cash outflow is the $50,000 cost of the project. Cash inflows consist of the reduction in operating costs, equal to $30,000(0.60) = $18,000 on an after-tax basis, and depreciation. The value of the depreciation cash flows generated by the project is the amount of tax savings. After-tax depreciation cash flows are found by multiplying the depreciable basis, $50,000, by the recovery percentage in each year, and then multiplying this product by the tax rate. The allowances in each year are 33, 45, and 15 percent, respectively, and the depreciation tax savings in each year are as follows:

$$\text{Dep}_1 = \$50,000(0.33)(0.40) = \$6,600.$$

$$\text{Dep}_2 = \$50,000(0.45)(0.40) = \$9,000.$$

$$\text{Dep}_3 = \$50,000(0.15)(0.40) = \$3,000.$$

The project's cash flows are placed on a time line as follows:

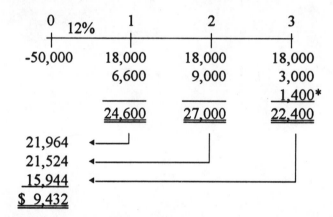

*Salvage value tax savings. National has taken $16,500 + $22,500 + $7,500 = $46,500 in total depreciation, and hence the book value at the end of Year 3 is $50,000 – $46,500 = $3,500. Since the salvage value is $0, National can reduce its taxable income by $3,500, producing a 0.4($3,500) = $1,400 tax savings.

4. e. In this case, the net income of the project is $61,257. Net cash flow = Net income + Depreciation = $61,257 + Depreciation. The depreciation allowed in each year is calculated as follows:

$Dep_1 = \$500,000(0.20) = \$100,000.$

$Dep_2 = \$500,000(0.32) = \$160,000.$

$Dep_3 = \$500,000(0.19) = \$95,000.$

$Dep_4 = \$500,000(0.12) = \$60,000.$

$Dep_5 = \$500,000(0.11) = \$55,000.$

$Dep_6 = \$500,000(0.06) = \$30,000.$

$Dep_{7-10} = \$0.$

In the final year (Year 10), the firm receives $35,000 from the sale of the machine. However, the book value of the machine is $0. Thus, the firm would have to pay 0.4($35,000) = $14,000 in taxes, and the net salvage value is $35,000 - $14,000 = $21,000. The time line is as follows:

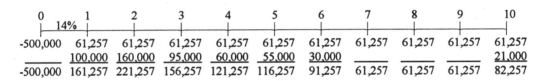

The project's NPV can be found by discounting each of the cash flows at the firm's 14 percent cost of capital. The project's NPV, found by using a financial calculator is $177,902.

5. d. The initial net investment is $730,000:

Price	($600,000)
Transportation	(60,000)
Installation	(40,000)
Change in net working capital	(30,000)
Initial net investment	($730,000)

The annual net cash flows are equal to the net after-tax increase in revenues, 0.6($120,000 - $20,000) = $60,000, plus the depreciation tax savings. In Year 10, the firm will recover its investment in net working capital and gain the net salvage value. The depreciable basis is $700,000, thus, the annual depreciation tax savings is calculated as follows:

$$Dep_1 = \$700,000(0.20)(0.4) = \$56,000.$$

$$Dep_2 = \$700,000(0.32)(0.4) = \$89,600.$$

$$Dep_3 = \$700,000(0.19)(0.4) = \$53,200.$$

$$Dep_4 = \$700,000(0.12)(0.4) = \$33,600.$$

$$Dep_5 = \$700,000(0.11)(0.4) = \$30,800.$$

$$Dep_6 = \$700,000(0.06)(0.4) = \$16,800.$$

$$Dep_{7-10} = \$0.$$

The net salvage value is $10,000(0.6) = $6,000. Therefore, the time line is as follows:

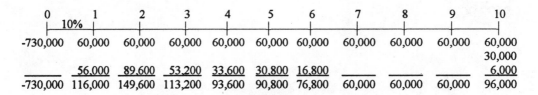

The project's NPV using a 10 percent cost of capital is -$130,961.

6. c.

Price of new machine	($300,000)
Installation	(50,000)
Sale of old machine	100,000
Tax on sale	(40,000)*
Increase in net working capital	(40,000)
	($330,000)

*The old machine has been depreciated down to zero, but can be sold for $100,000. The full $100,000 (purchase price minus book value) is treated as ordinary income and is taxed at 40 percent. Thus, Union Mills must pay a tax of 0.4($100,000) = $40,000 on the sale of the old asset.

7. a. The after-tax revenue/cost component is 0.6($40,000) = $24,000. As for the tax savings due to depreciation, the depreciable basis for the new machine is $350,000. Further, the MACRS depreciation allowance for Year 1 of a 5-year class asset is 20 percent. Thus, the depreciation expense on the new machine is 0.20($350,000) = $70,000. The old machine has been fully depreciated, so its depreciation expense in Year 1 is $0, and the change in depreciation due to the replacement decision is an increase of $70,000. The tax savings is 0.4($70,000) = $28,000. Therefore, the Year 1 net cash flow from operations is $24,000 + $28,000 = $52,000.

8. d. In the final year, Year 5, the net cash flow is composed of 0.6($40,000) = $24,000 in after-tax cost decrease and 0.4(0.11)($350,000) = $15,400 in depreciation tax savings, for a total of $39,400, plus the applicable nonoperating cash flows. Thus, we have the following:

From operations	$ 39,400
Salvage value of new machine	100,000
Tax on new machine salvage value	(31,600)
Salvage value of old machine	(50,000)
Tax on old machine salvage value	20,000
Change in working capital	40,000
	$117,800

Note that the salvage value of the old machine is a cash outflow. This is an opportunity cost, since buying the new machine deprives Union Mills of the salvage value of the old machine. Additionally, salvage tax effects must be considered. Also note that the change in working capital considered at t = 0, an outflow, is exactly offset by an inflow at the end of the project. This is because it is assumed that the project will terminate and the increase in working capital is no longer required.

9. d.

Year	Initial Investment & Operating Cash Flow	Abandonment Value in Year t
0	($5,000)	$5,000
1	2,000	3,500
2	2,000	2,000
3	2,000	0

NPV of project:

$-\$5,000 + \$2,000/(1.10)^1 + \$2,000/(1.10)^2 + \$2,000/(1.10)^3 = -\$26.30.$

NPV of project if abandoned after Year 1:

$-\$5,000 + \$2,000/(1.10)^1 + \$3,500/(1.10)^1 = \$0.$

NPV of project if abandoned after Year 2:

$-\$5,000 + \$2,000/(1.10)^1 + \$2,000/(1.10)^2 + \$2,000/(1.10)^2 = \$124.$

10. d. The first step is to recast the given data in nominal terms since the cost of capital is nominal:

Year	Revenue	Cost	Depreciation
0	$ 0	$90,000	$ 0
1	42,000	11,000	30,000
2	44,100	12,100	30,000
3	46,305	13,310	30,000

Now apply standard capital budgeting procedures. The initial investment is $90,000. The operating cash flows are 0.6($42,000 - $11,000) = $18,600 for Year 1, 0.6($44,100 - $12,100) = $19,200 for Year 2, and 0.6($46,305 - $13,310) = $19,797 for Year 3. The tax savings from depreciation is 0.4($30,000) = $12,000 in Years 1 through 3. Now putting this on a time line gives the following:

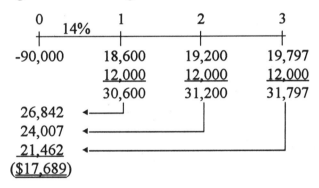

11. d. Project C (in millions):

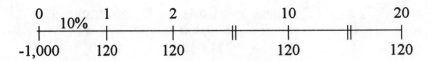

With a financial calculator, input the cash flows into the cash flow register, input I = 10, and then solve for NPV = $21.63 million.

Project G (in millions):

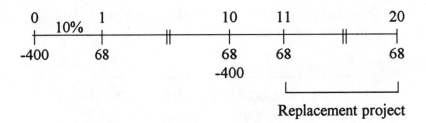

Replacement project

With a financial calculator, input the cash flows for the first replication of the project into the cash flow register, input I = 10, and then solve for NPV = $17.83 million. However, this NPV must be adjusted for a 20-year common life. The NPV for the next replication can be calculated by inputting N = 10, I = 10, PMT = 0, FV = 17.83, and then solving for PV = $6.87. Thus, the extended NPV for Project G = $17.83 + $6.87 = $24.70 million:

$$\text{Extended NPV}_G = \$17.83 + (\text{PVIF}_{10\%,10})\$17.83$$
$$= \$17.83 + \$6.87 = \$24.70 \text{ million.}$$

12. e. Plane A: Expected life = 5 years; Cost = \$200; NCF = \$60, COC = 14%.

Plane B: Expected life = 10 years; Cost = \$245; NCF = \$48, COC = 14%.

A:

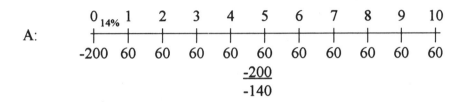

Enter these values into the cash flow register: $CF_0 = -200$; $CF_1 = 60$, 4 times; $CF_2 = -140$; $CF_3 = 60$, 5 times. Then enter I = 14, and press the NPV to get $NPV_A = \$9.0932 \approx \$9.09$.

B:

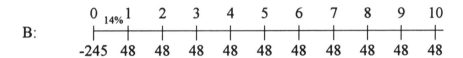

Enter these values into the cash flow register, along with the interest rate, and press the NPV key to get $NPV_B = -\$5.3736 \approx -\$5.37$.

Project A is the better project and will increase the company's value by \$9.09.

CHAPTER 11

RISK ANALYSIS AND THE OPTIMAL CAPITAL BUDGET

OVERVIEW

Risk analysis is important in all financial decisions, especially those relating to capital budgeting. As we saw in Chapter 5, the higher the risk associated with a security, the higher the rate of return needed to compensate for that risk. This is also true when the investor is a corporation and the investment is a capital project. This chapter discusses procedures for both assessing risk in a capital budgeting context and for incorporating it into capital budgeting decisions. In Chapter 8, we developed the concept of the weighted average,

or overall, cost of capital (WACC). Then, in Chapters 9 and 10, we saw how capital projects are evaluated. However, capital budgeting and the cost of capital are actually interrelated—we cannot determine the cost of capital unless we know the size of the capital budget, and we cannot determine the size of the capital budget unless we know the cost of capital. Therefore, as we show in this chapter, the cost of capital and the capital budget must be determined simultaneously.

OUTLINE

Risk relates to uncertainty about future events, and in capital budgeting, this means the future profitability of a project.

Three separate and distinct types of project risk can be defined: (1) stand-alone risk, (2) corporate (within-firm) risk, and (3) market risk.

- ■ *Stand-alone risk* is the riskiness of a project in isolation, that is, its riskiness when standing alone.
  - □ A project's stand-alone risk is measured by its variability of profitability. A common measure is the standard deviation of IRR.
  - □ Although a project's stand-alone risk is relatively easy to measure, projects are not held in isolation—firms hold portfolios of projects, and equity investors hold portfolios of firms.

- *Within-firm,* or *corporate, risk,* which views the risk of a project within the context of the firm's portfolio of projects, is the contribution of the project to the firm's total risk.
  - ☐ Conceptually, a project's within-firm risk can be found by regressing the project's returns against returns on the firm's other assets. In essence, this creates a characteristic line for the project, but the returns on the X axis are firm returns as opposed to market returns, and the slope of this line is the contribution of the project to the firm's riskiness.
  - ☐ A project's within-firm risk is conceptually measured by its within-firm beta:

  $$b_{\text{Within-firm}} = (\sigma_P/\sigma_F)r_{P,F} \ .$$

  Here σ_P is the standard deviation of project returns, σ_F is the standard deviation of firm returns, and $r_{P,F}$ is the correlation coefficient between the returns.
  - ☐ If the project's within-firm beta equals 1.0, then the project has the same amount of corporate risk as the firm's other assets. If the beta is greater than 1.0, the project has higher-than-average corporate risk, while the opposite is true if the beta is less than 1.0.

- *Market risk,* which views the risk of a project within the context of an investor's portfolio of stocks, is the contribution of the project to the riskiness of the portfolio.
  - ☐ Conceptually, a project's market risk can be found by regressing the project's returns against returns on a market portfolio. This creates a standard characteristic line for the project, and the slope of this line measures the project's market risk.
  - ☐ A project's market risk is conceptually measured by its market beta:

  $$b_{\text{Market}} = (\sigma_P/\sigma_M)r_{P,M} \ .$$

  - ☐ If the project's market beta is equal to the firm's market beta, then the project has the same amount of market risk as the firm's average project. If the beta is greater than the firm's beta, then the project has more market risk, and vice versa if the beta is less than the corporate beta.

- There are three determinants of a project's risk: (1) the standard deviation of the project's forecasted returns, σ_P, (2) the correlation of those returns with the firm's other assets, $r_{P,F}$, and (3) the correlation of the project's returns with the stock market, $r_{P,M}$.

- Most projects' returns are highly correlated with the returns on the firm's other assets, with the correlation being highest for projects in the firm's core business line. Thus, in general, projects with high stand-alone risk will also have high within-firm risk.

■ Most projects' returns are also highly correlated with the economy as a whole, and hence the return on the market. Thus, in general, projects with high stand-alone risk will also have high market risk.

It is occasionally argued that only a project's market risk should be considered, because managers should be acting to maximize shareholder wealth, and the risk that is relevant to shareholders is market risk. Here are some points to consider:

■ Undiversified stockholders, including owners of small businesses, are more concerned about corporate risk than about market risk.

■ Many financial theorists argue that even well-diversified stockholders consider corporate risk to be important, because the risk of financial distress is more related to corporate risk than to market risk.

■ The firm's stability is important to all the firm's stakeholders, including its managers, workers, customers, suppliers, creditors, and even the communities in which it operates.

The starting point for analyzing a project's riskiness is stand-alone risk analysis, which involves estimating the uncertainty inherent in the project's cash flows. There are four techniques commonly used to measure stand-alone risk: (1) sensitivity analysis, (2) scenario analysis, (3) Monte Carlo simulation, and (4) decision tree analysis.

■ *Sensitivity analysis* is a technique which indicates exactly how much a project's NPV or IRR will change in response to a given change in an input variable, other things held constant.
  □ The analysis begins with expected values for unit sales, sales price, fixed costs, and variable costs to give an expected, or base case, NPV. A series of "what if" questions may then be asked to find the change in NPV or IRR, given a change in one of the input variables. Typically, the input values are changed by fixed percentages such as +/- 10%, +/- 20%, and so on.
  □ Spreadsheet computer models such as *Lotus 1-2-3* are ideal for performing sensitivity analysis.
  □ Sensitivity analyses are often plotted; the steeper the plots, the greater the risk.
  □ Sensitivity analysis is very useful for identifying the critical input variables, but it is less useful for assessing risk, because sensitivity analysis does not consider the inherent uncertainty in the input variable.

- *Scenario analysis* provides a more complete analysis, because in addition to the sensitivity of NPV to changes in key variables, it considers the range of likely variable values.
  - ☐ Most likely, worst, and best case scenarios are estimated and the input values from these scenarios are used to find the corresponding NPVs.
  - ☐ Probabilities can be assigned to the scenarios, and the NPVs from each scenario used to find the expected NPV, standard deviation of NPV, and coefficient of variation of NPV.
  - ☐ The project's coefficient of variation can be compared to the coefficient of variation of the firm's "average" project to determine the relative stand-alone riskiness of the project.
  - ☐ Scenario analysis is useful, but it assumes that a project can have only a limited number of outcomes, usually three, while, in reality, there are an almost infinite number of possible outcomes.
  - ☐ Scenario analysis as it is commonly applied assumes that the variables treated as uncertain are perfectly positively correlated. Therefore, scenario analysis typically overstates the extremes.

- *Monte Carlo simulation* ties together sensitivities and input variable probabilities.
  - ☐ The computer repeatedly selects a random value for each uncertain variable based on its specified probability distribution, along with values for the certain variables. The end result is a continuous NPV probability distribution.
  - ☐ Simulation analysis is more comprehensive than scenario analysis, because it considers an infinite number of possible outcomes.

- A problem with both scenario and simulation analysis is the specification of each uncertain variable's distribution and the correlations among the distributions. Another problem is that even when the analysis has been completed, no clear-cut decision rule emerges. Finally, since scenario and simulation analysis both focus on a project's stand-alone risk, they ignore the effects of diversification, both among projects within the firm and by investors in their personal investment portfolios.

- *Decision tree analysis* is often used to evaluate projects that have several decision points.
  - ☐ The cash flows and their associated estimated probabilities are laid out on a grid called a "decision tree."
  - ☐ The joint probability of each branch is multiplied by the NPV of that branch and these products are summed to obtain the expected NPV.
  - ☐ The ability to abandon a project changes the branches of a decision tree, often resulting in decreased risk and a higher expected NPV for the project.

In the previous section, we described four methods for measuring a project's stand-alone risk. However, we know that the type of risk that is most relevant to the firm's managers, employees, creditors, and so on is the project's within-firm, or corporate, risk.

■ A project's *corporate risk* is the project's contribution to the firm's overall corporate risk, or, put another way, it reflects the impact of the project on the variability of the firm's total cash flows.

■ Corporate risk is a function of both the project's relative standard deviation and its correlation with the returns on the firm's other assets.

■ In practice, it is very difficult to estimate the returns distribution for a project with any confidence; thus, it is difficult to quantify a project's within-firm risk.

■ A subjective assessment is usually made regarding the correlation between the project's returns and the firm's returns. If the correlation is high, then the project's stand-alone risk assessment probably also applies to its within-firm risk; high stand-alone risk indicates high within-firm risk, and so on. If the correlation is zero or negative, then the stand-alone risk assessment overstates the project's within-firm risk.

Market risk measures risk from the standpoint of an equity investor holding a highly diversified portfolio.

■ Beta analysis can sometimes be used to determine the appropriate project cost of capital.
  □ The required rate of return on equity, k_s, is equal to the risk-free rate of return, k_{RF}, plus a risk premium equal to the firm's beta coefficient, b, times the market risk premium, $k_M - k_{RF}$:

$$k_s = k_{RF} + (k_M - k_{RF})b.$$

  □ For example, if a firm has a beta of 0.9, $k_M = 12\%$, and $k_{RF} = 7\%$, then its required rate of return would be $k_s = 7\% + (5\%)0.9 = 11.5\%$. Stockholders are willing to let the firm invest their money if the firm can earn 11.5 percent on their equity capital.
  □ If the firm's before-tax cost of debt is 8 percent, its marginal tax rate is 40 percent, and its target capital structure is 50 percent debt and 50 percent equity, then its weighted average cost of capital would be 8.2 percent:

$$WACC = w_d k_d(1 - T) + w_{ce}k_s = 0.5(8\%)(0.6) + 0.5(11.5\%) = 8.2\%.$$

- Average-risk projects for this firm should be evaluated using an 8.2 percent cost of capital as the discount rate in the NPV method or as the hurdle rate in the IRR and MIRR methods.

- It is often very difficult to estimate the beta for a particular project, and for some projects, such as a new computer billing system, the beta may not be meaningful.
  - One way of estimating project betas is the *pure play method*. Here the firm must find one or more companies which are exclusively engaged in the same business line as the product.
  - A second approach to estimating project betas is the *accounting beta method*. Here, a project's (or perhaps a division's) return on assets (ROA) is regressed against the average ROA of a large sample of firms, say the S&P 500. The resulting accounting beta is then used as a proxy for the project's market beta.

Most firms use the risk-adjusted discount rate method to incorporate differential project risk in the capital budgeting process, but another technique, the certainty equivalent method, can also be used.

- In the *risk-adjusted discount rate method*, differential risk is dealt with by changing the discount rate—average risk projects are discounted at the firms' WACC, above-average risk projects are discounted at a higher cost of capital, and below-average risk projects are discounted at a rate below the firms' WACC.

- In the *certainty equivalent method*, risky cash flows are scaled down each year to reflect project risk, and the riskier the flows, the lower their certainty equivalent values. The certainty equivalent cash flows are then discounted by the risk-free rate.

- The risk-adjusted discount rate method (RADR) is used more frequently in practice, because it is easier to estimate suitable discount rates than it is to derive certainty equivalent cash flows. The RADR assumes that risk increases with time, and will reward short-payoff alternatives over projects with longer payoffs. The assumption of increasing risk over time is usually valid, but some investments, e.g., many public utility projects, become less risky because in time the full capacity will be utilized.

The adjustment of the discount rate because of differences in risk and capital structure is usually a judgmental and somewhat arbitrary process.

- Because of differences in the financing of assets, some divisions might have a higher debt capacity than others. The WACC should be adjusted to account for these differences.

■ Divisions can also differ in risk, and the WACC should be adjusted to reflect risk differentials.

Many capital budgeting decisions are based on cost minimization rather than NPV maximization. For example, a firm might be choosing between two production methods. One method could use expensive robotics technology and minimal manpower, while the other method might use few robots but have high labor costs. The revenues, or cash inflows, would be the same under both methods. Thus, the method that minimizes costs will also maximize NPV, and cost minimization could be used as the selection criterion.

■ If two mutually exclusive projects are being evaluated based on costs alone, the project with the lower present value of costs should be chosen.

■ If these projects have the same risk as the firm's (or division's) average project, then the discount rate used is the firm's (or division's) marginal cost of capital.

■ However, if the projects have riskiness other than average, then the risk adjustment procedure is the opposite of that normally used in the NPV method. That is, projects with above-average risk will have a lower-than-average project cost of capital, while projects that are less risky than average will have a higher-than-average cost of capital.
   □ This adjustment procedure is followed because projects with above-average risk should be penalized, and to do so, the present value of costs must be increased. Decreasing the discount rate causes the project to become less attractive in comparison.
   □ Note that this reverse risk adjustment is also applicable for cash outflows in a normal NPV analysis. For example, a strip mining project might have a large cash outflow at the end of the project's life. If this outflow is significantly riskier than average, then its discount rate must be less than the rate used on the project's other cash flows.

The firm's investment opportunity schedule (IOS) plays an important role in determining the optimal capital budget.

■ The investment opportunity schedule is a plot of the firm's potential projects in descending order of IRR.

■ If the firm has mutually exclusive projects, then it also has multiple investment opportunity schedules—one for each different combination of projects.

The second element in the optimal capital budget process is the marginal cost of capital (MCC) schedule.

■ The marginal cost of capital schedule is a plot of the firm's weighted average cost of capital. (This concept was introduced in Chapter 8, but we will extend it here.)

■ Suppose that Firm B has a target capital structure of 40 percent debt and 60 percent equity; that its before-tax cost of debt, k_d, is 12 percent, its cost of retained earnings, k_s, is 17.5 percent, and its cost of new common stock, k_e, is 18.2 percent; and that its tax rate, T, is 40 percent.

   ☐ Therefore, its WACC using retained earnings as the common stock component is 13.4 percent:

$$WACC = w_d k_d(1 - T) + w_{ce}(k_s) = 0.4(12\%)(0.6) + 0.6(17.5\%) = 13.4\%.$$

   ☐ When new common stock must be used as the equity component, then Firm B's WACC rises to 13.8 percent:

$$WACC = w_d k_d(1 - T) + w_{ce}(k_e) = 0.4(12\%)(0.6) + 0.6(18.2\%) = 13.8\%.$$

■ The question now is at what point, or at what amount of new capital raised, does Firm B's WACC increase from 13.4 to 13.8 percent? Of course, the answer is when the retained earnings are exhausted. Suppose Firm B is projecting $40,000 in retained earnings during the planning period. We know that 60 percent of the capital raised will be raised as equity capital. If X is the total capital raised, then

$$Retained\ earnings = 0.6(Total\ capital) = 0.6X = \$40,000.$$

Solving for X, which is called the *retained earnings break point*, we obtain:

$$RE_{BP} = X = Retained\ earnings/0.6 = \$40,000/0.6 = \$66,667.$$

Thus, Firm B can raise $66,667 of new capital before it exhausts its retained earnings. Of the $66,667, 0.6($66,667) = $40,000 represents earnings retention and 0.4($66,667) = $26,667 represents debt financing supported by the earnings retention.

■ Firm B also has $100,000 in depreciation cash flow, and, as we learned in Chapter 8, depreciation cash flow pushes the retained earnings break point to the right. Thus, considering both retention and depreciation cash flows, Firm B's retained earnings breakpoint occurs at $66,667 + $100,000 = $166,667.

■ In general, firms have additional breakpoints beyond that for retained earnings. As more and more securities are issued during any planning period, the costs of debt, preferred stock, and new common stock will rise.

■ It is very difficult to precisely identify the new cost levels and break points. Thus, most firms do not attempt to quantitatively define the MCC schedule beyond what is shown here. However, firms will judgmentally increase the WACC if new capital requirements are extraordinarily large.

The optimal capital budget, along with the firm's marginal cost of capital, is found by combining the IOS and MCC schedules.

■ The intersection of the IOS and MCC schedules defines the firm's *marginal cost of capital.*
  □ All projects that have "average" risk should be evaluated at this cost of capital. Note that for independent projects, the IRR method can be used as a proxy for the NPV method since both lead to the same accept/reject decision. Thus, all independent projects of average risk with IRRs exceeding the firm's marginal cost of capital should be accepted.
  □ However, for mutually exclusive projects, the NPV method should be used, and the appropriate discount rate for average risk projects is the firm's marginal cost of capital.

The procedures set forth above are conceptually correct, and it is important that you understand the logic of this process. However, most companies use a more judgmental, less quantitative process for establishing their optimal capital budgets.

■ The approximate size of the capital budget is compared with the firm's capital costs to get a reasonably good approximation of the corporation's marginal cost of capital.

■ The corporate MCC is scaled up or down to reflect each division's target capital structure and riskiness.

■ Each project within each division is classified into one of three risk groups: high, low, or average risk.

■ Each project's cost of capital is then determined by adjusting the division's MCC to reflect project risk. All independent projects with positive NPVs are accepted. For mutually exclusive projects, the highest positive NPV projects are accepted.

Capital budgeting is normally an application of a classic economic principle: A firm should expand to the point where its marginal profits equal its marginal costs. In other words, keep

accepting projects as long as the benefits exceed the costs. However, some firms set an absolute limit on the size of their capital budgets. This is called capital rationing. Capital rationing is discussed in Appendix 11A. If a firm truly rations capital, its value is not being maximized. Project selection under capital rationing maximizes value subject to the constraint that the capital ceiling not be exceeded.

SELF-TEST QUESTIONS

Definitional

1. The _____ the risk associated with an investment, the greater the _____ ___ _____ needed to compensate investors.

2. Three types of risk have been identified in capital budgeting decisions: _____ risk, _____ risk, and _____-_____ risk.

3. A project's stand-alone risk is measured by its variability of _____.

4. _____ _____ _____ ties together sensitivities and input variable probabilities.

5. A commonly used method of risk analysis is based on constructing optimistic (best case), pessimistic (worst case), and most likely (base case) value estimates for the key variables. This method is called _____ _____.

6. In project analysis, changing one of the key input variables at a time and determining the effect of the change on NPV is known as _____ _____.

7. One purpose of sensitivity analysis is to determine which of the variables has the _____ influence on the project's NPV.

8. The required rate of return on a company's stock is equal to the _____-_____ rate plus a(n) _____ for risk.

9. The risk premium on a stock is equal to the stock's _____ _____ times the market risk premium.

10. One of the problems with both scenario and simulation analysis is that because they both focus on a project's stand-alone risk, they ignore the effects of _____, both among projects within the firm and by investors in their personal investment portfolios.

11. An increase in the overall beta coefficient will cause the firm's stock price to _____ unless this increase is offset by a(n) _____ expected rate of return.

12. A project with a high degree of corporate risk will not necessarily affect the firm's _____ risk to any great extent.

13. If two mutually exclusive projects are being evaluated based on costs alone, the project with the _____ present value of costs should be chosen.

14. Firms often measure a project's stand-alone risk, yet a project's market risk is more relevant. Stand-alone risk can also measure market risk if the two are highly _____.

15. Riskier projects should be evaluated with a higher _____ _____ than average-risk projects.

16. The _____ _____ _____ is a plot of the firm's proposed projects, ranked in descending order of IRR, versus the dollars of new capital required.

17. The marginal cost of capital schedule is a plot of the firm's _____ _____ _____ ____ _____ versus the dollars of new capital raised.

18. The _____ _____ ____ ____ is the point in the firm's MCC schedule at which the WACC _____ due to the fact that the retained earnings are exhausted.

19. The firm's _____ _____ ____ _____ is defined by the intersection of the MCC and IOS schedules.

20. All projects of _____ risk should be evaluated at the firm's marginal cost of capital.

21. In general, projects can be evaluated using the IRR method; however, _____ _____ projects must be evaluated by the NPV method.

22. The _____ capital budget is found by combining the IOS and MCC schedules.

23. _____ _____ occurs when firms set an absolute limit on the dollar amount of investment capital.

24. _____ _____ _____ is often used to evaluate projects that have several decision points.

25. Two approaches have been used for estimating the betas of individual assets: the _____ _____ method and the _____ _____ method.

26. One of the methods developed for incorporating project risk into the capital budgeting decision method is the _____ _____ method, in which the annual expected cash flows are adjusted to reflect project risk and then discounted by the risk-free rate.

Conceptual

27. Even if the beta of a project being considered has a value of zero, acceptance of the project will affect the market risk of the firm.

    a. True   b. False

28. When projects of different risk are to be considered in capital budgeting, any project will be acceptable to the firm if the project's IRR is greater than the firm's weighted average cost of capital.

    a. True   b. False

29. When using the pure play approach, the analyzing firm uses a proxy firm's beta as an estimate of the project's beta.

    a. True   b. False

30. If a cash outflow is judged to be riskier than average, then the firm's marginal cost of capital must be adjusted downward to reflect this differential.

    a. True   b. False

31. The firm's marginal cost of capital is determined by the intersection of the MCC and IOS schedules.

    a. True   **b.** False

32. In capital budgeting decisions, corporate (within-firm) risk will be of least interest to

    a. Employees.
    b. Stockholders with few shares.
    c. Institutional investors.
    d. Creditors.
    e. The local community.

33. Which of the following steps are commonly used in practice to establish a firm's optimal capital budget?

    a. Rough estimates of the MCC and IOS schedules are used to estimate the firm's MCC.
    b. The corporate MCC is scaled up or down to reflect each division's capital structure and risk characteristics.
    c. Each division's MCC is scaled up or down to reflect differential project risk.
    d. Each project's NPV is then determined using its appropriate risk-adjusted cost of capital.
    e. All the above steps are used.

34. The Pennsylvania Company is evaluating two mutually exclusive pollution control processes. Since the company's revenue stream will not be affected by the choice of control process, the projects are being evaluated by finding the PV of each set of costs. The firm's cost of capital is 10 percent, and it adds or subtracts 2 percentage points to adjust for project risk differences. Process A is judged to be a high-risk project—it might end up costing much more to operate than is expected. Process A's risk-adjusted cost of capital is

    a. 8 percent; this might seem illogical at first, but it correctly adjusts for risk where outflows, rather than inflows, are being discounted.
    b. 10 percent; the firm's cost of capital should not be adjusted when evaluating outflow-only projects.
    c. 12 percent; since A is more risky, its cash flows should be discounted at a higher rate because this correctly penalizes the project for its high risk.
    d. Somewhere between 8 and 12 percent, with the answer depending on the riskiness of the relevant inflows.
    e. Indeterminate, or, more accurately, irrelevant, because for such projects we would simply select the process that meets the requirements with the lowest required investment.

35. Which of the following statements is most *correct*?

   a. If a project's returns are negatively correlated with returns on most other assets in the economy, then stand-alone risk is a better proxy for market risk than would be true if the project's returns were positively correlated with most other assets' returns.
   b. In a sensitivity analysis, the steeper the lines relating NPV to changes in a variable, the less risky the project, other things held constant.
   c. It would be easier to use the pure-play method to assess the riskiness of a project such as a corporate aircraft than for a project which involves expanding into a new line of business, such as IBM's analysis of whether or not to go into the personal computer business.
   d. Normally, higher discount rates should be used to find the PV of riskier cash flows, but in the case of cash outflows, the greater the risk, the lower the discount rate used to find the present value of the cash flows.
   e. Statements a, b, c, and d are all true.

SELF-TEST PROBLEMS

   1. Initially, United Products has a beta of 1.30. The risk-free rate is 12 percent, and the required rate of return on the market is 18 percent. The firm now sells 10 percent of its assets, having a beta of 1.30, and uses the proceeds to purchase a new product line with a beta of 1.00. What is the new overall required rate of return for United Products?

   a. 15.11%   **b.** 16.24%   **c.** 17.48%   **d.** 18.00%   **e.** 19.62%

   2. Consolidated Inc. uses its marginal cost of capital of 12 percent to evaluate average-risk projects and adds/subtracts two percentage points to evaluate projects of greater/lesser risk. Currently, two mutually exclusive projects are under consideration. Both have a net cost of $200,000 and last 4 years. Project A, which is riskier than average, will produce yearly after-tax net cash flows of $71,000. Project B, which has less-than-average risk, will produce an after-tax net cash flow of $146,000 in Years 3 and 4 only. What should Consolidated do?

   a. Accept Project B with an NPV of $9,412.
   b. Accept both projects since both NPVs are greater than zero.
   c. Accept Project A with an NPV of $6,874.
   d. Accept neither project since both NPVs are less than zero.
   e. Accept Project A with an NPV of $15,652.

3. Universal Industries is considering the purchase of a plant that produces plastic products. The plant is expected to generate a rate of return of 17 percent, and the plant's estimated beta is 2.00. The risk-free rate is 12 percent, and the market risk premium is 6 percent. Universal has a target capital structure of 40 percent debt and 60 percent common equity. Its tax rate is 40 percent and its before-tax cost of debt is 14 percent. Universal should make the investment.

   a. True   **b.** False

4. Diversified Products (DP) is considering the formation of a new division which will double the assets of the firm. DP is an all-equity firm which has a current required rate of return of 20 percent. The risk-free rate is 10 percent, and the market risk premium is 5 percent. If DP wants to reduce its required rate of return to 18 percent, what is the maximum beta the new division could have?

   a. 1.00   **b.** 1.10   **c.** 1.20   **d.** 1.25   **e.** 1.30

5. Midwest Motors is choosing between two automobile washing/waxing machines on the basis of cost. The expected net costs of the two machines are as follows:

Year	Machine A	Machine B
0	($20,000)	($10,000)
1	(5,000)	(8,000)
2	(5,000)	(8,000)
3	(5,000)	(8,000)
4	(5,000)	(8,000)

   The firm's cost of capital is 10 percent. Machine B is judged to be a riskier-than-average project, while Machine A is considered less risky than average. The firm's policy is to add or subtract 2 percentage points to adjust for risk. The firm should choose Machine B.

   a. True   **b.** False

6. Western Industries' overall cost of capital (WACC) is 10 percent. Division HR is riskier than average, Division AR has average risk, and Division LR is less risky than average. Western adjusts for risk by adding or subtracting 2 percentage points. What is the risk-adjusted project cost of capital for a low-risk project in the HR division?

   a. 6%   **b.** 8%   **c.** 10%   **d.** 12%   **e.** 14%

(The following data apply to the next three problems.)

The Braxton Corporation has the following investment opportunities in the coming planning period:

Project	Net Investment	IRR
F	$300,000	18%
G	100,000	15
H	200,000	13
H*	200,000	12
I	100,000	10

Projects H and H* are mutually exclusive. The firm's MCC schedule is 10 percent up to $500,000 of new capital, and 11 percent thereafter.

7. What is the firm's marginal cost of capital?

   a. 10%   b. 11%   c. 12%   d. 13%   e. 15%

8. Assume that all projects have average risk. What is the dollar total of the firm's optimal capital budget?

   a. $300,000   b. $400,000   c. $500,000   d. $600,000   e. $700,000

9. Now assume that Project F is riskier than average and that Project I is less risky than average. The remaining projects have average risk. Braxton's policy is to adjust the marginal cost of capital up or down by 2 percentage points to account for risk. What is the effect of differential risk on Braxton's optimal capital budget?

   a. The capital budget is not changed.
   b. Project F is now unacceptable.
   c. The capital budget is now $700,000.
   d. Project I becomes acceptable.
   e. Both c and d are correct.

10. Protect Natural Resources Inc. (PNR) can control ground water pollution using either "Project Average" or "Project Risky." Both will do the job, but the actual costs involved with Project Risky could be much higher than the expected cost levels. The cash outflows associated with Project Average are about as uncertain as the cash flows associated with the firm's average project. PNR's cost of capital for average-risk projects is *normally* set at 12 percent, and the company adds 3 percent for high-risk projects but subtracts 3 percent for low-risk projects. The two projects in question meet the criteria for high and average risk, but the financial manager is concerned about applying the normal rule to such cost-only projects. You must decide which project to recommend, and you should recommend the one with the lower PV of costs. What is the PV of costs of the better project?

Year	Project Risky	Project Average
0	($1,000)	($400)
1	(210)	(400)
2	(210)	(400)
3	(210)	(400)
4	(210)	(400)

a. -$1,680.34   **b.** -$1,599.55   **c.** -$1,614.94   **d.** -$1,541.99   **e.** -$1,637.84

ANSWERS TO SELF-TEST QUESTIONS

1. higher; rate of return
2. market (beta); corporate (within-firm); stand-alone
3. profitability
4. Monte Carlo simulation
5. scenario analysis
6. sensitivity analysis
7. greatest
8. risk-free; premium
9. beta coefficient
10. diversification
11. decline; higher
12. market
13. lower
14. correlated
15. discount rate
16. investment opportunity schedule
17. weighted average cost of capital
18. retained earnings break point
19. marginal cost of capital (MCC)
20. average
21. mutually exclusive
22. optimal
23. Capital rationing
24. Decision tree analysis
25. pure play; accounting beta
26. certainty equivalent

27. a. The addition of an asset with a beta of zero will lower the beta of the firm, thus lowering the firm's market risk. (We assume that the starting beta of the firm is greater than zero.)

28. b. The only time this statement holds is when all projects being evaluated have the same risk as the firm's current average project. Otherwise, the cost of capital must be adjusted for project risk.

29. a. This is essentially true, but as we will note in Chapter 13, the proxy firm's beta must be adjusted to reflect the analyzing firm's target capital structure and tax rate.

30. a. The present value of a cash outflow (cash cost) must be increased to penalize it for above-average risk, and the present value will be increased only if the discount rate is decreased.

31. a. This intersection determines the marginal cost of capital for projects with average risk. The MCC is a function of the size of the capital budget, the firm's marginal capital component costs, and the firm's target capital structure.

32. c. Institutional investors are well diversified and, therefore, more concerned with market risk.

33. e. In fact, responses a through d are the steps normally followed, in the correct sequence.

34. a. When cash outflows are judged to be riskier than average, a project's cost of capital must be adjusted downward to reflect this fact.

35. d. Statement d is the correct statement. Using high discount rates for risky cash outflows produces misleading results. Statement a is incorrect; stand-alone risk is a good proxy for market risk if the asset's returns are positively correlated with returns on other assets. Statement b is incorrect; the steeper the lines relating NPV to changes in a variable, the riskier the project. Statement c is incorrect; the pure play method can only be used for investments where the investment itself has characteristics similar to publicly traded firms.

SOLUTIONS TO SELF-TEST PROBLEMS

1. e. $b_N = 0.9(1.30) + 0.1(1.00) = 1.27$.

New $k_s = 12\% + (18\% - 12\%)1.27 = 19.62\%$.

2. a. Look at the time lines:

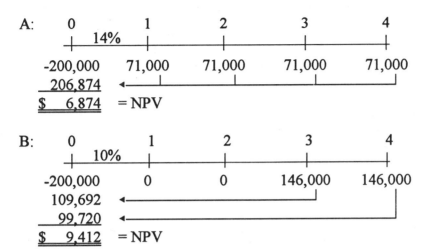

Note that both discount rates are adjusted for risk. Since the projects are mutually exclusive, the project with the higher NPV is chosen.

3. b. The project's required rate of return on equity is 24 percent:

$$k_{s(Project)} = 12\% + (6\%)2 = 24\%.$$

Thus, the project's cost of capital is 17.8 percent:

$$WACC_{(Project)} = 0.4(14\%)(0.6) + 0.6(24\%) = 17.8\%.$$

Since its expected return is only 17 percent, the plant should not be purchased.

4. c. First, find the current beta of the firm: $k_s = 10\% + (5\%)b = 20\%$; thus, $b = 2.00$.

Now find the beta required to lower the firm's required rate of return to 18 percent:

$$k_s = 10\% + (5\%)b = 18\%; b = 1.60.$$

Finally, if the firm doubles, 50 percent of the expanded firm's assets will be old, while 50 percent will be the new division. Thus, $0.5(2.00) + 0.5(b_{Div}) = 1.60$; $b_{Div} = 1.20$.

5. b. These are cash outflows, so the risk adjustment process is reversed. Thus, the project cost of capital for Machine A is 12 percent, while for B it is 8 percent.

k	PV Costs A	PV Costs B
10%	($35,849)	($35,359)
12	(35,187)	(34.299)
8	(36,561)	(36,497)

We see that with the correct risk adjustment, the PV of costs for Machine A is less than the PV of costs for Machine B, and hence Machine A should be selected. Note that the normal adjustment for risk would result in an incorrect decision.

6. c. $k_{s(HR)} = 10\% + 2\% = 12\%$.

$k_{s(Project)} = 12\% - 2\% = 10\%$.

7. b. First, plot the MCC and IOS schedules:

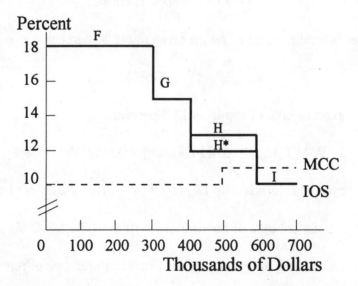

The intersection of the schedules defines the firm's marginal cost of capital. Thus, Braxton's MCC is 11 percent.

8. d. Since all projects have average risk, they are all evaluated at a project cost of capital of 11 percent. Clearly, Projects F and G are acceptable since their IRRs exceed 11 percent. (Since they are independent projects, it is permissible to use the IRR method as a proxy for the NPV method.) The decision between Projects H and H* must be made according to the NPV rule. Since we do not know the project cash flows, we cannot calculate their NPVs. However, one of the two would be chosen since both will have positive NPVs. Thus, the optimal capital budget consists of Projects F and G, and either Project H or H*, and totals $600,000.

9. e. Since Project F is riskier than average, its cost of capital must be adjusted upward to 11% + 2% = 13%. However, its IRR is 18 percent so Project F remains acceptable. On the other hand, Project I's cost of capital is adjusted downward to 9 percent, and hence it becomes acceptable. Thus, the optimal capital budget increases to $700,000. Note that Braxton's MCC remains at 11 percent.

10. c. Recognize that (1) risky *outflows* must be discounted at *lower* rates and (2) since Project Risky is risky, it must be discounted at a rate of 12% – 3% = 9%. Project Average must be discounted at 12 percent. At these rates:

$$NPV_R = -\$1,680.34 \text{ and } NPV_A = -\$1,614.94.$$

Thus, Project Average is the better project because it has the lower PV of costs.

CHAPTER 12

LONG-TERM FINANCIAL PLANNING

OVERVIEW

The previous chapters have dealt to a large extent with theory and strategic decision making. However, investment and financing decisions are not made in a vacuum; they are made within the guidelines set down by firms' operating and financial plans. In this chapter, long-term financial planning, which provides managers with a "road map" for some future period, is discussed.

Managers are vitally concerned with *future financial statements* and with the effects of alternative assumptions and policies on these *projected*, or *pro forma*, statements. The construction of pro forma statements begins with a *sales forecast*. On the basis of the sales forecast, the amount of assets necessary to support this sales level is determined. Although some liabilities will increase *spontaneously* with increased sales, if the sales growth rate is rapid, then external capital will be required to support the growth in sales.

Pro forma statements are important for two reasons. First, if projected operating results look poor, management can reformulate its plans for the coming year. Second, it is desirable to plan the acquisition of funds well in advance to insure that funds will be available when they are needed.

OUTLINE

Financial plans are developed within the framework of the firm's overall strategic plan.

■ Strategic planning charts the course for a firm over the long term. A strategic plan can take many forms, but most include the following items:

☐ The *corporate purpose* defines the firm's overall mission.

☐ The *corporate scope* defines a firm's lines of business and geographic areas of operations.

☐ The corporate purpose and scope outline the general philosophy and approach of the business. *Corporate objectives* set forth specific goals that management strives to attain.

☐ *Corporate strategies* are broad approaches to be taken to meet corporate objectives.

■ *Operating plans* provide detailed implementation guidance for management.
 □ Most firms use a five-year horizon for developing operating plans, with the first year of the plan being the most detailed, and with each succeeding year's plan becoming less specific.
 □ The operating plan explains in considerable detail who is responsible for what particular function and when specific tasks are to be accomplished.

The financial planning process can be broken down into five steps.

■ Set up a system of projected financial statements which can be used to analyze the effects of the operating plan on projected profits and other financial condition indicators.

■ Determine the funds needed to support the five-year plan.

■ Forecast the funds availability over the next five years by estimating the funds generated internally as well as those which can be obtained from external sources.

■ Establish and maintain a system of controls governing the allocation and use of funds within the firm.

■ Develop procedures for adjusting the basic plan if the economic forecasts upon which the plan was based do not materialize. This step is really a "feedback loop" which triggers modifications to the financial plan.

Well-run companies generally base their operating plans on a set of forecasted financial statements. A sales forecast for the next five years or so is developed, the assets required to meet the sales target are determined, and a decision is made concerning how to finance the required assets. These forecasts represent the "base case" and are a standard by which to judge alternate forecasts.

■ The sales forecast generally begins with a review of sales for the past 5 to 10 years.

■ If the sales forecast is off, the consequences can be serious. Thus, an accurate sales forecast is critical to the firm's well-being.

The first step in the financial plan is to develop a set of projected financial statements, with the sales forecast as the key input. The simplest technique to forecast financial statements is the constant ratio method.

■ The first step is to forecast next year's income statement.
  □ A sales forecast is needed.
  □ Assumptions about the operating cost ratio, the tax rate, interest charges, and the dividend payout ratio are made.
  □ In the simplest case, costs are assumed to increase at the same rate as sales; in more complicated situations, cost changes are forecasted separately.
  □ The primary objective is to determine how much income the company will earn and then retain for reinvestment in the business during the forecasted year.

■ The second step is to forecast next year's balance sheet.
  □ All asset accounts can be assumed to vary directly with sales unless the firm is operating at less than full capacity. If the firm is not operating at full capacity, then fixed assets will not vary directly with sales, but the cash, receivables, and inventory accounts will increase in proportion to the increase in sales.
  □ Liabilities, equity, or both must also increase if assets increase—asset expansions must be financed in some manner.
  □ Certain liability accounts, such as accounts payable and accruals, will increase *spontaneously* with sales. Retained earnings will increase, but not proportionately with sales. The new level of retained earnings will be the old level plus the addition to retained earnings, determined from the projected income statement.
  □ Other financing accounts, such as short-term debt, long-term debt, and common stock, are not directly related to sales. Changes in these accounts result from managerial decisions; they do not increase spontaneously as sales increase.
  □ The difference between projected total assets and projected liabilities and equity capital is the amount of additional funds needed (AFN).

■ The third step is the decision on how to finance the additional funds needed. Sometimes existing contractual agreements, such as a limit on the debt ratio, will restrict the firm's financing decisions. In addition, financial managers need to consider the firm's target capital structure and conditions in the debt and equity markets.

■ One complexity that arises in financial forecasting relates to *financing feedbacks*, which are the effects on the income statement and balance sheet of actions taken to finance asset increases. Financing feedbacks are incorporated into the pro forma financial statements through additional calculations, or *passes*, of the projected income statement and balance sheet.

■ Once the pro forma financial statements have been developed, the key ratios can be analyzed to determine whether the forecast meets the firm's financial targets as specified in the firm's financial plan. If the statements do not meet the targets, then elements of the forecast must be changed.

Although most firms' forecasts of capital requirements are made by constructing pro forma financial statements as described above, the following formula can be used to obtain an initial rough estimate of financial requirements:

■ The formula is as follows:

$$
\begin{array}{cccc}
\text{Additional} & \text{Required} & \text{Spontaneous} & \text{Increase in} \\
\text{funds} & = \text{increase} - & \text{increase} - & \text{retained} \\
\text{needed} & \text{in assets} & \text{in liabilities} & \text{earnings}
\end{array},
$$

or

$$\text{AFN} = (A^*/S)\Delta S - (L^*/S)\Delta S - MS_1(1 - d).$$

Here, A^*/S = assets that must increase if sales are to increase, expressed as a percentage of sales, or the required dollar increase in assets per \$1 increase in sales; L^*/S = liabilities that increase spontaneously with sales as a percentage of sales, or spontaneously generated financing per \$1 increase in sales; S_1 = total expected sales for the year in question (note that S_0 = last year's sales); ΔS = change in sales = $S_1 - S_0$; M = profit margin, or rate of profit per \$1 of sales; and d = the percentage of earnings paid out in dividends (dividend payout ratio).

■ Inherent in the formula are the assumptions (1) that each asset item must increase in direct proportion to sales increases, (2) that designated liability accounts also grow at the same rate as sales, and (3) that the profit margin and dividend payout are constant. Obviously, these assumptions do not always hold, so the formula does not always produce reliable results. Thus, the formula is used primarily to get a rough-and-ready forecast of financial requirements and as a supplement to the projected financial statement method.

■ The faster a firm's sales growth rate, the greater its need for additional financing.
   □ Higher growth rates require managers to plan very carefully to decide if the additional financing needed is actually available to the firm. Otherwise, they may need to reconsider their projected growth rate.
   □ Dividend policy, as reflected in the payout ratio, also affects external capital requirements: the higher the payout ratio, the smaller the addition to retained earnings, and hence the greater the requirements for external capital. Dividend policy may be changed to satisfy internal

financing requirements, but this may have a negative impact on stock price and may be met with resistance from investors.

☐ The amount of assets required per dollar of sales, A*/S, is often called the *capital intensity ratio*. This factor has a major effect on capital requirements per unit of sales growth. If the capital intensity ratio is low, then sales can grow rapidly without much outside capital. However, if a firm is capital intensive, even a small growth in output will require a great deal of outside capital.

☐ Profit margin, M, also has an effect on capital requirements. The higher the profit margin, the lower the funds requirement, and the lower the profit margin, the higher the requirement. Thus, highly profitable firms can raise most of their capital internally.

The forecasting process is greatly complicated if the ratios of balance sheet items to sales are not constant at all levels of sales.

■ Where *economies of scale* occur in asset use, the ratio of that asset to sales will change as the firm's size increases.

■ Technological considerations sometimes dictate that fixed assets be added in large, discrete units, often referred to as *lumpy assets*. This automatically creates excess capacity immediately after a plant expansion.

■ *Forecasting errors* can cause the actual asset/sales ratio for a given period to be quite different from the planned ratio. This situation can result in excess capacity.

If any of the above conditions apply (economies of scale, lumpy assets, or excess capacity), the A*/S ratio will not be a constant, and the constant ratio technique should not be used. Rather, other techniques must be used to forecast asset levels to determine additional financing requirements. These other techniques include excess capacity adjustments and regression analyses.

■ Since excess capacity may exist in fixed assets, the target fixed assets to sales ratio needs to be adjusted downward since it was estimated on the assumption of full capacity of fixed assets.

☐ Full capacity sales is defined as actual sales divided by the percentage of capacity at which the fixed assets operated to achieve these sales:

$$\text{Full capacity sales} = \frac{\text{Actual sales}}{\substack{\text{Percentage of capacity at which} \\ \text{fixed assets were operated}}}.$$

- ☐ The target fixed assets to sales ratio is equal to the current year's fixed assets divided by full capacity sales:

$$\text{Target fixed assets/Sales ratio} = \frac{\text{Actual fixed assets}}{\text{Full capacity sales}}.$$

- ☐ The required level of fixed assets is equal to the target fixed assets to sales ratio times projected sales:

$$\text{Required level of fixed assets} = \frac{\text{Target fixed assets}}{\text{Sales}} (\text{Projected sales}).$$

■ If one assumes that the relationship between a certain item or account and sales is linear, then simple linear regression techniques can be used to estimate the item or account level for any given sales increase. Linear regression is appropriate when the relationship is linear but does not pass through the origin.

- ☐ *Curvilinear regression* can be used to make a forecast if the relationship between an income statement item or balance sheet account and sales is a curve.
- ☐ If the relationship between a variable and sales has points that are widely scattered about the regression line, then there is a good chance that other factors, in addition to sales, affect the level of that variable. In this case, *multiple regression* might be used.
- ☐ A final approach to forecasting is to develop a specific model for each income statement and balance sheet variable to be forecasted. This method is called *specific variable forecasting* because each income statement item and balance sheet account is forecasted independently, given the sales forecast.

Although the types of financial forecasting described in this chapter can be done with a hand calculator, virtually all corporate forecasts are made using computerized forecasting models. Most models are based on a spreadsheet program, such as Lotus 1-2-3. Spreadsheet programs are easy to construct for forecasts extending over several years, and they are useful for instantaneously recomputing projected statements and ratios when one of the input variables is changed.

Financial forecasting and planning is vital to corporate success, but planning is for nought unless the firm has a control system that (1) ensures implementation of the planned policies and (2) provides an information feedback loop which permits rapid adjustments if the conditions upon which the plan is based change.

- In a financial control system, the key question is "How is the firm doing in 199X as compared with our forecasts, and if actual results differ from the budget, what can we do to get back on track?"

- The basic tools of financial control are *budgets* and *pro forma financial statements*. These express management's targets and are compared with actual corporate performance to determine *variances*, the difference between actual and target values.

- By focusing on variances, managers can *manage by exception*, concentrating on those variables that are most in need of improvement and leaving alone those operations that are running smoothly.

SELF-TEST QUESTIONS

Definitional

1. The construction of pro forma statements begins with a(n) _____ _____.

2. Those asset items that typically increase proportionately with higher sales are _____, _____, and _____. _____ assets are frequently not used to full capacity and hence do not increase in proportion to sales.

3. If various asset categories increase, _____ and/or _____ must also increase.

4. Typically, certain liabilities will rise _____ with sales. These include accounts _____ and _____.

5. _____ and _____ _____ are examples of accounts that do not increase automatically with higher levels of sales.

6. As the dividend _____ _____ is increased, the amount of earnings available to finance new assets is _____.

7. Retained earnings depend not only on next year's sales level and dividend payout ratio but also on the _____ _____.

8. The amount of assets required per dollar of sales, A*/S is often called the _____ _____ _____.

9. A capital intensive industry will require large amounts of _____ capital to finance increased growth.

10. The constant ratio method assumes that the _____ of balance sheet items to _____ is _____ at all levels of sales.

11. The constant ratio assumption may not be accurate when assets must be added in discrete amounts, called _____ assets, or when _____ of scale are considered.

12. The _____ _____ defines the firm's overall mission.

13. One complexity that arises in financial forecasting relates to _____ _____, which are the effects on the income statement and balance sheet of actions taken to finance asset increases.

14. The basic tools of financial control are _____ and pro forma financial statements. These express management's targets and are compared with actual corporate performance to determine _____, the difference between actual and target values.

Conceptual

15. An increase in a firm's inventories will call for additional financing unless the increase is offset by an equal or larger *decrease* in some other asset account.

    a. True   b. False

16. If the capital intensity ratio of a firm actually decreases as sales increase, use of the AFN formula method will typically *overstate* the amount of additional funds required, other things held constant.

    a. True   b. False

17. If the dividend payout ratio is 100 percent, all ratios are held constant, and the firm is operating at full capacity, then any increase in sales will require additional financing.

   a. True   **b.** False

18. One of the first steps in the constant ratio method is to identify those asset and liability accounts which increase spontaneously with retained earnings.

   a. True   **b.** False

19. Which of the following would *reduce* the additional funds needed if all other things are held constant?

   a. An increase in the dividend payout ratio.
   b. A decrease in the profit margin.
   c. An increase in the capital intensity ratio.
   d. An increase in the expected sales growth rate.
   e. A decrease in the firm's tax rate.

20. Which of the following statements is most *correct*?

   a. Suppose economies of scale exist in a firm's use of assets. Under this condition, the firm should use the regression method of forecasting asset requirements rather than the constant ratio method.
   b. If a firm must acquire assets in lumpy units, it can avoid errors in forecasts of its need for funds by using the linear regression method of forecasting asset requirements because all the points will lie on the regression line.
   c. If economies of scale in the use of assets exist, then the AFN formula rather than the constant ratio method should be used to forecast additional funds needed.
   d. Notes payable to banks are included in the AFN formula, along with a projection of retained earnings.
   e. One problem with the AFN formula is that it does not take account of the firm's dividend policy.

SELF-TEST PROBLEMS

1. Southern Products Inc. has the following balance sheet:

Current assets	$ 5,000	Accounts payable	$ 1,000
		Notes payable	1,000
Net fixed assets	5,000	Long-term debt	4,000
		Common equity	4,000
Total assets	$10,000	Total liabilities and equity	$10,000

Business has been slow; therefore, fixed assets are vastly underutilized. Management believes it can double sales next year with the introduction of a new product. No new fixed assets will be required, and management expects that there will be no earnings retained next year. What is next year's AFN?

   a. $0   **b.** $4,000   **c.** $6,000   **d.** $13,000   **e.** $19,000

2. The 1996 balance sheet for American Pulp and Paper is shown below (in millions of dollars):

Cash	$ 3.0	Accounts payable	$ 2.0
Accounts receivable	3.0	Notes payable	1.5
Inventory	5.0		
Current assets	$11.0	Current liabilities	$ 3.5
Fixed assets	3.0	Long-term debt	3.0
		Common equity	7.5
Total assets	$14.0	Total liabilities and equity	$14.0

In 1996, sales were $60 million. In 1997, management believes that sales will increase by 20 percent to a total of $72 million. The profit margin is expected to be 5 percent, and the dividend payout ratio is targeted at 40 percent. No excess capacity exists. What is AFN (in millions) for 1997 using the formula method?

   a. $0.36   **b.** $0.24   **c.** $0   **d.** -$0.24   **e.** -$0.36

3. Refer to Self-Test Problem 2. How much can sales grow above the 1997 level of $60 million without requiring any additional funds?

   a. 12.28%   **b.** 14.63%   **c.** 15.75%   **d.** 17.65%   **e.** 18.14%

4. Smith Machines Inc. has a net income this year of $500 on sales of $2,000 and is operating its fixed assets at full capacity. Management expects sales to increase by 25 percent next year and is forecasting a dividend payout ratio of 30 percent. The profit margin is not expected to change. If spontaneous liabilities are $500 this year and next year's AFN is expected to be zero, what are Smith's total assets this year?

a. $1,000   b. $1,500   c. $2,250   d. $3,000   e. $3,500

(The following data apply to the next three problems.)

Crossley Products Company's 1996 financial statements are shown below:

Crossley Products Company
Balance Sheet as of December 31, 1996
(Thousands of Dollars)

Cash	$ 600	Accounts payable	$ 2,400
Receivables	3,600	Notes payable	1,157
Inventories	4,200	Accruals	840
Total current assets	$ 8,400	Total current liabilities	$ 4,397
		Mortgage bonds	1,667
		Common stock	667
Net fixed assets	7,200	Retained earnings	8,869
Total assets	$15,600	Total liabilities and equity	$15,600

Crossley Products Company
Income Statement for December 31, 1996
(Thousands of Dollars)

Sales	$12,000
Operating costs	10,261
Earnings before interest and taxes	$ 1,739
Interest	339
Earnings before taxes	$ 1,400
Taxes (40%)	560
Net income	$ 840
Dividends (60%)	$504
Addition to retained earnings	$336

5. Assume that the company was operating at full capacity in 1996 with regard to all items except fixed assets; fixed assets in 1996 were being utilized to only 75 percent of capacity. By what percentage could 1997 sales increase over 1996 sales without the need for an increase in fixed assets?

   a. 33%   **b.** 25%   **c.** 20%   **d.** 44%   **e.** 50%

6. Now suppose 1997 sales increase by 25 percent over 1996 sales. How much AFN (in thousands) will be required? Assume that Crossley cannot sell any fixed assets. Use the constant ratio method to develop a pro forma balance sheet and income statement. Assume that any required financing is borrowed as notes payable. Do not include any financing feedbacks, and use a pro forma income statement to determine the addition to retained earnings.

   a. $825   **b.** $925   **c.** $750   **d.** $900   **e.** $850

7. Use the financial statements developed in Self-Test Problem 6 to incorporate the financing feedback which results from the addition of notes payable. (That is, do the next financial statement iteration.) For purposes of this part, assume that the notes payable interest rate is 12 percent. What is the AFN (in thousands) for this iteration?

   a. $28   **b.** $30   **c.** $20   **d.** $24   **e.** $36

(The following data apply to the next two problems.)

Taylor Technologies Inc.'s 1996 financial statements are shown below:

Taylor Technologies Inc.
Balance Sheet as of December 31, 1996

Cash	$ 90,000	Accounts payable		$ 180,000
Receivables	180,000	Notes payable		78,000
Inventories	360,000	Accruals		90,000
Total current assets	$ 630,000	Total current liabilities		$ 348,000
		Common stock		900,000
Net fixed assets	720,000	Retained earnings		102,000
Total assets	$1,350,000	Total liabilities and equity		$1,350,000

Taylor Technologies Inc.
Income Statement for December 31, 1996

Sales	$1,800,000
Operating costs	1,639,860
EBIT	$ 160,140
Interest	10,140
EBT	$ 150,000
Taxes (40%)	60,000
Net income	$ 90,000
Dividends (60%)	$54,000
Addition to retained earnings	$36,000

8. Suppose that in 1997 sales increase by 10 percent over 1996 sales. Construct the pro forma financial statements using the constant ratio method. How much is AFN? Assume the firm operated at full capacity in 1996. Do not include financing feedbacks.

   a. $72,459   **b.** $70,211   **c.** $68,157   **d.** $66,445   **e.** $63,989

9. Now assume that 50 percent of AFN will be financed by selling common stock and the remainder by borrowing as notes payable. Assume that the interest rate on notes payable is 13 percent. Do the next iteration of financial statements incorporating financing feedbacks. What is the AFN for this iteration?

   a. $1,063   **b.** $957   **c.** $1,124   **d.** $927   **e.** $1,185

10. Your company's sales were $2,000 last year, and they are forecasted to rise by 50 percent during the coming year. Here is the latest balance sheet:

Cash	$ 100		Accounts payable	$ 200
Receivables	300		Notes payable	200
Inventories	800		Accruals	20
Total current assets	$1,200		Total current liabilities	$ 420
			Long-term debt	780
			Common stock	400
Net fixed assets	800		Retained earnings	400
Total assets	$2,000		Total liabilities and equity	$2,000

Fixed assets were used to only 80 percent of capacity last year, and year-end inventory holdings were $100 greater than were needed to support the $2,000 of sales. The other current assets (cash and receivables) were at their proper levels. All assets would be a constant percentage of sales if excess capacity did not exist; that is, all assets would increase at the same rate as sales if no excess capacity existed. The company's profit margin will be 3 percent, and its payout ratio will be 80 percent. If all additional funds needed (AFN) are raised as notes payable, what will the current ratio be at the end of the coming year? Ignore the effects of financing feedbacks on the income statement.

   a. 2.47   **b.** 1.44   **c.** 1.21   **d.** 1.00   **e.** 1.63

11. The Bouchard Company's sales are forecasted to increase from $500 in 1996 to $1,000 in 1997. Here is the December 31, 1996, balance sheet:

Cash	$ 50	Accounts payable	$ 25
Receivables	100	Notes payable	75
Inventories	100	Accruals	25
Total current assets	$250	Total current liabilities	$125
		Long-term debt	200
		Common stock	50
Net fixed assets	250	Retained earnings	125
Total assets	$500	Total liabilities and equity	$500

Bouchard's fixed assets were used to only 50 percent of capacity during 1996, but its current assets were at their proper levels. All assets except fixed assets should be a constant percentage of sales, and fixed assets would also increase at the same rate if the current excess capacity did not exist. Bouchard's profit margin is forecasted to be 8 percent, and its payout ratio will be 40 percent. What is Bouchard's additional funds needed (AFN) for the coming year? Ignore financing feedbacks.

   a. $102   **b.** $152   **c.** $197   **d.** $167   **e.** $183

ANSWERS TO SELF-TEST QUESTIONS

1. sales forecast
2. cash; receivables; inventories; Fixed
3. liabilities; equity

4. spontaneously; payable; accruals
5. Bonds; common stock (or preferred stock, or retained earnings)

6. payout ratio; decreased

7. profit margin

8. capital intensity ratio

9. external

10. ratio; sales; constant

11. lumpy; economies

12. corporate purpose

13. financing feedbacks

14. budgets; variances

15. a. When an increase in one asset account is not offset by an equivalent decrease in another asset account, then financing is needed to reestablish equilibrium on the balance sheet. Note, though, that this additional financing may come from a spontaneous increase in accounts payable or from retained earnings.

16. a. A decreasing capital intensity ratio, A*/S, means that fewer assets are required, proportionately, as sales increase. Thus, the external funding requirement is overstated. Always keep in mind that the AFN formula method assumes that the asset/sales ratio is constant regardless of the level of sales.

17. a. With a 100 percent payout ratio, there will be no retained earnings. When operating at full capacity, *all* assets are spontaneous, but *all* liabilities cannot be spontaneous since a firm must have common equity. Thus, the growth in assets cannot be matched by a growth in spontaneous liabilities, so additional financing will be required in order to keep the financial ratios (the debt ratio in particular) constant.

18. b. The first step is to identify those accounts which increase spontaneously with sales.

19. e. Answers a through d would increase the additional funds needed, but a decrease in the tax rate would raise the profit margin and thus increase the amount of available retained earnings.

20. a. Statement a is correct; economies of scale cause the ratios to change over time, which violates the assumption of the constant ratio method. Statement b is false; the points will not all lie on the regression line. Statement c is false; the AFN formula requires constant ratios over time. Statement d is false; the AFN formula includes only spontaneous liabilities, and notes payable do not spontaneously increase with sales. Statement e is false; the AFN formula includes the dividend payout, so dividend policy is included.

SOLUTIONS TO SELF-TEST PROBLEMS

1. b. Look at next year's balance sheet:

Current assets	$10,000	Accounts payable	$ 2,000
Net fixed assets	5,000	Notes payable	1,000
		Current liabilities	$ 3,000
		Long-term debt	4,000
		Common equity	4,000
			$11,000
		AFN	4,000
Total assets	$15,000	Total liabilities and equity	$15,000

With no retained earnings next year, the common equity account remains at $4,000. Thus, the AFN is $15,000 – $11,000 = $4,000.

2. b. None of the items on the right side of the balance sheet rises spontaneously with sales except accounts payable. Therefore,

$$AFN = (A*/S)(\Delta S) - (L*/S)(\Delta S) - MS_1(1 - d)$$
$$= (\$14/\$60)(\$12) - (\$2/\$60)(\$12) - (0.05)(\$72)(0.6)$$
$$= \$2.8 - \$0.4 - \$2.16 = \$0.24 \text{ million.}$$

The firm will need $240,000 in additional funds to support the increase in sales.

3. d. Note that g = Sales growth = $\Delta S/S$ and $S_1 = S(1 + g)$. Then,

$$AFN = A*g - L*g - M[(S)(1 + g)](1 - d) = 0$$
$$\$14g - \$2g - 0.05[(\$60)(1 + g)](0.6) = 0$$
$$\$12g - 1(\$3 + \$3g)(0.60) = 0$$
$$\$12g - \$1.8 - \$1.8g = 0$$
$$\$10.20g = \$1.80$$
$$g = 0.1765 = 17.65\%.$$

4. c. $\text{AFN} = (A^*/S)(\Delta S) - (L^*/S)(\Delta S) - MS_1(1 - d)$

$0 = (A^*/\$2,000)(\$500) - (\$500/\$2,000)(\$500)$
$\quad - (\$500/\$2,000)(\$2,500)(1 - 0.3)$

$0 = (\$500A^*/\$2,000) - \$125 - \$437.50$

$0 = (\$500A^*/\$2,000) - \$562.50$

$\$562.50 = 0.25A^*$

$A^* = \$2,250.$

5. a. $\dfrac{\text{Full}}{\text{capacity}} = \dfrac{\text{Actual sales}}{\% \text{ of capacity at which}} = \dfrac{\$12,000}{0.75} = \$16,000.$
$\quad\text{sales} \qquad\qquad \text{FA were operated}$

$\dfrac{\text{Percent}}{\text{increase}} = \dfrac{\text{New sales} - \text{Old sales}}{\text{Old sales}} = \dfrac{\$16,000 - \$12,000}{\$12,000} = 0.33 = 33\%.$

Therefore, sales could expand by 33 percent before Crossley Products would need to add fixed assets.

6. e.

Crossley Products Company
Pro Forma Income Statement
December 31, 1997
(Thousands of Dollars)

	1996	$(1 + g)$	1st Pass 1997
Sales	$12,000	(1.25)	$15,000
Operating costs	10,261	(1.25)	12,826
EBIT	$ 1,739		$ 2,174
Interest	339		339
EBT	$ 1,400		$ 1,835
Taxes (40%)	560		734
Net income	$ 840		$ 1,101
Dividends (60%)	$504		$661
Addition to RE	$336		$440

Crossley Products Company
Pro Forma Balance Sheet
December 31, 1997
(Thousands of Dollars)

	1996	(1 + g)	1997	AFN	1997 After AFN
Cash	$ 600	(1.25)	$ 750		$ 750
Receivables	3,600	(1.25)	4,500		4,500
Inventories	4,200	(1.25)	5,250		5,250
Total current assets	$ 8,400		$10,500		$10,500
Net fixed assets	7,200		7,200[b]		7,200
Total assets	$15,600		$17,700		$17,700
Accounts payable	$ 2,400	(1.25)	$ 3,000		$ 3,000
Notes payable	1,157		1,157	+850	2,007
Accruals	840	(1.25)	1,050		1,050
Total current liabilities	$ 4,397		$ 5,207		$ 6,057
Mortgage bonds	1,667		1,667		1,667
Common stock	667		667		667
Retained earnings	8,869	440[a]	9,309		9,309
Total liabilities and equity	$15,600		$16,850		$17,700

AFN = $850

Notes:
[a]See income statement on previous page.
[b]From Self-Test Problem 5 we know that sales can increase by 33 percent before additions to fixed assets are needed.

7. d.

Crossley Products Company
Pro Forma Income Statement
December 31, 1997
(Thousands of Dollars)

	1st Pass 1997	Financing Feedback	2nd Pass 1997
Sales	$15,000		$15,000
Operating costs	12,826		12,826
EBIT	$ 2,174		$ 2,174
Interest	339	+102[a]	441
EBT	$ 1,835		$ 1,733
Taxes (40%)	734		693
Net income	$ 1,101		$ 1,040
Dividends (60%)	$661		$624
Addition to RE	$440		$416

Notes:
[a]Change in interest = $850(0.12) = $102.

	1st Pass 1997	Financing Feedback	2nd Pass 1997
Total assets	$17,700		$17,700
Accounts payable	$ 3,000		$ 3,000
Notes payable	2,007		2,007
Accruals	1,050		1,050
Total current liabilities	$ 6,057		$ 6,057
Mortgage bonds	1,667		1,667
Common stock	667		667
Retained earnings	9,309	-24[b]	9,285
Total liabilities and equity	$17,700		$17,676
AFN =			$24
Cumulative AFN (two passes) =		$874	

Notes:
[b]Change in RE addition = $416 – $440 = -$24.

8. c. The first pass balance sheet indicates that the AFN = $68,157. This AFN ignores financing feedbacks.

Taylor Technologies Inc.
Pro Forma Income Statement
December 31, 1997

	1996	(1 + g)	1st Pass 1997	AFN Effects	2nd Pass 1997
Sales	$1,800,000	(1.10)	$1,980,000		$1,980,000
Operating costs	1,639,860	(1.10)	1,803,846		1,803,846
EBIT	$ 160,140		$ 176,154		$ 176,154
Interest	10,140		10,140	+4,430[a]	14,570
EBT	$ 150,000		$ 166,014		$ 161,584
Taxes (40%)	60,000		66,406		64,634
Net income	$ 90,000		$ 99,608		$ 96,950
Dividends (60%)	$54,000		$59,765		$58,170
Addition to RE	$36,000		$39,843		$38,780

Notes:
[a]Change in interest = $34,079(0.13) = $4,430.

Taylor Technologies Inc.
Pro Forma Balance Sheet
December 31, 1997

	1996	(1 + g)	1st Pass 1997	AFN Effects	2nd Pass 1997
Cash	$ 90,000	(1.10)	$ 99,000		$ 99,000
Receivables	180,000	(1.10)	198,000		198,000
Inventories	360,000	(1.10)	396,000		396,000
Total current assets	$ 630,000		$ 693,000		$ 693,000
Fixed assets	720,000	(1.10)	792,000		792,000
Total assets	$1,350,000		$1,485,000		$1,485,000
Accts. payable	$ 180,000	(1.10)	$ 198,000		$ 198,000
Notes payable	78,000		78,000	+34,079	112,079
Accruals	90,000	(1.10)	99,000		99,000
Total current liabilities	$ 348,000		$ 375,000		$ 409,079
Common stock	900,000		900,000	+34,078	934,078
Ret. earnings	102,000	39,843[a]	141,843	-1,063[b]	140,780
Total liabilities and equity	$1,350,000		$1,416,843		$1,483,937
AFN =			$68,157		$1,063
Cumulative AFN (two passes) =				$69,220	

Notes:
[a]See 1st pass income statement.
[b]Change in addition to RE = $38,780 − $39,843 = -$1,063.

9. a. See the AFN line in the final column of the projected balance sheet above. This AFN is the result of the change to retained earnings due to the increased interest expense from the addition of notes payable.

10. e.

	Current Year	(1 + g)	1st Pass	AFN	2nd Pass
Cash	$ 100	× 1.5	$ 150		$ 150
Receivables	300	× 1.5	450		450
Inventories	800	+ 250[a]	1,050		1,050
Total curr. assets	$1,200		$1,650		1,650
Net fixed assets	800	+ 160[b]	960		960
Total assets	$2,000		$2,610		$2,610
Accounts payable	$ 200	× 1.5	$ 300		$ 300
Notes payable	200		200	+ 482	682
Accruals	20	× 1.5	30		30
Total curr. liab.	$ 420		$ 530		$1,012
Long-term debt	780		780		780
Common stock	400		400		400
Retained earnings	400	+ 18[c]	418		418
Total liab./equity	$2,000		$2,128		$2,610

AFN $482

Notes:

[a]Target inventory/assets = ($800 – $100)/$2,000 = 35%.
Target inventory level = 0.35($3,000) = $1,050.
Since we already have $800 of inventories, we need:
Additional inventories = $1,050 – $800 = $250.

[b]Capacity sales = Sales/Capacity factor = $2,000/0.8 = $2,500.
Target FA/S ratio = FA/Capacity sales = $800/$2,500 = 32%.
Required FA = Target ratio × Forecasted sales = 0.32($3,000) = $960.
Since we already have $800 of fixed assets, we need:
Additional fixed assets = $960 – $800 = $160.

[c]Additions to RE = S_1(M)(1 – Payout ratio) = $3,000(0.03)(0.2) = $18.

The problem asks for the forecasted current ratio which is calculated as:
Forecasted current ratio = $1,650/$1,012 = 1.6304.

11. b.

	1996	$(1 + g)$	1st Pass 1997
Cash	$ 50	×2	$100
Receivables	100	×2	200
Inventories	100	×2	200
Total current assets	$250		$500
Net fixed assets	250	+0[a]	250
Total assets	$500		$750
Accounts payable	$ 25	×2	$ 50
Notes payable	75		75
Accruals	25	×2	50
Total current liabilities	$125		$175
Long-term debt	200		200
Common stock	50		50
Retained earnings	125	+48[b]	173
Total claims	$500		$598
AFN =			$152

Notes:

[a]Capacity sales = Actual sales/Capacity factor = $500/0.5 = $1,000.

Target FA/S ratio = $250/$1,000 = 0.25.

Target FA = 0.25($1,000) = $250 = Required fixed assets.

Since Bouchard currently has $250 of FA, no new FA will be required.

[b]Addition to RE = $M(S_1)(1 - \text{Payout ratio}) = 0.08(\$1,000)(0.6) = \$48$.

CHAPTER 13

CAPITAL STRUCTURE DECISIONS: THE BASICS

OVERVIEW

One of the most perplexing issues facing financial managers is the relationship between *capital structure*, which is a mix of debt and equity financing, and stock prices. Should different industries and different firms within industries have different capital structures, and, if so, what factors lead to these differences.

In Chapters 13 and 14, we will discuss both the theories that underlie capital structure decisions and more pragmatic approaches to the problem. Although the capital structure decision is far from precise, an understanding of Chapters 13 and 14 will help you deal with the issues involved.

OUTLINE

Capital structure decisions involve the tradeoff between risk and expected return.

■ Debt financing increases the riskiness of a firm, but the use of financial leverage can increase the expected return to shareholders.

■ The optimal capital structure balances risk and return to maximize the stock price.

Business risk, in a stand-alone risk sense, is a function of the uncertainty inherent in projections of a firm's future rate of return on assets (ROA). It is the riskiness of the firm's assets if it uses no debt.

■ The business risk of a *leverage-free firm* can be measured by the standard deviation of its expected ROE, because its assets will be all-equity financed so ROA = ROE.

■ Business risk depends on several factors:
  □ Demand variability
  □ Sales price variability
  □ Input cost variability

    ☐ Ability to adjust output prices for changes in input costs
    ☐ Ability to develop new products in a timely, cost-effective manner
    ☐ Extent to which costs are fixed: operating leverage

■ Operating leverage is the degree to which a firm uses fixed cost inputs (as opposed to variable cost inputs) in its production processes.
    ☐ Firms that have a higher percentage of fixed costs are said to have a high degree of operating leverage.
    ☐ Higher fixed costs are generally associated with more highly automated, capital intensive firms and industries.
    ☐ High operating leverage implies that a relatively small change in sales will result in a large change in ROE.
    ☐ In general, the higher a firm's operating leverage, the higher its standard deviation of ROE, and hence the higher its business risk (in a stand-alone sense).
    ☐ Production technology limits control over the amount of fixed costs and hence operating leverage. However, firms do have some control over the type of production processes they employ. Therefore, a firm's capital budgeting decisions will have an impact on its business risk.
    ☐ The breakeven quantity, Q_{BE}, is calculated as $Q_{BE} = F/(P - V)$.

Financial risk is the additional risk placed on the common stockholders as a result of the decision to finance with debt and/or preferred stock.

■ The use of financial leverage concentrates the firm's inherent business risk of a smaller equity base.

■ The σ_{ROE} at any debt level is a measure of the stand-alone risk borne by the common stockholders.

■ If the firm does not use any financial leverage, then $\sigma_{ROE} = \sigma_{ROE(U)}$.

■ However, if the firm does use financial leverage, then $\sigma_{ROE} > \sigma_{ROE(U)}$, and the difference is a measure of financial risk:

$$\text{Financial risk} = \text{Stand-alone risk} - \text{Business risk} = \sigma_{ROE} - \sigma_{ROE(U)}.$$

■ Financial leverage will be "favorable" and, hence, "leverage up" shareholder returns if the return on assets measured as EBIT/Total assets is greater than the cost of debt. However, the stand-alone risk to stockholders will also increase as leverage increases.

- Operating and financial leverage normally work in the same way; both generally increase expected ROE, but they also increase the risk borne by stockholders. Operating leverage affects the firm's business risk, financial leverage affects the firm's financial risk, and both influence the firm's stand-alone risk.

Modern capital structure theory began in 1958, when Professors Franco Modigliani and Merton Miller (MM) published what has been called the most influential finance article ever written.

- MM proved, under a very restrictive set of assumptions, that a firm's value is unaffected by its capital structure. Their theory produces what is often referred to as the "irrelevance result."

- MM provided us with some clues about what is required for capital structure to be relevant and hence to affect a firm's value. Consequently, MM's work was only the beginning of capital structure research, and subsequent research has focused on relaxing the MM assumptions to develop a more realistic theory of capital structure.

- MM published a follow-up paper in which they relaxed the assumption that there are no corporate taxes. MM demonstrated that if all of their other assumptions hold, the asymmetry of the tax deductibility of interest versus the non-deductibility of dividend payments leads to a situation which calls for 100 percent debt financing.

- Merton Miller then analyzed the effects of personal taxes. While an increase in the corporate tax rate makes debt look better to corporations because interest is tax deductible, an increase in the personal tax rate encourages additional equity financing because of the favorable capital gains tax treatment on stocks.

- Bankruptcy-related problems are more likely to arise the more debt a firm includes in its capital structure. Therefore, bankruptcy costs discourage firms from pushing their use of debt to excessive levels.
  - ☐ Bankruptcy-related costs have three components: (1) the probability of their occurring, (2) the costs they produce given that financial distress has arisen, and (3) the adverse effects on current operations.

- The "trade-off theory of leverage" recognizes that firms trade off the *benefits* of debt financing (favorable corporate tax treatment) against the *costs* of debt financing (higher interest rates and bankruptcy costs).

- Signaling theory recognizes the fact that investors and managers do *not* have the same information regarding a firm's prospects, as was assumed by trade-off theory. This is called *asymmetric information*, and it has an important effect on the optimal capital structure.
  - ☐ As a result, one would expect a firm with very favorable prospects to try to avoid selling stock and to attempt to raise any required new capital by other means, including using debt beyond the normal target capital structure.
  - ☐ The announcement of a stock offering by a mature firm that seems to have financing alternatives is taken as a signal that the firm's prospects as seen by its management are not bright.
  - ☐ The implications of the signaling theory for capital structure decisions is that firms should, in normal times, maintain a *reserve borrowing capacity* which can be used in the event that some especially good investment opportunity comes along.

- Agency conflicts are particularly likely when the firm's managers have too much cash at their disposal. Firms can reduce cash flow in a variety of ways:
  - ☐ Funnel cash back to shareholders through higher dividends or stock repurchases.
  - ☐ Shift the capital structure toward more debt in the hope that higher debt service requirements will force managers to become more disciplined. A leveraged buyout (LBO) is one way to achieve this.

- Increasing debt and reducing free cash flow has its downside: It increases the risk of bankruptcy, which can be costly.

- In practice, capital structure decisions must be made by combining judgment and numerical analysis.

Capital structure theory suggests that each firm has an optimal capital structure, one that maximizes its value and minimizes its overall cost of capital. Research on capital structure theory also points out that there are many contradictory issues regarding capital structure decisions, and that theory cannot enable us to specify a precisely optimal structure for any firm. However, one can get an idea of the capital structure range by quantitative analysis.

- First, the costs of debt and equity are estimated for different debt levels, holding total assets constant.

- As more debt is used, the estimated costs of debt and equity will rise, because the riskiness of these capital components is increasing.

■ The estimated component costs are then combined to find the weighted average cost of capital at each debt level.

■ The debt amount which produces the lowest overall weighted average cost of capital (WACC) is optimal, and this is the firm's target capital structure, because that capital structure which minimizes a firm's weighted average cost of capital also maximizes its stock price.

■ If one assumes that the firm's cash flows are perpetuities (a no-growth firm), the following equations can be used to determine a firm's total market value at different capital structures, and then to use this information to establish the firm's stock price as a function of its capital structure. This analysis focuses on the impact of leverage on a firm's total value and its stock price.
  □ Firm value: $V = D + S$.
  □ Equity value: $S = [(EBIT - k_d D)(1 - T)]/k_s$.
  □ Stock price: $P_0 = DPS/k_s = EPS/k_s$.
  □ Cost of capital: $WACC = (D/V)(k_d)(1 - T) + (S/V)(k_s)$.

■ Quite obviously, the situation in the real world is much more complex and less exact.

■ Although expected EPS is much higher if the firm uses financial leverage, the risk of low, or even negative, EPS is also higher if debt is used. Using leverage involves a risk/return trade-off—higher leverage increases expected EPS, but more leverage also increases the firm's risk. It is this increasing risk that causes k_s and k_d to increase at higher amounts of financial leverage.

■ Price per share and EPS will not both be maximized at the same debt level. Since management is primarily interested in maximizing shareholder wealth, the optimal capital structure should be based on value, or share price, and not on EPS.

■ Although conceptually simple, it is impossible to place much faith in the results, since it is just not possible to estimate the values for k_d and k_s at different debt levels with any degree of precision and the models are very sensitive to input estimates.

Since one cannot determine a precise optimal capital structure, managers must apply judgment to their quantitative analyses. The judgmental analysis involves several different factors that should be taken into account.

■ Managers must refrain from using leverage to the point where the firm's *long-run viability* is endangered. Long-run viability may conflict with stock price maximization and cost of capital minimization.

■ Managers often view financial distress with more concern than well-diversified investors because managers are typically not well diversified, and their careers, and thus the present value of their expected earnings, can be seriously affected by the onset of financial distress. Thus, it is not difficult to imagine that managers might be more "conservative" (*managerial conservatism*) in their use of leverage and might set a lower target capital structure than the one which maximizes stock price that the average stockholder would desire.

■ *Lenders' and rating agencies' attitudes* are frequently important determinants of financial structures.

    □ Lenders and rating agencies generally focus on the risk of default. Accordingly, they place considerable importance on a firm's times-interest-earned (TIE) ratio:

$$TIE = EBIT/\text{Interest charges}.$$

    □ Another measure that is often used to estimate default probability is the fixed charge coverage (FCC) ratio:

$$FCC = \frac{EBIT + \text{Lease payments}}{\text{Interest charges} + \text{Lease payments} + \frac{\text{Sinking fund payments}}{1 - T}}.$$

    □ Sinking fund payments are mandatory payments made to redeem debt. Note that this definition "grosses up" the sinking fund payments in recognition of the fact that these payments are made with after-tax dollars. Also note that lump-sum principal repayments might be included along with the sinking fund payments.

■ Firms should maintain *reserve borrowing capacity and financing flexibility* to preserve their ability to issue debt on favorable terms. To maintain reserve borrowing capacity that permits new debt financings at favorable terms on short notice, firms generally use less debt under "normal" conditions, thus presenting a stronger financial picture than they would otherwise have. This is not suboptimal from a long-run standpoint.

■ The effect on a management's control position may also influence the capital structure decision. If a firm's management just barely has voting control, then there could be an inclination to use more debt financing. Control considerations do not necessarily suggest the use of debt or of equity, but if management does not have majority control, the effects of capital structure on control will certainly be taken into account.

■ The following additional considerations are relevant to the capital structure decision:

☐ *Asset structure*. Firms with assets that are suitable as collateral for loans tend to use more debt than firms without such assets.

☐ *Growth rate*. Firms with high growth rates need lots of capital. Since flotation costs are generally considerably lower for debt than for equity, high-growth firms tend to use more debt than do slow-growth firms.

☐ *Profitability*. Firms that are highly profitable often have very low debt ratios. Although there is no theoretical justification, such firms simply do not need to sell much debt—they can do most of their financing through retained earnings.

☐ *Taxes*. The higher the firm's marginal tax rate, the greater the advantage of using debt.

A pragmatic approach to setting the target capital structure requires judgmental assumptions, but it also allows managers to consider how alternative capital structures would affect future profitability, coverage, and external financing requirements under a variety of assumptions.

■ The starting point for the analysis is a forecasting model that is set up to test the effects of capital structure changes.

■ The financial manager begins by entering base year values plus data on expected unit sales growth rates, expected inflation rates, and other known or estimated operating input data.

■ Next, the debt/equity mix, the debt maturity mix, and the component costs of the capital must be entered. Note that the component costs must reflect the particular capital structure being analyzed—the higher the debt ratio, the higher the component costs.

■ The model then forecasts balance sheets and income statements, as well as ROE, EPS, DPS, WACC, and projected stock prices for a specified number of years.

■ The model is then used to analyze alternative scenarios. This analysis takes two forms: (1) changing the financing inputs to get some idea of how the financing mix affects the key outputs and (2) changing the operating inputs to see how the firm's basic business risk affects the key outputs under various financing strategies. The model's outputs must be reviewed and analyzed, and a decision must be made as to the best capital structure.

■ It should be noted that while capital structure decisions do affect the prices of companies' stocks, those effects are small in comparison to the effects of operating decisions. Financial arrangements can facilitate or hamper operations, but the best of financial plans cannot overcome deficiencies in the operations area.

SELF-TEST QUESTIONS

Definitional

1. Capital structure decisions involve the tradeoff between _____ and _____ _____.

2. High operating leverage implies that a relatively _____ change in sales will result in a large change in ROE.

3. Business risk, in a stand-alone risk sense, is a function of the uncertainty inherent in projections of a firm's future _____ _____ _____ _____ _____.

4. Some of the factors that influence a firm's business risk include (1) demand variability, (2) sales price variability, (3) input cost variability, (4) ability to adjust output prices for changes in input costs, (5) ability to develop new products, and (6) the extent to which costs are fixed, which is called _____ _____.

5. Business risk represents the riskiness of the firm's operations if it uses no _____; financial risk represents the risk concentrated on the common stockholders as a result of using _____.

6. Financial leverage will be favorable and, hence, leverage up shareholder returns if the return on assets measured as EBIT/Total assets is greater than the _____ _____ _____.

7. Up to some point, expected EPS _____ as the debt/assets ratio increases.

8. MM proved, under a very restrictive set of assumptions, that a firm's value is unaffected by its _____ _____. Their theory produces what is often referred to as the _____ _____.

9. Higher fixed costs are generally associated with more _____ _____ firms and industries.

10. MM demonstrated that if they relaxed the no tax assumption, and if all of their other assumptions held, the asymmetry of the tax deductibility of interest versus the non-deductibility of dividend payments leads to a situation which calls for 100 percent _____ financing.

11. While an increase in the corporate tax rate makes _____ look better to corporations because _____ is tax deductible, an increase in the personal tax rate encourages additional _____ financing.

12. _____ _____ discourage firms from pushing their use of debt to excessive levels.

13. The _____-_____ theory of leverage recognizes the benefits of debt financing, favorable corporate tax treatment, versus the costs of debt financing, higher interest rates and bankruptcy costs.

14. _____ theory recognizes the fact that investors and managers do not have the same information regarding a firm's prospects. This is called _____ _____, and it has an important effect on the optimal capital structure.

15. The implications of the signaling theory for capital structure decisions is that firms should, in normal times, maintain _____ _____ _____ which can be used in the event that some especially good investment opportunity comes along.

16. _____ _____ are particularly likely when the firm's managers have too much cash at their disposal.

17. Firms with assets that are suitable as collateral for loans tend to use _____ debt than firms without such assets.

18. The higher the firm's marginal tax rate, the _____ the advantage of using debt.

19. While capital structure decisions do affect the prices of companies' stocks, those effects are small in comparison to the effects of _____ decisions.

20. The same debt ratio that maximizes firm value also _____ the firm's cost of capital.

Conceptual

21. Firm A has higher business risk than Firm B. Firm A can offset this by increasing its operating leverage.

    a. True   **b.** False

22. Two firms, although operating in different industries, have the same expected ROE and the same standard deviation of expected ROE. Thus, in a stand-alone risk, sense, the two firms must have the same financial risk.

    a. True   b. False

23. Assume a firm has zero debt. The use of some debt is bound to increase ROE.

    a. True   b. False

24. If a firm does use financial leverage, then $\sigma_{ROE} > \sigma_{ROE(U)}$, and the difference between the two is a measure of financial risk.

    a. True   b. False

25. Both price per share and EPS will be maximized at the same debt level; therefore the optimal capital structure is determined at the debt level where both price and EPS are maximized.

    a. True   b. False

26. A decrease in the debt ratio will have no effect on

    a. Financial risk.
    b. Stand-alone risk.
    c. Business risk.
    d. Market risk.
    e. Company-specific risk.

27. As a general rule, the capital structure that maximizes stock price also

    a. Maximizes the weighted average cost of capital.
    b. Maximizes EPS.
    c. Maximizes bankruptcy costs.
    d. Minimizes the weighted average cost of capital.
    e. Minimizes the required rate of return on equity.

28. Which of the following statements is most *correct*?

    a. If a firm is exposed to a high degree of business risk as a result of its high operating leverage, then it probably should offset this risk by using a larger-than-average amount of financial leverage. This follows because debt has a lower after-tax cost than equity.

    b. Financial risk can be reduced by replacing common equity with preferred stock.

    c. MM proved, under a very restrictive set of assumptions, that a firm's value is affected by its capital structure; therefore, it does matter how a firm finances its operations.

    d. In the text it was stated that the capital structure which minimizes the WACC also maximizes the firm's stock price and its total value, but generally not its expected EPS. One reason given for why debt is beneficial is that it shelters operating income from taxes, while it was stated that a disadvantage of excessive debt has to do with costs associated with bankruptcy and financial distress generally.

    e. All of the above statements are false.

SELF-TEST PROBLEMS

1. The Fisher Company will produce 50,000 10-gallon aquariums next year. Variable costs will equal 40 percent of dollar sales, while fixed costs total $100,000. At what price must each aquarium be sold for the firm's EBIT to be $90,000?

    a. $5.00   **b.** $5.33   **c.** $5.50   **d.** $6.00   **e.** $6.33

2. The Diamond Company has identified two methods of producing playing cards. One method involves using a machine having a fixed cost of $20,000 and variable costs of $1.00 per deck. The other method would use a less expensive machine having a fixed cost of $5,000, but it would require variable costs of $2.00 per deck. If the selling price per deck will be the same under each method, at what level of output would the two methods produce the same net operating income (EBIT)?

    a. 5,000   **b.** 10,000   **c.** 15,000   **d.** 20,000   **e.** 25,000

3. Brown Products is a new firm just starting operations. The firm will produce backpacks which will sell for $22.00 each. Fixed costs are $500,000 per year, and variable costs are $2.00 per unit of production. The company expects to sell 50,000 backpacks per year, and its effective federal-plus-state tax rate is 40 percent. Brown needs $2 million to build facilities, obtain working capital, and start operations. If Brown borrows part of the money, the interest charges will depend on the amount borrowed as follows:

Amount Borrowed	Percentage of Debt in Capital Structure	Interest Rate on Total Amount Borrowed
$ 200,000	10%	9.00%
400,000	20	9.50
600,000	30	10.00
800,000	40	15.00
1,000,000	50	19.00
1,200,000	60	26.00

Assume that stock can be sold at a price of $20 per share on the initial offering, regardless of how much debt the company uses. Then after the company begins operating, its price will be determined as a multiple of its earnings per share. The multiple (or the P/E ratio) will depend upon the capital structure as follows:

Debt/Assets	P/E	Debt/Assets	P/E
0.0	12.5	40.0	8.0
10.0	12.0	50.0	6.0
20.0	11.5	60.0	5.0
30.0	10.0		

What is Brown's optimal capital structure, which maximizes stock price, as measured by the debt/assets ratio?

a. 10%   **b.** 20%   **c.** 30%   **d.** 40%   **e.** 50%

(The following data apply to the next six problems.)

United Producers (UP), an unleveraged firm, has a total market value of $10 million, consisting of 500,000 shares of common stock selling at $20 per share. Management is considering issuing $2 million of debt at a before-tax cost of 12 percent, and using the proceeds to repurchase stock at the new equilibrium market price. If the plan is carried out, the required rate of return on equity will increase by 2 percentage points to 16 percent. UP's marginal tax rate is 40 percent, and it pays out all earnings as dividends.

4. What are UP's earnings before interest and taxes (EBIT) in millions of dollars?

    a. $1.4   **b.** $2.3   **c.** $3.0   **d.** $3.6   **e.** $4.2

5. Regardless of your answer to Self-Test Problem 4, assume that UP's EBIT is $2,800,000. What is the value of the firm in millions of dollars if the restructuring occurs?

    a. $9.76   **b.** $10.00   **c.** $10.56   **d.** $11.00   **e.** $11.60

6. Suppose a tax law change occurs which causes UP's marginal tax rate to decline to 30 percent. UP's EBIT remains at $2.8 million. Under these conditions, what is the value of the firm in millions of dollars at zero debt?

    a. $10   **b.** $11   **c.** $12   **d.** $13   **e.** $14

7. Under the conditions of Self-Test Problem 6, what is the value of the firm in millions of dollars if restructuring occurs?

    a. $13.2   **b.** $14.0   **c.** $14.2   **d.** $14.6   **e.** $14.8

8. Disregard the tax change in Self-Test Problem 6 and refer to the data in the original problem. Assume these data are correct, including an assumed EBIT of $2.8 million, except that use of financial leverage will increase the required rate of return on equity to only 15 percent, rather than 16 percent. What is the value of the firm in millions of dollars if the restructuring occurs?

    a. $9.4   **b.** $10.0   **c.** $12.2   **d.** $13.0   **e.** $13.1

9. Under the conditions of Self-Test Problem 8, what will be the new number of shares outstanding if the restructuring occurs? (Hint: $P_1 = [V_1 - D_0]/n_0$.)

    a. 500,000   **b.** 478,642   **c.** 438,231   **d.** 418,301   **e.** 396,547

(The following data apply to the next four problems.)

Union Brick Inc. (UBI) has a total market value of $200 million, consisting of 2 million shares of common stock selling for $50 per share and $100 million of 10 percent perpetual bonds currently selling at par. UBI pays out all earnings as dividends, and its marginal tax rate is 40 percent. The firm's earnings before interest and taxes (EBIT) are $30 million. Management is considering increasing UBI's debt to $140 million. The additional funds will be used to repurchase stock at the new equilibrium price. At a debt level of $140 million UBI's cost of debt is estimated at 12 percent and its cost of equity is estimated to be 15 percent.

10. What is UBI's required rate of return on equity at its current debt level of $100 million?

    a. 11.0%   **b.** 12.0%   **c.** 13.0%   **d.** 14.0%   **e.** 15.0%

11. Assume that UBI will increase its outstanding debt by calling in the old debt and issuing new debt, resulting in a debt level of $140 million. What would be UBI's new firm value in millions of dollars?

    a. $52.8   **b.** $100.0   **c.** $140.0   **d.** $192.8   **e.** $200.0

12. Refer to Self-Test Problem 11. What would be UBI's new stock price? (Hint: $P_1 = [V_1 - D_0]/n_0$.)

    a. $40.00   **b.** $46.40   **c.** $50.00   **d.** $50.40   **e.** $52.60

13. Now assume that UBI will increase its outstanding debt by issuing $40 million of new debt--the debt outstanding will not be called. What would be UBI's new stock price? (Hint: $P_1 = [V_1 - D_0]/n_0$.)

    a. $40.00   **b.** $46.40   **c.** $50.00   **d.** $50.40   **e.** $52.60

(The following data apply to the next four problems.)

Tapley Dental Supplies Inc. is in a stable, no-growth situation. Its $1,000,000 of debt consists of perpetuities which have a 10 percent coupon and sell at par. Tapley's EBIT is $500,000, its cost of equity is 15 percent, it has 100,000 shares of common stock outstanding that sell for $16 per share, all earnings are paid out as dividends, and its federal-plus-state tax rate is 40 percent. Tapley could borrow an additional $500,000 at an interest rate of 13 percent without having to retire the original debt, and it would use the proceeds to repurchase stock at the new equilibrium price. The increased risk from the additional leverage will raise the cost of equity to 17 percent.

14. What is the firm's current value in millions of dollars at a debt level of $1 million?

   a. $1.6   **b.** $2.0   **c.** $2.6   **d.** $1.8   **e.** $2.3

15. What is the firm's new value in millions of dollars at a debt level of $1.5 million, assuming that the original debt is not retired?

   a. $2.25   **b.** $2.45   **c.** $2.68   **d.** $1.75   **e.** $1.18

16. If the recapitalization takes place, what is Tapley's new stock price? (Hint: $P_1 = [V_1 - D_0]/n_0$.)

   a. $16.50   **b.** $16.23   **c.** $17.10   **d.** $16.82   **e.** $17.45

17. After the recapitalization takes place, how many shares of common stock will remain?

   a. 70,273   **b.** 69,697   **c.** 70,760   **d.** 71,347   **e.** 69,193

ANSWERS TO SELF-TEST QUESTIONS

1. risk, expected return
2. small
3. rate of return on assets
4. operating leverage
5. debt (leverage); debt (leverage)
6. cost of debt
7. increases

8. capital structure; irrelevance result
9. capital intensive
10. debt
11. debt; interest; equity
12. Bankruptcy costs
13. trade-off
14. Signaling; asymmetric information

15. reserve borrowing capacity
16. Agency conflicts
17. more

18. greater
19. operating
20. minimizes

21. b. Increasing operating leverage will increase Firm A's business risk.

22. b. The two firms would have the same stand-alone risk. Each could have different combinations of business and financial risk.

23. b. Debt financing only increases ROE if the cost of the debt is less than the return on the assets.

24. a. This statement is correct.

25. b. Price per share and EPS will not both be maximized at the same debt level. The optimal capital structure occurs where price per share is maximized.

26. c. Business risk is solely dependent upon the basic riskiness of the assets, and not the financing mix.

27. d. The optimal capital structure balances risk and return to maximize the stock price. The structure that maximizes stock price also minimizes the firm's cost of capital.

28. d. Statement a is false; if a firm is exposed to a high degree of business risk this implies that it should offset this risk by using a lower amount of financial leverage. Statement b is false; preferred stock is a fixed-income security, and as such, would increase financial risk. Statement c is false; MM proved exactly the opposite—under a very restrictive set of assumptions, a firm's value is not affected by its capital structure. Statement d is the correct choice.

SOLUTIONS TO SELF-TEST PROBLEMS

1. e. $\text{EBIT} = PQ - VQP - F$
$\$90,000 = P(50,000) - 0.4(50,000)P - \$100,000$
$30,000P = \$190,000$
$P = \$6.33.$

2. **c.** For the first method: EBIT = PQ - $1.00Q - $20,000.
For the second method: EBIT = PQ - $2.00Q - $5,000.

Now, equate the EBITs:
PQ - $1.00Q - $20,000 = PQ - $2.00Q - $5,000; $1.00Q = $15,000; Q = 15,000.

3. **b.** The first step is to calculate EBIT:

Sales in dollars [50,000($22)]	$1,100,000
Less: Fixed costs	500,000
Variable costs [50,000($2)]	100,000
EBIT	$ 500,000

The second step is to calculate the EPS at each debt/assets ratio using the formula:

$$\text{EPS} = \frac{(\text{EBIT} - \text{I})(1 - \text{T})}{\text{Shares outstanding}}.$$

Recognize (1) that I = Interest charges = (Dollars of debt)(Interest rate at each D/A ratio), and (2) that shares outstanding = (Assets − Debt)/Initial price per share = ($2,000,000 − Debt)/$20.00.

D/A	EPS	D/A	EPS
0%	$3.00	40%	$3.80
10	3.21	50	3.72
20	3.47	60	2.82
30	3.77		

Finally, the third step is to calculate the stock price at each debt/assets ratio using the following formula: Price = (P/E)(EPS).

D/A	Price	D/A	Price
0%	$37.50	40%	$30.40
10	38.52	50	22.32
20	39.91	60	14.10
30	37.70		

Thus, a debt/assets ratio of 20 percent maximizes stock price. This is the optimal capital structure.

4. b. $V_0 = S_0 = 500,000(\$20) = \$10,000,000$.

$$S_0 = \frac{(EBIT - k_dD)(1 - T)}{k_s} = \frac{EBIT(1 - T)}{k_s}\ .$$

Thus,

$$\$10,000,000 = \frac{EBIT(0.6)}{0.14}$$

$$0.6(EBIT) = \$1,400,000$$

$$EBIT = \$2,333,333\ .$$

5. e. $S_1 = \dfrac{(EBIT - k_dD)(1 - T)}{k_s}$

$$= \frac{[\$2,800,000 - 0.12(\$2,000,000)]0.6}{0.16} = \$9,600,000\ .$$

$V_1 = D_1 + S_1 = \$2,000,000 + \$9,600,000 = \$11,600,000$.

6. e. $S_0 = \dfrac{(EBIT - k_dD)(1 - T)}{k_s}$

$$= \frac{(\$2,800,000 - \$0)(0.7)}{0.14} = \$14,000,000 = V_0\ .$$

Now, less money is paid in taxes, more remains for the shareholders, and the value of the firm is higher.

7. a. $S_1 = \dfrac{(EBIT - k_dD)(1 - T)}{k_s}$

$$= \frac{[\$2,800,000 - 0.12(\$2,000,000)]0.7}{0.16} = \$11,200,000\ .$$

$V_1 = D_1 + S_1 = \$2,000,000 + \$11,200,000 = \$13,200,000$.

8. c. $S_1 = \dfrac{(EBIT - k_dD)(1 - T)}{k_s}$

$= \dfrac{[\$2,800,000 - 0.12(\$2,000,000)]0.6}{0.15} = \$10,240,000.$

$V_1 = D_1 + S_1 = \$2,000,000 + \$10,240,000 = \$12,240,000.$

9. d. First, find the equilibrium stock price:

$P_1 = \dfrac{V_1 - D_0}{n_0} = \dfrac{\$12,240,000 - \$0}{500,000} = \$24.48.$

Then, find the number of shares repurchased:

Shares repurchased $= \dfrac{\$2,000,000}{\$24.48} = 81,699.$

Finally, determine the shares remaining:

Shares remaining $= 500,000 - 81,699 = 418,301.$

10. b. $k_s = \dfrac{(EBIT - k_dD)(1 - T)}{S} = \dfrac{[\$30 - 0.10(\$100)]0.6}{\$100} = 12.0\%.$

11. d. $S_1 = \dfrac{(EBIT - k_dD)(1 - T)}{k_s} = \dfrac{[\$30 - 0.12(\$140)]0.6}{0.15} = \$52.8 \text{ million.}$

$V_1 = D_1 + S_1 = \$140 + \$52.8 = \$192.8 \text{ million.}$

12. b. $P_1 = \dfrac{V_1 - D_0}{n_0} = \dfrac{\$192.8 - \$100}{2} = \$46.40.$

Note that stock price decreases with the increase in leverage. Thus, the change should not be made.

13. d. $S_1 = \dfrac{(EBIT - k_dD - k_{d_1}D_1)(1 - T)}{k_s}$

$= \dfrac{[\$30 - 0.10(\$100) - 0.12(\$40)]0.6}{0.15} = \$60.8$ million.

$V_1 = S_1 + D_0 + D_1$.

But the value of the old debt, D_0, decreases because its riskiness has increased:

$D_0 = \dfrac{0.1(\$100)}{0.12} = \$83.33$ million.

Thus, $V_1 = \$60.8 + \$83.33 + \$40 = \$184.13$ million. Finally,

$P_1 = \dfrac{V_1 - D_0}{n_0} = \dfrac{\$184.13 - \$83.33}{2} = \$50.40$.

Note that the change should be made under these circumstances. Here some of the wealth of the old bondholders is being transferred to the shareholders.

14. c. $S_0 = \dfrac{(EBIT - k_dD)(1 - T)}{k_s} = \dfrac{(\$500,000 - \$100,000)(0.6)}{0.15} = \$1.6$ million.

$V_0 = S_0 + D_0 = \$1.6$ million $+ \$1.0$ million $= \$2.6$ million.

15. b. $S_1 = \dfrac{[EBIT - k_dD - k_{d_1}D_1][1 - T]}{k_s}$

$= \dfrac{[\$500,000 - \$100,000 - \$65,000](0.6)}{0.17} = \$1,182,353$.

$V_1 = S_1 + D_0 + D_1$

$D_0 = 0.1(\$1,000,000)/0.13 = \$769,231$.

$V_1 = \$1,182,353 + \$769,231 + \$500,000 = \$2,451,584$.

16. d. $P_1 = (\$2,451,584 - \$769,231)/100,000 = \$16.82$.

17. a. Shares remaining $= 100,000 - \$500,000/\$16.82 = 70,273$.

CHAPTER 14

CAPITAL STRUCTURE DECISIONS: EXTENSIONS

OVERVIEW

Chapter 13 presented the basic material necessary to understand capital structure concepts, including a brief introduction to capital structure theory. We saw that debt financing concentrates a firm's business risk on its stockholders, but debt also increases the expected return on equity. We also saw that there is some optimal level of debt that maximizes a company's stock price, but that it is very difficult to identify the optimal capital structure. In this chapter, we go into more detail on capital structure theory, which will give you a better understanding of the benefits and costs associated with debt financing.

OUTLINE

Beginning in 1958, Modigliani and Miller (MM) addressed the capital structure issue in a rigorous, scientific fashion. The result is the well-known MM propositions.

■ MM began with a set of assumptions including constant debt costs, zero brokerage costs, perpetual cash flows, and zero growth. Initially, they also assumed zero taxes. MM used an arbitrage proof to develop two propositions.

 ☐ Proposition I:

$$V_L = V_U = EBIT/WACC = EBIT/k_{sU},$$

where V_L = value of a leveraged firm and V_U = value of an unleveraged firm in the same risk class.

  ▸ Proposition I tells us that the value of a firm is established by capitalizing the expected net operating income at the firm's weighted average cost of capital which is a constant equal to the cost of equity of an unleveraged (zero debt) firm. Thus, Proposition I implies that the value of a firm is independent of its leverage.

  ▸ Proposition I also implies (1) that a firm's WACC is completely independent of its capital structure, and (2) that the WACC for any firm, regardless of the amount of debt it uses, is equal to the cost of equity it would have if it used no debt.

☐ Proposition II:

$$k_{sL} = k_{sU} + \text{Risk premium} = k_{sU} + (k_{sU} - k_d)(D/S).$$

- ▸ Here we see that the cost of equity to a leveraged firm, k_{sL}, is equal to the cost of equity to an unleveraged firm in the same risk class, k_{sU}, plus a risk premium whose size depends on both the differential between the costs of equity and debt to an unleveraged firm and the amount of leverage used.
- ▸ Proposition II states that as the firm's use of debt increases, its cost of equity also rises, and in a mathematically precise manner.

■ Taken together, the two MM propositions imply that the inclusion of more debt in the capital structure will not increase a firm's value because the benefits of lower cost debt will be exactly offset by an increase in the riskiness, hence, in the cost of equity. Thus, the MM theory implies that in a world without taxes, both the value of a firm and its overall cost of capital are unaffected by its capital structure.

■ MM used an *arbitrage proof* to support their propositions. They showed that, under their assumptions, if two companies differed only (1) in the way they are financed and (2) in their total market values, then investors would sell shares of the higher-valued firm, buy those of the lower-valued firm, and continue this process until the companies had exactly the same market value.

MM reworked their theory in 1963 by adding corporate taxes. The result was two additional propositions. With corporate income taxes, they concluded that leverage will increase a firm's value. This occurs because interest on debt is a tax-deductible expense, hence more of a leveraged firm's operating income flows through to investors.

■ Proposition I:

$$V_L = V_U + TD = EBIT(1 - T)/k_{sU} + TD.$$

- ☐ Thus, the value of a leveraged firm is equal to the value of the unleveraged firm in the same risk class plus the gain from leverage, the value of the tax savings which equals the corporate tax rate times the amount of debt used.
- ☐ Note that for an unleveraged firm with perpetual cash flows, $EBIT(1 - T)$ = Net income = Total dividends. Thus, the value of the unleveraged firm is equal to the perpetual dividend divided by k_{sU}.
- ☐ Also note that the differential between V_U and V_L increases as the firm's use of debt increases, so a firm's value is maximized at virtually 100 percent debt financing.

■ Proposition II:

$$k_{sL} = k_{sU} + (k_{sU} - k_d)(1 - T)(D/S).$$

☐ Now, the cost of equity for a leveraged firm is still equal to the cost of equity for an unleveraged firm plus a risk premium, but the risk premium is reduced by the term $(1 - T)$.

☐ Thus, when corporate taxes are introduced, the cost of equity rises at a slower rate than it did in the absence of corporate taxes. Further, the cost of debt is reduced by the tax deductibility of interest payments. These two factors combine to produce the increase in firm value which is shown by Proposition I.

☐ MM's model with corporate taxes leads to the conclusion that firms should use almost 100 percent debt. However, firms do not follow this prescription, and hence theorists have been searching for other models which better describe actual behavior.

In our discussion of business and financial risk, we focused on stand-alone risk. Now we shift our focus from a stand-alone risk to a market risk perspective.

■ Robert Hamada, using the Capital Asset Pricing Model (CAPM) and MM with corporate taxes model, developed an expression for the cost of equity to a leveraged firm:

$$\begin{aligned} k_{sL} &= \text{Risk-free rate} + \text{Business risk premium} + \text{Financial risk premium} \\ &= k_{RF} + (k_M - k_{RF})b_U + (k_M - k_{RF})b_U(1 - T)(D/S). \end{aligned}$$

■ Equating the SML equation with Hamada's equation for k_{sL}, we ultimately obtain:

$$b = b_U[1 + (1 - T)(D/S)].$$

■ Thus, under the MM and CAPM assumptions, the beta of a leveraged firm is equal to the beta the firm would have if it used zero debt, adjusted upward by a factor that depends on (1) the corporate tax rate and (2) the amount of financial leverage employed.

■ A firm's market risk, which is measured by b, depends on both the firm's business risk as reflected by b_U, and its financial risk as measured by $b_U(1 - T)(D/S)$.

■ Within a market risk context, a firm's business risk is measured by its unleveraged beta, b_U, its overall risk is measured by its leveraged beta, b, and its financial risk is measured by the difference, $b - b_U$.

■ The Hamada relationship can also be used to estimate the cost of equity for a firm or division by leveraging up or down the betas of comparable proxy firms to reflect the firm's or division's capital structure and tax rate.

In 1976, Miller presented a capital structure model which includes not only corporate taxes, but personal taxes as well.

■ The *Miller Model* takes this form:

$$V_U = \frac{EBIT(1 - T_c)(1 - T_s)}{k_{sU}}, \text{ and}$$

$$V_L = V_U + [1 - \frac{(1 - T_c)(1 - T_s)}{(1 - T_d)}]D.$$

☐ Here T_c is the corporate tax rate, T_s is the personal tax rate on stock income, and T_d is the personal tax rate on income from debt.

☐ The term in brackets, multiplied by D, is the gain from leverage. The bracketed term replaces the factor $T = T_c$ in the MM model with corporate taxes.

☐ If all taxes are ignored, then $T_c = T_s = T_d = 0$, and the model reduces to the original MM model without taxes.

☐ If we ignore personal taxes, then $T_s = T_d = 0$, and the model reduces to the MM model with corporate taxes.

■ The gain from leverage in the Miller model depends on the values of T_c, T_s, and T_d as well as the amount of debt financing.

☐ Because taxes on capital gains are deferred (and capped at 28 percent), the effective tax rate on stock income is normally less than the effective tax rate on bond income.

☐ When $T_s < T_d$, the bracketed term is less than T_c, and the value of financial leverage is less than it would be in the absence of personal taxes.

■ Thus, Miller's model confirms the earlier MM conclusion that the use of corporate debt increases the value of a firm, but the advantage is clearly less than TD, and hence personal taxes reduce the benefits of corporate debt. Note, however, that the Miller model still prescribes close to 100 percent debt as the value-maximizing capital structure.

While the conclusions of the two MM models and the Miller model follow logically from the initial assumptions, these theories lack support because (1) their assumptions do not reflect

actual market conditions, and (2) more important, their prescriptions are not followed. Some of the main objections include the following:

■ Both MM and Miller assumed that personal and corporate leverage are perfect substitutes.

■ Brokerage costs are assumed away, making the switch from leveraged to unleveraged costless.

■ To reach the conclusions of MM and Miller, one must assume that both corporations and investors can borrow at the risk-free rate.

■ Miller concluded that equilibrium would be reached, but to reach equilibrium the tax benefit from corporate debt must be the same for all firms and must be constant for an individual firm regardless of the amount of leverage used.

■ MM and Miller assumed that there are no financial distress costs and they ignore agency costs.

■ MM and Miller assume that all market participants have identical information about firms' prospects.

A potential problem with the MM and Miller models is that they ignore financial distress and agency costs. Quite a few firms go bankrupt every year, and the costs of financial distress, as well as agency costs, can be significant.

■ Actual bankruptcy results in extraordinary costs such as forced sale of assets at below-market prices, deterioration of property, and court and administrative costs. The threat of financial distress also involves costs, since managers must spend more time on fending off bankruptcy than on making good operating decisions, as well as taking costly actions in attempts to ward off distress.

■ In general, the probability of financial distress increases as more debt is used. The greater the use of debt financing, and the larger the fixed interest charges, the greater the probability that a decline in earnings will lead to financial distress, hence the higher the probability that the costs of financial distress will be incurred.

■ Agency costs also tend to increase as more and more debt is used.

■ When these costs are considered, MM's Proposition I, with corporate taxes, becomes:

$$V_L = V_U + TD - \text{(PV of expected financial distress costs)} - \text{(PV of agency costs)}.$$

■ This relationship is shown in Figure 1.

Figure 1
Debt Usage versus Firm Value

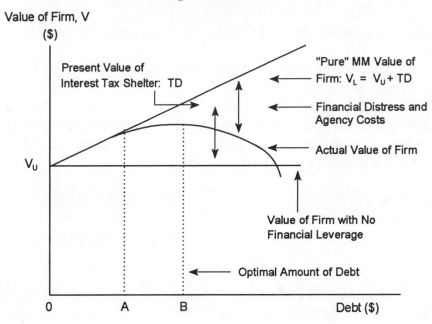

■ Here we see that the tax shelter effect dominates until debt reaches Point A. After Point A, the financial distress and agency costs begin to offset the tax advantages of debt financing. At Point B, the marginal tax benefits of debt are exactly offset by the marginal financial distress and agency costs, and beyond Point B, the disadvantages of using debt outweigh the benefits. However, the financial distress and agency costs cannot be estimated easily, and it is very difficult, if not impossible, to identify Point B in practice with any precision.

■ Note that financial distress and agency costs can also be added to the Miller model. When these are added, the relationship between value and debt is the same as when these costs are added to the MM with corporate taxes model. However, the "`Pure' MM Value of Firm" line would be less steep under Miller since the value of debt financing is reduced. Further, the Y intercept would be lowered because the addition of personal taxes reduces the value of the unleveraged firm.

Both the MM with corporate taxes and Miller models modified to include financial distress and agency costs are called trade-off models. That is, the optimal capital structure is found

by balancing the tax shield benefits of leverage against the costs of leverage, and hence the costs and benefits are "traded off" against one another.

■ The trade-off models cannot be used to specify a firm's precise optimal capital structures, but they can enable us to make three statements about leverage:
  ☐ Firms with inherently risky assets experience higher variability of returns and therefore face a greater probability of financial distress at any debt level. Given the higher probability of financial distress at any level of debt, firms with higher business risk should borrow less than firms with lower business risk.
  ☐ Specialized assets, intangible assets, and growth opportunities lose more value in financial distress, and hence firms using these types of assets should use less debt than firms employing standardized, tangible assets.
  ☐ Firms paying taxes at the highest rates gain the most benefit from debt financing and, hence, should carry more debt than firms in lower tax brackets.

■ Although the trade-off models present a logical framework for thought, empirical support for the trade-off models is not strong, suggesting that factors that are not incorporated into the models are at work.

The asymmetric information theory of capital structure was developed in an attempt to reconcile the MM/Miller theories with the pecking order method of financing observed by Professor Gordon Donaldson. By allowing that asymmetric (or different) information exists for different groups of market participants, certain actions may be implied for corporate financial policy.

■ Donaldson observed that there is a "pecking order" of financing, not the balanced approach that would result if the trade-off models accurately described real-world behavior.

■ The asymmetric information theory attempts to explain this "pecking order."
  ☐ Information asymmetries often exist between managers and investors.
  ☐ When such situations exist, a firm will issue new stock only when its stock price is overvalued by the market. If its stock is undervalued, the firm will issue debt.
  ☐ Because investors recognize all this, they tend to mark down a company's share price when it announces plans to issue new shares, since chances are that the announcement is signaling bad news, not good news.
  ☐ If managers believe that new stock sales will be regarded as negative signals, then they should maintain some "reserve borrowing capacity," so they can always issue debt on favorable terms if external financing is needed.

- Industries which hold a significant amount of proprietary information, such as pharmaceutical or semiconductor industries, will have a higher degree of asymmetric information than retailing or trucking industries. Although asymmetric information theory is applicable to all firms, its impact on managerial decisions varies from firm to firm.

- Emerging firms with limited capital but good growth opportunities are recognized as having to use external financing, so the announcement of new stock offerings by a new company is not viewed with as much concern by investors as are offerings by mature firms with limited growth opportunities.

The great contribution of the trade-off models developed by MM and Miller is that these models identified the specific costs and benefits of using debt. Prior to these models, no capital structure theory existed, and we had no systematic approach to analyzing the effects of financial leverage.

- The trade-off view is summarized graphically in Figure 2.

Figure 2
The Effects of Debt Financing

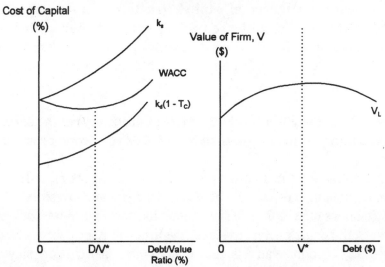

- The left-hand graph shows the relationship between the debt ratio and capital costs. Both the cost of equity and cost of debt rise steadily with increasing leverage, but the rate of increase accelerates sharply at higher debt levels. The weighted average cost of capital first declines, then hits a minimum, and then begins to rise. Note, however, that the WACC curve is shallow, indicating the debt ratio does not have a pronounced effect on WACC over a fairly wide range of values.

☐ The right-hand graph shows that firm value first rises with debt usage, hits a peak, and then falls. Again, the relationship is such that small deviations from the optimal debt ratio do not have a large impact on value.

☐ Note in the figure that the same debt ratio that minimizes the cost of capital also maximizes firm value. Thus, the optimal capital structure can be defined in terms of either cost minimization or value maximization because the same capital structure does both.

■ Little disagreement exists in either business or academic circles that the general situation described above is correct. However, details can only be discovered by empirical testing. Unfortunately, firms which differ only in capital structure do not exist, and future earnings are not known with any certainty. Thus, empirical tests have not produced conclusive results.

■ We believe that there is a net benefit to debt financing, at least out to some point, but we also believe that firms should maintain a borrowing reserve. Thus, firms use debt on the basis of their tax rates, asset structures, and inherent riskiness, but they also try to maintain the ability to issue new debt at favorable rates if it becomes necessary to raise external capital when chaotic market conditions exist.

Wide variations in the use of financial leverage occur both across industries and among the individual firms in each industry. In addition, capital structures also change over time.

Firms should focus on market value capital structures and base their cost of capital calculations on market value weights. Because market values do change, it would be impossible to keep the actual capital structure on target at all times, but this fact in no way detracts from the validity of market value targets.

SELF-TEST QUESTIONS

Definitional

1. The addition of financial distress and agency costs leads to a WACC curve which first _____, then reaches a _____, and then _____.

2. The optimal capital structure is that structure at which the marginal _____ of leverage equal the marginal _____.

3. The asymmetric information theory relaxes the MM models' assumption that _____ _____ exists.

4. By allowing for asymmetric information, Donaldson's _____ _____ method of financing can be explained.

5. Difficulties in estimating the relationship between _____ ratios and the costs of _____ and _____ have made some managers reluctant to rely heavily on quantitative analysis to set the target capital structure.

6. Conservative financial managers may try to maintain a target capital structure that is _____ than optimal.

7. External capital is particularly important to firms with high _____ _____.

8. Owner/managers may prefer additional _____ as opposed to common stock in order to maintain _____ of the company.

9. A firm's cost of capital should be based on _____ _____ weights. However, these weights are based on its _____ capital structure rather than its current capital structure.

Conceptual

10. While asymmetric information theory applies to all firms, its impact on managerial decisions varies from firm to firm.

   a. True   b. False

11. As a general rule, the capital structure which maximizes stock price (firm value) also

   a. Maximizes earnings per share.
   b. Minimizes the probability of financial distress.
   c. Minimizes both the cost of equity and the cost of debt.
   d. Answers a, b, and c above are all correct.
   e. Answers a, b, and c above are all incorrect.

12. Firms should use more debt if

    a. They are in a lower tax bracket.
    b. They have stable expected returns on their assets (low business risk).
    c. They employ standardized, tangible assets.
    d. Answers b and c above are correct.
    e. Answers a, b, and c above are correct.

13. If information asymmetries exist, then management is motivated to issue new stock only if the stock is

    a. Overvalued.
    b. Undervalued.
    c. Fairly valued.

14. Which of the following statements is most *correct*?

    a. The "pure MM" theory of capital structure, when income taxes are considered, suggests that the value of a firm rises as it uses more and more debt and that this increase is due to tax savings. Thus, the optimal capital structure under MM theory calls for 100 percent debt.
    b. When the "pure MM" theory is modified to include bankruptcy costs, an optimal capital structure with some debt, but less than 100 percent debt, is found for the "typical" firm.
    c. Under the signaling, or asymmetric information theory, the issuance of new common stock by a mature company is taken by investors as bad news. As a result, new stock issues depress the stock price. This implies that firms should, under normal conditions, use less debt than they otherwise might so as to have a reserve borrowing capacity which would enable them to avoid issuing stock under most conditions.
    d. The above statements are all true.
    e. The above statements are all false.

SELF-TEST PROBLEMS

(The following data apply to the next two problems.)

A firm with no debt financing has a firm value of $20 million. It has a corporate marginal tax rate of 34 percent. The firm's investors are estimated to have marginal tax rates of 31 percent on interest income and a weighted average of 28 percent on stock income. The firm is planning to change its capital structure by issuing $10 million in debt, and repurchasing $10 million of common stock.

1. According to the Modigliani-Miller view with corporate taxes, what is the value in millions of dollars of the leveraged firm?

    a. $20.00   **b.** $22.44   **c.** $23.40   **d.** $26.40   **e.** $30.00

2. According to the Miller view with corporate and personal taxes, what is the gain from leverage in millions of dollars?

    a. $0.00   **b.** $3.10   **c.** $4.60   **d.** $6.40   **e.** $8.00

(The following data apply to the next three problems.)

The Ensyder Trading Company (ETC) is a zero growth firm with an EBIT of $250,000 and a corporate tax rate of 40 percent. ETC uses $1 million of debt financing, and the cost of equity of an unleveraged firm in the same risk class is 15 percent. The personal tax rates of ETC's investors are 30 percent on interest income and 20 percent (on average) on income from common stocks.

3. What is the value of ETC according to MM with corporate taxes?

    a. $1,000,000   **b.** $1,114,000   **c.** $1,314,000   **d.** $1,400,000   **e.** $2,000,000

4. What is ETC's value according to Miller (including personal taxes)?

    a. $1,000,000   **b.** $1,114,000   **c.** $1,314,000   **d.** $1,600,000   **e.** $2,000,000

5. Suppose that the present value of financial distress costs is estimated to be $800,000, and that, at a debt level of $1 million, ETC has a 20 percent probability of going bankrupt. Further, assume that the present value of agency costs are $50,000 at a $1,000,000 debt level. What is the firm's value if these costs are added to the Miller model?

   a. $904,000   **b.** $1,114,000   **c.** $1,314,000   **d.** $1,600,000   **e.** $2,000,000

(The following data apply to the next five problems.)

Unleveraged Corporation (Firm U) has a total market value of $500,000, a tax rate of 40 percent, and earnings before interest and taxes (EBIT) of $100,000. Leveraged Corporation (Firm L) is identical in all respects to Firm U, but Firm L has $200,000 market (and book) value of debt outstanding. Firm L pays total annual interest of $16,000 on this debt. Both firms satisfy the MM assumptions.

6. What is the value of Firm L according to MM's Proposition I with corporate taxes?

   a. $500,000   **b.** $520,000   **c.** $540,000   **d.** $560,000   **e.** $580,000

7. What is Firm U's cost of equity?

   a. 10.00%   **b.** 10.34%   **c.** 11.00%   **d.** 12.00%   **e.** 13.26%

8. What is Firm L's cost of equity?

   a. 10.00%   **b.** 10.34%   **c.** 11.00%   **d.** 12.00%   **e.** 13.26%

9. What is Firm L's weighted average cost of capital?

   a. 10.00%   **b.** 10.34%   **c.** 11.00%   **d.** 12.00%   **e.** 13.26%

10. An alternative equation for a firm's cost of capital is

$$\text{WACC} = \frac{\text{EBIT}(1-T)}{V}.$$

What is Firm L's weighted average cost of capital according to this formula?

   a. 10.00%   **b.** 10.34%   **c.** 11.00%   **d.** 12.00%   **e.** 13.26%

ANSWERS TO SELF-TEST QUESTIONS

1. declines; minimum; rises
2. benefits; costs
3. perfect information
4. pecking order
5. debt; debt; equity

6. less
7. growth rates
8. debt; control
9. market value; target

10. a. This statement is correct.

11. e. The capital structure which maximizes stock price also minimizes the firm's weighted average cost of capital. The probability of financial distress is minimized at zero debt. Also, note that neither the cost of debt nor the cost of equity is minimized at the optimal capital structure.

12. d. Firms gain the most benefits from using debt when they are in the highest tax bracket. Firms with highly variable expected returns and intangible, specialized assets should use lower levels of debt.

13. a. Management will want to issue new stock only if the excess value will benefit the existing stockholders and not be passed on to new investors.

14. d. Statements a, b, and c are all correct; therefore, statement d is the proper choice.

SOLUTIONS TO SELF-TEST PROBLEMS

1. c. $V_L = V_U + TD = \$20 + 0.34(\$10) = \$20 + \$3.4 = \$23.4$ million.

2. b. Gain from leverage $= [1 - \dfrac{(1 - T_c)(1 - T_s)}{(1 - T_d)}]D$

$= [1 - \dfrac{(1 - 0.34)(1 - 0.28)}{(1 - 0.31)}]\$10$

$= [1 - 0.689]\$10 = 0.311(\$10) = \$3.11$ million.

Note that the gain from leverage is reduced when personal taxes are added.

3. d. $V_L = V_U + TD = \dfrac{EBIT(1 - T)}{k_{sU}} + TD$

$= \dfrac{\$250,000(0.6)}{0.15} + 0.4(\$1,000,000) = \$1,000,000 + \$400,000 = \$1,400,000.$

4. b. $V_L = V_U + [1 - \dfrac{(1 - T_c)(1 - T_s)}{(1 - T_d)}]D$

$= V_U + [1 - \dfrac{0.6(0.8)}{0.7}]\$1,000,000$

$= V_U + 0.314(\$1,000,000) = V_U + \$314,000.$

Now, the addition of personal taxes also reduces the value of V_U:

$$V_U = \dfrac{EBIT(1 - T_c)(1 - T_s)}{k_{sU}} = \dfrac{\$250,000(0.6)(0.8)}{0.15} = \$800,000.$$

Thus, $V_L = \$800,000 + \$314,000 = \$1,114,000.$

5. a. $V_L = V_{Miller} - PV$ (Financial distress costs) - PV (Agency costs)
   $= \$1,114,000 - 0.2(\$800,000) - \$50,000 = \$904,000.$

6. e. $V_L = V_U + TD = \$500,000 + 0.4(\$200,000) = \$500,000 + \$80,000 = \$580,000.$

7. d. $V_U = \dfrac{EBIT(1 - T)}{k_{sU}};$ $\$500,000 = \dfrac{\$100,000(0.6)}{k_{sU}};$ $k_{sU} = \dfrac{\$60,000}{\$500,000} = 12.0\%.$

8. e. First, note that Firm L's cost of debt is 8.0 percent:

k_d = \$16,000/\$200,000 = 8.0%.

Next, note that V_L = \$580,000 and D = \$200,000. Thus, Firm L's equity value is S = \$580,000 - \$200,000 = \$380,000. Finally,

k_{sL} = k_{sU} + (k_{sU} - k_d)(1 - T)(D/S)
    = 12.0% + (12.0% - 8.0%)(0.6)(\$200,000/\$380,000)
    = 12.0% + 1.26% = 13.26%.

9. b. WACC = $w_d k_d$(1 - T) + $w_{ce} k_s$
        = (\$200,000/\$580,000)(8.00%)(0.6) + (\$380,000/\$580,000)(13.26%)
        = 10.34%.

10. b. WACC = EBIT(1 - T)/V = \$100,000(0.6)/\$580,000 = 10.34%.

CHAPTER 15

DIVIDEND POLICY

OVERVIEW

Dividend policy involves the decision whether to pay out earnings as dividends or to retain and reinvest them in the firm, and it has two key elements: (1) What fraction of earnings should be paid out, on average, over time? This is the *target payout policy* decision. (2) Should the firm attempt to maintain a steady, stable dividend growth rate, or should it vary its dividend payments from year to year depending on its internal need for funds and on its cash flows? This is the *dividend stability policy*. We also examine two related issues: stock repurchases and stock splits.

OUTLINE

Dividend policy theories attempt to establish the relationship between a firm's payout policy and its value. In essence, they attempt to determine whether investors prefer dividends or capital gains.

- ■ Modigliani and Miller (MM) argue that a firm's value is determined solely by its basic earnings power and its business risk. Thus, the value of the firm depends on the earning power of its assets rather than on how the assets are financed or how the firm's earnings are split between dividends and retained earnings. This is called *dividend irrelevance*.
  - □ MM prove their proposition, but only under a set of restrictive assumptions, including (1) zero taxes, (2) zero flotation and transactions costs, (3) independence between dividend policy and equity costs, and (4) symmetric information.
  - □ Obviously, firms and investors do pay taxes, and firms do incur flotation costs. Thus, the MM conclusions on dividend irrelevance may not be valid under real-world conditions.

- ■ Another theory, the *bird-in-the-hand theory*, has been proposed by Myron Gordon and John Lintner.
  - □ Gordon and Lintner argue that k_s increases as the dividend payout is reduced because investors view dividend payments as more certain than the capital gains that presumably result from retained earnings.

☐ MM call the Gordon-Lintner argument the "bird-in-the-hand fallacy" because, in MM's view, most investors simply reinvest their dividends in the same or similar firms, and the riskiness of the firm's cash flows to investors in the long run is determined by the riskiness of the firm's cash flows from operating assets.

■ A third theory, the *tax preference theory*, is based on the fact that capital gains are effectively taxed at a lower rate than dividend income because taxes on capital gains are capped at 28 percent and are deferred until the end of the holding period.

☐ Because of the tax deferral feature on capital gains (and the fact that capital gains taxes are capped at 28 percent), investors should require higher rates of return on high dividend yield stocks than they do on low dividend yield stocks, other things held constant.

☐ Under the old tax laws before 1986, capital gains were taxed at a significantly lower rate as well as deferred, making the yield differentials even more pronounced.

■ Note that each of these theories leads to a different prescription for financial managers.

☐ According to MM, there is no optimal dividend payout policy.

☐ Gordon and Lintner argue that firms should set high dividend payout ratios to maximize stock price.

☐ The tax preference theory leads to the opposite conclusion: Firms should set low dividend payout ratios.

■ Unfortunately, empirical testing has not produced definitive results regarding which theory is correct.

There are three other issues which have a bearing on optimal dividend policy.

■ It has been observed that an announcement of a dividend increase is often accompanied by an increase in the price of the stock.

☐ This might be interpreted by some that investors prefer dividends over capital gains, thus supporting the Gordon-Lintner hypothesis.

☐ However, MM argue that a dividend increase is a "signal" to investors that the firm's management forecasts good future earnings. Thus, MM argue that investors' reactions to dividend announcements do not necessarily show that investors prefer dividends to retained earnings. Rather, the fact that the stock price changes merely indicates that there is an important *information, or signaling, content* in dividend announcements.

■ MM also suggest that a *clientele effect* might exist.
   □ Some stockholders prefer current income; they would want the firm to pay out a high percentage of its earnings.
   □ Other stockholders have no need for current income; they would simply reinvest any dividends received, after first paying income taxes on the dividend income. These stockholders would want the firm to retain most of its earnings.
   □ Thus, a firm attracts a specific clientele that is drawn to its dividend policy.
   □ Empirical evidence supports the contention that a clientele effect does exist, but MM argue that one clientele is as good as another, so the existence of clienteles does not imply that one payout policy is better than another. However, MM offer no proof that the aggregate makeup of investors permits firms to disregard clientele effects.

■ The relationship between dividend policy and agency costs has a bearing on the optimal dividend policy. One of the most perplexing issues in dividend policy is why firms pay dividends and then issue new securities.
   □ One potential answer is the *signaling value* inherent in dividends. However, it is hard to imagine that the value produced by signaling is greater than the costs associated with new security issues.
   □ A second explanation for paying dividends relates to *agency costs*. An agency conflict exists between managers and stockholders, and because of this potential agency conflict, stockholders are willing to incur agency costs to monitor managerial actions. The monitoring problem is substantially reduced when firms must frequently raise external capital.
   □ For any given level of investment, the higher the dividend payout, the more frequently the firm must issue new securities. A higher payout policy thus forces firms to undergo the frequent scrutiny of the capital markets, and this appraisal process *mitigates* the agency problem. If the costs of paying dividends (which includes flotation for additional securities) are less than the value inherent in the additional monitoring, then large dividend payouts make sense.

As we noted at the beginning of the chapter, the decision as to how stable over time a firm's dividend should be is an important issue.

■ Firms' profits and cash flows vary over time, as do their investment opportunities. Taken alone, this suggests that corporations should vary their dividends over time.

■ However, many stockholders rely on dividends to meet expenses. Further, dividend cuts could be interpreted by investors as signals of bad news.

■ How should the balance be struck; that is, how stable and dependable should a firm attempt to make its dividends? Although it is impossible to give a definitive answer to this question, the following points are relevant:

☐ Virtually every publicly owned company makes a 5- to 10-year financial forecast of earnings and dividends. For a "normal" company, such forecasts typically project higher earnings and dividends.

☐ Years ago, when inflation was not persistent, the term "stable dividend policy" meant a policy of paying the same dollar dividend year after year. Today, most companies and stockholders expect earnings and dividends to grow over time as a result of both inflation and retentions. Thus, today a *stable dividend policy* generally means increasing the dollar dividend at a reasonably steady rate.

☐ Companies with volatile earnings and cash flows would be reluctant to make a commitment to increase the dividend each year, but they would still plan to increase dividends when the situation warrants.

■ Dividend stability has two components:

☐ How dependable is the growth rate?

☐ How dependable is the current dividend; that is, can investors at least count on receiving the current dividend in the future?

■ Most observers believe that *dividend stability* is desirable, even though statistical problems prevent empirical tests from proving the point. If this position is correct, then:

☐ Investors would prefer a stock that pays more predictable dividends to one that has the same expected present value of dividends but pays them in a more erratic manner.

☐ This means that the cost of equity would be minimized, and shareholder wealth maximized, if a firm stabilizes its dividends as much as possible, given its requirements to support capital growth.

In the preceding sections we have seen that investors may or may not prefer dividends to capital gains, but they do seem to prefer predictable to unpredictable dividends. Given this situation, how should firms set their basic dividend policies?

■ The *residual dividend model* is based on the premise that investors prefer to have a firm retain and reinvest earnings rather than pay them out in dividends if the rate of return the firm can earn on reinvested earnings exceeds the rate of return investors can obtain for themselves on other investments of comparable risk. Further, it is less expensive for the firm to use retained earnings than it is to issue new common stock. A firm using the residual model would follow these four steps:

☐ Determine the optimal capital budget.

☐ Determine the amount of equity required to finance the optimal capital budget, recognizing that the funds used will consist of both equity and debt to preserve the optimal capital structure.

☐ To the extent possible, use retained earnings to supply the equity required.

☐ Pay dividends only if more earnings are available than are needed to support the optimal capital budget.

■ Since both investment opportunities and earnings vary from year to year, strict adherence to the residual dividend model would result in dividend variability—one year the firm might declare zero dividends because investment opportunities were good (or profitability poor), and the next year it might pay a large dividend because investment opportunities were poor (or profitability good).

■ Because annual use of the residual model leads to unstable dividends, it is not used to set annual dividend payments. However, it is used, in conjunction with a firm's 5-year forecast, to determine a *long-run target payout ratio*.

■ Note that dividends are paid from cash flow, and not from earnings, so target payout ratios are set more on the basis of *cash flows* than on earnings. Cash flows reflect a firm's ability to pay dividends, while current earnings are heavily influenced by accounting practices and do not necessarily reflect the ability to pay dividends.

■ The actual payment procedure is as follows:

☐ On the *declaration date* the directors meet and declare the regular dividend.

☐ At the close of the business on the *holder-of-record* date, the company closes its stock transfer books and makes up a list of shareholders as of that date.

☐ The securities industry has set up a convention of declaring that the right to the dividend remains with the stock until four business days prior to the holder-of-record date. The date when the right to the dividend leaves the stock is called the *ex-dividend date*.

☐ The company actually mails the checks to the holders of record on the *payment date*.

Firms should try to establish a rational dividend policy and then stick with it. Dividend policy can be changed, but this can cause problems because such changes can inconvenience the firm's existing stockholders, send unintended signals, and convey the impression of dividend instability, all of which can have negative implications for stock prices. Still, economic circumstances do change, and occasionally such changes may dictate that a firm alter its dividend policy.

During the 1970s, most large companies instituted dividend reinvestment plans (DRPs), whereby stockholders can automatically reinvest their dividends in the stock of the paying corporation.

■ There are two types of dividend reinvestment plans:
- ☐ In an *old stock plan*, a bank (acting as trustee) takes the total amount of dividends designated for the plan, purchases the company's stock on the open market, and distributes the shares to the investors on a pro rata basis. The transactions costs are low because of the large transaction, and hence, the participating shareholders benefit.
- ☐ In a *new stock plan*, the company merely issues stock to investors in the plan in lieu of cash dividends. Often, the stock is offered at a 3 to 5 percent discount from market price.

■ One interesting aspect of DRPs is that they are forcing corporations to reexamine their basic dividend policies. A high participation rate in a DRP suggests that stockholders might be better off if the firm simply reduced cash dividends to save stockholders some personal income taxes.

■ Companies may change from one type of DRP to the other, depending on their needs for additional equity capital.

In addition to the theories and issues discussed so far, a number of other factors influence the dividend decision.

■ *Bond indentures* often contain provisions that restrict dividend policy.

■ Typically, common dividends cannot be paid if the company has *omitted (passed) its preferred dividend.*

■ Dividend payments cannot exceed the balance sheet value for retained earnings. This restriction, called the *impairment of capital rule*, is designed to protect creditors.

■ Dividends must be paid with cash, and hence, *a cash shortage may restrict dividends.*

■ The IRS can penalize a firm if it believes that the firm is *improperly accumulating earnings,* that is, withholding dividends for the sole purpose of investor tax avoidance.

■ If management is concerned about *control*, then it may be reluctant to sell new common stock, and hence may retain more earnings than it otherwise would, rather than pay dividends.

■ Managers can and do use dividends to *signal* the firm's situation.

Setting dividend policy is truly an exercise in informed judgment, and not a decision that can be based on a precise mathematical model. In practice, dividend policy is not an independent decision—the dividend decision is made jointly with the capital structure and capital investment decisions.

■ In setting dividend policy, managers first consider the firm's future investment opportunities, expected internal cash flows, and target capital structure. This gives them an idea of the residual earnings that might be available for dividends. In effect, managers use the residual dividend model, but applied to a long planning period.

■ An actual dollar dividend per share is then selected so that there is an extremely low probability that the dividend, once set, will have to be lowered, or worse yet, omitted.

■ If there is a great deal of uncertainty in the forecasted inflows and required outflows of the firm, a conservative dividend policy (low dollar dividend and low projected growth rate) will be adopted.

Firms may distribute income to stockholders by repurchasing their own stock. These repurchased shares are called treasury stock.

■ When outstanding shares are repurchased, the earnings per share on the remaining shares will increase, resulting in a higher market price per share. Capital gains are substituted for dividends.

■ Many very large repurchase programs are part of a general corporate restructuring plan whereby excess capital from asset sales or the issuance of new debt is distributed to stockholders through a major one-time stock repurchase. A "regular" stock repurchase is merely a substitute for cash dividends.

■ Advantages to repurchases include:
   □ Repurchase announcements are viewed as positive signals by investors because the repurchase is often motivated by management's belief that firm's shares are undervalued.
   □ Stockholders have a choice when the firm repurchases stock, while they must accept dividend payments and pay the resulting tax.
   □ Repurchases can remove a large block of stock that is overhanging the market and keeping the price per share down.

- ☐ If the excess cash flow is believed to be temporary, management can make the distribution in the form of share repurchase rather than declare an increased cash dividend that cannot be maintained.
- ☐ Repurchases can be used to produce large-scale changes in capital structures.

- ■ Disadvantages to repurchases include:
  - ☐ The stock price may benefit more from cash dividends than from repurchases because stockholders may not be indifferent between dividends and capital gains.
  - ☐ Selling stockholders may not be fully aware of all the implications of a repurchase.
  - ☐ The corporation may pay too high a price for the repurchased stock, to the detriment of remaining stockholders.

- ■ There are pros and cons regarding stock repurchases. Some general observations can be made:
  - ☐ Because of uncertainties about their tax treatment, repurchases on a regular, systematic, dependable basis are probably not a good idea.
  - ☐ However, repurchases do offer investors an opportunity to save taxes, and, for this reason, they should be given careful consideration.
  - ☐ Repurchases can be especially valuable to a firm that wants to make a large shift in its capital structure within a short period of time.

Stock dividends and stock splits are often used to lower a firm's stock price and, at the same time, to conserve its cash resources.

- ■ The effect of a stock split is an increase in the number of shares outstanding and a reduction in the par, or stated, value of the shares. For example, if a firm had 1,000 shares of stock outstanding with a par value of $100 per share, a 2-for-1 split would reduce the par value to $50 per share and increase the number of shares to 2,000.
  - ☐ The total net worth of the firm remains unchanged.
  - ☐ The stock split does not involve any cash payment, only additional certificates representing new shares.

- ■ Although the economic effects of stock splits and stock dividends are virtually identical, accountants treat them somewhat differently.

- ■ Stock dividends and splits "divide a given amount of pie into smaller slices."

■ The rationale behind using stock splits and dividends to reduce share prices lies in the belief in an *optimal trading range* within which large numbers of investors will be able to purchase the stock and the price will be maximized.

■ Unless the total amount of dividends paid on shares is increased, any upward movement in the stock price following a stock split or dividend is likely to be temporary. The price will normally fall in proportion to the dilution in per share earnings and dividends unless earnings and dividends rise.

SELF-TEST QUESTIONS

Definitional

1. MM argue that a firm's dividend policy has _____ _____ on shareholder wealth.

2. Gordon and Lintner hypothesize that investors value a dollar of _____ more highly than a dollar of expected _____ _____.

3. The tax differential theory implies that firms should set _____ dividend payout ratios.

4. A company may be forced to increase its _____ ratio in order to avoid a tax on retained earnings deemed to be unnecessary for the conduct of the business.

5. Some stockholders prefer dividends to _____ _____ because of a need for current _____.

6. If a firm's stock _____ increases with the announcement of an increase in dividends, investors may be reacting to the _____ content in the dividend announcement rather than to a preference for dividends over capital gains.

7. The hypothesis that some investors prefer a high dividend payout while others prefer a low payout is called the _____ effect.

8. The residual dividend policy is based on the fact that new common stock is _____ _____ than retained earnings.

9. The _____ _____ _____ decision involves the question of what fraction of earnings should be paid out, on average, over time.

10. The stock transfer books of a corporation are closed on the _____-___-_____ date, and dividends are paid to shareholders as of that date.

11. The ____-_____ date occurs four business days prior to the holder-of-record date and provides time for stock transfers to be recorded on the books of the firm.

12. Actual payment of a dividend is made on the _____ date as announced by the firm's _____ ___ _____ .

13. Many firms have instituted _____ _____ plans whereby stockholders purchase additional shares of the company's stock in lieu of receiving dividends.

14. Stock repurchases substitute _____ _____ for cash dividends.

15. Firms often repurchase stock with funds from the sale of _____ or the issuance of new _____ when restructuring occurs.

16. A stock split involves a reduction in the _____ _____ of the common stock, but no accounting transfers are made between accounts.

17. Stock repurchased by the firm which issued it is called _____ _____.

18. A(n) _____ _____ _____ generally means increasing the dollar dividend at a reasonably steady rate.

19. The _____ _____ _____ is based on the premise that investors prefer to have a firm retain and reinvest earnings rather than pay them out in dividends if the rate of return the firm can earn on reinvested earnings exceeds the rate of return investors can obtain for themselves on other investments of comparable risk.

20. The rationale behind using stock splits and dividends to reduce share prices lies in the belief in a(n) _____ _____ _____ within which large numbers of investors will be able to purchase the stock and the price will be maximized.

Conceptual

21. An increase in cash dividends will always result in an increase in the price of the common stock because D_1 will increase in the stock valuation model.

   a. True   **b.** False

22. If investors are indifferent between dividends and capital gains, the farther to the left the IOS and MCC schedule intersect, the *higher* the dividend payout ratio should be.

   a. True   **b.** False

23. Which of the following is a possible disadvantage to stock repurchases?

   a. The shareholder may or may not decide to sell.
   b. The price of the stock may be undervalued.
   c. EPS will increase.
   d. The repurchase may be viewed as a signal of poor growth opportunities.
   e. All of the above.

24. If investors prefer dividends to capital gains, then

   a. The required rate of return on equity, k_s, will not be affected by a change in dividend policy.
   b. The cost of capital will not be affected by a change in dividend policy.
   c. k_s will increase as dividends are reduced.
   d. k_s will decrease as the retention rate increases.
   e. A policy conforming to the residual theory of dividends will maximize stock price.

25. A stock split will affect the amounts shown in which of the following balance sheet accounts?

   a. Common stock
   b. Paid-in capital
   c. Retained earnings
   d. Cash
   e. None of the above accounts

26. Which of the following statements is most *correct*?

    a. Modigliani and Miller's theory of the effect of dividend policy on the value of a firm has been called the "bird-in-the-hand" theory, because MM argued that a dividend in the hand is less risky than a potential capital gain in the bush. After extensive empirical tests, this theory is now accepted by most financial experts.
    b. According to proponents of the "dividend irrelevance theory," if a company's stock price rises after the firm announces a greater-than-expected dividend increase, the price increase occurs because of signaling effects, not because of investors' preferences for dividends over capital gains.
    c. Both statements a and b are correct.
    d. Both statements a and b are false.

27. Which of the following statements is most *correct*?

    a. The residual dividend policy calls for the establishment of a fixed, stable dividend (or dividend growth rate) and then for the level of investment each year to be determined as a residual equal to net income minus the established dividends.
    b. According to the residual dividend policy, for any given MCC schedule and level of earnings, the further to the right the IOS schedule cuts the MCC schedule, the lower the optimal dividend payout ratio.
    c. According to the text, a firm would probably maximize its stock price if it established a specific dividend payout ratio, say 40 percent, and then paid that percentage of earnings out each year because stockholders would then know exactly how much dividend income to count on when they planned their spending for the coming year.
    d. If you buy a stock after the ex-dividend date but before the dividend has been paid, then you, and not the seller, will receive the next dividend check the company sends out.
    e. Each of the above statements is false.

28. Which of the following statements is most *correct*?

   a. According to the asymmetric information, or signaling, hypothesis, the announcement of a new stock issue by a mature firm would generally lead to an *increase* in the price of the firm's stock.

   b. According to the asymmetric information, or signaling, hypothesis, the announcement of a new stock issue by a mature firm would generally lead to a *decrease* in the price of the firm's stock.

   c. If Firm A's managers believe in the asymmetric information theory, but Firm B's managers do not, then, other things held constant, Firm A would probably have the *higher* normal target debt ratio.

   d. There is no such thing as the asymmetric information hypothesis, at least according to the text.

   e. Statements b and c are both true.

29. Which of the following statements is most *correct*?

   a. According to the tax preference theory, investors prefer dividends and, as a result, the higher the payout ratio, the higher the value of the firm.

   b. According to the "bird-in-the-hand" theory, investors prefer cash to paper (stock), so if a company announces that it plans to repurchase some of its stock, this causes the price of the stock to increase.

   c. According to the dividend irrelevance theory developed by Modigliani and Miller, stock dividends (but not cash dividends) are irrelevant because they "merely divide the pie into thinner slices."

   d. According to the information content, or signaling, hypothesis, the fact that stock prices generally increase when an increase in the dividend is announced demonstrates that investors prefer higher to lower payout ratios.

   e. According to the text, the residual dividend policy is more appropriate for setting a company's long-run target payout ratio than for determining the payout ratio on a year-to-year basis.

30. Which of the following statements is most *correct*?

   a. Stock prices generally rise on the ex-dividend date, and that increase is especially great if the company increases the dividend.
   b. Dividend reinvestment plans are popular with investors because investors who do not need cash income can have their dividends reinvested in the company's stock and thereby avoid having to pay income taxes on the dividend income until they sell the stock.
   c. In the past, stock dividends and stock splits were frequently used by corporations which wanted to lower the prices of their stocks to an "optimal trading range." However, recent empirical studies have demonstrated that stock dividends and stock splits generally cause stock prices to decline, so companies today rarely split their stock or pay stock dividends.
   d. Statements a, b, and c are all false.
   e. Statements a, b, and c are all true.

SELF-TEST PROBLEMS

1. Express Industries' expected net income for next year is $1.0 million. The company's target, and current, capital structure is 40 percent debt and 60 percent common equity. The optimal capital budget for next year is $1.2 million. If Express uses the residual dividend policy to determine next year's dividend payout, what is the expected payout ratio?

   a. 0% b. 10% c. 28% d. 42% e. 56%

2. Amalgamated Shippers has a current, and target, capital structure of 30 percent debt and 70 percent equity. This past year Amalgamated, which uses the residual dividend policy, had a dividend payout ratio of 47.5 percent and net income of $800,000. What was Amalgamated's capital budget?

   a. $400,000 b. $500,000 c. $600,000 d. $700,000 e. $800,000

3. The Aikman Company's optimal capital structure calls for 40 percent debt and 60 percent common equity. The interest rate on its debt is a constant 12 percent; its cost of common equity from retained earnings is 16 percent; the cost of equity from new stock is 18 percent; and its federal-plus-state tax rate is 40 percent. Aikman has the following investment opportunities:

Project A: Cost = $5 million; IRR = 22%.
Project B: Cost = $5 million; IRR = 14%.
Project C: Cost = $5 million; IRR = 11%.

Aikman expects to have net income of $7 million. If Aikman bases its dividends on the residual policy, what will its payout ratio be?

   a. 22.62%   **b.** 14.29%   **c.** 31.29%   **d.** 25.62%   **e.** 18.75%

ANSWERS TO SELF-TEST QUESTIONS

1. no effect
2. dividends; capital gains
3. low
4. payout
5. capital gains; income
6. price; information
7. clientele
8. more costly
9. target payout policy
10. holder-of-record

11. ex-dividend
12. payment; board of directors
13. dividend reinvestment
14. capital gains
15. assets; debt
16. par value
17. treasury stock
18. stable dividend policy
19. residual dividend model
20. optimal trading range

21. b. A dividend increase could also be perceived by investors as leading to lower growth in future earnings, thus reducing g in the model. The net effect on stock price is uncertain.

22. a. If investors are indifferent, firms should follow the residual theory. Thus, the smaller the optimal capital budget, the higher the dividend payout ratio.

23. d. From the shareholder's point of view, the repurchase may signal that the stock is undervalued and will therefore rise in price, providing a capital gain. It is an advantage to the stockholder to have the option to sell or not. Repurchases will increase EPS to the remaining shareholders, but a repurchase could be viewed as a signal that the firm has limited growth opportunities available.

24. c. This is the Gordon-Lintner hypothesis. If investors view dividends as being less risky than potential capital gains, then the cost of equity is inversely related to the payout ratio.

25. e. A stock split will affect the par value and number of shares outstanding. However, no dollar values will be affected.

26. b. Statement a is false; the proponents of this theory were Gordon and Lintner and empirical tests have not proven any of the dividend theories. Statement b is correct.

27. b. Statement a is false; the residual dividend policy calls for the determination of the optimal capital budget and then the dividend is established as a residual of net income minus the amount of retained earnings necessary for the capital budget. Statement b is correct. Statement c is false; a constant payout policy would lead to uncertainty of dividends due to fluctuating earnings. Statement d is false; if a stock is bought after the ex-dividend date the dividend remains with the seller of the stock.

28. b. The asymmetric information hypothesis suggests that investors regard the announcement of a stock sale as bad news: If the firm had really good investment opportunities, it would use debt financing so that existing stockholders would get all the benefits from the good projects. Therefore, the announcement of a stock sale leads to a decline in the price of the firm's stock. In order to reduce the chances of having to issue stock, firms therefore set low target debt ratios, which give them "reserve borrowing capacity."

29. e. Statements a, b, c, and d are false, but statement e is true.

30. d. The statements are all false.

SOLUTIONS TO SELF-TEST PROBLEMS

1. c. The $1,200,000 capital budget will be financed using 40 percent debt and 60 percent equity. Therefore, the equity requirement will be 0.6($1,200,000) = $720,000. Since the expected net income is $1,000,000, $280,000 will be available to pay as dividends. Thus, the payout ratio is expected to be $280,000/$1,000,000 = 0.28 = 28%.

2. c. Of the $800,000 in net income, 0.475($800,000) = $380,000 was paid out as dividends. Thus, $420,000 was retained in the firm for investment. This is the equity portion of the capital budget, or 70 percent of the capital budget. Therefore, the total capital budget was $420,000/0.7 = $600,000.

3. b. Maximum BP_{RE} = NI/Equity ratio = $7,000,000/0.6 = $11,666,667.

   $WACC_1 = 0.4(12\%)(0.6) + 0.6(16\%) = 12.48\%.$

   $WACC_2 = 0.4(12\%)(0.6) + 0.6(18\%) = 13.68\%.$

   We see that the capital budget should be $10 million because the IRRs of Projects A and B are greater than $WACC_2$. We know that 60 percent of the $10 million should be equity. Therefore, the company should pay dividends of:

   Dividends = NI - Needed equity = $7,000,000 - $6,000,000 = $1,000,000.

   Payout ratio = $1,000,000/$7,000,000 = 0.1429 = 14.29%.

CHAPTER 16

COMMON STOCK AND
THE INVESTMENT BANKING PROCESS

OVERVIEW

In this chapter, we consider in some detail the decisions financial managers must make regarding stock financings. As a part of this analysis, we also examine in detail the procedures used to raise new long-term capital, or the investment banking process.

Common stock constitutes the ownership position in a firm. As owners, the common stockholders have certain rights and privileges, including (1) the right to control the firm through election of directors and (2) the right to the firm's residual earnings. Firms generally begin their corporate life as closely held companies, with all the common stock held by the founding managers. Then, as the company grows, it is often necessary to sell stock to the general public (that is, go public) to raise more funds. At this point, the firm's managers must be familiar with securities markets, including their regulation by the Securities and Exchange Commission (SEC). Eventually, the firm may choose to list its stock on one of the organized exchanges.

OUTLINE

Common stock represents the ownership of an incorporated business. It corresponds to the proprietor's capital or the partners' capital for an unincorporated business.

- Legal and accounting terminology is vital to both investors and financial managers if they are to avoid misinterpretations and possibly costly mistakes.
  - Shares of common stock are authorized by the owners of a business and issued by management.
  - *Par value* is the minimum amount for which new shares can be issued.
  - Any difference between the par value and what stockholders paid for common stock is shown on the balance sheet as *additional paid-in capital.*
  - *Retained earnings* represent the net income earned over the years that has been reinvested in the business rather than paid out as dividends.

□ The *book value per share* is equal to the company's net worth, or common equity (stockholder's equity), consisting of the sum of common stock, retained earnings, and paid-in capital, divided by the number of shares of common stock outstanding.

■ The corporation's common stockholders have certain rights and privileges.
  □ Common stockholders have control of the firm through their election of the firm's directors, who in turn select officers to manage the business.
    ‣ In a large, publicly owned firm, neither the managers nor any individual shareholder normally has the 51 percent necessary for absolute control of the company.
    ‣ Thus, stockholders must vote for directors, and the voting process is regulated by both state and federal laws.
    ‣ Stockholders who are unable to attend annual meetings may still vote by means of a *proxy*. Proxies can be solicited by any party seeking to control the firm.
  □ The *preemptive right* gives the current shareholders the right to purchase any new shares issued, in proportion to their current holdings.
    ‣ The preemptive right may or may not be required by state law.
    ‣ When granted, the preemptive right enables current owners to maintain their proportionate share of ownership and control of the business.
    ‣ It also prevents the sale of shares at low prices to new stockholders, which would dilute the value of the previously issued shares.

■ Although most firms have only one type of common stock, in some instances *classified stock* is used by a firm to meet special needs and circumstances. If two classes of stock were desired, one would normally be called "Class A" and the other "Class B."
  □ Class A might be entitled to receive dividends before dividends can be paid on Class B stock, but carry no voting rights for a certain number of years.
  □ Class B might have the exclusive right to vote, but not entitled to dividends until the company has established its earning power by building up retained earnings to a designated level. This would be the typical situation for *founders' shares*.
  □ Note that Class A and Class B have no standard meanings.

The United States has highly developed markets for buying and selling common stocks. Institutional investors have long dominated the bond market, and in recent years they have become a major factor in the stock market. Pension funds and other institutional investors now own about 50 percent of the stocks of large, publicly held firms, but they represent about 80 percent of the trading volume.

- The stocks of smaller companies are generally owned by management groups, or only a few people, and are referred to as *closely held*, or *privately owned*, corporations. The stocks of larger firms are generally held by a large number of investors. These companies are called *publicly held* corporations.

- The stocks of smaller publicly owned firms are not listed on an exchange; they trade in the *over-the-counter (OTC)* market. The companies and their stocks are said to be *unlisted*.

- Stock market transactions may be separated into three distinct categories.
  - [ ] The primary market handles *initial public offerings (IPOs)* of shares in firms that were formerly closely held. Here, capital for a firm can be raised by going public, and this market is often termed the *new issue market*.
  - [ ] The *primary market* also handles additional shares sold by established, publicly owned companies. Companies can raise additional capital by selling in this market.
  - [ ] The *secondary market* deals with trading in previously issued, or outstanding, shares of established, publicly owned companies. The company receives no new money when sales are made in the secondary market.

- *Going public* has the following advantages:
  - [ ] The original owners are able to *diversify* their holdings by selling some of their stock in a public offering.
  - [ ] Public ownership *increases* the stock's *liquidity*.
  - [ ] New corporate cash is more *easily raised* by a publicly owned company.
  - [ ] Going public *establishes the firm's value* in the marketplace.

- Going public has the following disadvantages:
  - [ ] A publicly owned company must file quarterly and annual reports with various governmental agencies. These reports can be *costly*.
  - [ ] Publicly owned firms must *disclose* operating and ownership data.
  - [ ] The opportunities for owners/managers to engage in questionable, but legal, *self-dealings are reduced*.
  - [ ] If a publicly held firm is very small, and if its shares will be *traded infrequently*, then its stock will not really be liquid, and the market price may be lower than the stocks' true value.
  - [ ] Managers of publicly owned firms with *less than 50 percent* control must be concerned about tender offers and proxy fights. This sometimes leads to operating decisions that are not in the best long-run interests of the shareholders.

Stocks traded on organized exchanges are called listed stocks. While the decision to go public is significant, the decision to list is not a major event. In order to have a listed stock, a company must apply to an exchange, pay a relatively small fee, and meet the exchange's minimum requirements.

■ The company will have to file a few new reports with an exchange.

■ It will have to abide by the exchange's rules.

■ Firms benefit from listing their stock by *gaining liquidity, status,* and *free publicity.* These factors may cause an increase in the stock's value. However, due to improvements in telecommunications and computer technologies, the differences between the OTC market and the exchanges have become less distinct.

If stock is to be sold to raise new capital, the new shares may be sold in one of five ways:

■ If stockholders have a preemptive right, or if the firm chooses to do so, it can sell the additional stock to existing stockholders as a *rights offering.* Each shareholder is issued an option to buy a certain number of new shares, and the terms of the option are listed on a certificate called a *stock purchase right,* or simply a *right.*

■ If the preemptive right does not exist, the company can choose between a rights offering and a *public offering.*

■ In a *private placement,* securities are sold to one or a few investors, generally institutional investors. The primary advantages are lower flotation costs and greater speed, since the shares will not have to go through the SEC registration process.
  □ One particular type of private placement that is occurring with increasing frequency is the situation in which a large company makes an equity investment in a smaller supplier.
  □ The primary disadvantage of a private placement is that the securities generally will not have gone through the SEC registration process, so they cannot be sold except to another large, "sophisticated" purchaser in the event the original buyer wants to sell them.

■ Many companies have plans that allow employees to purchase stock on favorable terms.
  □ First, under executive *incentive stock option plans,* key managers are given options to purchase stock. If they perform well, the stock will go up, and the options will become valuable.

☐ Second, there are plans for lower-level employees in which they can allocate part of their salary to buy newly issued shares below market value.

☐ A third type of plan is an *Employee Stock Ownership Plan (ESOP)*, in which the stock bought for the employees is purchased out of a share of the company's profits. ESOPs have the following advantages: (1) tax breaks, (2) anti-takeover defense, (3) pension cost control, and (4) productivity enhancement. Potential disadvantages are: (1) no productivity enhancement, (2) the balance of power is altered, (3) legal considerations regarding ESOP abuses, (4) retiree benefits becoming so dependent on the stock's price that retirees are vulnerable, and (5) private companies with ESOPs must repurchase stock at the current appraised value when employees quit or retire in a given year.

■ Stock can be sold through dividend reinvestment plans which were discussed in Chapter 15.

Common stock financing has advantages and disadvantages.

■ Financing with common stock has the following advantages to the corporation:
   ☐ Common stock *does not obligate* the firm to make *fixed payments* to investors.
   ☐ Common stock carries *no fixed maturity date*.
   ☐ Common stock *increases the creditworthiness* of the firm, thus increasing the future availability of debt at a lower cost and establishing a reserve borrowing capacity.
   ☐ Common stock can often be *sold more easily* than debt if the firm's prospects look potentially good, but risky.

■ Financing with common stock has the following disadvantages to the corporation:
   ☐ Issuing common stock *extends voting rights*, and thus *control*, to new stockholders.
   ☐ Common stock means that *more stockholders share in the firm's net profits* rather than a fixed payment as with creditors.
   ☐ The *cost of underwriting* and distributing common stock is high.
   ☐ The sale of new common stock may be perceived by investors as a *negative signal*, hence may cause the stock price to fall.

In a going private transaction, the entire equity of a publicly held firm is purchased by a small group of investors, which usually includes the firm's current senior management.

■ Such deals almost always involve substantial borrowing, and thus are commonly known as *leveraged buyouts (LBOs)* or *leveraged managerial buyouts (MBOs)*.

■ The primary advantages to going private are:

   □ *Administrative cost savings* because the firm does not have stockholder servicing costs, and top management is free from meetings with security analysts, government hearings, and so on.

   □ An even larger potential gain comes from the *improvement in the incentives for high-level managerial performance*. Heavy interest payments combined with a knowledge that success will bring large wealth does a lot to improve decisions.

   □ The *increased flexibility* available to managers of private firms.

   □ An *increase in shareholder participation*.

   □ The *increased use of financial leverage* reduces taxes and forces managers to increase revenues and/or reduce costs to insure that the firm has sufficient cash flow to meet its obligations.

■ Not all firms are privately held, because the advantages of access to public capital markets dominate the advantage of going private for most firms.

Most participants in the securities markets, including the organized exchanges, brokers, investment bankers, and dealers, are regulated by the federal government through the Securities and Exchange Commission (SEC) and, to a lesser extent, by state governments.

■ The SEC has jurisdiction over all interstate offerings to the public in amounts of $1.5 million or more.

■ New issues must be registered at least 20 days before they are offered to the public. A *prospectus* describing the company and the securities to be offered must be sent to prospective purchasers of the new issue. The *registration statement* provides financial, legal, and technical information about the company to the SEC.

■ The SEC also regulates all national security exchanges. Firms listed on these exchanges must file financial reports with both the SEC and the exchanges.

■ The Federal Reserve System controls the flow of credit (margin credit) that may be used in purchasing securities.

■ The SEC also monitors the stock transactions of corporate *insiders*.

■ The securities industry realizes the importance of stable markets, sound brokerage firms, and the absence of stock manipulation. Therefore, the various exchanges and trade organizations work closely with the regulatory agencies to police the markets and protect customers.

■ The purpose of regulation is to insure that adequate and accurate information is available concerning securities offered to the public, and to prevent fraud. Regulation cannot insure that investments will be successful or that investors will exercise good judgment.

The financial manager must have a knowledge of the investment banking process, the process by which new securities are issued. Investment banking decisions take place in two stages.

■ At *Stage I*, the firm makes some initial, preliminary decisions on its own.
   ☐ The *dollar amount* of new capital required is established.
   ☐ The *type of securities* to be offered is specified. Further, if common stock is to be issued, managers must decide whether a rights offering should be used.
   ☐ The basis on which to deal with the investment bankers, either by a *competitive bid* or a *negotiated deal*, is determined.
   ☐ Finally, the *investment banking firm* must be *selected*.

■ The *Stage II* decisions are made jointly by the firm and the selected investment banker.
   ☐ First, the two parties will *reevaluate the Stage I decisions*.
   ☐ The firm and its investment banker must decide whether the banker will work on a "best efforts" basis or will "underwrite" the issue.
      ▸ On a *best efforts basis*, the banker does not guarantee that the securities will be sold or that the company will get the cash it needs.
      ▸ On an *underwritten issue*, the company does get a guarantee. Essentially, the banker purchases the issue from the company, then resells the securities at a higher price. The banker bears significant risks in underwritten offerings.
   ☐ The investment banker's *compensation* must be *negotiated*.
   ☐ The *offering price* must be set. The investment banker will have an easier job if the issue is priced relatively low, while the issuer naturally wants as high a price as possible.
   ☐ If pressure from the new shares and/or *negative signaling effects* drives down the stock's price, all shares outstanding, not just the new shares, are affected.

Once the company and its investment banker have decided how much money to raise, the type of securities to issue, and the basis for pricing the issue, they will prepare and file an SEC Registration statement and a prospectus.

- If the sum of money involved is large and the risk of a price fluctuation is substantial, investment bankers form *underwriting syndicates* in an effort to minimize the risk each banker carries. The banking house which sets up the deal is called the *lead*, or *managing, underwriter*.

- A new selling procedure has recently emerged. It's called an *unsyndicated stock offering*, and it does not require an underwriting syndicate. The managing underwriter, acting alone, sells the issue entirely to institutional investors, thus bypassing both retail stockbrokers and individual investors.

- Large well-known public companies which issue securities frequently may file a master registration statement with the SEC and then update it with a short-form statement just prior to each individual offering.
  - ☐ This procedure is known as a *shelf registration* because, in effect, the company puts its new securities on the "shelf," and then sells them to investors when it feels the market is right.
  - ☐ Shelf registrations have two advantages over standard registrations: (1) Lower flotation costs and (2) firms have more control over the timing of the issue.

- For new issues involving small companies, the investment banker will normally *maintain a market* in the shares after the public offering. This is done in order to provide liquidity for the shares and to maintain a good relationship with both the issuer and the investors who purchased the shares.

SELF-TEST QUESTIONS

Definitional

1. Ownership interest in a corporation is reflected on the balance sheet by the _____ _____ accounts.

2. Amounts paid by stockholders in excess of the par value are shown as "additional _____ - ____ _____."

3. One of the fundamental rights of common stockholders is to elect a firm's _____, who in turn select the operating management.

4. If a stockholder cannot vote in person, participation in the annual meeting is still possible through a(n) _____.

5. The preemptive right protects stockholders against loss of _____ of the corporation as well as _____ of market value from the sale of new shares below market value.

6. Firms may find it desirable to separate the common stock into different _____. Generally, this classification is designed to differentiate stock in terms of the right to receive _____ and the right to _____.

7. A(n) _____ _____ or _____ _____ corporation is one whose stock is held by a small group, normally its management.

8. The trading of previously issued shares of a corporation takes place in the _____ market, while new issues are offered in the _____ market.

9. _____ _____ refers to the sale of shares of a closely held business to the general public. Such a sale is also called a(n) _____ _____ _____.

10. Going public establishes the firm's _____ in the marketplace.

11. Securities traded on an organized exchange are known as _____ securities.

12. Before an interstate issue of stock amounting to $1.5 million or more can be sold to the public, it must be _____ with and approved by the _____.

13. The _____ _____ gives the current shareholders the right to purchase any new shares issued, in proportion to their current holdings.

14. In a(n) _____ _____ securities are sold to one or a few investors, generally institutional investors. The primary advantages are lower flotation costs and greater speed.

15. Setting the _____ price for a stock issue may present a conflict of interest between the issuer and the _____ _____.

16. In order to spread the risk of underwriting a sizable common stock issue, investment bankers will form a(n) _____ _____.

17. Credit used to buy stock is known as _____ credit, and its use is controlled by the _____ _____ _____.

18. In a(n) _____ _____ _____ plan stock is bought for the employees out of a share of the company's profits.

19. In a(n) _____ _____ _____ the managing underwriter, acting alone, sells the issue entirely to institutional investors, thus bypassing both retail stockbrokers and individual investors.

20. On a(n) _____ _____ _____, the investment banker does not guarantee that the securities will be sold or that the company will get the cash it needs; while on a(n) _____ issue the company does get a guarantee.

Conceptual

21. A firm may go public, yet the firm itself may not receive any additional funds in the process.

    a. True   **b.** False

22. Flotation costs are generally higher for bond issues than for stock issues.

    a. True   **b.** False

23. When new shares are being sold, if it appears that the investment bankers will be unable to sell the entire issue at the initial offering price, the only way the entire issue can be sold is to lower the price.

    a. True   **b.** False

24. A change in the dividend payout ratio will have the most direct (most immediate) effect on a firm's

    a. Common stock account.
    b. Earnings per share.
    c. Paid-in capital account.
    d. Net operating income.
    e. Retained earnings account.

25. When stockholders assign their right to vote to another party, this is called

    a. A privilege.
    b. A preemptive right.
    c. An ex right.
    d. A proxy.
    e. A prospectus

26. In a going private transaction, the entire equity of a publicly held firm is purchased by a small group of investors. Such deals which involve substantial borrowing to purchase the equity are called

    a. Initial public offerings (IPOs).
    b. Leveraged buyouts (LBOs).
    c. Rights offerings.
    d. ESOPs.
    e. None of the above.

27. Which of the following statements is most *correct*?

    a. The preemptive right gives current stockholders the right to purchase a pro rata share of any new stock that the firm decides to issue. This is a fundamental right, and all stockholders have it.
    b. Whenever a publicly-owned firm decides to issue new common stock, it must register the stock with the SEC, and prospective stockholders must be given a copy of the prospectus. The SEC must approve the prospectus, and one key aspect of this approval is that the SEC must agree that the price at which the shares are to be offered is fair to investors.
    c. Once a company "goes public," it must file periodic statements with the SEC. These periodic statements are called "prospectuses," or, sometimes, "red herring prospectuses."
    d. One important recent innovation is "shelf registration," whereby large companies can register securities in advance, in effect putting them "on the shelf" of an investment banking house, which can then sell them at any time, in whole or in part, when the market is receptive to the securities. Theoretically, either stock or bonds could be sold through shelf registrations, but, because of the preemptive right, as a practical matter, only bonds are involved.
    e. All of the above statements are false.

28. Which of the following statements is most *correct*?

    a. Large companies such as IBM and Exxon are exempt from SEC listing requirements, but small companies (assets below $10 million) are not. Hence, small companies have listed stock, while large companies have unlisted stock.

    b. If a company's stock is publicly owned, and if its price has been established in the market and is quoted in a source such as *The Wall Street Journal*, then the price of any new issue of stock will be based on the current market price. However, if the stock is not traded, and if the company is issuing shares in an "initial public offering," or IPO, then the Securities and Exchange Commission (SEC) must approve the price at which the stock is to be offered to the public.

    c. In the United States, most new stock issues are sold through the investment banking departments of large commercial banks, such as Barnett Bank or Citibank.

    d. The SEC must normally approve the prospectuses relating to new stock offerings by companies whose securities are listed on the New York Stock Exchange before the new stock can be sold to the public.

    e. Statements b and d are both correct.

SELF-TEST PROBLEMS

(The following data apply to the next three problems.)

McCollough Company
Stockholders' Equity Accounts

Common stock (100,000 shares authorized	
80,000 shares outstanding, $1 par)	$ 80,000
Additional paid-in capital	720,000
Retained earnings	1,200,000
Total common stockholders' equity	$2,000,000

1. If all 80,000 shares outstanding were sold at one offering, how much did McCollough receive for each share?

    a. $1   **b.** $5   **c.** $10   **d.** $20   **e.** $25

2. What is the current book value per share?

    a. $1   **b.** $5   **c.** $10   **d.** $20   **e.** $25

3. Suppose the firm sold the remaining authorized shares and netted $20.00 per share from the sale. What is the new book value per share?

    a. $23   **b.** $24   **c.** $25   **d.** $26   **e.** $27

ANSWERS TO SELF-TEST QUESTIONS

1. stockholders' equity (common equity)
2. paid-in capital
3. directors
4. proxy
5. control; dilution
6. classes; dividends; vote
7. closely held; privately owned
8. secondary; primary
9. Going public; initial public offering
10. value
11. listed
12. registered; SEC
13. preemptive right
14. private placement
15. offering; investment banker
16. underwriting syndicate
17. margin; Federal Reserve Board
18. employee stock ownership
19. unsyndicated stock offering
20. best efforts basis; underwritten

21. **a.** An example, that of the Ford Foundation selling stock to the general public, is given in the text. Also, a firm may go public if its managers sell off a portion of their stock holdings. Then, the funds obtained go to the managers rather than the firm.

22. **b.** The investment banker normally must expend greater effort in selling stocks, thus must charge a higher fee. Also, a new common stock issue may lower stock price because of negative signaling effects and/or supply/demand price pressure.

23. **b.** The investment bankers may be able to increase the demand for the stock by "promoting" the issue. If not, then a price reduction may be required.

24. **e.** Although a change in the dividend payout would, in the long run, affect every item listed, retained earnings would be affected most directly.

25. d. Recently, there has been a spate of proxy fights, whereby a dissident group of stockholders solicits proxies in competition with the firm's management. If the dissident group gets a majority of the proxies, then it can gain control of the board of directors and oust existing management.

26. b. Leveraged buyouts often involve up to 90 percent debt financing.

27. e. Statement a is false; stockholders *often* have this right, but not always. Statement b is false; the SEC is responsible for making sure the information in the registration and prospectus is adequate; however, it does not determine the fairness of the offering price. Statement c is false; prospectuses accompany any sales solicitations. Statement d is false; shelf registrations are also applicable to common stock. Thus, statement e is the correct choice.

28. d. All companies are subject to the SEC's listing requirements, which makes statement a false. The SEC does not have to approve offering prices for IPOs. Therefore, statement b is false. Finally, statement c is false because commercial banks are barred from participating in investment bank activities at the present time.

SOLUTIONS TO SELF-TEST PROBLEMS

1. c. The offering of 80,000 shares resulted in the firm collecting $80,000 in par value and $720,000 in additional paid-in capital for a total of $800,000. Thus, each share must have brought the firm $800,000/80,000 = $10.

2. e. The total common equity of $2,000,000 represents the total investment of the 80,000 shares outstanding. Thus, the book value per share is $2,000,000/80,000 = $25.

3. b. The firm now sells the remaining 20,000 shares and nets $20 per share for a total of $400,000. Thus, the new total common equity is $2,400,000, and 100,000 shares are outstanding. The new book value per share is $2,400,000/100,000 = $24. Note that selling new shares below book value results in a lower book value on all shares. The opposite holds if new shares are sold above book value.

CHAPTER 17

LONG-TERM DEBT

OVERVIEW

As noted in Chapter 13, the use of debt financing is generally required to maximize shareholder wealth. In this chapter, we discuss long-term debt, including its different forms, typical provisions in debt contracts, securitization, bond ratings, and the various factors that influence a firm's decision to use debt financing at a particular point in time. Refunding operations are covered in the appendix to this chapter.

OUTLINE

There are many types of long-term debt. In this section, we briefly review the traditional long-term debt instruments.

- A *term loan* is a contract under which a borrower agrees to make a series of interest and principal payments, on specific dates, to a lender. Term loans are generally negotiated between the borrowing firm and a financial institution, generally a bank, an insurance company, or a pension fund.
    - The maturity of a term loan is generally from 3 to 15 years, but it may be as short as 2 or as long as 30 years.
    - Term loans are usually amortized in equal installments over the life of the loan.
    - Term loans have several advantages over public offerings: speed, flexibility, and low issuance costs. Also, because they are negotiated directly between the lender and the borrower, formal documentation is minimized.
    - Term loans are actually private placements of debt. Private placements are often called *story credit*, because each placement has a "story" which explains the company's need for funds.

- A *bond* is also a long-term debt contract, but it differs from a term loan in that it is generally offered to the public rather than to a single lender or a small group of lenders.
    - When real estate or other property is pledged as collateral for a bond issue, the bond is referred to as a *mortgage bond*. In case of bankruptcy, the mortgage bondholders have first claim on the proceeds from the sale of the pledged assets.

- ☐ A *debenture* is an unsecured bond, and holders are general creditors of the corporation. The use of debentures depends on the firm's general credit strength and the nature of its assets.
- ☐ *Subordinated debt* has claims on assets, in the event of bankruptcy, only after *senior debt* as named in the subordinate debt's indenture has been paid off. *Second mortgage bonds* are subordinate to first mortgage bonds. Also, *subordinated debentures* may be subordinated to designated notes payable, or to all other debt.
- ☐ There are several other important types of bonds.
  - ▸ *Convertible bonds* are securities that can be converted into a fixed number of shares of common stock at the option of the bondholder.
  - ▸ *Bonds issued with warrants* provide the investor with an option to buy the firm's common stock at a stated price. The warrants are detachable from the bonds, and the bonds remain outstanding even after the warrants have been exercised.
  - ▸ *Income bonds* pay interest only when covered by the firm's earnings.
  - ▸ *Indexed,* or *purchasing power, bonds* have their coupon rates tied to an inflation index, such as the consumer price index.

Zero coupon bonds pay no interest but are offered at a substantial discount below their par values and hence provide capital appreciation rather than interest income.

- ■ The advantages to the issuer are that no cash outlays are required until maturity, and these bonds often have a lower required rate of return than coupon bonds.

- ■ The advantages for investors are that there is little danger of a call, and zeros guarantee a "true" yield to maturity since there is no reinvestment rate risk.

There have been other innovations in long-term financing.

- ■ When interest rates are volatile, lenders are reluctant to lend long term. Thus, they charge very high maturity risk premiums. On the other hand, borrowers, in general, would rather borrow long term so that they do not have to worry about having to continually refund their debt. The answer to the dilemma is *long-term floating rate debt*.
  - ☐ The floating rate bond may have a 5- or 10-year maturity, but the interest rate changes periodically to reflect current market conditions.
  - ☐ Floating rate debt is advantageous to lenders because it causes the debt's market value to be stabilized, and it provides lenders with more income to meet their own obligations.
  - ☐ Floating rate debt is also advantageous to corporations because they can obtain debt with a long maturity without committing themselves to paying an historically high interest rate for

the entire term of the loan. However, if interest rates rise, borrowers will face increasing interest expense.

■ Bonds that are *redeemable at par* at the holder's option also protect the holder against interest rate changes.
  □ Typically, these bonds are not callable by the company, but holders can turn them in for redemption at any time during the first 5 or so years.
  □ *Poison put* bonds are bonds that are redeemable at par if the company restructures or engages in a leveraged buyout that significantly lowers the credit rating of the debt. The risk of an event of this nature is called *event risk*.

■ Another type of bond is the *junk bond*, a high-risk, high-yield bond issued to finance a leveraged buyout, a merger, or a troubled company.
  □ The development of the junk bond market has effectively extended the bounds of firm's debt capacities beyond the earlier limits.

■ *Project financing* is another type of debt that has been used extensively in recent years.
  □ In project financing, the holders of the debt generally have claims only against the sponsor's equity in the project and the cash flows generated from the project, and not against the firm or firms that own the project (the sponsors).
  □ Project financings increase the number and type of investment opportunities; hence they make capital markets "more complete."
  □ Project financing is often used in conjunction with joint ventures and other types of business combinations where more than one firm is involved.

■ As the term is generally used, a *security* refers to a publicly traded financial instrument. Thus securities tend to have high liquidity. In recent years, various types of debt have been *securitized*, which means turned into liquid securities.
  □ Securitization has occurred in two ways.
    ▸ Some debt instruments that were formerly never traded are now being widely traded. Examples are commercial paper and junk bonds.
    ▸ In *asset securitization*, individual assets are pledged as collateral, but then typically combined into pools to reduce risk. The oldest type of asset securitization is the mortgage-backed security, but today, such things as accounts receivable and automobile loans are also used as collateral.
  □ The process of securitization has, in general, lowered costs and increased the availability of funds to borrowers, decreased risks to lenders, and created new investment opportunities for many investors.

The cost of a debt security to the issuer is a function of the specific features of the debt contract. These features determine the debt's riskiness.

■ An *indenture* is the legal document which spells out the rights of both the bondholders and the issuing corporation. It contains the basic terms of the issue as well as any special provisions such as restrictive covenants, call provisions, and sinking funds. A *trustee*, the person or institution who represents the bondholders, makes certain that terms of the indenture are carried out.

■ A *restrictive covenant* is a provision in a bond issue that requires the issuer to meet certain stated conditions.
  □ Standard provisions typically include minimum levels for the current ratio and the debt-to-assets ratio, conditions under which the issuer can pay off the bonds prior to maturity, and restrictions against the payment of dividends unless earnings meet certain specifications.
  □ These requirements are designed to help insure that the credit standing of the firm and the bond issue remains high.

■ A *call provision* gives the issuing corporation the right to call the entire bond issue for redemption before its regular maturity.
  □ When a bond is called, the company must normally pay an amount greater than the par value. This extra payment over par is referred to as a *call premium*.
  □ Bonds are frequently called when the issuing firm can *refund* the issue at a lower interest rate. The call premium is thus a penalty for depriving investors of the higher interest rate.

■ A *sinking fund* provision requires that a firm retires a portion of a bond issue each year. Its purpose is like that of an amortization schedule for a term loan.
  □ Failure to make a sinking fund payment constitutes *technical default,* so lenders can require immediate payment on the entire issue and possibly force the firm into bankruptcy.
  □ Generally, sinking funds permit the firm to call a specific number of bonds for redemption or to buy the required number of bonds in the open market. The firm will select whichever method is the least costly.
  □ Note that a sinking fund call involves a *small percentage* of the issue, say one-thirtieth of a 30-year issue, while a regular call involves the entire issue. Further, *no premium* is paid on sinking fund calls, the bonds are *redeemed at par*.
  □ Although the sinking fund is designed to protect the bondholders by assuring that the issue is retired in an orderly fashion, it must be recognized that the sinking fund may at times work to the detriment of the bondholders.

- ☐ On balance, securities that provide for a sinking fund and continuing redemption are regarded as being safer than bonds without sinking funds, so adding a sinking fund provision to a bond issue will lower the bond's interest rate.

Bond issues are normally assigned quality ratings by both Moody's Investors Service and Standard & Poor's Corporation. These ratings reflect the probability that a bond will go into default. Aaa (Moody's) and AAA (S&P) are the highest ratings.

- ■ *Bond ratings* influence investors' perceptions of default risk and therefore have an impact on the interest rate paid, and hence on the firm's cost of capital.

- ■ Institutions are often limited to investing in *investment grade securities,* that is, those rated BBB or Baa, or higher. It is important, therefore, that a firm maintains a good quality rating on its bond issues.

- ■ Rating assignments are based on qualitative and quantitative factors, including the firm's debt/assets ratio, current ratio, and coverage ratios.

- ■ Rating agencies review outstanding bonds on a periodic basis and occasionally *upgrade* or *downgrade* a bond as the issuer's circumstances change. Also, if a company issues more bonds, this will trigger a review by the rating agencies.

- ■ A change in a firm's bond rating will have a significant effect on its *ability to borrow* long-term capital, and on the *cost of that capital.*

Long-term debt financing has several advantages and disadvantages to the issuer.

- ■ The major advantages are as follows:
  - ☐ The cost of debt is fixed (even floating rate debt is relatively fixed), so debtholders do not participate in the gains if profits soar.
  - ☐ The effective risk-adjusted cost of debt is lower than the risk-adjusted cost of equity when corporate taxes are considered.
  - ☐ The corporate owners do not share their control with debtholders.

- ■ The primary disadvantages are as follows:
  - ☐ Since debt service requirements are fixed, a reduction in revenues could lead to financial distress or bankruptcy.

- ☐ Financial leverage increases the firm's riskiness, and hence increases both the costs of debt and equity.
- ☐ Debt has a fixed maturity, and hence the firm must repay the principal at some future date.
- ☐ Long-term debt indenture agreements are much more stringent than in a short-term credit agreement.
- ☐ Widely accepted credit standards dictate the maximum amount of debt that is considered "reasonable," and the cost of debt beyond this limit becomes exorbitant.

Long-term financing decisions are difficult because they are influenced by many factors, most of which are subjective. Additionally, these factors vary among firms at any point in time and for any given firm over time.

- ■ One of the foremost considerations is the firm's *target (optimal) capital structure.*
  - ☐ Over the long haul, firms try to maintain their target structures.
  - ☐ However, from year to year, firms may stray from the target to minimize flotation costs, to take advantage of market conditions, or because of their own internal situation. As examples, a firm would not want to issue long-term debt if it was convinced that its bond rating would be upgraded in the near future, and it would not want to issue stock if it felt that its earnings were about to rise sharply, and more than the public anticipated.

- ■ Firms also must consider the *maturity of the assets being financed.*
  - ☐ If a firm uses 30-year bonds to finance 10-year assets, the bond payments would continue long after the assets were retired.
  - ☐ If a firm uses 10-year bonds to finance 30-year assets, it would have to "roll over" the debt after 10 years.
  - ☐ Each of the above strategies involves significant risks. In general, the best all-around strategy is to match the maturity of the debt to the maturity of the assets being financed.

- ■ Current interest rate levels and forecasts of future interest rates also play an important role in the financing decision.
  - ☐ If current rates are high, and are expected to drop, it might be wise to use short-term financing until rates drop, and then lock in the lower rates with long-term financing.
  - ☐ Conversely, if current rates are low and expected to rise, use long-term financing now to lock in the rates.
  - ☐ However, interest rates are difficult, if not impossible, to forecast. Thus, pursuing one of the above strategies could prove to be disastrous if the forecasts were wrong.

- ■ The firm's current condition and earnings outlook also have an effect on the choice of securities.

☐ A firm may delay debt financing which would trigger a review by the rating agencies.

☐ Debt issued when in a poor financial condition would probably cost more and have more severe restrictive covenants.

■ The amount of financing required and the availability of assets which could be pledged as collateral also impact the financing decision.

Corporations that issue callable debt or preferred stock during high interest rate periods often replace the issue with a lower cost issue when interest rates drop. This operation is called refunding, and is explained in Appendix 17A.

SELF-TEST QUESTIONS

Definitional

1. A(n) _____ loan is a contract to pay _____ and _____ on specific dates to a lender.

2. Term loans are generally negotiated directly with a(n) _____, _____ _____, or _____ _____. They are not sold to the _____ at large.

3. The process of paying off a term loan in equal _____ over the life of the loan is called _____.

4. _____ _____ _____ are offered at a discount below their par values and pay no coupon payments.

5. _____ are unsecured bonds, and holders of these securities are general creditors of the corporation.

6. A high yield, high risk bond is called a(n) _____ _____.

7. The oldest type of asset securitization is the _____-_____ _____.

8. A(n) _____ is a long-term contract that is generally offered to the public and under which the _____ agrees to make payments of interest and principal to the holders.

9. The legal document setting forth the terms and conditions of a bond issue is known as the _____.

10. The _____ represents the bondholders and sees that the terms of the indenture are carried out.

11. A bond secured by real estate is known as a(n) _____ bond.

12. Failure to make a sinking fund payment places the company in _____ _____, and could ultimately lead to _____.

13. In meeting its sinking fund requirements, a firm may _____ the bonds or purchase them on the _____ _____.

14. Except when the call is for sinking fund purposes, when a bond issue is called, the firm must pay a(n) _____ _____, or an amount in excess of the _____ value of the bond.

15. A restrictive _____ is a provision in the bond's _____ which requires the issuer to meet certain stated conditions.

16. Firms issue various securities because investors have different _____/_____ trade-offs.

17. Over the long run, a firm should finance in accordance with its _____ _____ _____.

18. The least risky financing strategy is to match the _____ of the debt with the _____ of the asset being financed.

19. It is very _____, if not _____, to forecast interest rates.

20. _____ _____ has claims on assets, in the event of bankruptcy, only after senior debt has been paid off.

21. _____ _____ pay interest only when covered by the firm's earnings.

22. _____ _____ bonds are bonds that are redeemable at par if the company restructures or engages in a leveraged buyout that significantly lowers the credit rating of the debt.

23. _____ _____ influence investors' perceptions of default risk and therefore have an impact on the interest rate paid, and hence on the firm' cost of capital.

24. With _____ _____ debt, the interest rate changes periodically to reflect current market conditions which causes the debt's market value to be stabilized..

25. In _____ _____, the holders of the debt generally have claims only against the sponsor's equity in the project and the cash flows generated from the project, and not against the firm or firms that own the project.

Conceptual

26. There is a direct relationship between bond ratings and the required rate of return on bonds; that is, the higher the rating, the higher is the required rate of return.

    a. True   **b.** False

27. The "penalty" for having a low bond rating is less severe when the Security Market Line is relatively steep than when it is not so steep.

    a. True   **b.** False

28. Which of the following would tend to increase the coupon interest rate on a bond that is to be issued?

    a. Adding a sinking fund.
    b. Adding a restrictive covenant.
    c. Adding a call provision.
    d. A change in the bond's rating from Aa to Aaa.
    e. Both a and c above.

29. Zero coupon bonds have become quite popular over the last several years. These bonds are advantageous to the issuer because

    a. The bond is, in effect, not callable.
    b. These bonds generally have a higher yield to maturity than normal coupon bonds.
    c. The bond's cash outflows are spread over the life of the bond.
    d. The bonds are initially sold above par value.
    e. None of the above statements is correct.

30. Which of the following statements is most *correct*?

    a. A first mortgage bond is secured by a company's assets, whereas a debenture is a type of bond that is secured by a second mortgage, meaning that it will only be paid off, in the event of bankruptcy, after the first mortgage bondholders have been paid in full.
    b. Bonds have three major advantages over term loans—speed, flexibility, and low issuance costs.
    c. Company X is planning to issue new bonds. If the bonds of a U.S. company have a sinking fund, this means that the company must deposit funds with a trustee, who invests the funds and lets the amount on deposit build up to an amount sufficient to pay off the bonds when they mature. Sinking funds are set up differently in Europe, where the funds in the sinking fund are used either to buy bonds on the open market or else to call in a small fraction of the issue each year. The results of both American and European sinking funds are the same, though; the bond obligation is paid off systematically rather that in one lump sum at maturity.
    d. Each of the above statements is true.
    e. Each of the above statements is false.

31. Which of the following statements is most *correct*?

   a. If a company decides to use callable bonds, the interest rate on the bonds will be higher than if it made the bonds noncallable. Therefore, only weak companies whose interest rate would be high anyway tend to issue callable bonds.

   b. Sinking fund provisions as spelled out in the indenture normally give the firm the right to call bonds for sinking fund purposes at par. This is bad for bondholders if interest rates have fallen. Therefore, if a company insists on including a sinking fund provision on its new bond issue, the interest rate will be higher than if the issue does not have a sinking fund.

   c. The primary advantage of zero coupon bonds to investors, especially to wealthy individual investors, is that the investor gets his or her returns in the form of capital gains rather than interest income. Since capital gains (1) are taxed at relatively low rates and (2) are deferred until the bond matures or is sold, zero coupon corporate bonds have a significant advantage over regular coupon bonds.

   d. The bond refunding decision is analyzed like a capital budgeting decision. The investment cost consists of the call premium plus the flotation cost on the new issue, and the cash flow benefits consist of the interest saved each year as a result of substituting low rate debt for high rate debt. Rational companies constantly monitor the situation, and they call callable bonds immediately if the NPV on the refunding decision is positive.

   e. The above statements are all false.

32. Assume that a new company will raise $100,000, all of which will be used to construct a new office building. The company will, by the terms of its charter, *never* raise any additional capital of any type or make any other investments. Tentatively, the company plans to issue $50,000 of first mortgage bonds and $50,000 of debentures. Which of the following statements is most correct?

   a. If the company issues $100,000 of first mortgage bonds rather than $50,000 of mortgage bonds and $50,000 of debentures, then the interest rate on the mortgage bonds will increase.

   b. If the company issues $10,000 of first mortgage bonds and $90,000 of debentures rather than $50,000 of mortgage bonds and $50,000 of debentures, then the interest rate on the debentures will probably decrease.

   c. If the company can never do any additional financing, there is no compelling reason to believe that the WACC would be materially affected by the mix between debentures and mortgage bonds.

   d. Statements a, b, and c are all true.

   e. Statements a, b, and c are all false.

SELF-TEST PROBLEMS

1. J.C. Nickel is planning a zero coupon bond issue. The bond has a par value of $1,000, matures in 10 years, and will be sold at an 80 percent discount, or for $200. The firm's marginal tax rate is 40 percent. What is the annual after-tax cost of debt to Nickel on this issue? (Hint: You will need to use a financial calculator.)

   a. 10.48%   **b.** 10.00%   **c.** 11.62%   **d.** 14.79%   **e.** 17.46%

   (The following data apply to the next two problems.)

   Ten years ago, the Privy Company issued a 10-year bond with a 10 percent annual coupon. The $100,000 issue sold at its par value of $1,000 per bond. The indenture had a sinking fund provision which stipulated that one-tenth of the issue must be redeemed at the end of each year.

2. Assume that interest rates fell after the issue date, causing the market value of the bonds to rise, and that Privy exercised the sinking fund provision by calling one-tenth of the issue (10 bonds) each year. What was the realized before-tax cost of the issue?

   a. 8.0%   **b.** 9.2%   **c.** 10.0%   **d.** 11.2%   **e.** 12.0%

3. Now assume that interest rates rose after the issue date, causing the market value of bonds to fall, and that the firm retired the issue over time by buying 10 of the bonds outstanding each year on the open market. Further, assume that Privy repurchased each bond (with a face value of $1,000) for $950, so its total expenditure to purchase 10 bonds was $9,500. Now what was the realized before-tax cost of the issue?

   a. 8.0%   **b.** 9.2%   **c.** 10.0%   **d.** 11.2%   **e.** 12.0%

4. Assume that the City of Miami sold an issue of $1,000 maturity value, tax exempt (muni), zero coupon bonds 10 years ago. The bonds had a 30-year maturity when they were issued, and the interest rate built into the issue was a nominal 12 percent, but with semiannual compounding. The bonds are now callable at a premium of 12 percent over the accrued value. What effective annual rate of return would an investor who bought the bonds when they were issued and who still owns them earn if they are called today? (Hint: You will need to use a financial calculator.)

   a. 13.33%   **b.** 12.00%   **c.** 12.37%   **d.** 11.76%   **e.** 13.64%

Appendix 17A

A-1. The City of Tampa issued $1,000,000 of 12 percent coupon, 25-year, semiannual payment, tax-exempt muni bonds 10 years ago. The bonds had 10 years of call protection, but now Tampa can call the bonds if it chooses to do so. The call premium would be 11 percent of the face amount. New 15-year, 10 percent, semiannual payment bonds can be sold at par, but flotation costs on this issue would be 3 percent, or $30,000. What is the net present value of the refunding?

    a. $13,011   **b.** $12,262   **c.** $15,121   **d.** $13,725   **e.** $14,545

A-2. Assume that the Tennessee Valley Power Authority (which is exempt from income taxes) issued $100,000 of 30-year maturity, 10 percent coupon, semiannual payment, tax-exempt bonds on January 1, 1987. The bonds were callable after 10 years, or after January 1, 1997, at a price that is 10 percent above the bonds' par value. On January 1, 1997, the Power Authority learns that it can issue $100,000 of new 20-year, semiannual payment, 8 percent coupon bonds at par. Costs associated with selling the new issue will amount to $2,000. What is the NPV of the refunding decision?

    a. -$7,485.46   **b.** $9,285.48   **c.** -$4,334.60   **d.** $7,792.77   **e.** $6,982.74

A-3. Assume that the City of Pensacola has $10 million of 12 percent, 20-year, $1,000 par value, semiannual payment bonds outstanding that can be called at a price of $1,100 per bond. New 20-year, 10 percent, semiannual payment bonds can be sold at a flotation cost of $600,000, or 6 percent. What is the NPV of the refunding operation?

    a. $115,909   **b.** $120,606   **c.** $125,505   **d.** $130,707   **e.** $135,808

ANSWERS TO SELF-TEST QUESTIONS

1. term; interest; principal
2. bank; insurance company; pension fund; public
3. installments (amounts); amortization
4. Zero coupon bonds
5. Debentures
6. junk bond
7. mortgage-backed security
8. bond; borrower
9. indenture
10. trustee
11. mortgage
12. technical default; bankruptcy
13. call; open market

14.	call premium; par	**20.**	Subordinated debt
15.	covenant; indenture	**21.**	Income bonds
16.	risk/return	**22.**	Poison put
17.	target capital structure	**23.**	Bond ratings
18.	maturity; maturity	**24.**	floating rate
19.	difficult; impossible	**25.**	project financing

26. b. The relationship is inverse. The higher the rating, the lower the default risk, and hence the lower the required rate of return. Aaa/AAA is a high rating, and as we go down the alphabet, the ratings are lower.

27. b. A steeper SML implies a higher risk premium on risky securities, and thus a greater "penalty" on lower-rated bonds.

28. c. Sinking funds, restrictive covenants, and an improvement in the bond rating all indicate lower risk for the bond, and hence would lower the coupon rate.

29. e. The primary advantages to the issuer are (1) that zero coupons have a lower required rate of return, and (2) that annual interest payments are avoided.

30. e. Statement a is false; a debenture is unsecured. Statement b is false; these are the advantages of term loans not bonds. Statement c is false; sinking funds are used either to buy bonds on the open market or to call in a small fraction of the issue each year. Therefore, the correct choice is statement e.

31. e. Statement a is false; the second sentence of this statement is incorrect. Statement b is false; sinking fund provisions make a bond issue less risky, and thus, lower the coupon rate on the issue. Statement c is false; investors must impute interest income in each year on zero coupon bonds even though the interest is not received until maturity. The advantage to investors is that there is no reinvestment rate risk with zeros. Statement d is false; companies do not necessarily call callable bonds immediately if the NPV on the refunding decision is positive because if interest rates decrease further it may be beneficial to wait awhile. Therefore, the correct choice is statement e.

32. d. As the firm uses more and more mortgage bonds, less and less collateral will lie behind each bond, so the riskiness and hence the interest rate on the mortgage bonds will increase. Thus, statement a is true. Second, if the company issued relatively few mortgage bonds, then more of the property would be available to the debentures in the event of bankruptcy, so the debentures would be less risky and would have a lower interest rate. Thus, statement b is also true. Third, the overall cost of debt will be a weighted average of the costs of mortgage bonds and debentures. As the use of mortgage bonds goes up, the costs of both types of bonds will increase, but the weight of the lower cost bonds (mortgage bonds) will increase, and the net result could well be a constant average cost of debt. In that case, the WACC would not be affected by the mortgage/debenture mix. Therefore, statement c is also true, which makes statement d the correct answer.

SOLUTIONS TO SELF-TEST PROBLEMS

1. a. Maturity = N = 10; Issue price = PV = 200; PMT = 0; Maturity value = FV = 1000; Corporate tax rate = 40%.

Enter into a financial calculator: N = 10, PV = -200, PMT = 0, and FV = 1000, and then solve for k_d = I = 17.46%. However, this is a before-tax cost of debt. $k_d(1 - T) = 17.46\%(1 - 0.4) = 10.48\%$.

Alternatively, set the analysis up on a time line:

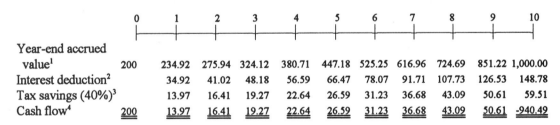

	0	1	2	3	4	5	6	7	8	9	10
Year-end accrued value[1]	200	234.92	275.94	324.12	380.71	447.18	525.25	616.96	724.69	851.22	1,000.00
Interest deduction[2]		34.92	41.02	48.18	56.59	66.47	78.07	91.71	107.73	126.53	148.78
Tax savings (40%)[3]		13.97	16.41	19.27	22.64	26.59	31.23	36.68	43.09	50.61	59.51
Cash flow[4]	200	13.97	16.41	19.27	22.64	26.59	31.23	36.68	43.09	50.61	-940.49

After-tax cost of debt: 10.48%.

Notes:
[1]Year-end accrued value = Issue price $\times (1 + k_d)^n$.
[2]Interest in Year n = Accrued value$_n$ – Accrued value$_{n-1}$.
[3]Tax savings = (Interest deduction)(T).
[4]Cash flow in Year 10 = Tax savings – Maturity value.

2. c. Each year, Privy retired $10,000 face value in bonds. Thus, its interest expense also decreased by one-tenth each year:

Year	Debt Outstanding at Beginning of Year	Interest Expense
1	$100,000	$10,000
2	90,000	9,000
--	----	----
9	20,000	2,000
10	10,000	1,000

Thus, Privy paid 10 percent on the outstanding balance throughout the life of the issue and it was retired at par value. Thus, its realized before-tax cost was also 10 percent.

3. b. To answer this, you must lay out the cash flows over the life of the issue:

Year	Debt Outstanding at Beg of Year	Interest Expense	Sinking Fund Expense	Total Service Requirement
1	$100,000	$10,000	$9,500	$19,500
2	90,000	9,000	9,500	18,500
3	80,000	8,000	9,500	17,500
4	70,000	7,000	9,500	16,500
5	60,000	6,000	9,500	15,500
6	50,000	5,000	9,500	14,500
7	40,000	4,000	9,500	13,500
8	30,000	3,000	9,500	12,500
9	20,000	2,000	9,500	11,500
10	10,000	1,000	9,500	10,500

Now, the firm received $100,000 at Time 0, and paid out the cash flows shown above in the right-hand column. The IRR of this cash flow stream, 9.2 percent, was Privy's realized before-tax cost of debt in this case. The ability to repurchase the bonds at less than par reduced the cost of the issue. (Note that Privy would not actually be able to repurchase the final $10,000 worth of bonds for $9,500. At maturity, it must pay the full par value. This would change the total service requirement in Year 10 to $11,000, and the resultant before-tax cost of debt would increase slightly from 9.196% to 9.248%.)

4. e.

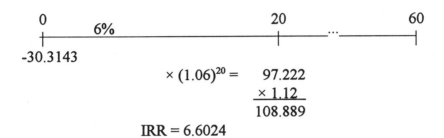

Periodic rate = 6.6024%.

EAR = $(1.066024)^2 - 1 = 0.1364 = 13.64\%$.

The solution to this problem requires three steps:

(1) Solve for the PV of the original issue. Using a financial calculator, enter N = 60, I = 6, PMT = 0, and FV = 1000, and then solve for PV = $30.3143.

(2) Determine the accrued value at the end of 20 periods, and multiply by the call premium.

$$\$30.3143 \times (1.06)^{20} \times 1.12 = \$108.889.$$

(3) Solve for the EAR to an investor if the bonds are called today. Using a financial calculator, enter N = 20, PV = -30.3143, PMT = 0, and FV = 108.889, and then solve for $k_d/2 = I = 6.6024$.

$$EAR = (1.066024)^2 - 1 = 0.1364 = 13.64\%.$$

Appendix 17A

A-1. d. Interest on old bond per 6 months: $120,000/2 = \$ 60,000

Interest on new bond per 6 months: $100,000/2 = \underline{\quad 50,000}

Savings per six months \underline{\$ \ 10,000}

Cost: Call premium = 11% = \quad\quad\quad\quad $110,000

Flotation cost = 3% = \quad\quad\quad\quad \underline{\quad 30,000}

Total investment outlay \quad\quad \underline{\$140,000}

$k_d/2 = 10\%/2 = 5\%$ per 6 months.

$$NPV = \sum_{t=1}^{30} \frac{\$10,000}{(1.05)^t} - \$140,000 = \$153,725 - \$140,000 = \$13,725.$$

Alternatively, input the cash flows into the cash flow register, enter I = 5, and then solve for NPV = $13,725.

A-2. d. Cost of refunding = Call premium + Flotation cost

$\quad\quad\quad\quad\quad\quad = 0.10(\$100,000) + \$2,000 = \$12,000.$

Savings each 6 months = Interest on old bonds – Interest on new bonds

$\quad\quad\quad\quad\quad\quad\quad\quad = 0.05(\$100,000) - 0.04(\$100,000)$

$\quad\quad\quad\quad\quad\quad\quad\quad = \$5,000 - \$4,000 = \$1,000.$

$k_d/2 = 8.0\%/2 = 4.0\%$ = Discount rate for NPV.

```
       0    4%    1        2        3           40     Periods
       ├─────────┼────────┼────────┼─── ··· ───┤
    -12,000    1,000    1,000    1,000        1,000
```

$$NPV = \sum_{t=1}^{40} \frac{\$1,000}{(1.04)^t} - \$12,000 = \$19,792.77 - \$12,000 = \$7,792.77.$$

A-3. a. Cost of refunding = Call premium + Flotation cost
$$= (\$1,100 - \$1,000)10,000 + \$600,000 = \$1,600,000.$$

Savings each 6 months = Interest on old bonds – Interest on new bonds
$$= 0.06(\$1,000)(10,000) - 0.05(\$1,000)(10,000)$$
$$= \$100,000.$$

Using a time line, the cash flows are shown below:

```
      0            1            2            40    Periods
         5%
      +------------+------------+------...----+
  -1,600,000   100,000      100,000      100,000
```

$$NPV = \sum_{t=1}^{40} \frac{\$100,000}{(1.05)^t} - \$1,600,000.$$

Using a financial calculator, input the cash flows into the cash flow register, enter I = 5, and then solve for NPV = $115,908.64 ≈ $115,909.

CHAPTER 18

LEASE FINANCING

OVERVIEW

Firms generally own fixed assets and hence report them on their balance sheets, but it is the use of the fixed assets that is important, not their ownership. One way of obtaining the use of facilities and equipment is to buy them, but an alternative is to lease them. Prior to the 1950s, leasing was generally associated with real estate—land and buildings. Today, however, it is possible to lease virtually any kind of asset, and about 30 percent of all new capital equipment acquired by businesses is financed through lease arrangements.

OUTLINE

There are two parties (at least) to every lease agreement, and there are several different types of leases.

■ The *lessor* is the owner of the leased property. The lessor receives the tax benefit of ownership through depreciation tax savings.

■ The *lessee* buys the right to use the property by making lease payments to the lessor.

■ There are four common types of leasing arrangements.
   □ *Operating leases.* These leases include both financing and maintenance services.
   ▸ Operating leases ordinarily call for the lessor to maintain and service the leased equipment; the cost of maintenance is built into the lease payments.
   ▸ The lease contract is written for less than the useful life of the equipment; that is, the lease is not fully amortized.
   ▸ The lessor expects to recover the cost of the equipment by subsequent renewal payments, by re-leasing the equipment to other lessees, or by sale of the equipment.
   ▸ Operating leases often contain a cancellation clause to protect the lessee against obsolescence.
   □ *Financial, or capital, leases.* These leases are fully amortized; however, they do not provide for maintenance and are not cancelable.
   ▸ They differ from a sale and leaseback in that the equipment is new.

- ► Equipment is purchased by the lessor from the manufacturer or distributor, and the lessee simultaneously executes an agreement to lease the equipment from the financial institution.
- ► The lessee generally pays the property taxes and insurance on the leased property. Since the lessor receives a return after, or net of, these payments, this type of lease is often called a "net, net" lease.
- ☐ *Sale and leaseback*. In this type of lease, a firm owning an asset sells the property to a leasing company and simultaneously leases it back for a specified period at specific terms.
  - ► The sale and leaseback is an alternative to simply borrowing against the property on a mortgage loan basis.
  - ► The seller receives the purchase price but retains the use of the property in exchange for rental payments.
  - ► The lease payments are sufficient to return the purchase price to the lessor plus provide a specified return on the investment.
  - ► A sale and leaseback may be thought of as a special type of financial lease.
- ☐ *Combination leases*. This type of lease contains features of both operating and financial leases.

Lease payments are deductible expenses for income tax purposes, provided the IRS agrees that the contract is a genuine lease and not an installment sale called a lease.

- ■ The IRS would consider the transaction to be a *sale* if any of these conditions hold:
  - ☐ The lease payments are made over a relatively short period and approximate the price of the asset.
  - ☐ The lessee may continue to use the asset for a relatively nominal (small) payment.
  - ☐ A purchase option at a favorable price is written into the lease contract.

- ■ These restrictions prevent a company from using a lease arrangement to depreciate equipment over a much shorter period than its MACRS class life.

- ■ A lease that complies with all the IRS requirements for a genuine lease is called a *guideline*, or *tax-oriented, lease*. The main purpose of the tax guidelines are as follows:
  - ☐ The lease term must not exceed 80 percent of the estimated useful life of the equipment at the commencement of the lease transaction.
  - ☐ The equipment's estimated residual value at the expiration of the least must equal at least 20 percent of its value at the start of the lease.
  - ☐ Neither the lessee nor any related party can have the right to purchase the property from the lessor at a fixed price predetermined at the lease's inception.

- ☐ Neither the lessee nor any related party can pay or guarantee payment of any part of the price of the leased equipment.
- ☐ The leased equipment must not be "limited use" property, defined as equipment that can only be used by the lessee or a related party at the end of the lease.

- ■ In a guideline lease, the tax benefits of ownership belong to the lessor, and the lessee can deduct the full amount of the lease payment.

- ■ A lease that does not meet the tax guidelines is called a *non-tax-oriented lease*. For this type of lease, the tax benefits of ownership accrue to the lessee, but the lessee can only deduct the implied interest portion of each lease payment.

Lease financing is financially comparable to debt financing because both subject the firm to a contractual series of payments and failure to make these payments could lead to bankruptcy.

- ■ Leasing is sometimes referred to as *off balance sheet financing* because, under certain conditions, neither the leased assets nor the lease liabilities appear directly on the firm's balance sheet.

- ■ A firm with extensive lease arrangements not appearing directly on the firm's balance sheet would have both its assets and its liabilities understated in comparison with a firm which borrowed to purchase the assets, and hence, the firm that leases would show a lower debt ratio. Note, however, that these lease obligations must be disclosed in the notes to the financial statements.

- ■ FASB #13 requires firms to *capitalize* certain financial leases and thus to restate their balance sheets if certain conditions exist. A lease is capitalized if one or more of the following conditions exist:
  - ☐ Ownership of the property is effectively transferred from the lessor to the lessee.
  - ☐ The lessee can purchase the property at less than its true market value when the lease expires.
  - ☐ The lease runs for a period equal to or greater than 75 percent of the asset's life.
  - ☐ The present value of the lease payments is equal to or greater than 90 percent of the initial value of the asset.

- ■ When a lease is capitalized, leased assets must be reported under fixed assets, and the present value of future lease payments must be shown as a debt obligation.

- ■ Leased assets are equivalent to assets purchased using all debt financing. Suppose a firm's target capital structure is 50 percent debt and 50 percent equity. Further, assume that 50 percent of the firm's assets are leased. Then, to maintain its target capital structure, the firm must use all-equity financing for the nonleased assets.

■ The lease decision is a *financing decision*, and not a capital budgeting decision. Thus, lease analysis is not generally conducted unless the decision has already been made to acquire the asset.

Leases must be evaluated by both the lessee and the lessor. For the lessee, the analysis focuses on whether leasing the asset is less costly than borrowing and buying the asset, and the lessor must decide what the lease payments must be to produce a target rate of return on invested funds .

■ In an NPV-type analysis, the lessee estimates the cost of leasing and the cost of owning, assuming that the asset is financed solely with debt. If the cost of leasing is less than the cost of owning, the asset should be leased.
   □ All cash flows must reflect tax effects.
   □ Since leasing is a substitute for debt financing, and since lease cash flows have approximately the same risk as debt cash flows, the *appropriate discount rate is the after-tax cost of debt*.
   □ In a lease analysis, the PV cost of owning less the PV cost of leasing is called the *net advantage to leasing (NAL)*.

■ The lease versus purchase decision can also be analyzed using an IRR approach.
   □ The IRR of the lease is the after-tax cost rate of the lease.
   □ The asset should be leased if the IRR of the lease is less than the after-tax cost of debt.
   □ If the cost of leasing is less than the cost of debt, the overall cost of capital for an asset with lease financing would be less than that for a nonleased asset of similar risk. Thus, assets that were marginally unacceptable could have a positive NPV if lower cost lease financing were available.

■ The final way to analyze a lease from the lessee's perspective is through the *equivalent loan method*. With this method the lessee considers the dollar amount of the loan that it could obtain if it paid the cash flows to a lender instead of the lessor. The difference in the financing amounts is equal to the NAL.

■ The NPV, IRR, and equivalent loan approaches will always lead to the same decision.

The lessor views the lease transaction as an investment, and hence, the lessor's analysis focuses on the return on the lease transaction.

■ The lessor compares the return on the lease with the return available on alternative investments of similar risk. If the return expected on the lease is greater than that available on alternatives of similar risk, the lease should be written.

■ The analysis is similar to that of the lessee, in that the cash flows are laid out on a time line.
- ☐ All tax effects must be considered.
- ☐ If the lessor's NPV is positive, then the lease should be written.
- ☐ The lessor's IRR can also be examined, and if it is greater than the after-tax return on comparable investments, the lease transaction should be completed.

■ When the lessor borrows to purchase the leased property, the lease is called a *leveraged lease*.
- ☐ Whether or not a lease is leveraged is unimportant from the lessee's standpoint.
- ☐ Typically, leveraged leases provide the lessor with higher expected rates of return (IRRs) and higher NPVs per dollar of invested capital than unleveraged leases. However, the riskiness to the lessor is increased by the leveraging.

Other issues often arise in leasing decisions.

■ The value of the asset at lease termination is called its *residual value*.
- ☐ It might first appear that assets with large residual values would most likely be owned since the owner gets the residual value.
- ☐ However, competition among leasing companies forces lease contracts to reflect expected residual values. Thus, large residual value assets are not necessarily more suitable for buying than for leasing.

■ It is sometimes argued that firms which lease a significant portion of their assets can get more favorable debt terms than firms which do not.
- ☐ This premise rests upon the assumption that credit analysts do not recognize the full impact of leasing on a firm's financial strength.
- ☐ However, this contention is of *questionable validity* for firms with audited financial statements.
- ☐ Leasing can be a way to circumvent existing loan covenants. If restrictive covenants prohibit a firm from issuing more debt but fail to restrict lease payments, then the firm could effectively increase its leverage by leasing additional assets.
- ☐ Firms in very poor financial condition and facing possible bankruptcy may be able to obtain lease financing at a lower cost than comparable debt financing, because lessors often have a more favorable position than lenders should the lessee actually go bankrupt.

- ■ Tax considerations are an important motive behind many nonoperating leases that are written today.
  - □ A firm that is unprofitable, or that is expanding rapidly and generating large depreciation writeoffs, cannot immediately use the full tax benefits of ownership.
  - □ On the other hand, firms in the highest marginal tax bracket gain the most tax benefits from owning.
  - □ Therefore, companies that make extensive use of lease financing are typically doing poorly and are unable to effectively use tax benefits, while lessors include highly profitable companies which can fully use the tax benefits.

- ■ The ability to structure leases that are advantageous to both lessor and lessee depends in large part on tax laws. The four major factors that influence leasing are (1) investment tax credits, (2) depreciation rules, (3) tax rates, and (4) alternative minimum taxes.
  - □ The *investment tax credit (ITC)* is a direct reduction of taxes that occurs when a firm purchases new capital equipment.
  - □ Owners recover their investments in capital assets through *depreciation*, which is tax deductible. Recent tax laws have tended to slow depreciation write-offs, and hence to reduce the value of ownership.
  - □ The value of depreciation depends on the firm's *tax rate*, because the depreciation tax savings equals the amount of depreciation multiplied by the tax rate. Higher tax rates mean greater ownership tax savings, and hence more incentive for tax-driven leases.
  - □ The *alternative minimum tax (AMT)* also impacts leasing activity.
    - ‣ Previously, some corporations were able to pay little or no taxes by using accelerated depreciation for tax purposes, and yet report high earnings to stockholders by using straight line depreciation. The AMT now requires companies to pay a minimum tax equal to approximately 20 percent of their reported earnings.
    - ‣ A company can reduce its reported income, and hence its AMT liability, by using short-term, fully amortized leases on long-term assets--such leases need not meet the requirements for ordinary tax deductibility.

In addition to tax motivations, there are many other reasons why firms might lease assets rather than purchase them.

- ■ Many assets are leased, particularly through operating leases, because it is less risky for the firm to lease the asset than to commit to ownership.
  - □ Assets that face rapid and uncertain *technological obsolescence* are often leased. Lessees benefit because they are more easily able to acquire the most advanced equipment. Although the risk of obsolescence is passed to the lessor, lessors may be better able to bear this risk

because of (1) diversification across a wide variety of assets and (2) being better able to assess residual values and market the used assets.

☐ If the life of the project is in doubt, then it may be better to lease the asset, since it might be easier to dispose of the asset in the event of *premature termination* of the project.

■ The leasing industry recently introduced a type of lease that transfers some of a project's operating risk from the lessee to the lessor.

☐ In the health care industry, such leases are called per-procedure leases.

☐ Instead of making a fixed rental payment, the lessee pays a fee each time the leased equipment is used. By using a per-procedure lease, the company is converting a fixed cost for the equipment into a variable cost, hence reducing the machine's operating leverage and breakeven point.

SELF-TEST QUESTIONS

Definitional

1. Conceptually, leasing is similar to _____, and it provides the same type of financial _____.

2. Under a(n) _____ _____ _____ arrangement, the seller receives the purchase price of the asset but retains the _____ of the property.

3. _____ leases include both financing and maintenance arrangements.

4. A(n) _____, or _____, lease is similar to a sale and leaseback arrangement, but generally apply to the purchase of _____ equipment directly from the manufacturer.

5. The IRS would disallow a "lease" which pays for the asset in a relatively _____ period, and then permits the lessee to retain the asset for a(n) _____ payment.

6. If the IRS allows the lease, then the _____ _____ is fully deductible.

7. FASB #13 requires that firms _____ certain financial leases, and hence restate their _____ _____.

8. Capitalizing a lease requires that the asset be listed under _____ _____, and that the _____ _____ of the future lease payments be shown as _____.

9. The value of an asset at the end of the lease term is referred to as its _____ _____.

10. _____ among leasing companies will tend to force leasing rates down to the point where _____ values are fully reflected in the lease rates.

11. Since some leases do not appear on the _____ _____, a firm may be able to use more _____ than if it did not lease.

12. The leasing decision is a(n) _____ decision rather than a(n) _____ _____ decision.

13. Both the lessee and the lessor can use the _____ or _____ technique to evaluate a lease.

14. _____ _____ are often an important motive behind financial leases.

15. The _____ _____ is designed to insure that corporations reporting high earnings will pay some taxes.

16. _____ leases contain features of both operating and financial leases.

17. A lease that complies with all the IRS requirements for a genuine lease is called a(n) _____, or _____-_____, lease.

18. Since leasing is a substitute for debt financing, and since lease cash flows have approximately the same risk as debt cash flows, the appropriate discount rate is the _____-_____ _____ _____ _____.

19. When the lessor borrows to purchase the leased property, the lease is called a(n) _____ lease.

20. Assets that face rapid and uncertain _____ _____ are often leased.

Conceptual

21. Capital leases typically include both financing and maintenance arrangements.

    a. True   **b.** False

22. Leveraged leases typically provide the lessor with higher NPVs per dollar of investment than do unleveraged leases.

    a. True   **b.** False

23. When one is evaluating a lease proposal, cash flows should be discounted at a relatively high rate because lease flows are fairly certain.

    a. True   **b.** False

24. Generally, operating leases are fully amortized, and the lease is written for the expected life of the asset.

    a. True   **b.** False

25. A firm which uses extensive lease financing may have a substantially lower reported debt ratio than a firm which borrows to finance its assets.

    a. True   **b.** False

26. Firms may or may not capitalize a financial lease.

    a. True   **b.** False

27. The more stringent alternative minimum tax (AMT) has generated new leasing business.

    a. True   **b.** False

28. Which of the following statements is most *correct*?

    a. Some years ago leasing was called "off balance sheet financing" because the leased asset and the corresponding lease obligation did not appear directly on the balance sheet. Today, though, that situation has changed materially because *all leases* must be capitalized and reported on the balance sheet, along with the value of the leased asset.

    b. In a lease versus purchase analysis, cash flows should generally be discounted at the weighted average cost of capital (WACC).

    c. Each of the above statements is true.

    d. Each of the above statements is false.

SELF-TEST PROBLEMS

(The following data apply to the next four problems.)

Treadmill Trucking Company is negotiating a lease for five new tractor/trailer rigs with Leasing International. Treadmill has received its best offer from Betterbilt Trucks for a total price of $1 million. The terms of the lease offered by International Leasing call for a payment of $205,000 at the beginning of each year of the 5-year lease. As an alternative to leasing, the firm can borrow from a large insurance company and buy the trucks. The $1 million would be borrowed on an amortized term loan at a 10 percent interest rate for 5 years. The trucks fall into the MACRS 5-year class and have an expected residual value of $100,000. Maintenance costs would be included in the lease. If the trucks are owned, a maintenance contract would be purchased at the beginning of each year for $10,000 per year. Treadmill plans to buy a new fleet of trucks at the end of the fifth year. Leasing International has a 40 percent federal-plus-state marginal tax rate, while Treadmill Trucking has a total tax rate of 20 percent.

1. What is Treadmill's present value of the cost of owning?

    a. $802,468   **b.** $805,265   **c.** $807,189   **d.** $817,197   **e.** $829,668

2. What is Treadmill's present value of the cost of leasing?

    a. $702,468   **b.** $705,265   **c.** $707,189   **d.** $729,668   **e.** $735,419

3. Treadmill should lease the trucks.

   a. True   **b.** False

4. Assume that the lessor's alternative to leasing is to invest in a 5-year certificate of deposit which pays 9 percent before taxes. The lessor should

   a. Write the lease; it has an IRR of 3 percent.
   b. Not write the lease; it has an IRR of 3 percent.
   c. Write the lease; its NPV is $78,625.
   d. Not write the lease; its NPV is -$78,625.
   e. Be indifferent between the lease and the alternative investment.

(The following data apply to the next four problems.)

Walton Publishing Company (WPC) is evaluating a potential lease agreement on a printing press that costs $250,000 and falls into the MACRS 3-year class. The loan rate would be 8 percent, if WPC decided to borrow and buy rather than lease. The press has a 4-year economic life, and its estimated residual value is $25,000 at the end of Year 4. If WPC buys the press, it would purchase a maintenance contract which costs $5,000 per year, payable at the beginning of each year. The lease terms, which include maintenance, call for a $71,000 lease payment at the beginning of each year. WPC's tax rate is 40 percent. (Hint: Use a financial calculator.)

5. Should the firm lease or buy?

   a. Lease; it costs $842 less than buying.
   b. Lease; it costs $1,576 less than buying.
   c. Buy; it costs $1,576 less than leasing.
   d. Buy; it costs $842 less than leasing.
   e. Neither lease nor buy; the truck's NPV is negative.

6. Assume that the lessor is in the 40 percent tax bracket. Further, the lessor's investment alternatives of similar risk yield 8 percent before taxes. Should the lessor write the lease?

   a. Yes, its NPV is $1,577.   **d.** No, its NPV is -$842.
   b. No, its NPV is -$1,577.   **e.** The lessor is indifferent.
   c. Yes, its NPV is $842.

7. At what lease payment would the lessee be indifferent between owning and leasing?

   a. $42,178   **b.** $68,348   **c.** $69,572   **d.** $70,898   **e.** $70,296

8. Assume that the lessor's NPV on the lease investment is $1,600. Further, assume that the lessor could obtain financing on 80 percent of his cost of $250,000. If the lessor leverages, assume his NPV on the lease investment would drop to $800. Should the lessor leverage the lease?

   a. Yes   **b.** No

ANSWERS TO SELF-TEST QUESTIONS

1. borrowing; leverage
2. sale and leaseback; use
3. Operating
4. financial; capital; new
5. short; small (nominal)
6. lease payment
7. capitalize; balance sheets
8. fixed assets; present value; debt (liability)
9. residual value
10. Competition; residual

11. balance sheet; leverage (debt)
12. financing; capital budgeting
13. NPV; IRR
14. Tax considerations
15. alternative minimum tax
16. Combination
17. guideline; tax-oriented
18. after-tax cost of debt
19. leveraged
20. technological obsolescence

21. b. Operating leases include both financing and maintenance arrangements, while financial, or capital, leases typically do not provide maintenance services. However, many leases written today are combination leases, which combine some of the features of both operating and financial leases.

22. a. However, this only holds true if the cost of leveraging is less than the return on the lease. Further, note that leveraging increases the lessor's risk.

23. b. The cash flows are fairly certain, so they should be discounted at a relatively low rate, generally, the after-tax cost of debt.

24. b. Operating leases are not fully amortized. The lessor expects to recover all costs either in subsequent leases or through the sale of the used equipment at its residual value.

25. a. But analysts would recognize that leases are as risky as debt financing, and thus include the impact of lease financing on the firm's debt costs and capital structure.

26. b. FASB #13 spells out in detail the conditions under which leases must be capitalized.

27. a. Firms have been seeking ways to lower their AMT liability. Leasing for short periods and hence making high lease payments will reduce the company's reported earnings and meet this need.

28. d. Statement a is false; only certain leases that meet the FASB #13 criteria for capitalization have to be reported on the balance sheet. Statement b is false; the discount rate in a borrow-versus-lease decision is the after-tax cost of debt because the cash flows are fairly certain. Therefore, statement d is the correct choice.

SOLUTIONS TO SELF-TEST PROBLEMS

1. d. Place the cash flows associated with ownership on a time line:

	0	1	2	3	4	5
		8%				
Outlay	-1,000,000					
Dep. tax savings[a]		40,000	64,000	38,000	24,000	22,000
Maintenance (AT)[b]	-8,000	-8,000	-8,000	-8,000	-8,000	
Residual value (AT)[c]						92,000
	-1,008,000	32,000	56,000	30,000	16,000	114,000

[a]Depreciation schedule:

Year	Factor	Depreciation Expense	Tax Savings
1	0.20	$ 200,000	$ 40,000
2	0.32	320,000	64,000
3	0.19	190,000	38,000
4	0.12	120,000	24,000
5	0.11	110,000	22,000
6	0.06	60,000	12,000
		$1,000,000	$200,000

Notes:
[b]After-tax maintenance cash flow = $10,000(1 - T) = $8,000.
[c]Net residual value = $100,000 - ($100,000 - $60,000)(T) = $92,000.

PV cost of owning at the firm's 8 percent after-tax cost of debt is $817,197.

2. c. Place the cash flows associated with leasing on a time line:

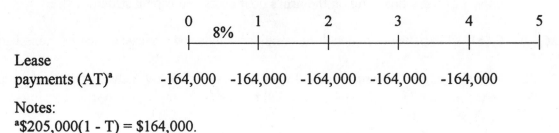

Notes:
[a] $205,000(1 - T) = $164,000.

PV cost of leasing at the firm's 8 percent after-tax cost of debt is $707,189.

3. a. The Net Advantage to Leasing (NAL) is $817,197 - $707,189 = $110,008, and hence the trucks should be leased.

4. d. Place the lessor's cash flows on a time line:

	0	1	2	3	4	5
		5.4%				
Outlay[a]	-1,000,000					
Dep. tax savings[b]		80,000	128,000	76,000	48,000	44,000
Lease payment (AT)[c]	123,000	123,000	123,000	123,000	123,000	
Residual value (AT)[d]						84,000
Maintenance (AT)[e]	-6,000	-6,000	-6,000	-6,000	-6,000	
	-883,000	197,000	245,000	193,000	165,000	128,000

Notes:
[a] Cost of purchasing the trucks.
[b] This is each year's depreciation expense times the lessor's tax rate of 40 percent.
[c] After-tax lease payment = $205,000(1 - 0.40) = $123,000.
[d] After-tax residual value = $100,000 - ($100,000 - $60,000)(T) = $84,000.
[e] After-tax maintenance payment = $10,000(1 - T).

The lessor's NPV of the lease investment is the PV of the net cash flows when discounted at the after-tax opportunity cost of capital or 9%(1 - T) = 9%(0.6) = 5.4%. NPV = -$78,625.

5. c. Cost of owning: Net investment = $250,000.

Year	Factor	Depreciation
1	0.33	$ 82,500
2	0.45	112,500
3	0.15	37,500
4	0.07	17,500
	1.00	$250,000

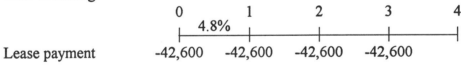

	0	1	2	3	4
Net cost	-250,000				
Maintenance (AT)	-3,000	-3,000	-3,000	-3,000	
Dep. tax savings		33,000	45,000	15,000	7,000
Residual value (AT)					15,000
	-253,000	30,000	42,000	12,000	22,000

PV cost of owning at 4.8% = $157,470.

Cost of leasing:

	0	1	2	3	4
Lease payment	-42,600	-42,600	-42,600	-42,600	

PV cost of leasing at 4.8% = $159,046.

Thus, owning is $157,470 - $159,046 = $1,576 less costly than leasing, so the firm should purchase the printing press.

6. a. Lessor's analysis:

	0	1	2	3	4
		4.8%			
Net cost	-250,000				
Maintenance	-3,000	-3,000	-3,000	-3,000	
Dep. tax savings		33,000	45,000	15,000	7,000
Net residual value					15,000
Lease payment	42,600	42,600	42,600	42,600	
	-210,400	72,600	84,600	54,600	22,000

The lessor's NPV at 4.8 percent = $1,577.

7. e. The lessee would be indifferent if the cost of leasing were equal to $157,470, the PV of owning. Thus,

$$\$157,470 = PMT(PVIFA_{4.8\%,4})(1.048)$$
$$PMT = \$42,177.74.$$

Lease payment = $42,177.74/0.6 = $70,296.23 ≈ $70,296.

8. a. If the lessor can finance 80 percent of his cost, the lease would only require an investment of 0.2($250,000) = $50,000. Thus, the lessor could write 5 leases for the same $250,000 original investment, and his total NPV would be 5($800) = $4,000, which is significantly higher than the assumed $1,600 NPV available on the $250,000 unleveraged lease.

CHAPTER 19

HYBRID FINANCING: PREFERRED STOCK, WARRANTS, AND CONVERTIBLES

OVERVIEW

In the three preceding chapters, we examined the use of common stock, various types of long-term debt, and leasing. In this chapter, we examine three other sources of long-term capital: preferred stock, which is a hybrid security that represents a cross between debt and common equity; warrants, which are derivative (option) securities that are issued by firms; and convertibles, which are hybrids between debt or preferred stock and warrants.

OUTLINE

Preferred stock is a hybrid—it is similar to bonds in some respects and to common stock in others. Preferred stock resembles bonds in that it has a par value, and like a bond's coupon payments, preferred dividends are fixed in amount and must be paid before common stock dividends. On the other hand, if earnings are not sufficient to cover the preferred dividend, the directors can omit the dividend without subjecting the company to potential bankruptcy.

- Accountants generally view preferred stock as equity and show it on the balance sheet as an equity account. Financial managers view preferred stock as being somewhere between debt and common equity—it imposes a fixed charge and thus increases the firm's financial leverage, yet if the preferred dividend is omitted, the company may not be forced into bankruptcy.

- Some of the major provisions of preferred stock issues are featured below.
  - ☐ Preferred stockholders have priority over common stockholders with regard to earnings and assets.
  - ☐ Preferred stock has an established par value which represents the amount due the preferred stockholders in the event of liquidation.
  - ☐ Most preferred stock provides for *cumulative dividends*, whereby all preferred dividends in arrears must be paid before common dividends can be paid.

■ Occasionally other provisions are encountered in preferred stock issues.
  ☐ Preferred stockholders are generally given voting rights after management has missed a specified number of dividend payments.
  ☐ Most newly issued preferred stocks now have sinking funds and/or call provisions.
  ☐ Because of these provisions, most preferred stocks now have finite maturity dates and hence are not perpetual.
  ☐ Preferred stock may be convertible into common stock.

■ Two important innovations in preferred stock financing have occurred in recent years.
  ☐ *Floating*, or *adjustable rate, preferred stocks (ARPs)* tie their dividends to the rate on Treasury securities instead of paying fixed dividends.
  ☐ *Money market,* or *market auction, preferred stocks* are, from the investor's point of view, a low risk 7-week maturity security which can be sold between auction dates at close to par value.

■ Preferred stock financing has both advantages and disadvantages.
  ☐ By using preferred, the firm can avoid sharing either control or earnings with new investors, yet limit the possibility of bankruptcy if earnings are not sufficient to meet the dividend payment.
  ☐ However, since preferred dividends are not tax deductible, preferred stock usually has a higher after-tax cost than debt financing. In addition, preferred dividends are considered to ba a fixed cost, hence the use of preferred stock, like debt, increases the financial risk of the firm and thus increases the cost of common equity.

■ Preferred stock also has its benefits and drawbacks to investors.
  ☐ Because 70 percent of preferred dividends received by corporations are exempt from taxes, preferred stock offers high after-tax returns to corporations, and hence, most nonconvertible preferred stock is owned by corporations.
  ☐ For the individual investor, after-tax bond yields are generally higher than those of riskier preferred stock.

A warrant is a call option issued by a company which gives the holder the right to buy a stated number of shares of the company's stock at a specified price.

■ Often warrants are attached to debt instruments as an incentive for investors to buy the combined issue at a lower interest rate than would otherwise be the case. Additionally, warrants may eliminate the need for extremely restrictive indenture provisions.

■ Warrants were originally used as "sweeteners" by small, risky firms to make their bonds or preferred stocks more attractive. However, after AT&T became the first large and financially strong corporation to use warrants, their use by such firms became commonplace.

■ Most warrants are *detachable* and can be traded separately from the bond or preferred stock with which they were issued.

■ Warrants generate additional equity capital when they are exercised.
   □ The *exercise price* on warrants is generally set 10 to 30 percent above the market price of the stock at the time the warrant is issued.
   □ If the market price is above the exercise price, and the warrants are about to expire, holders will exercise their options and purchase stock.
   □ Since warrants pay no dividends, holders will be inclined to exercise them and obtain common stock as the common dividend is increased.
   □ A stepped-up exercise price will also induce holders to exercise their warrants.

■ Warrants generally produce needed funds as the company grows and as the stock price increases over the exercise price.

■ The component cost of an issue with warrants can be estimated by placing the expected cash flows associated with the issue on a time line and then calculating the IRR of the stream.

■ Although the interest rate on the bond will be less than the rate on a similar straight debt issue, the total cost rate of the issue, including the opportunity cost of the warrants, will usually be somewhere between the firm's costs of straight debt and equity because the riskiness of a bond with warrants falls between that of debt and equity.

Convertible securities are bonds or preferred stocks which can be exchanged for common stock at the option of the holder and under specified terms and conditions.

■ Conversion of a bond or preferred stock, unlike the exercise of a warrant, does not produce additional funds for the firm. However, conversion does lower the debt ratio.

■ The *conversion ratio (CR)* specifies the number of common shares that will be received for each bond or share of preferred stock that is converted.

■ The *conversion price,* P_c, is the effective price paid for the common stock when conversion occurs. For example, if a bond is issued at its par value of $1,000 and can be converted into 40 shares of common stock, the conversion price would be

$$P_c = \$1,000/CR = \$1,000/40 = \$25 \text{ per share.}$$

Someone buying the bond and then converting it would, in effect, be paying $25 per share for the stock.

■ The conversion price of a bond is typically set at about 10 to 30 percent above the market price of common stock when the convertible issue is sold. Thus, if the common stock is selling for $20.83 at the time the convertible is issued, the conversion price might be set at 1.2($20.83) = $25. This would produce a conversion ratio of CR = 40:

$$CR = \$1,000/P_c = \$1,000/\$25 = 40.$$

■ Convertible issues have certain advantages and disadvantages to the issuing corporation.
  □ By giving investors an opportunity to realize capital gains, a firm can sell debt with a lower interest rate or preferred stock with a lower dividend yield.
  □ Convertibles provide a way of selling common stock in the future at prices higher than those currently prevailing.
  □ However, if the stock price does not increase, investors will not convert and the company will be stuck with debt (or preferred) rather than equity in its capital structure. However, the interest rate on this debt will be comparatively low and will be lost when conversion occurs.
  □ If the stock price does rise, the company can force conversion by including a call feature in the bond's indenture or on the preferred stock.
  □ Note that if the firm's stock price rises sharply, it would have been better off to have waited and sold the common shares at the higher price.

■ The actual market price of a convertible bond will always be equal to or greater than the higher of its straight debt value or its conversion value. The higher of those two values is called the *floor price*.

■ Like a bond with warrants, the expected cost rate on convertible debt can be estimated by placing the issue's expected cash flows on a time line. Also, like debt with warrants, the costs should lie between the issuing firm's cost of straight debt and its cost of common stock, because, from the investors' viewpoint, a convertible is riskier than straight debt but less risky than common stock.

■ When convertible debt is issued, actions to increase the company's riskiness may increase the convertible debt's value as well as the common stock's value. Thus, some of the gains to shareholders from taking on high-risk projects may be transferred to convertible bondholders. This reduction in benefits to shareholders decreases the incentive for managers to substitute assets, and hence lowers agency costs.

Most convertible issues have provisions that allow the issuer to call the issue prior to maturity.

■ If a convertible is called when its conversion value is less than the stock price, convertible holders will elect to receive the call price. In this stiuation, the firm will have to pay out cash to redeem the issue, and no new equity will appear on the balance sheet.

■ If the call is made when the conversion value exceeds the stock price, convertible holders will convert their bonds. In this case, the firm will not need to use cash to retire the convertibles, and a balance sheet transfer will be made from debt or preferred to common equity.
   □ When a convertible is converted into common stock, the difference between the conversion price and the stock's current market price constitutes a wealth transfer from current stockholders to convertible holders.
   □ The optimal call policy is to call the convertible issue as soon as the issue's conversion value reaches the call price.

Convertible debt can be thought of as straight debt with nondetachable warrants. Thus, it might appear that debt with warrants and convertible debt are more or less interchangeable. However, a closer examination reveals differences.

■ The exercise of warrants brings in new equity capital, while the conversion of convertibles results only in an accounting transfer.

■ Most convertible issues contain a call provision that allows the issuer either to refund the debt or to force conversion, depending on the relationship between the conversion value and call price. However, most warrants are not callable, so firms generally must wait until maturity for the warrants to generate new equity capital.

■ Warrants typically have much shorter maturities than convertibles, and warrants typically have much shorter maturities than their accompanying debt.

■ Warrants usually provide for fewer future common shares than do convertibles.

■ Bonds with warrants typically require issuance costs that are about 120 basis points more than the flotation costs for convertibles.

Firms with warrants or convertible securities outstanding must reflect these securities when they report earnings per share to stockholders. A firm could report earnings per share in one of three ways:

■ *Simple EPS,* where earnings available to common stockholders are divided by the average number of shares actually outstanding during the period.

■ *Primary EPS,* where earnings available are divided by the average number of shares that would be outstanding if those warrants and convertibles likely to be exercised or converted had actually been exercised or converted.

■ *Fully diluted EPS,* which is similar to primary EPS except that all warrants and convertibles are assumed to be exercised or converted regardless of the likelihood of this occurring.

■ For firms with large amounts of warrants and/or convertibles outstanding, there can be substantial differences between EPS calculations. Thus, the SEC requires that both primary and fully diluted earnings be shown.

Securities innovation is the development of new securities that not only are different but also enable issuers or investors to do something they could not do before, or to do the same thing in a more cost-effective way.

■ Value can be created in several ways by securities innovation:
  □ Reallocation of risk from one class of investors to another class that is less risk sensitive. Interest rate swaps are an example of this type of value creation.
  □ Reduction of transactions costs paid to third parties, or increased liquidity for investors. The development of the junk bond market illustrates these points.
  □ Reduction of investors' taxes without increasing the corporate tax rate liability, or vice versa. Leasing provides a good example of this point.

■ One recent innovation is Merrill Lynch's *Liquid Yield Option Note*, or *LYON*. The LYON is a zero coupon variant of the traditional form of the convertible debt. The LYON promises a return with no reinvestment rate risk, plus the potential appreciation of common stock.

SELF-TEST QUESTIONS

Definitional

1. Preferred stock has characteristics similar to both _____ and _____ _____.

2. The _____ _____ feature means that preferred stockholders must receive all dividends in arrears before common dividends may be paid.

3. Warrants and convertibles may make a company's securities more attractive to a broader range of _____ and hence lower its _____ _____ _____.

4. A(n) _____ is an option to buy a stated number of shares of _____ _____ at a specified _____.

5. Warrants are often attached to a(n) _____ issue in order to make it salable at a relatively low _____ rate.

6. Warrants are _____ options as opposed to _____ options.

7. The _____ price of a warrant is generally set at about _____ to _____ percent above the stock's market price.

8. When they are exercised, warrants add additional _____ _____ to a firm's capital structure.

9. Warrants will certainly be exercised if the stock's market price is above the _____ price and the warrant is about to _____.

10. Holders of warrants will have an extra incentive to convert to _____ _____ as the company increases the _____ on its common shares.

11. Almost all warrants are _____ and can be traded separately from the debt or preferred stock with which they were issued.

12. Convertible bonds or preferred stocks may be exchanged for _____ _____ at the option of the _____.

13. The _____ _____ specifies the number of shares of common stock that will be received for each bond that is converted.

14. The _____ _____ is the effective price paid for one share of common stock upon conversion.

15. When a convertible bond is issued, the conversion price is determined by dividing the _____ _____ of the bond by the number of shares received on conversion.

16. Selling a convertible issue may have the effect of selling _____ _____ at a price higher than the market price prevailing at the time the convertible is issued.

17. If a firm's stock price does increase, the company can force _____ of convertible bonds by including a(n) _____ _____ in the bond indenture.

18. It may be unwise for a firm to sell a convertible issue if it anticipates that its _____ _____ will increase rapidly in the near future.

19. In reporting its earnings, a firm with warrants and convertible securities must report both _____ EPS and _____ _____ EPS.

20. The higher of a convertible bond's straight debt value or its conversion value is called the _____ _____.

21. The _____ _____ _____ _____ promises a return with no reinvestment rate risk, plus the potential appreciation of common stock.

22. _____, or _____ _____, _____ _____ tie their dividends to the rate on Treasury securities instead of paying fixed dividends.

Conceptual

23. Preferred stock is generally viewed as equity by bondholders and as debt by common stockholders.

    a. True   b. False

24. The coupon interest rate on convertible bonds is generally set higher than the rate on similar nonconvertible issues.

    a. True   **b.** False

25. Primary EPS shows what EPS would have been if all warrant and convertibles had been converted prior to the reporting date.

    a. True   **b.** False

26. Investors are willing to accept lower interest (or dividend) yields on convertible securities in the hopes of later realizing capital gains.

    a. True   **b.** False

27. The conversion of a convertible bond replaces debt with common equity on a firm's balance sheet, but it does not bring in any additional capital.

    a. True   **b.** False

28. The market price of a warrant may be substantially above its expiration value.

    a. True   **b.** False

29. The advantage to the corporation of using preferred stock financing is:

    a. Preferred dividends are tax deductible.
    b. Preferred stockholders bear no risk of ownership.
    c. The returns on preferred stock are always higher than on bonds.
    d. The firm can retain control and limit the profit sharing of new investors.
    e. Preferred stockholders always have voting rights.

SELF-TEST PROBLEMS

1. The Clayton Corporation has warrants outstanding that permit the holder to purchase one share of common stock per warrant at $30. What is the expiration value of Clayton's warrants if the common stock is currently selling at $20 per share?

    a. -$20   **b.** -$10   **c.** $5   **d.** $10   **e.** $20

2. Refer to Self-Test Problem 1. Calculate the expiration value if the common stock is now selling at $40 per share.

    a. -$20   **b.** -$10   **c.** $0   **d.** $10   **e.** $20

3. White Corporation has just sold a bond issue with 10 warrants attached to each bond. The bonds have a 20-year maturity, an annual coupon rate of 12 percent, and they sold at the $1,000 initial offering price. The current yield to maturity on bonds of equal risk, but without warrants, is 15 percent. What is the value of each warrant?

    a. $22.56   **b.** $21.20   **c.** $20.21   **d.** $19.24   **e.** $18.78

    The following data apply to the next four problems.

    Central Food Brokers is considering issuing a 20-year convertible bond that will be priced at its par value of $1,000 per bond. The bonds have a 12 percent annual coupon interest rate, and each bond could be converted into 40 shares of common stock. The stock currently sells at $20 per share, has an expected annual dividend of $3.00, and is growing at a constant 5 percent per year. The bonds are callable after 10 years at a price of $1,050, with the price declining by $5 per year thereafter. If, after 10 years, the conversion value exceeds the call price by at least 20 percent, management will call the bonds.

4. What is the conversion price?

    a. $20   **b.** $25   **c.** $33   **d.** $40   **e.** $50

5. If the yield to maturity on similar nonconvertible bonds is 16 percent, what is the straight-debt value?

    a. $1,000.00   **b.** $907.83   **c.** $812.22   **d.** $762.85   **e.** $692.37

6. What is the conversion value in Year 10?

   a. $800.73   **b.** $1,000.50   **c.** $1,148.01   **d.** $1,222.18   **e.** $1,303.12

7. If an investor expects the bond issue to be called in Year 10, and he plans on converting it at that time, what is the investor's expected rate of return upon conversion?

   a. 12.0%   **b.** 12.2%   **c.** 13.6%   **d.** 14.4%   **e.** 15.3%

ANSWERS TO SELF-TEST QUESTIONS

1. bonds (debt); common stock (equity)
2. cumulative dividends
3. investors; cost of capital
4. warrant; common stock; price
5. debt; interest
6. call; put
7. exercise (striking); 10; 30
8. common equity
9. exercise (striking); expire
10. common stock; dividend
11. detachable
12. common stock; holder
13. conversion ratio
14. conversion price
15. par value
16. common stock
17. conversion; call provision
18. stock price
19. primary; fully diluted
20. floor price
21. liquid yield option note
22. floating; adjustable rate preferred stock

23. a. Preferred stock is treated as debt by common stockholders since preferred dividends must be paid before common dividends. Bondholders have a priority claim on cash flows over preferred stockholders and also priority in the event of liquidation and therefore view preferred stock as equity.

24. b. The coupon interest rate is lower because investors expect some capital gains return upon conversion. Note, however, that the overall required rate of return is higher for the convertible issue.

25. b. Primary EPS includes only those shares from warrants and convertibles likely to be converted in the near future. Fully diluted EPS includes all shares.

26. a. However, the investor is including the expected capital gain as part of his required return, so the total required return on convertibles is higher than on a straight security with similar other features.

27. a. The bond is turned in to the company and replaced with common stock. No cash is exchanged.

28. a. A warrant is a call option, and hence its value depends not only on its expiration value, but also on its time to maturity, the price volatility of the underlying stock, and the risk-free rate.

29. d. By setting a fixed dividend, management can limit the degree of profit sharing by preferred stockholders and also retain control since preferred stockholders normally do not have voting rights.

SOLUTIONS TO SELF-TEST PROBLEMS

1. b. Expiration value = Market price - Exercise price. When $P_0 = \$20$, the Expiration value = $\$20 - \$30 = -\$10$.

2. d. When $P_0 = \$40$, the Expiration value = $\$40 - \$30 = \$10$.

3. e. First, find the straight-debt value:

$$V = INT(PVIFA_{k,n}) + M(PVIF_{k,n}) = \$120(PVIFA_{15\%,20}) + \$1,000(PVIF_{15\%,20}) = \$812.22.$$

Thus the value of the attached warrants is $\$1,000 - \$812.22 = \$187.78$. Since each bond has 10 warrants, each warrant must have a value of $\$18.78$.

4. b. P_c = Par value/Shares received = $\$1,000/40 = \$25.00$.

5. d. $V = INT(PVIFA_{k,n}) + M(PVIF_{k,n}) = \$120(PVIFA_{16\%,20}) + \$1,000(PVIF_{16\%,20}) = \$762.85$.

6. e. $C_t = P_t CR$; $C_{10} = P_{10} CR = \$20(1.05)^{10}(40) = \$1,303.12$.

7. c. This is solved by finding the value of k_c in the equation:

Price paid = INT($PVIF_{k_c,n}$) + Expected conversion value ($PVIF_{k_c,n}$)

$\$1,000$ = $\$120(PVIF_{k_c,10})$ + $\$1,303.12(PVIF_{k_c,10})$

k_c = 13.6%.

CHAPTER 20

CURRENT ASSET MANAGEMENT

OVERVIEW

About 60 percent of a typical financial manager's time is devoted to working capital management, and many students' first jobs will involve working capital. This is particularly true in smaller businesses, where most new jobs are being created.

Working capital policy involves two basic questions: (1) What is the appropriate amount of current assets for the firm to carry, both in total and for each specific account, and (2) how should current assets be financed? This chapter addresses the first question, while Chapter 21 addresses the second.

OUTLINE

It is useful to begin by reviewing some basic definitions and concepts.

■ *Working capital*, sometimes called *gross working capital*, is defined as current assets, while *net working capital* is defined as current assets minus current liabilities.

■ The *current ratio*, which is calculated as current assets divided by current liabilities, is intended to measure a firm's liquidity. The *quick ratio*, which also attempts to measure liquidity, is calculated as current assets less inventories, divided by current liabilities.

■ The most comprehensive picture of a firm's liquidity is obtained by examining its *cash budget*, which forecasts a firm's cash inflows and outflows, and thus focuses on what really counts, the firm's ability to generate the cash inflows required to meet its required cash outflows.

■ *Working capital policy* refers to the firm's basic policies regarding target levels for each category of current assets and how current assets will be financed.

■ *Working capital management* involves the administration of current assets and current liabilities.

A firm's current asset levels rise and fall with business cycles and seasonal trends. At the peak of such cycles, businesses carry their maximum amounts of current assets.

■ There are three alternative policies regarding the total amount of current assets carried. Each policy differs in that different amounts of current assets are carried to support a given level of sales.

☐ A *relaxed current asset investment policy* is one in which large amounts of cash, marketable securities, and inventories are carried, and where sales are stimulated by the use of a liberal credit policy.

☐ A *restricted current asset investment policy* is one in which holdings of cash, securities, inventories, and receivables are minimized.

☐ A *moderate current asset investment policy* is between the two extremes.

☐ Generally, the decision on the current assets level involves a risk/return tradeoff. The relaxed policy minimizes risk, but it also has the lowest expected return. On the other hand, the restricted policy offers the highest expected return coupled with the highest risk. The moderate policy falls in between the two extremes in terms of expected risk and return.

☐ Changing technology can lead to dramatic changes in the optimal current asset investment policy.

■ Working capital consists of four main components: cash, marketable securities, inventory, and accounts receivable.

■ For each type of asset, firms face a fundamental tradeoff: current assets are necessary to conduct business, and the greater the holdings of current assets, the smaller the danger of running out, hence the lower the firm's operating risk. However, holding working capital is costly; so, there is pressure to hold the amount of working capital carried to the minimum consistent with running the business without interruption.

In today's world of intense global competition, working capital management is receiving increasing attention from managers striving for peak efficiency. The goal of many leading companies today is zero working capital.

■ This concept has its own definition of working capital: Inventories + Receivables - Payables.

■ Reducing working capital, and thus increasing turnover, has two major financial benefits.

☐ Every dollar freed up by reducing inventories or receivables, or generated by increasing payables, results in a one-time one dollar contribution to cash flow.

☐ A movement toward zero working capital permanently raises a company's earnings.

- ☐ In addition to the financial benefits, reducing working capital forces a company to produce and deliver faster than its competitors, which helps it gain new business and charge premium prices for filling rush orders.

- ■ Focusing on minimizing receivables and inventories while maximizing payables will help a firm lower its working capital, reduce its cash conversion cycle, and achieve financial and production economies.

Cash is a nonearning asset. Excessive cash balances reduce the rate of return on equity and hence a firm's stock value. Thus, the goal of cash management is to minimize the amount of cash the firm must hold in order to conduct its normal business.

- ■ Firms hold cash for two primary reasons:
  - ☐ *Transactions balances* are held to provide the cash needed to conduct normal business operations.
  - ☐ *Compensating balances* are often required by banks for providing loans and services.

- ■ Two secondary reasons are also cited:
  - ☐ *Precautionary balances* are held in reserve for random fluctuations in cash inflows and outflows.
  - ☐ *Speculative balances* are held to enable the firm to take advantage of bargain purchases.

- ■ Most firms do not segregate funds for each of these motives, but they do consider them in setting their overall cash positions.

- ■ An ample cash balance should be maintained to take advantage of trade discounts and favorable business opportunities, to help the firm maintain its credit rating, and to meet emergency needs.

A cash budget projects cash inflows and outflows over some specified period of time.

- ■ The basis for a cash budget is the sales forecast and the level of fixed assets and inventory that will be required to meet the forecasted sales level.

- ■ Cash budgets can be created for any interval, but firms typically use a monthly cash budget for the coming year, a weekly budget for the coming month, and a daily budget for the coming week, or something similar.

- ■ A typical cash budget consists of three sections.

□ The *collections and purchases worksheet* summarizes the firm's cash collections from sales and cash purchases for materials.

□ The *cash gain or loss section* lays out the cash inflows and outflows, and the "bottom line" of this section is the net cash gain or loss.

□ The *cash surplus or loan requirement section* summarizes the firm's cumulative need for loans and cumulative surplus cash.

■ If the firm's inflows and outflows are not uniform over the budget interval, say monthly, the cash budget will overstate or understate the firm's cash needs.

■ The cash budget can be used to help set the firm's *target cash balance*. This is accomplished by incorporating uncertainty into the budget, and then setting a target balance which provides a cushion against adverse conditions.

■ Computer spreadsheet programs are particularly well suited for preparing and analyzing the cash budget.

■ Note that the cash budget focuses on the physical movement of cash, and hence depreciation cash flow does not appear directly on the budget. It does, however, affect the amount of taxes shown.

Cash management has changed significantly over the last two decades as a result of interest rates and new technology.

■ From the early 1970s to the mid-1980s, there was a clear upward trend in interest rates which increased the opportunity cost of holding cash, and therefore, encouraged financial managers to search for more efficient ways of managing the firm's cash.

■ New technology, particularly computerized electronic funds transfer mechanisms, have improved cash management efficiency.

■ Cash management techniques encompass (1) cash flow synchronization, (2) using float, (3) accelerating collections, (4) getting available funds to where they are needed, and (5) controlling disbursements.

■ Synchronizing cash inflows and outflows permits a reduction in the firm's cash balances, decreases its bank loans, lowers its interest expense, and increases profits.

■ Net float is the difference between the balance shown in a firm's checkbook and the balance on the bank's records. A firm's net float is a function of its ability to speed up collections on checks received (*collections float*) and to slow down collections on checks written (*disbursement float*).
  □ Delays that cause float arise because it takes time for checks to travel through the mail (mail float), to be processed by the receiving firm (processing float), and to clear through the banking system (clearing, or availability, float).

Several techniques are now used to speed collections and to get funds where they are needed.

■ A *lockbox plan* is a procedure which speeds up collections and reduces float through the use of post office boxes in payers' local areas.
  □ Customers mail checks to a post office box in a specified city. A local bank then collects the checks, deposits them, starts the clearing process, and notifies the selling firm that payment has been received.
  □ Processing time is further reduced because it takes less time for banks to collect local checks.

■ Firms are increasingly demanding payments of larger bills by wire, or even by automatic electronic debits.

Marketable securities typically provide much lower yields than a firm's operating assets, yet they are often held in sizable amounts.

■ In many cases companies hold marketable securities for the same reasons they hold cash.

■ While these securities are not as liquid as cash, in most cases they can be converted to cash in a very short period of time.

■ Marketable securities provide at least a modest return, while cash yields nothing.

■ William Baumol first recognized that the tradeoff between cash and marketable securities is similar to the one firms face when setting the optimal inventory level.
  □ His model suggests that cash holdings should be higher if it costs a lot and takes a long time to liquidate marketable securities, but lower if interest rates are low.

Inventory, which may be classified as raw materials, work-in-process, and finished goods, is essential to the operation of most businesses.

■ Inventory is greatly influenced by the level of sales. Since inventory is acquired before sales can take place, an accurate sales forecast is critical to effective inventory management.

■ Proper inventory management requires close coordination among the sales, purchasing, production, and finance departments. The sales/marketing department is generally the first to spot changes in demand. These changes must be worked into the company's purchasing and manufacturing schedules, and the financial manager must arrange any financing that will be needed to support the inventory buildup. Improper coordination among departments, poor sales forecasts, or both, can lead to disaster.

The goal of inventory management is to insure that the inventories needed to sustain operations are available, but to hold the costs of ordering and carrying inventories to the lowest possible level.

■ Inventory costs are divided into three categories: carrying costs, ordering and receiving costs, and the costs that are incurred if the firm runs short of inventory.

    □ *Carrying costs* generally rise in direct proportion to the average amount of inventory held. Carrying costs associated with inventory include cost of the capital tied up, storage and handling costs, insurance, property taxes, and depreciation and obsolescence.

    □ *Ordering costs*, which are considered to be fixed costs, decline as average inventory increase, that is, as the number of orders decrease. Ordering costs include the costs of placing and receiving orders.

    □ The *costs of running short* include loss of sales, loss of customer goodwill, and disruption of production schedules.

Inventory management also involves the establishment of an inventory control system. These systems vary from the extremely simple to the very complex.

■ One simple control procedure is the *redline method*. A red line is drawn inside the bin where the inventory is stocked. When the red line shows, an order is placed.

■ The *two-bin method* has inventory items stocked in two bins. When the working bin is empty, an order is placed and inventory is drawn from the second bin.

■ Large companies employ much more sophisticated *computerized inventory control systems*. The computer starts with an inventory count in memory. As withdrawals are made, they are recorded by the computer, and the inventory balance is revised. Orders are automatically placed once the reorder point is reached.

■ The *just-in-time (JIT) system* coordinates a manufacturer's production with suppliers' so that raw materials arrive from suppliers just as they are needed in the production process. It also requires that component parts be perfect; therefore, JIT inventory management has been developed in conjunction with total quality management (TQM).

■ Another important development related to inventory is *out-sourcing*, which is the practice of purchasing components rather than making them in-house. Out-sourcing is often combined with just-in-time systems to reduce inventory levels.

■ A final point relating to inventory levels is the relationship between production scheduling and inventory levels. Inventory policy must be coordinated with the firm's manufacturing and procurement policies, because the ultimate goal is to minimize total production and distribution costs, and inventory costs are just one part of the picture.

Carrying receivables has both direct and indirect costs, but it also has an important benefit—granting credit will increase sales.

■ *Accounts receivable* are created when a firm sells goods or performs services on credit rather than on a cash basis. When cash is received, accounts receivable are reduced by the same amount.

■ The total amount of accounts receivable outstanding is determined by (1) the volume of credit sales and (2) the average length of time between sales and collections.

■ The investment in receivables, like any asset, must be financed in some manner; however, the entire amount of the receivable does not have to be financed because the profit portion does not represent a cash outflow.

Receivables must be actively managed to insure that the firm's receivables policy is effective. There are two commonly used methods to monitor a firm's receivables.

■ The *days sales outstanding (DSO)*, also sometimes called the average collection period (ACP), measures the average length of time it takes a firm's customers to pay off their credit purchases.
   □ The DSO is calculated by dividing the receivables balance by average daily credit sales.
   □ The DSO can be compared with the industry average and the firm's own credit terms to get an indication of how well customers are adhering to the terms prescribed and how customers' payments, on average, compare with the industry average.

■ An *aging schedule* breaks down a firm's receivables by the ages of the accounts, and it points out the percentage of receivables due that are attributable to late paying customers.

■ Both the DSO and aging schedule can be distorted if sales are seasonal or if a firm is growing rapidly. A deterioration in either the DSO or the aging schedule should be taken as a signal to investigate further, but not necessarily as a sign that the firm's credit policy has weakened.

The major controllable variables that affect sales are sales price, product quality, advertising, and the firm's credit policy. The credit policy consists of (1) the credit period, (2) credit standards, (3) collection policy, and (4) discounts.

■ The *credit period* is the length of time for which credit is granted. Increasing the credit period often stimulates sales, but there is a cost involved in carrying the increased receivables.

■ *Credit standards* refer to the strength and creditworthiness a customer must exhibit in order to qualify for credit.
  □ Two major sources of external credit information are available: credit associations and credit-reporting agencies such as Dun & Bradstreet and TRW.

■ *Collection policy* refers to the procedures the firm follows to collect past-due accounts. The collection process can be expensive in terms of both direct costs and lost goodwill, but at least some firmness is needed to prevent an undue lengthening of the collection period and to minimize outright losses.

■ The last variable in the credit policy decision is the firm's *cash discount policy*. Cash discounts attract customers and encourage early payment but reduce the dollar amount received on each discount sale.

■ Other conditions may also influence a firm's overall credit policy.
  □ It is sometimes possible to sell on credit and assess a carrying charge on the receivables that are outstanding, making credit sales more profitable than cash sales.
  □ It is illegal for a firm to charge prices or to set credit terms that discriminate between customers unless these differential prices are cost-justified.

SELF-TEST QUESTIONS

Definitional

1. Current assets are also referred to as _____ _____.

2. _____ working capital is defined as _____ assets minus current _____.

3. The goal of cash management is to _____ the amount of _____ the firm must hold in order to conduct its normal business activities.

4. Precautionary balances are maintained in order to allow for random, unforeseen fluctuations in cash _____ and _____.

5. _____ balances are maintained to pay banks for services they perform.

6. Efficient cash management is often concerned with speeding up the _____ of checks received and slowing down the _____ of checks issued.

7. One method for speeding the collection process is the use of a(n) _____ system.

8. The difference between a firm's balance on its own books and its balance as carried on the bank's books is known as net _____.

9. Inventory is usually classified as _____ _____, _____ - ___ - _____, and _____ _____.

10. The goal of inventory management is to provide the inventory needed for operations at the _____ _____.

11. Storage costs, obsolescence, and other costs that _____ with larger inventory are known as _____ costs.

12. Ordering and receiving costs are _____ related to average inventory size.

13. Inventory control systems that require suppliers to deliver items as they are needed are called _____ - ___ - _____ systems.

14. _____ _____ are created when goods are sold or services are performed on credit.

15. A firm's outstanding accounts receivable will be determined by the _____ of credit sales and the length of time between _____ and _____.

16. Sales volume and the collection period will be affected by a firm's _____ _____.

17. Extremely strict credit standards will result in lost _____.

18. Credit terms generally specify the _____ for which credit is granted and any _____ _____ that is offered for early payment.

19. The optimal credit terms involve a tradeoff between increased _____ and the cost of carrying additional _____ _____.

20. _____ policy refers to the manner in which a firm tries to obtain payment from past-due accounts.

21. Two popular methods for monitoring receivables are _____ _____ and the _____ _____ _____.

22. Credit sales may be especially profitable if a(n) _____ charge is assessed on accounts receivable.

23. A(n) _____ current asset investment policy is one in which large amounts of cash, marketable securities, and inventories are carried, and where sales are stimulated by the use of a liberal credit policy.

24. A(n) _____ _____ projects cash inflows and outflows over some specified period of time.

25. _____-_____ is the practice of purchasing components rather than making them in-house.

Conceptual

26. A firm changes its credit policy from 2/10, net 30, to 3/10, net 30. The change is to meet competition, so no increase in sales is expected. The firm's average investment in accounts receivable will probably increase as a result of the change.

    a. True   **b.** False

27. An aging schedule is constructed by a firm to keep track of when its accounts payable are due.

    a. True   **b.** False

28. If a credit policy change increases the firm's accounts receivable, the entire increase must be financed by some source of funds.

    a. True   **b.** False

29. Which of the following actions would not be consistent with good cash management?

    a. Increasing the synchronization of cash flows.
    b. Using lockboxes in funds collection.
    c. Maintaining an average cash balance equal to that required as a compensating balance or that which minimizes total cost.
    d. Minimizing the use of float.

30. The goal of credit policy is to

    a. Minimize bad debt losses.
    b. Minimize DSO.
    c. Maximize sales.
    d. Minimize collection expenses.
    e. Extend credit to the point where marginal profits equal marginal costs.

SELF-TEST PROBLEMS

1. The Mill Company has a daily average collection of checks of $250,000. It takes the company 4 days to convert the checks to cash. Assume a lockbox system could be employed which would reduce the cash conversion period to 3 days. The lockbox system would have a net cost of $25,000 per year, but any additional funds made available could be invested to net 8 percent per year. Should Mill adopt the lockbox system?

   a. Yes; the system would free $250,000 in funds.
   b. Yes; the benefits of the lockbox system exceed the costs.
   c. No; the benefit is only $10,000.
   d. No; the firm would lose $5,000 per year if the system were used.
   e. The benefits and costs are equal; hence the firm is indifferent toward the system.

   (The following data apply to the next three Self-Test Problems.)

   Simmons Brick Company sells on terms of 3/10, net 30. Gross sales for the year are $1,200,000 and the collections department estimates that 30 percent of the customers pay on the tenth day and take discounts; 40 percent pay on the thirtieth day; and the remaining 30 percent pay, on average, 40 days after the purchase. Assume 360 days per year.

2. What is the days sales outstanding?

   a. 10 days   b. 13 days   c. 20 days   d. 27 days   e. 40 days

3. What is the current receivables balance?

   a. $60,000   b. $70,000   c. $75,000   d. $80,000   e. $90,000

4. What would be the new receivables balance if Simmons toughened up on its collection policy, with the result that all nondiscount customers paid on the thirtieth day?

   a. $60,000   b. $70,000   c. $75,000   d. $80,000   e. $90,000

ANSWERS TO SELF-TEST QUESTIONS

1. working capital
2. Net; current; liabilities
3. minimize; cash
4. inflows; outflows
5. Compensating
6. collection; payment
7. lockbox
8. float
9. raw materials; work-in-process; finished goods
10. lowest cost
11. increase; carrying
12. inversely
13. just-in-time
14. Accounts receivable
15. volume; sales; collections
16. credit policy
17. sales
18. period; cash discount
19. sales; accounts receivable
20. Collection
21. aging schedules; days sales outstanding (DSO)
22. carrying
23. relaxed
24. cash budget
25. Out-sourcing

26. b. No new customers are being generated. The current customers pay either on Day 10 or Day 30. The increase in trade discount will induce some customers who are now paying on Day 30 to pay on Day 10. Thus, the days sales outstanding is shortened which, in turn, will cause a decline in accounts receivable.

27. b. The aging schedule breaks down accounts receivable according to how long they have been outstanding.

28. b. Receivables are based on sales price which presumably includes some profit. Only the actual cash outlays associated with receivables must be financed. The remainder, or profit, appears on the balance sheet as an increase in retained earnings.

29. d. Management should try to maximize float.

30. e. The goal of credit policy is to maximize overall profits. This is achieved when the marginal profits equal the marginal costs.

SOLUTIONS TO SELF-TEST PROBLEMS

1. d. Currently, Mill has 4($250,000) = $1,000,000 in unavailable collections. If lockboxes were used, this could be reduced to $750,000. Thus, $250,000 would be available to invest at 8 percent, resulting in an annual return of 0.08($250,000) = $20,000. If the system costs $25,000, Mill would lose $5,000 per year by adopting the system.

2. d. 0.3(10 days) + 0.4(30 days) + 0.3(40 days) = 27 days.

3. e. Receivables = (DSO)(Sales/360) = 27($1,200,000/360) = $90,000.

4. d. New days sales outstanding = 0.3(10) + 0.7(30) = 24 days.
   Sales per day = $1,200,000/360 = $3,333.33.
   Receivables = $3,333.33(24 days) = $80,000.00.

   Thus, the average receivables would drop from $90,000 to $80,000. Furthermore, sales may decline as a result of the tighter credit and reduce receivables even more. Also, some additional customers may now take discounts, which would further reduce receivables.

CHAPTER 21

SHORT-TERM FINANCING

OVERVIEW

Working capital policy involves decisions relating to current assets, including decisions about financing them. Since about half of the typical firm's capital is invested in current assets, working capital policy and management are important to the firm and its shareholders. In fact, about 60 percent of a financial manager's time is devoted to working capital policy and management, and many finance students' first assignments on the job will involve working capital. For these reasons, working capital policy is a vitally important topic.

OUTLINE

A firm's current asset levels and financing requirements rise and fall with business cycles and seasonal trends. At the peak of such cycles, businesses carry their maximum amounts of current assets. Similar fluctuations in financing needs can occur over these cycles, typically, financing needs contract during recessions, and they expand during booms.

■ Current assets rarely drop to zero, and this fact has led to the development of the idea of *permanent current assets*. These are the current assets on hand at the low point of the year.

■ Seasonal current assets are defined as *temporary current assets*.

■ The manner in which the permanent and temporary current assets are financed is called the firm's *current asset financing policy*.
   □ The *moderate, or maturity matching, approach* matches asset and liability maturities. Defined as a moderate current asset financing policy, this would use permanent financing for permanent assets (permanent current assets and fixed assets), and use short-term financing to cover seasonal and/or cyclical temporary assets (fluctuating current assets). This strategy minimizes the risk that the firm will be unable to pay off its maturing obligations.
   □ The *aggressive approach* is used by a firm which finances all of its fixed assets with long-term capital but part of its permanent current assets with short-term, nonspontaneous credit.

□ A *conservative approach* would be to use permanent capital to meet some of the cyclical demand, and then hold the temporary surpluses as marketable securities at the trough of the cycle. Here, the amount of permanent financing exceeds permanent assets.

There are advantages and disadvantages to the use of short-term financing.

■ A short-term loan can be obtained much faster than long-term credit.

■ Short-term debt is more flexible since it may be repaid if the firm's financing requirements decline. Long-term debt can be retired, but this will probably involve a prepayment penalty. In addition, long-term loan agreements always contain provisions, or covenants, which constrain the firm's future actions, while short-term credit agreements are generally much less onerous in this regard.

■ Short-term interest rates are normally lower than long-term rates. Therefore, financing with short-term credit usually results in lower interest costs.

■ Short-term debt is generally more risky than long-term debt for two reasons.
  □ Short-term interest rates fluctuate widely while long-term rates tend to be more stable and predictable, and hence the interest rate on short-term debt could increase dramatically in a short period.
  □ Short-term debt comes due every few months. If a firm does not have the cash to repay debt when it comes due, and if it cannot refinance the loan, it may be forced into bankruptcy.

Different types of short-term funds have different characteristics. One source of short-term funds is accrued wages and taxes (accruals), which increase and decrease spontaneously as a firm's operations expand and contract. This type of debt is "free" in the sense that no interest is paid on funds raised through accruals. Firms use all the accruals they can, but they have little control over the levels of these accounts.

Accounts payable, or trade credit, is the largest single category of short-term debt. Trade credit is a spontaneous source of funds in that it arises from ordinary business transactions. Most firms make purchases on credit, recording the debt as an account payable.

■ An increase in sales will be accompanied by an increase in inventory purchases, which will automatically generate additional financing.

■ The cost of trade credit is made up of discounts lost by not paying invoices within the discount period.

☐ For example, if credit terms are 2/10, net 30, the cost of 20 additional days credit is 2 percent of the dollar value of the purchases made.

☐ The following equation may be used to calculate the nominal percentage cost, on an annual basis, of not taking discounts:

$$\text{Nominal percentage cost} = \frac{\text{Discount \%}}{100 - \text{Discount \%}} \times \frac{360}{\text{Days credit is outstanding} - \text{Discount period}}.$$

☐ For example, the nominal cost of not taking the discount when the credit terms are 2/10, net 30, is

$$\text{Nominal percentage cost} = \frac{2}{98} \times \frac{360}{30 - 10} = 0.0204(18) = 0.367 = 36.7\%.$$

☐ In effective annual interest terms, the rate is even higher. Note that the first term on the right-hand side of the nominal cost equation is the periodic cost, and the second term is the number of periods per year. Thus, the effective annual rate is $(1.0204)^{18} - 1.0 = 1.438 - 1.0 = 43.8\%$.

■ Trade credit can be divided into two components: *Free trade credit* is that credit received during the discount period. *Costly trade credit* is obtained by foregoing discounts. This costly component should be used only when it is less expensive than funds obtained from other sources.

☐ Financial managers should always use the free component, but they should use the costly component only after analyzing the cost of this capital to make sure that it is less than the cost of funds which could be obtained from other sources.

☐ Competitive conditions may permit firms to do better than the stated credit terms by taking discounts beyond the discount period or by simply paying late. Such practices, called *stretching accounts payable*, reduce the cost of trade credit, but they also result in poor relationships with suppliers.

Bank loans appear on a firm's balance sheet as notes payable and represent another important source of short-term financing. Bank loans are not generated spontaneously but must be negotiated and renewed on a regular basis.

■ About two-thirds of all bank loans mature in a year or less, although banks do make longer-term loans.

■ When a firm obtains a bank loan, a promissory note specifying the following items is signed: the amount borrowed, the percentage interest rate, the repayment schedule, any collateral offered as security, and other terms of the loan.

■ Banks normally require regular borrowers to maintain *compensating balances* equal to 10 to 20 percent of the face value of loans. Such required balances generally increase the effective interest rate on the loan.

■ A *line of credit* is an informal agreement between a bank and a borrower indicating the maximum credit the bank will extend to the borrower.

■ A *revolving credit agreement* is a formal line of credit often used by large firms. Normally, the borrower will pay the bank a commitment fee to compensate the bank for guaranteeing that the funds will be available. This fee is paid in addition to the regular interest charge on funds actually borrowed.
  □ Note that a revolving credit agreement is very similar to a line of credit, but with an important difference: The bank has a legal obligation to honor a revolving credit agreement, and it receives a commitment fee. Neither the legal obligation nor the fee exists under the informal line of credit.

The cost of bank loans varies for different types of borrowers at any given point in time and for all borrowers over time. Interest rates are higher for riskier borrowers, and rates are also higher on smaller loans because of the fixed costs involved in making and servicing loans.

■ If a firm can qualify as a "prime credit" because of its size and financial strength, it can borrow at the *prime rate*, which has traditionally been the lowest rate banks charge. Rates on other loans are generally scaled up from the prime rate, but loans to very large, strong customers are made at rates below prime.

■ The terms on a short-term bank loan to a business are spelled out in the promissory note. The key elements include the following:
  □ *Interest only versus amortized.* Loans are either *interest-only*, meaning that only interest is paid during the life of the loan with the principal amount being repaid when the loan matures, or *amortized*, meaning that some principal is repaid one each payment date. Amortized loans are called *installment loans*.
  □ *Collateral.* If the loan is secured by some specific collateral this fact is indicated in the note.
  □ *Loan Guarantees.* If the borrower is a small corporation, its bank will probably insist that the larger stockholders personally guarantee the loan.

☐ *Nominal, or stated, interest rate.* The interest rate can be either *fixed* or *floating*.

☐ *Frequency of interest payments.* If the note is on an interest-only basis, it will indicate how frequently interest must be paid.

☐ *Maturity.* Long-term loans always have specific maturity dates, while short-term loans may or may not have specified maturity dates.

☐ *Discount interest.* Most loans call for interest to be paid after it has been earned, but *discount loans* require that interest be paid in advance.

☐ *Add-on basis installment loans.* Interest charges over the life of the loan are calculated and then added to the face amount of the loan.

☐ *Other cost elements.* Some loans require compensating balances, and revolving credit agreements often require commitment fees. Both raise the effective cost of a loan above its stated nominal rate.

■ *Regular, or simple, interest.* For business loans, this is the most common procedure.

☐ The interest rate per day is calculated as the nominal rate divided by the number of days in a year. (The denominator can either be 365 or 360.)

☐ The interest charge for the period is calculated as the number of days in the period multiplied by the interest rate per day multiplied by the amount of the loan.

☐ The effective interest rate on a loan depends on how frequently interest must be paid—the more frequently, the higher the effective rate. To determine the effective rate, the loan amount received and the interest and principal payments are put on a time line. The data is input into a financial calculator to solve for the effective interest rate.

☐ The effective interest rate for a $10,000 loan at a nominal interest rate of 12 percent, with a 365-day year and interest paid quarterly, is calculated as follows:

Interest payments:
Quarter 1 (91 days) = (0.12/365)(91)($10,000) = $299.18.
Quarter 2 (91 days) = (0.12/365)(91)($10,000) = $299.18.
Quarter 3 (92 days) = (0.12/365)(92)($10,000) = $302.47.
Quarter 4 (91 days) = (0.12/365)(91)($10,000) = $299.18.

0	1	2	3	4 Qtrs
10,000	-299.18	-299.18	-302.47	-299.18
				-10,000.00
				-10,299.18

If you enter the cash flows in the time line above into the CF_j register and solve for the IRR, you obtain the periodic rate, 3% per quarter. The effective anual rate is calculated as $(1.03)^4 - 1 = 12.55\%$.

■ *Discount interest.* Under this method, the bank deducts interest in advance. The effective rate on a discount loan is always higher than the rate on an otherwise similar simple interest loan.

☐ The effective interest rate for a $10,000 loan at a discount interest rate of 12 percent for one year is calculated as follows:

Discount interest = 0.12 × $10,000 = $1,200.

With a financial calculator, enter N = 1, PV = 8800, PMT = 0, and FV = -10000, and then press I to obtain the effective cost of the discount loan, 13.64%.

☐ If the discount loan matured in one quarter, the effective interest rate would be calculated as follows:

Discount interest = 0.12/4 × $10,000 = $300.

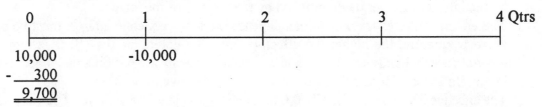

With a financial calculator, enter N = 1, PV = 9700, PMT = 0, and FV = -10000, and then press I to find the periodic rate, 3.092784% per quarter, which corresponds to an effective annual rate of $(1.03092784)^4 - 1 = 12.96\%$.

☐ Shortening the period of a discount loan lowers the effective rate of interest. This occurs because there is a delay in paying interest relative to a longer-term discount loan.

■ *Effects of Compensating Balances.* If the bank requires a compensating balance, and if the amount of the required balance exceeds the amount the firm would normally hold on deposit, then the excess must be deducted at t = 0 and then added back when the loan matures. This has the effect of raising the effective rate on the loan.

■ *Installment loans: add-on interest.* Interest charges are calculated and then added on to the funds received to determine the face value of the note, which is paid off in equal installments. The borrower has use of the full amount of the funds received only until the first installment is paid.

The approximate annual rate is double the stated rate, because the average amount of the loan outstanding is only about half the face amount borrowed.

$$\text{Approximate annual rate}_{\text{Add-on}} = \frac{\text{Interest paid}}{(\text{Amount received})/2}.$$

☐ To determine the effective rate of an add-on loan, proceed as follows:
- ▸ Add the total interest to the principal amount to determine the PV of the loan.
- ▸ Divide the PV of the loan by 12 months to determine the monthly payment.
- ▸ Place the PV of the loan and the monthly payments on a time line. Then, with a financial calculator, enter N = 12, PV = PV of the loan calculated above, PMT = loan payment calculated above, FV = 0, and then press I to obtain the monthly interest rate.
- ▸ Convert the monthly rate to an effective rate.

Choosing a bank involves an analysis of the following variables:

■ *Willingness to assume risks.* Some banks are quite conservative, while others are more willing to make risky loans.

■ *Advice and counsel.* A bank's ability to provide counsel is particularly important to firms in their formative years.

■ *Loyalty to customers.* This variable deals with a bank's willingness to support customers during difficult economic times.

■ *Specialization.* A bank may specialize in making loans to a particular type of business. Firms should seek out a bank which is familiar with their particular type of business.

■ *Maximum loan size.* This is an important consideration for large companies when establishing a borrowing relationship because most banks cannot lend to a single customer more than 15 percent of the total amount of the bank's capital.

■ *Merchant banking.* Originally the term applied to banks which not only loaned depositors' money but also provided its customers with equity capital and financial advice. In recent years, commercial banks have been attempting to get back into merchant banking, in part because of their foreign competitors. Currently, the larger banks, often through holding companies, are being permitted to get back into merchant banking, at least to a limited extent.

■ *Other services.* The availability of services such as lockbox systems should also be taken into account when selecting a bank.

Commercial paper, another source of short-term credit, is an unsecured promissory note. It is generally sold to other business firms, to insurance companies, to banks, and to money market mutual funds. Only large, financially strong firms are able to tap the commercial paper market.

■ Maturities of commercial paper range from a few days to nine months, with an average of about five months.

    ☐ Interest rates on prime commercial paper generally range from 1 ½ to 3 percentage points below the stated prime rate, and about 1/8 to 1/2 of a percentage point above the T-bill rate. However, rates fluctuate daily with supply and demand conditions in the marketplace, and since no compensating balance is required, the effective cost is even lower in comparison to bank loans.

    ☐ The use of commercial paper is restricted to a comparatively small number of very large concerns that are exceptionally good credit risks. Dealers prefer to handle the paper of firms whose net worth is $100 million or more and whose annual borrowing exceeds $10 million.

    ☐ A disadvantage of the commercial paper market vis-a-vis bank loans is that the impersonal nature of the market makes it difficult for firms to use commercial paper at times when they are in temporary financial distress.

For a strong firm, borrowing on an unsecured basis is generally cheaper and simpler than on a secured loan basis because of the administrative costs associated with the use of security. However, lenders will refuse credit without some form of collateral if a borrower's credit standing is questionable.

SELF-TEST QUESTIONS

Definitional

1. In the maturity matching approach to working capital financing, permanent assets should be financed with _____ capital, while _____ assets should be financed with short-term credit.

2. Some firms use short-term financing to finance permanent assets. This approach maximizes _____ _____, but also has the _____ _____.

3. Short-term borrowing provides more _____ for firms that are uncertain about their _____ borrowing needs.

4. Short-term borrowing will be less expensive than borrowing long-term if the yield curve is _____ sloping.

5. Short-term interest rates fluctuate _____ than long-term rates.

6. _____ wages and taxes are a common source of short-term credit. However, most firms have little control over the _____ of these accounts.

7. Accounts payable, or _____ _____, is the largest single source of short-term credit for most businesses.

8. Trade credit is a(n) _____ source of funds in the sense that it automatically increases when sales increase.

9. Trade credit can be divided into two components: _____ trade credit and _____ trade credit.

10. Free trade credit is that credit received during the _____ period.

11. _____ trade credit should only be used when the cost of the trade credit is less than the cost of _____ sources.

12. The instrument signed when bank credit is obtained is called a(n) _____ _____.

13. Many banks require borrowers to keep _____ _____ on deposit with the bank equal to 10 or 20 percent of the face value of the loan.

14. Maturities on commercial paper generally range from _____ to _____ months, with interest rates set about 1 1/2 to 3 percentage points _____ the _____ rate.

15. A(n) _____ loan is one where collateral such as _____ or _____ have been pledged in support of the loan.

16. A(n) _____ _____ _____ is an informal agreement between a bank and a borrower indicating the maximum credit the bank will extend to the borrower.

17. The fee paid to a bank to secure a revolving credit agreement is known as a(n) _____ fee.

18. If interest charges are deducted in advance, this is known as _____ interest, and the effective rate is higher than the _____ interest rate.

19. With a(n) _____ loan, the average amount of the usable funds during the loan period is equal to approximately _____ - _____ of the face amount of the loan.

20. Commercial paper can only be issued by _____, _____ _____ firms.

Conceptual

21. The matching of asset and liability maturities is considered desirable because this strategy minimizes interest rate risk.

    a. True   **b.** False

22. Accruals are "free" in the sense that no interest must be paid on these funds.

    a. True   **b.** False

23. The effect of compensating balances is to decrease the effective interest rate of a loan.

    a. True   **b.** False

24. Which of the following statements concerning commercial paper is most *correct*?

    a. Commercial paper is secured debt of large, financially strong firms.
    b. Commercial paper is sold primarily to individual investors.
    c. Maturities of commercial paper generally exceed nine months.
    d. Commercial paper interest rates are typically 1 1/2 to 3 percentage points above the stated prime rate.
    e. None of the above statements is correct.

25. Which of the following statements is most *correct?*

    a. If you had just been hired as Working Capital Manager for a firm with but one stockholder, and that stockholder told you that she had all the money she could possibly use, hence that her primary operating goal was to avoid even the remotest possibility of bankruptcy, then you should set the firm's working capital financing policy on the basis of the "Maturity Matching Approach."

    b. Due to the existence of positive maturity risk premiums, at most times short-term debt carries lower interest rates than long-term debt. Therefore, if a company finances primarily with short-term as opposed to long-term debt, its expected TIE ratio, hence its overall riskiness, will be lower than if it finances with long-term debt. Therefore, the more conservative the firm, the greater its reliance on short-term debt.

    c. If a firm buys on terms of 2/10, net 30, and pays on the 30th day, then its accounts payable may be thought of as consisting of some "free" and some "costly" trade credit. Since the percentage cost of the costly trade credit is lowered if the payment period is reduced, the firm should try to pay earlier than on Day 30, say on Day 25.

    d. Suppose a firm buys on terms of 2/10, net 30, but it normally pays on Day 60. Disregarding any "image" effects, it should, if it can borrow from the bank at an effective rate of 14 percent, take out a bank loan and start taking discounts.

    e. Each of the above statements is false.

SELF-TEST PROBLEMS

(The following data apply to the next three Self-Test Problems.)

A firm buys on terms of 2/10, net 30, but generally does not pay until 40 days after the invoice date. Its purchases total $1,080,000 per year.

1. How much "non-free" trade credit does the firm use on average each year?

    a. $120,000   **b.** $90,000   **c.** $60,000   **d.** $30,000   **e.** $20,000

2. What is the nominal cost of the "non-free" trade credit?

    a. 16.2%   **b.** 19.4%   **c.** 21.9%   **d.** 24.5%   **e.** 27.4%

3. What is the effective annual rate of the costly credit?

    a. 16.2%   **b.** 19.4%   **c.** 21.9%   **d.** 24.5%   **e.** 27.4%

4. Lawton Pipelines Inc. has developed plans for a new pump that will allow more economical operation of the company's oil pipelines. Management estimates that $2,400,000 will be required to put this new pump into operation. Funds can be obtained from a bank at 10 percent discount interest one-year loan, or the company can finance the expansion by delaying payment to its suppliers. Presently, Lawton purchases under terms of 2/10, net 40, but management believes payment could be delayed 30 additional days without penalty; that is, payment could be made in 70 days. Which means of financing should Lawton use? (Use the nominal cost of trade credit.)

    a. Trade credit, since the cost is about 12.24 percent.
    b. Trade credit, since the cost is about 3.13 percentage points less than the bank loan.
    c. Bank loan, since the cost is about 1.13 percentage points less than trade credit.
    d. Bank loan, since the cost is about 3.13 percentage points less than trade credit.
    e. The firm could use either since the costs are the same.

(The following data apply to the next four Self-Test Problems.)

You plan to borrow $10,000 from your bank, which offers to lend you the money at a 10 percent nominal, or stated, rate on a 1-year loan.

5. What is the effective interest rate if the loan is a discount loan?

    a. 11.1%   **b.** 13.3%   **c.** 15.0%   **d.** 17.5%   **e.** 20.0%

6. What is the approximate interest rate if the loan is an add-on interest loan with 12 monthly payments?

    a. 11.1%   **b.** 13.3%   **c.** 15.0%   **d.** 17.5%   **e.** 20.0%

7. What is the effective interest rate if the loan is a discount loan with a 15 percent compensating balance? (Assume the firm would not otherwise hold this compensating balance on deposit.)

    a. 11.1%   **b.** 13.3%   **c.** 15.0%   **d.** 17.5%   **e.** 20.0%

8. Under the terms of the previous problem, how much would you have to borrow to have the use of $10,000?

   a. $10,000   **b.** $11,111   **c.** $12,000   **d.** $13,333   **e.** $15,000

9. Gibbs Corporation needs to raise $1,000,000 for one year to supply working capital to a new store. Gibbs buys from its suppliers on terms of 4/10, net 90, and it currently pays on the 10th day and takes discounts, but it could forego discounts, pay on the 90th day, and get the needed $1,000,000 in the form of costly trade credit. Alternatively, Gibbs could borrow from its bank for one year on a 15 percent discount interest rate basis. What is the effective annual cost rate of the lower cost source?

   a. 20.17%   **b.** 18.75%   **c.** 17.65%   **d.** 18.25%   **e.** 19.50%

ANSWERS TO SELF-TEST QUESTIONS

1. permanent (long-term); temporary
2. expected return; greatest risk
3. flexibility; future
4. upward
5. more
6. Accrued; size (amount)
7. trade credit
8. spontaneous
9. free; costly
10. discount
11. Costly; alternative
12. promissory note
13. compensating balances
14. one; nine; below; prime
15. secured; receivables; inventory
16. line of credit
17. commitment
18. discount; simple (or nominal or stated)
19. installment; one-half
20. large; financially strong

21. b. The matching of maturities minimizes default risk, or the risk that the firm will be unable to pay off its maturing obligations, and reinvestment rate risk, or the risk that the firm will have to roll over the debt at a higher rate.

22. a. Neither workers nor the IRS require interest payments on wages and taxes that are not paid as soon as they are earned.

23. b. Compensating balances increase the effective rate because the firm is required to maintain excess non-interest-bearing balances.

24. e. Commercial paper is the unsecured debt of strong firms. It generally has a maturity from one to nine months and is sold primarily to other corporations and financial institutions. Rates on commercial paper are typically below the prime rate.

25. d. Statement a is false; the conservative approach would be the safest current asset financing policy. Statement b is false; short-term debt fluctuates more than long-term debt, thus, the greater the firm's reliance on short-term debt, the riskier the firm. Statement c is false; it makes no difference in the cost if the firm pays on Day 25 versus Day 30 in this instance. Statement d is true; if the firm can "stretch" its payables the nominal cost is 14.69% (the effective cost is 15.66%). Thus, the firm should obtain the 14% bank loan to take discounts as this is the lowest cost to the firm.

SOLUTIONS TO SELF-TEST PROBLEMS

1. b. $1,080,000/360 = $3,000 in purchases per day. Typically, there will be $3,000(40) = $120,000 of accounts payable on the books at any given time. Of this, $3,000(10) = $30,000 is "free" credit, while $3,000(30) = $90,000 is "non-free" credit.

2. d. $$\text{Nominal cost} = \frac{\text{Discount \%}}{100 - \text{Discount \%}} \times \frac{360}{\substack{\text{Days credit is} \\ \text{outstanding}} - \substack{\text{Discount} \\ \text{period}}}$$

$$= \frac{2}{100 - 2} \times \frac{360}{40 - 10} = \frac{2}{98} \times \frac{360}{30} = 24.5\% \ .$$

3. e. The periodic rate is $2/98 = 2.04\%$, and there are $360/30 = 12$ periods per year. Thus, the effective annual rate is 27.4 percent:

$$\left(1 + \frac{k_{Nom}}{m}\right)^{12} - 1.0 = (1.0204)^{12} - 1.0$$
$$= 1.2742 - 1.0 = 0.2742 = 27.4\% \ .$$

4. c. Discount interest = (0.10)($2,400,000) = $240,000.

```
        0                              1 Year
        ├─────────────────────────────┤
    2,400,000                      -2,400,000
   -  240,000
    2,160,000
```

With a financial calculator, enter N = 1, PV = 2160000, PMT = 0, and FV = -2400000, then press I to obtain I = 11.11%.

Credit terms are 2/10, net 40, but delaying payments 30 additional days is the equivalent of 2/10, net 70. Assuming no penalty, the nominal cost is as follows:

$$\text{Nominal cost} = \frac{\text{Discount \%}}{100 - \text{Discount \%}} \times \frac{360}{\text{Days credit is} - \text{Discount}}$$
$$\text{outstanding} \quad \text{period}$$

$$= \frac{2}{100 - 2} \times \frac{360}{70 - 10}$$

$$= \frac{2}{98} \times \frac{360}{60} = 0.0204(6) = 12.24\% .$$

Therefore, the loan cost is 1.13 percentage points less than trade credit.

5. a. Discount interest = (0.10)($10,000) = $1,000.

```
        0                              1 Year
        ├─────────────────────────────┤
     10,000                        -10,000
    -  1,000
      9,000
```

With a financial calculator, enter N = 1, PV = 9000, PMT = 0, and FV = -10000, then press I to obtain I = 11.11%.

6. e. Approximate annual rate = $1,000/$5,000 = 20.0%.

7. b. Discount interest = 0.10($10,000) = $1,000.
15% compensating balance = 0.15($10,000) = $1,500.

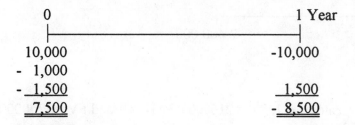

0   1 Year

10,000   -10,000
- 1,000
- 1,500   1,500
7,500   - 8,500

With a financial calculator, enter N = 1, PV = 7500, PMT = 0, and FV = -8500, then press I to obtain I = 13.33%.

8. d.

$$\frac{\$10,000}{1 - 0.15 - 0.10} = \$13,333.$$

0.15($13,333) = $2,000 is required for the compensating balance, and 0.10($13,333) = $1,333 is required for the immediate interest payment.

9. c. Accounts payable: EAR cost = $[1+(0.04/0.96)]^{4.5}$ - 1.0 = 20.17%.

Cost of notes payable:

Discount interest = 0.15($1,000,000) = $150,000.

0   1 Year

1,000,000   -1,000,000
- 150,000
850,000

With a financial calculator, enter N = 1, PV = 850000, PMT = 0, and FV = -1000000, then press I to obtain I = 17.65%.

CHAPTER 22

OTHER TOPICS IN WORKING CAPITAL MANAGEMENT

OVERVIEW

In Chapters 20 and 21, we presented the basics of current asset management and short-term financing. Those chapters should have provided you with a solid overview of working capital management. Now, in Chapter 22, we present a more in-depth treatment of several working capital topics, including (1) the cash conversion cycle, (2) setting the target cash balance, (3) accounting for inventory, (4) the EOQ model, (5) monitoring the receivables position, and (6) secured financing.

OUTLINE

The concept of working capital management originated with the old Yankee peddler, who would borrow to buy inventory, sell the inventory to pay off the bank loan, and then repeat the cycle. That general concept has been applied to more complex businesses, and the cash flow cycle concept is used for analyzing the effectiveness of a firm's working capital management.

■ The cash conversion cycle model focuses on the length of time between when the company makes payments and when it receives cash inflows.

■ The *inventory conversion period* is the average length of time required to convert materials into finished goods and then to sell those goods.

■ The *receivables collection period* is the average length of time required to convert the firm's receivables into cash, that is, to collect cash following a sale.

■ The *payables deferral period* is the average length of time between the purchase of materials and labor and the payment of cash for them.

- The *cash conversion cycle* nets out the inventory conversion period, the receivables collection period, and the payables deferral period.
  - ☐ It equals the length of time between the firm's actual cash expenditures to pay for productive resources and its own cash receipts from the sale of products—the average length of time a dollar is tied up in current assets.
  - ☐ Cash conversion cycle = Inventory conversion period + Receivables collection period
    - Payables deferral period.

One of the key elements in a firm's cash budget is the target cash balance. The target cash balance is normally set as the larger of the firm's transactions balances plus precautionary balances or its required compensating balances. The Baumol model applies inventory methodology (EOQ model) to cash balances.

- The optimal cash holdings to be transferred from marketable securities or to be borrowed, C*, can be found by the equation:

$$C^* = \sqrt{\frac{2(F)(T)}{k}}.$$

  Here, F = fixed costs of borrowing or of converting marketable securities into cash, T = total amount of net new cash needed for transactions over the entire period, usually a year, and k = the opportunity cost of holding cash.

- Assuming no precautionary balances, the optimal average cash balance is C*/2.

- The optimal cash balance increases less than proportionately with increases in the amount of cash needed for transactions. This suggests that there are economies of scale in holding cash balances, and this in turn gives larger firms an edge over smaller ones.

- The Baumol model is simplistic in many respects, but it can provide a useful starting point for establishing a target cash balance.

- Although the Baumol model and other theoretical models provide insights into the optimal cash balance, they are generally not practical for actual use. Rather, firms generally set their target cash balances as some "safety stock" of cash that reduces their risk of running out of money to some acceptably low level. One commonly used method for setting the target cash balance is Monte Carlo simulation.

When finished goods are sold, the firm must assign a cost of goods sold. Four methods can be used to value the cost of goods sold, and hence to value remaining inventory.

■ Under *specific identification*, a unique cost is attached to each item in inventory.
 □ This method is used only when the items are high cost and move relatively slowly.

■ In the *first-in, first-out (FIFO)* method, the units sold during a given period are assumed to be the first units that were placed in inventory. As a result, the cost of goods sold is based on the cost of the older inventory items, and the remaining inventory consists of the newer goods.

■ The *last-in, first-out (LIFO)* method is the opposite of FIFO. The cost of goods sold is based on the last units placed in inventory, while the remaining inventory consists of the first goods placed in inventory.

■ The *weighted average* method involves the computation of the weighted average unit cost of goods available for sale from inventory, and this average cost is then applied to the goods sold to determine the cost of goods sold.

Inventories are obviously necessary; however, a firm's profitability will suffer if it has too much or too little inventory. As a starting point in the process, it is useful for managers to consider the insights provided by the economic ordering quantity (EOQ) model.

■ *Carrying costs* generally rise in direct proportion to the average amount of inventory held.
 □ Carrying costs include the following: Cost of the capital tied up in inventories, storage costs, insurance costs, property taxes, and depreciation and obsolescence.
 □ If TCC = total carrying cost, C = annual carrying cost as a percentage of inventory value, P = purchase price per unit of inventory, and A = average number of units held in inventory, then

$$TCC = (C)(P)(A).$$

■ *Ordering costs*, which are considered to be fixed costs, decline as average inventories increase, that is, as the number of orders decrease.
 □ Ordering costs include the costs of placing and receiving orders.
 □ If TOC = total ordering cost, F = fixed cost associated with placing and receiving an order, and N = the number of orders placed per year, then

$$TOC = (F)(N).$$

■ The costs of running short of inventory, or *stock-out costs*, may well be the most important element of inventory costs. These costs will be added later, when safety stocks are discussed.

■ Total inventory costs, TIC, equal the sum of total carrying costs and total ordering costs:

$$TIC = TCC + TOC = (C)(P)(A) + (F)(N).$$

☐ Now recognize that if Q units are ordered each time an order is placed, and assuming that inventories are used evenly over the year and inventory levels are run down to zero immediately prior to receipt of the next order, then the average inventory level is one-half the number ordered:

$$A = Q/2.$$

☐ Further, if Q units are ordered each time, and S units are required over the year, then

$$N = S/Q.$$

☐ Using these relationships for A and N, the total inventory cost equation can be rewritten as

$$TIC = (C)(P)\left(\frac{Q}{2}\right) + (F)\left(\frac{S}{Q}\right).$$

■ The *EOQ model*, which is derived by minimizing total inventory costs, is

$$EOQ = \sqrt{\frac{2(F)(S)}{(C)(P)}},$$

where:
☐ EOQ is the optimal quantity to be ordered each time an order is placed.
☐ F = fixed costs of placing and receiving an order.
☐ S = annual sales in units.
☐ C = carrying cost expressed as a percentage of inventory value.
☐ P = purchase price the firm must pay per unit of inventory.

■ The assumptions of the model are as follows:
☐ There is no uncertainty in sales forecasts.
☐ Inventory usage is evenly distributed over time.
☐ Orders are received without delay.
☐ All carrying costs are completely variable and all ordering costs are completely fixed.

■ With instantaneous order delivery, the order point is zero. However, if the instantaneous order delivery assumption is dropped, the order point is found as follows:
  □ Find the daily rate of usage.
  □ The lead time is the number of days required to place an order and receive delivery.
  □ Order point equals daily usage times lead time.

■ Demand, rate of usage, and order lead time cannot always be known with certainty. Therefore, firms add a *safety stock* to their inventories to avoid running out of inventory and suffering stock-out costs.
  □ At the optimal level of safety stock, the probable cost of running out of inventory is just offset by the cost of carrying the additional inventory.
  □ The optimal safety stock increases with the uncertainty of demand forecasts, with the costs that result from inventory shortages, and with the probability that delays will occur in receiving shipments.
  □ The costs of a stock-out include customer ill will, production delays, and lost sales.
  □ The probability of a stock-out is influenced by fluctuations in usage rate and delivery time.
  □ Inclusion of a safety stock does not affect the EOQ.
    ▸ The average inventory with the safety stock is

$$A = (EOQ/2) + \text{Safety stock}.$$

    ▸ The order point is increased by the amount of the safety stock.
    ▸ Total inventory costs are increased by the carrying cost of the safety stock.

■ Suppliers often offer discounts for ordering large quantities; such discounts are called *quantity discounts*. To evaluate taking or not taking a quantity discount, the savings of the quantity discount is compared against the increased costs of ordering (and holding) a nonoptimal amount.

■ Moderate inflation—3% per year—can largely be ignored for purposes of inventory management, but higher inflation rates must be explicitly considered.
  □ If the inflation rate in the types of goods the firm stocks tends to be relatively constant, it can be dealt with quite easily—simply deduct the expected annual rate of inflation from the carrying cost percentage and use this modified version of the EOQ model to establish the ordering quantity.
  □ On balance, there is no evidence that inflation either raises or lowers the optimal inventories of firms in the aggregate. Inflation should still be explicitly considered, however, for it will raise the individual firm's optimal holdings if the inflation rate for its own inventories is above average.

■ For most firms, it is unrealistic to assume that demand for an inventory item is uniform throughout the year. Thus, the EOQ model cannot be used on an annual basis, but it can be used on a seasonal basis, with inventories either run down or built up during the transition between seasons.

■ Small deviations from the EOQ quantity do not appreciably increase the cost of ordering and carrying inventories, and hence, the optimal ordering quantity should be viewed more as a range than as a single value.

The days sales outstanding and aging schedules are useful receivables monitoring methods, especially for monitoring an individual customer's account, but neither method is totally suitable for monitoring the aggregate payment performance of all a firm's credit customers, especially for a firm that experiences fluctuating credit sales.

■ The primary point in analyzing the aggregate accounts receivable situation is to see if customers, on average, are slowing down their payments.
   □ The DSO and aging schedules are useful in monitoring credit operations, but both are affected by increases and decreases in a firm's sales level.

■ Changes in sales levels, including normal seasonal or cyclical changes, can change a firm's DSO and aging schedule even though its customers' payment behavior has not changed at all. For this reason, the *payments pattern approach* has been developed to measure any changes that might be occurring in customers' payment behavior.
   □ The payments pattern approach permits us to remove the effects of seasonal and/or cyclical sales variation and to construct an accurate measure of customers' payments patterns.

■ Another basic tool used to monitor receivables is the *uncollected balances schedule*. At the end of each quarter, the dollar amount of receivables remaining from each of the three month's sales is divided by the month's sales to obtain three receivables-to-sales ratios. The sum of the receivables-to-sales ratio, the total uncollected balances percentage, is obtained and if it has increased it will alert the firm's managers that customers are paying more slowly.
   □ The uncollected balances schedule permits a firm to monitor its receivables better, and it can also be used to forecast future receivables balances.

Changes in credit policy must be analyzed. For example, easing the credit policy normally stimulates sales. As sales rise, costs also rise (1) to produce the extra required goods, (2) to carry the additional receivables outstanding, and (3) because bad debt expenses may rise.

■ The question to answer when considering a credit policy change, therefore, is whether sales revenues will rise more than costs.

■ One way to answer this question is to compare projected income statements and, hence, focus on the *incremental changes* in expected sales revenues and costs that would result from a proposed change in the credit policy.
  □ In this analysis, determine the firm's *cost of carrying receivables* before and after the change in credit policy.
  □ The cost of carrying receivables is the product of the days sales outstanding, sales per day, the variable cost ratio, and the cost of funds.

$$\text{Cost of carrying receivables} = \text{DSO} \times \frac{\text{Sales}}{\text{per day}} \times \frac{\text{Variable}}{\text{cost ratio}} \times \frac{\text{Cost of}}{\text{funds}} .$$

  □ Only *variable costs* are considered because only this portion needs to be financed; the remainder is profit.
  □ The change in the level of *bad debt losses* and the dollar value of the *discounts* taken must also be determined.
  □ If expected sales revenues less expected expenses are greater after the proposed change in credit policy than before, the change in credit policy should be undertaken, unless the riskiness of the change is disproportionate to the benefits.

■ There is quite a bit of uncertainty in credit policy change analysis because the variables are very difficult to estimate. Further, the end result depends on the reactions of competitors. Thus, the final decision is based on the quantitative analysis plus a great deal of informed judgment.

For a strong firm, borrowing on an unsecured basis is generally cheaper and simpler than on a secured loan basis because of the administrative costs associated with the use of security. However, lenders will refuse credit without some form of collateral if a borrower's credit standing is questionable.

■ Most secured short-term business borrowing involves the use of accounts receivable and inventories as collateral.

■ The legal procedures for establishing loan security have been standardized and simplified in the *Uniform Commercial Code*.

■ The heart of the Uniform Commercial Code is the *security agreement*, a standardized document on which the specific pledged assets are listed.

Accounts receivable financing involves either the pledging of receivables or the selling (factoring) of receivables.

■ The *pledging of accounts receivable* is characterized by the fact that the lender not only has a claim against the receivables but also has recourse to the borrower. If the person or firm that bought the goods does not pay, the selling firm must take the loss. Thus, the risk of default on the pledged accounts receivable remains with the borrower.

■ *Factoring, or selling accounts receivable,* involves the purchase of accounts receivable by the lender, generally without recourse to the borrower, which means that if the purchaser of the goods does not pay for them, the lender rather than the seller of the goods takes the loss.

A substantial amount of credit is secured by business inventories.

■ The *inventory blanket lien* gives the lending institution a lien against all of the borrower's inventories. However, the borrower is free to sell inventories, which reduces the value of the collateral.

■ A *trust receipt*, or *security instrument*, is an instrument acknowledging that the goods are held in trust for the lender. The borrower may keep the goods in his possession, but he must remit the proceeds of the sale of the specific goods to the lender at the end of each day.

■ Like trust receipts, *warehouse receipt financing* uses inventory as security. A *public warehouse* is an independent third-party operation engaged in the business of storing goods.

■ Because of the bulkiness of goods and the expense of transporting them to and from the borrower's place of business, a *field warehouse* may be established at the borrower's place of business. To provide inventory supervision, the lending institution employs a third party, a field warehouse company, which acts as an agent for the lending institution.

SELF-TEST QUESTIONS

Definitional

1. The _____ _____ applies inventory methodology (the EOQ model) to cash balances.

2.   The _____ _____ period is the average length of time required to convert materials into finished goods and then to sell those goods.

3.   The _____ _____ period is the average length of time required to convert the firm's receivables into cash, that is, to collect cash following a sale.

4.   The _____ _____ period is the average length of time between the purchase of materials and labor and the cash payment for them.

5.   The _____ _____ _____ is the average length of time a dollar is tied up in current assets.

6.   The optimal cash balance increases _____ than proportionately with increases in the amount of cash needed for transactions. This suggests that there are _____ _____ _____ in holding cash balances, and this in turn gives _____ firms and edge over _____ firms.

7.   Besides using the Baumol model to give insights into the optimal cash balance, a commonly used method for setting the target cash balance is _____ _____ simulation.

8.   Under _____ _____, a unique cost is attached to each item in inventory.

9.   In the _____-____, _____-_____ method, the units sold during a given period are assumed to be the first units that were placed in inventory.

10.   _____ costs generally rise in direct proportion to the average amount of inventory held.

11.   _____ costs, which are considered to be fixed costs, decline as average inventories increase.

12.   Besides the payments pattern approach, another basic tool used to monitor receivables is the _____ _____ _____. With this method, at the end of each quarter, the dollar amount of receivables remaining from each of the three month's sales is divided by the month's sales to obtain receivables-to-sales ratios.

13.   _____ the credit policy normally stimulates sales.

14. If expected sales revenues less expected expenses are _____ after the proposed change in credit policy than before, the change in credit policy should be undertaken.

15. The legal procedures for establishing loan security have been standardized and simplified in the _____ _____ _____.

16. A(n) _____ loan is one where collateral such as _____ or _____ have been pledged in support of the loan.

17. _____ occurs when accounts receivable are purchased by the lender, generally without recourse to the borrower, which means that if the purchaser of the goods does not pay for them, the lender rather than the seller of the goods takes the loss.

18. A(n) _____ _____ lien gives the lender a lien against all inventories of the borrower.

19. The _____ _____ approach removes the effects of seasonal and/or cyclical sales variations and measures any changes that might be occurring in customers' payment behavior.

20. The _____ _____ quantity minimizes the total costs of ordering and holding inventories.

21. When the level of inventories reaches the _____ _____, the EOQ amount should be ordered.

22. _____ _____ must be maintained in order to allow for shipping delays and uncertainty in the rate of _____.

23. Running out of an item of inventory is called a(n) _____-_____.

24. The optimal ordering quantity should be thought of more as a(n) _____ than as a point value.

Conceptual

25. The economic ordering quantity is the order quantity that provides the minimum total cost; that is, both the ordering and carrying cost components are minimized.

   a. True   **b.** False

26. To evaluate taking or not taking a quantity discount, the savings of the quantity discount should be compared against the increased costs of ordering and holding a non optimal amount.

    a. True   **b.** False

27. There is evidence to suggest that inflation lowers the optimal inventories of firms in the aggregate.

    a. True   **b.** False

28. The costs of a stock-out do not include

    a. Disruption of production schedules.
    b. Loss of customer goodwill.
    c. Depreciation and obsolescence.
    d. Loss of sales.
    e. Answers c and d above.

29. The addition of a safety stock to the EOQ model

    a. Increases the EOQ proportionately.
    b. Raises the order point.
    c. Lowers the order point.
    d. Does not change the total inventory costs.
    e. Results in greater variability in the time required to receive deliveries.

SELF-TEST PROBLEMS

1. The Ryder Company has been practicing cash management for some time by using the Baumol model to determine cash balances. Recently, when the interest rate on marketable securities was 10 percent, the model called for an average cash balance of $1,000. A rapid increase in interest rates has driven this rate up to 15 percent. The firm incurs a cost of $20 per transaction. Ryder does not carry any precautionary balances. What is the appropriate average cash balance now?

    a. $596.97   **b.** $604.73   **c.** $816.50   **d.** $1,632.99   **e.** $1,333.33

(The following data apply to the next three problems.)

Stanton Industries projects that cash outlays of $1.5 million will occur uniformly throughout the year. Stanton plans to meet its cash requirements by periodically selling marketable securities from its portfolio. The firm's marketable securities are invested to earn 9 percent, and the cost per transaction of converting securities to cash is $18.

2. Using the Baumol model, what is the optimal transaction size for transfers from marketable securities to cash?

    a. $24,495   **b.** $33,271   **c.** $20,876   **d.** $23,154   **e.** $27,989

3. What will be Stanton's average cash balance?

    a. $13,994.50   **b.** $16,635.50   **c.** $11,577.00   **d.** $10,438.00   **e.** $12,247.50

4. How many transfers per year will be required?

    a. 45.08   **b.** 61.24   **c.** 53.59   **d.** 71.85   **e.** 64.78

(The following data apply to the next two problems.)

Douglas Industries needs an additional $500,000, which it plans to obtain through a factoring arrangement. The factor would purchase Douglas's accounts receivable and advance the invoice amount, minus a 4 percent commission, on the invoices purchased each month. Douglas sells on terms of net 30 days. In addition, the factor charges a 14 percent annual interest rate on the total invoice amount, to be deducted in advance.

5. What amount of accounts receivable must be factored to net $500,000?

    a. $527,241   **b.** $515,464   **c.** $530,441   **d.** $525,367   **e.** $518,989

6. If Douglas can reduce credit expenses by $10,000 per month and avoid bad debt losses of 3.5 percent on the factored amount, what is the total annual dollar cost of the savings that results from the use of the factoring arrangement?

    a. $12,353   **b.** $11,076   **c.** $14,544   **d.** $13,767   **e.** $11,841

(The following data apply to the next three problems.)

Furston Inc., a retail firm, currently has sales of $1 million. Its credit period and days sales outstanding are both 30 days, and 1 percent of its sales end up as bad debts. Furston's credit manager estimates that, if the firm extends its credit period to 45 days so that its days sales outstanding increases to 45 days, sales will increase by $100,000, but its bad debt losses on the incremental sales would be 3 percent. Variable costs are 40 percent, and the cost of carrying receivables, k, is 15 percent. Assume a tax rate of 40 percent and 360 days per year.

7. What would be the *incremental* investment required to finance the increase in receivables if the change were made?

   a. $3,250   **b.** $41,667   **c.** $21,667   **d.** $50,000   **e.** $56,667

8. What would be the *incremental* cost of carrying receivables?

   a. $5,000   **b.** $3,250   **c.** $8,250   **d.** $10,000   **e.** $0

9. What would be the *incremental* change in net income?

   a. $32,250   **b.** $26,875   **c.** $20,000   **d.** $10,550   **e.** $15,875

(The following data apply to the next two problems.)

Hodes Furniture currently has annual sales of $2,000,000. Its days sales outstanding is 40 days, and bad debts are 5 percent of sales. The credit and collection manager is considering instituting a stricter collection policy, whereby bad debts would be reduced to 2 percent of total sales, and the days sales outstanding would fall to 30 days. However, sales would also fall by an estimated $250,000 annually. Variable costs are 60 percent of sales and the cost of carrying receivables is 12 percent. Assume a tax rate of 40 percent and 360 days per year.

10. What would be the *incremental* investment required to finance the increase in receivables if the change were made?

   a. -$16,667   **b.** -$27,167   **c.** -$48,611   **d.** -$45,833   **e.** -$72,431

11. What would be the *incremental* change in net income?

   a. -$16,667   **b.** -$17,700   **c.** -$20,250   **d.** -$25,750   **e.** -$15,000

(The following data apply to the next four problems.)

The South Florida Lawn Supply Company is reviewing its inventory policy regarding lawn seed. The following relationships and conditions exist:

(1) Orders must be placed in multiples of 100 bags.
(2) Requirements for the year are 16,200 bags.
(3) The purchase price per bag is $5.00.
(4) The carrying cost is 20 percent of inventory value.
(5) The fixed costs per order are $25.
(6) The desired safety stock is 300 units; this amount is on hand initially.
(7) Five days are required for delivery.
(8) Assume 360 days per year.

12. What is the economic ordering quantity?

    a. 600 bags   **b.** 700 bags   **c.** 800 bags   **d.** 900 bags   **e.** 1,000 bags

13. How many orders should South Florida Lawn Supply place each year?

    a. 22   **b.** 20   **c.** 18   **d.** 16   **e.** 14

14. What is the order point?

    a. 750 bags   **b.** 525 bags   **c.** 345 bags   **d.** 300 bags   **e.** 225 bags

15. What is the average inventory level?

    a. 750 bags   **b.** 525 bags   **c.** 345 bags   **d.** 300 bags   **e.** 225 bags

(The following data apply to the next six problems.)

The Magnuson Company is trying to determine its optimal inventory policy. The following relationships and conditions exist for the firm:

(1) Annual sales are 120,000 units.
(2) The purchase price per unit is $500.
(3) The carrying cost is 20 percent of inventory value.
(4) The fixed costs per order are $600.
(5) The optimal safety stock is 500 units, which are already on hand.
(6) Assume 360 days per year.

16. What is the economic ordering quantity?

   a. 600 units   **b.** 800 units   **c.** 1,000 units   **d.** 1,200 units   **e.** 1,400 units

17. What is the maximum inventory the company will hold?

   a. 1,300 units   **b.** 1,400 units   **c.** 1,500 units   **d.** 1,600 units   **e.** 1,700 units

18. What is the average inventory the company will hold?

   a. 600 units   **b.** 850 units   **c.** 1,100 units   **d.** 1,200 units   **e.** 1,700 units

19. How often will the company order?

   a. Every 2.0 days   **d.** Every 2 weeks
   b. Every 3.60 days   **e.** Continually
   c. Every 5.25 days

20. What are the firm's annual total inventory costs disregarding the safety stock?

   a. $50,000   **b.** $120,000   **c.** $150,000   **d.** $170,000   **e.** $200,000

21. What are the annual total inventory costs including the safety stock?

   a. $50,000   **b.** $120,000   **c.** $150,000   **d.** $170,000   **e.** $200,000

22. The Hamilton Company has a variable operating cost ratio of 60 percent, its cost of capital is 12 percent, and current sales are $20,000. All of its sales are on credit, and it currently sells on terms of net 30. Its accounts receivable balance is $3,000. Hamilton is considering a new credit policy with terms of net 45. Under the new policy, sales will increase to $24,000, and accounts receivable will rise to $5,000. If Hamilton changes its credit policy to net 45, by how much will its cost of carrying receivables increase? Assume a 360-day year.

    a. $144   **b.** $127   **c.** $118   **d.** $135   **e.** $168

23. Your company sells on terms of net 40, sales (all on credit) are $500 per year, and accounts receivable average $50. You are considering a new credit policy, with terms of net 20, under which you expect sales of $475 and an average receivables balance of $25. Your variable cost ratio is 80 percent, and your cost of capital is 10 percent. Use 360 days per year, assume that fixed costs are the same under each credit policy, and assume all dollars are in millions. By how much would your *pre-tax profits* (in millions) change if the new credit policy is employed?

    a. $1.00   **b.** -$2.00   **c.** -$1.00   **d.** $3.00   **e.** -$3.00

ANSWERS TO SELF-TEST QUESTIONS

1.	Baumol model	
2.	inventory conversion	
3.	receivables collection	
4.	payables deferral	
5.	cash conversion cycle	
6.	less; economies of scale; larger; smaller	
7.	Monte Carlo	
8.	specific identification	
9.	first-in first-out	
10.	Carrying	
11.	Ordering	
12.	uncollected balances schedule	

13. Easing
14. greater
15. Uniform Commercial Code
16. secured; receivables; inventories
17. Factoring
18. inventory blanket
19. payments pattern; uncollected balances
20. economic ordering
21. order point
22. Safety stocks; usage
23. stock-out
24. range

25. b. The total cost, or sum of ordering and carrying costs, is minimized, but neither of the component costs is minimized. For example, to minimize carrying costs, no inventory would be kept on hand at all.

26. a. This is a correct statement.

27. b. On balance, there is no evidence that inflation either raises or lowers the optimal inventories of firms in the aggregate. Inflation should still be explicitly considered, however, for it will raise the individual firm's optimal holdings if the inflation rate for its own inventories is above average.

28. c. Depreciation and obsolescence are inventory carrying costs.

29. b. The addition of a safety stock increases the order point by the amount of the safety stock.

SOLUTIONS TO SELF-TEST PROBLEMS

1. c. The model is

$$C^* = \sqrt{\frac{2(F)(T)}{k}}.$$

Initially, the average cash balance, $C^*/2$, is $1,000, thus $C^* = \$2,000$. Therefore,

$$\$2,000 = \sqrt{\frac{2(\$20)(T)}{0.10}}$$

$$\$4,000,000 = \frac{2(\$20)(T)}{0.10}$$

$$\$4,000,000 = \$400T$$

$$\$10,000 = T.$$

Therefore, the new average cash balance is

$$C^* = \sqrt{\frac{2(\$20)(\$10,000)}{0.15}}$$

$$C^* = \$1,632.99$$

$$C^*/2 = \$816.50.$$

2. a. $C^* = \sqrt{\dfrac{2(F)(T)}{k}}$ = Optimal transaction size.

   F = \$18; T = \$1,500,000; k = 9\%.

   $C^* = \sqrt{\dfrac{2(\$18)(\$1,500,000)}{0.09}} = \$24,494.90 \approx \$24,495.$

3. e. Average cash balance = \$24,495/2 = \$12,247.50.

4. b. Transfers per year = \$1,500,000/\$24,495 = 61.24.

5. a. X = Amount needed to factor.

$$\$500,000 = X - \left(\dfrac{0.14}{12}X + 0.04X \right)$$

$$\$500,000 = X\left[1 - \left(\dfrac{0.14}{12} + 0.04 \right) \right]$$

$$\$500,000 = 0.9483X$$

$$\$527,240.77 = X$$

$$X \approx \$527,241.$$

6. c. Monthly costs:

Commission = \$527,241(0.04) =	\$21,090
Interest = \$527,241(0.14/12) =	6,151
	\$27,241

Monthly savings:

Credit expense =	\$10,000
Bad debt losses = \$527,241(0.035) =	18,453
	\$28,453

The factoring arrangement will result in a savings of \$28,453 − \$27,241 = \$1,212 per month, or \$1,212(12) = \$14,544 per year.

7. c. The incremental receivable investment is calculated as follows:

$$\text{Old credit policy: } DSO \times \frac{\text{Sales}}{\text{per day}} \times \frac{\text{Variable}}{\text{cost ratio}}$$

$$(30)\left(\frac{\$1,000,000}{360}\right)(0.4) = \$33,333.$$

$$\text{New credit policy: } DSO \times \frac{\text{Sales}}{\text{per day}} \times \frac{\text{Variable}}{\text{cost ratio}}$$

$$(45)\left(\frac{\$1,100,000}{360}\right)(0.4) = \$55,000.$$

The incremental investment in receivables is $55,000 - $33,333 = $21,667.

8. b. The incremental cost of carrying receivables would be calculated as follows:

$$\text{Old credit policy: } DSO \times \frac{\text{Sales}}{\text{per day}} \times \frac{\text{Variable}}{\text{cost ratio}} \times \frac{\text{Cost of}}{\text{funds}}.$$

$$(30)\left(\frac{\$1,000,000}{360}\right)(0.4)(0.15) = \$5,000.$$

or $\qquad \$33,333(0.15) = \$5,000.$

New credit policy:

$$(45)\left(\frac{\$1,100,000}{360}\right)(0.4)(0.15) = \$8,250.$$

or $\qquad \$55,000(0.15) = \$8,250.$

Thus, the incremental cost is $8,250 - $5,000 = $3,250.

9. a.

	Income Statement under Current Policy	Effect of Change	Income Statement under New Policy
Gross sales	$1,000,000	$ 100,000	$1,100,000
Less discounts	0	0	0
Net sales	$1,000,000	$ 100,000	$1,100,000
Production costs	400,000	40,000	440,000
Profit before credit costs and taxes	$ 600,000	$ 60,000	$ 660,000
Credit related costs:			
Cost of carrying receivables	5,000	3,250	8,250
Collection expenses			
Bad debt losses	10,000	3,000	13,000
Profit before taxes	$ 585,000	$ 53,750	$ 638,750
Taxes (40%)	234,000	21,500	255,500
Net income	$ 351,000	$ 32,250	$ 383,250

10. d. The incremental change in receivable investment would be calculated as follows:

$$\text{Old credit policy: } \text{DSO} \times \frac{\text{Sales}}{\text{per day}} \times \frac{\text{Variable}}{\text{cost ratio}}$$

$$(40)\left(\frac{\$2,000,000}{360}\right)(0.6) = \$133,333.$$

$$\text{New credit policy: } \text{DSO} \times \frac{\text{Sales}}{\text{per day}} \times \frac{\text{Variable}}{\text{cost ratio}}$$

$$(30)\left(\frac{\$1,750,000}{360}\right)(0.6) = \$87,500.$$

The incremental change in receivables is $87,500 - $133,333 = -$45,833.

11. b.

	Income Statement under Current Policy	Effect of Change	Income Statement under New Policy
Sales	$2,000,000	($250,000)	$1,750,000
Less discounts	0	0	0
Net sales	$2,000,000	($250,000)	$1,750,000
Production costs	1,200,000	(150,000)	1,050,000
Profit before credit costs and taxes	$ 800,000	($100,000)	$ 700,000
Credit related costs:			
Cost of carrying receivables	16,000	(5,500)	10,500
Collection expenses			
Bad debt losses	100,000	(65,000)	35,000
Profit before taxes	$ 684,000	($ 29,500)	$ 654,500
Taxes (40%)	273,600	(11,800)	261,800
Net income	$ 410,400	($ 17,700)	$ 392,700

12. d. $\text{EOQ} = \sqrt{\dfrac{2(F)(S)}{(C)(P)}} = \sqrt{\dfrac{2(\$25)(16,200)}{0.20(\$5)}} = \sqrt{\dfrac{\$810,000}{\$1.00}} = 900 \text{ bags.}$

13. c. $\dfrac{16,200 \text{ bags per year}}{900 \text{ bags per order}} = 18 \text{ orders per year.}$

14. b. Daily rate of use = 16,200/360 = 45 bags.

Order point = 300 + 5(45) = 525 bags.

Thus, South Florida Lawn Supply Company will have 1,200 bags on hand immediately after a shipment is received, will use 45 bags per day, will reorder when the stock is down to 525 bags (which is 5 days' requirement, plus the safety stock), and will be down to 300 bags just before a shipment arrives.

15. a. Average inventory level = EOQ/2 + Safety stock = 900/2 + 300 = 750 bags.

Note that the inventory fluctuates between 1,200 and 300 bags.

16. d. $\text{EOQ} = \sqrt{\dfrac{2(F)(S)}{(C)(P)}} = \sqrt{\dfrac{2(\$600)(120,000)}{0.20(\$500)}} = \sqrt{\dfrac{\$144,000,000}{\$100}} = 1,200$ units.

17. e. Maximum inventory = EOQ + Safety stock = 1,200 + 500 = 1,700 units.

18. c. Average inventory = EOQ/2 + Safety stock = 600 + 500 = 1,100 units.

19. b. $\dfrac{120,000 \text{ units per year}}{1,200 \text{ units per order}} = 100$ orders per year.

$\dfrac{360 \text{ days per year}}{100 \text{ orders per year}} = 3.60$ days.

The firm must place one order every 3.60 days.

20. b. $\text{TIC} = (C)(P)(Q/2) + \dfrac{(F)(S)}{Q} = 0.2(\$500)(1,200/2) + \dfrac{\$600(120,000)}{1,200}$

$= \$60,000 + \$60,000 = \$120,000.$

Note that total carrying costs equal total ordering costs at the EOQ.

21. d. Now, the average inventory is EOQ/2 + Safety stock = 1,100 units rather than EOQ/2 = 600 units.

$\text{TIC} = 0.2(\$500)(1,100) + \dfrac{\$600(120,000)}{1,200} = \$110,000 + \$60,000 = \$170,000.$

Another way of looking at this is

TIC = Cost of working inventory + Cost of safety stock
$= \$120,000 + 500(\$500)(0.2) = \$120,000 + \$50,000 = \$170,000.$

22. a. Cost of carrying accounts receivable at present:

DSO = Receivables/(Sales/360) = \$3,000/(\$20,000/360) = 54 days.

Cost of carrying receivables under current policy = DSO(Sales/360)(V)(k) = 54(\$55.556)(0.6)(0.12) = \$216.

Cost of carrying accounts receivable if credit policy is changed:

DSO = \$5,000/(\$24,000/360) = \$5,000/\$66.667 = 75 days.

Credit cost of new policy = 75(\$66.667)(0.6)(0.12) = \$360.

Change in cost of carrying accounts receivable = \$360 – \$216 = \$144.

23. e. Cost of carrying accounts receivable (in millions) at present:

DSO = Receivables/(Sales/360) = \$50/(\$500/360) = \$50/\$1.389 = 36 days.

Credit cost (in millions) at present = DSO(Sales/360)(V)(k) = 36(\$1.389)(0.8)(0.1) = \$4.00.

Cost of carrying receivables (in millions) if credit policy is changed:

DSO = \$25/(\$475/360) = \$25/\$1.319 = 18.95 days.

Credit cost (in millions) of new policy = 18.95(\$1.319)(0.8)(0.1) = \$2.00.

Change in cost of carrying accounts receivable = \$2.00 - \$4.00 = -\$2.00.

Here are the partial income statements (in millions):

	Current Policy	Change	New Policy
Sales	\$500	(\$25)	\$475
Variable costs (80%)	400	(20)	380
Fixed costs	NA	NA	NA
Pretax profit before credit costs	\$100	(\$ 5)	\$ 95
Credit costs	4	(2)	2
Pretax profit after credit costs	\$ 96	(\$ 3)	\$ 93

Change (in millions) in pre-tax profits: -\$3.00.

CHAPTER 23

DERIVATIVES AND
RISK MANAGEMENT

OVERVIEW

Risk management can mean many things, but in business it involves identifying events that could have adverse financial consequences for the firm and then undertaking actions to prevent and/or minimize the damage caused by these events. Years ago, corporate risk managers dealt primarily with insurance. More recently, however, the scope of risk management has been broadened to include such things as controlling the costs of key inputs or protecting against changes in interest rates or exchange rates. In addition, risk managers try to insure that actions designed to hedge against risks are not actually raising risks.

Since one of the most important tools used in risk management is derivative securities, we begin the chapter with a discussion of options and other derivatives. *Direct claim securities*, are pieces of paper that represent claims against real assets such as land, plant and equipment, and even whole businesses. *Indirect claim securities*, or *derivatives*, are securities whose values are determined, in whole or in part, by the market price (or interest rate) of some other security (or market). Derivatives include options, whose values depend on the price of some underlying stock; interest rate and exchange rate futures and swaps, whose values depend on interest rate and exchange rate levels; and commodity futures, whose values depend on commodity prices.

OUTLINE

An historical perspective is useful when studying derivatives. One of if not the first formal markets for derivatives was the futures market for wheat.

- ■ The earliest futures dealings were between two parties who arranged transactions between themselves. Soon, though, middlemen came into the picture, and trading in futures was established.
  - □ The Chicago Board of Trade was an early marketplace for this dealing, and futures dealers helped make a market in futures contracts. This improved the efficiency and lowered the cost of hedging operations.

■ Speculators then entered the scene. Speculators add capital and players to the derivatives market, and this stabilizes the market. Risk to the speculators themselves is high, but their bearing that risk probably makes the derivatives markets more stable for the hedgers.

■ *Natural hedges* are situations where aggregate risk can be reduced by derivatives transactions between two parties (called *counterparties*).

■ *Hedging* can also be done in situations where no natural hedge exists. Here one party wants to reduce some type of risk, and another party agrees to sell a contract which protects the first party from a specific event or situation.

■ The derivatives markets have grown more rapidly than any other major market in recent years for a number of reasons.
   □ Analytical techniques have been developed to help establish "fair" prices, which make the counter-parties more comfortable with deals.
   □ Computers and electronic communications make it much easier for counter-parties to deal with one another.
   □ Globalization has greatly increased the importance of currency markets, and the need for reducing the exchange rate risks brought on by global trade.

■ Derivatives do have a potential downside. These instruments are highly leveraged, so small miscalculations can lead to huge losses.

An option is a contract which gives its holder the right to buy or sell an asset at some predetermined price within a specified period of time.

■ *Pure options* are instruments that are created by outsiders rather than the firm, are bought and sold primarily by investors and speculators, and are of greater importance to individual investors than to financial managers.

■ The *striking*, or *exercise*, *price* is the price that must be paid (buying or selling) for a share of common stock when an option is exercised.

■ The seller of an option is called the *option writer*.

■ An investor who "writes" call options against stock held in his or her portfolio is said to be selling *covered options*. Options sold without the stock to back them up are called *naked options*.

■ When the exercise price exceeds the current stock price, a call option is said to be *out-of-the-money*. When the exercise price is less than the current price of the underlying stock, a call option is *in-the-money*.

■ An option which gives you the right to sell a stock at a specified price within some future period is called a *put option*.

■ There at least three factors which affect a call option's value:
  ☐ For a given striking price, the higher the stock's market price in relation to the strike price, the higher will be the call option price.
  ☐ For a given stock price, the higher the striking price, the lower will be the call option price.
  ☐ The longer the option period, the higher will be the option price, because the longer the time before expiration, the greater the chance that the stock price will climb substantially above the exercise price.

■ A call option's *formula value* is equal to the current stock price less the striking price.

■ In addition to the stock price and the exercise price, the price of an option depends on three other factors: (1) the option's term to maturity, (2) the variability of the stock price, and (3) the risk-free rate.
  ☐ The longer an option has to run, the greater its value and the larger its premium.
  ☐ An option on an extremely volatile stock will be worth more than one on a very stable stock.
  ☐ Because of the first two points, if everything else were constant, then the longer an option's life, the higher its market price is above its formula value.

Investors can, in principle, create riskless portfolios by buying stocks and selling call options against those stocks, and the return on such portfolios should be the risk-free rate. If call options are not priced to reflect this condition, arbitrageurs will actively trade stocks and options until option prices do reflect such equilibrium conditions.

The Black-Scholes Option Pricing Model (OPM) is widely used by option traders to estimate the value of a call option.

■ Option theory provides insights to valuing all securities subject to contingent claims, including warrants, convertibles, and even the equity of a levered firm.

- The assumptions made in the OPM are:
  - ☐ The stock underlying the call option provides no dividends or other distributions during the life of the option.
  - ☐ There are no transaction costs in buying or selling either the stock or the option.
  - ☐ The short-term, risk-free interest rate is known and is constant during the life of the option.
  - ☐ Any purchaser of a security may borrow any fraction of the purchase price at the short-term, risk-free interest rate.
  - ☐ Short selling is permitted without penalty, and the short seller will receive immediately the full cash proceeds of today's price for a security sold short.
  - ☐ The call option can be exercised only on its expiration date.
  - ☐ Trading in all securities takes place in continuous time, and the stock price moves randomly in continuous time.

- The Black-Scholes model consists of the following three equation:

$$V = P[N(d_1)] - Xe^{-k_{RF}t}[N(d_2)].$$

$$d_1 = \frac{\ln(P/X) + [k_{RF} + (\sigma^2/2)]t}{\sigma\sqrt{t}}.$$

$$d_2 = d_1 - \sigma\sqrt{t}.$$

  - ☐ V = current value of a call option with time t until expiration.
  - ☐ P = current price of the underlying stock.
  - ☐ $N(d_i)$ = probability that a deviation less than d_i will occur in a standard normal distribution.

    Thus, $N(d_1)$ and $N(d_2)$ represent areas under a standard normal distribution function.
  - ☐ X = exercise, or striking, price of the option.
  - ☐ $e \approx 2.7183$.
  - ☐ k_{RF} = risk-free interest rate.
  - ☐ t = time until the option expires (the option period).
  - ☐ ln(P/X) = natural logarithm of P/X.
  - ☐ σ^2 = variance of the rate of return on the stock.

Put and call options represent an important class of derivative securities, but there are other types of derivatives, including futures, swaps, structured notes, inverse floaters, and a host of other "exotic" contracts.

- *Futures* are contracts which require the holder to buy or sell something at a specified price on a specific future date. Futures were originally used for commodities, but today more trading is done in foreign exchange and interest rate futures.

- In a *swap* two parties agree to swap something, generally obligations to make specified payments. Most swaps today involve either interest payments or currencies.
  - ☐ Originally, swaps were arranged between companies by money center banks, which would match up counterparties. Such matching still occurs, but today most swaps are between companies and banks, with the banks then taking steps to ensure that their own risks are hedged.

- A *structured note* often means a debt obligation which is derived from some other debt obligation.
  - ☐ Zeroes formed by stripping T-bonds were one of the first types of structured notes.
  - ☐ Another important type of structured note is backed by the interest and principal payments on mortgages, *collateralized mortgage obligations*.

- A floating rate note has an interest rate that rises and falls with some interest rate index. With an *inverse floater*, the rate paid on the note moves counter to market rates.
  - ☐ Thus, if interest rates in the economy rose, the interest rate paid on an inverse floater would fall, lowering its cash interest payments. At the same time, the discount rate used to value the inverse floater's cash flows would rise along with other rates. The combined effect would lead to a very large decline in the value of the inverse floater. Thus, inverse floaters are exceptionally vulnerable to increases in interest rates.

Risk can be classified in many ways and different classifications are commonly used in different industries.

- Here's one list that provides an idea of the wide variety of risks to which a firm can be exposed: speculative risks, pure risks, demand risks, input risks, financial risks, property risks, personnel risks, environmental risks, liability risks, and insurable risks.

Firms often use the following three-step approach to risk management: (1) identify the risks faced by the firm, (2) measure the potential impact of the risks identified, and (3) decide how each relevant risk should be minimized.

- There are several techniques to help minimize risk exposure:
  - ☐ *Transfer the risk to an insurance company.* Often, it is advantageous to insure against, and hence transfer, a risk. However, insurability does not necessarily mean that a risk should be covered by insurance. Thus, it might be better for the company to *self-insure*, which means bearing the risk directly rather than paying to have another party bear the risk.

    ☐ *Transfer the function that produces the risk to a third party.* In some situations, risks can be reduced most easily by passing them on to some other company that is not an insurance company.

    ☐ *Reduce the probability of occurrence of an adverse event.* In some instances, it is possible to take action to reduce the probability that an adverse event will occur.

    ☐ *Reduce the magnitude of the loss associated with an adverse event.*

    ☐ *Totally avoid the activity that gives rise to the risk.*

■ Risk management decisions, like all corporate decisions, should include a rigorous cost/benefit analysis for each feasible alternative. The same financial management techniques that are applied to other corporate decisions also can be applied to risk management decisions.

Risk identification and measurement involves systematically and continuously identifying the potential losses confronting the firm, and then measuring these potential losses by estimating their likelihoods of occurrence and loss potentials.

■ Most corporate risk managers use a prepared checklist to identify risks; smaller firms often rely on risk management services of insurance companies to identify and measure the risks that they face.

■ After the risks have been identified, it is necessary to measure the firm's degree of exposure to each risk. This involves estimating *loss frequency* (the probability of a loss) and *loss severity* (the dollar value of each loss).

    ☐ In general, loss exposure is more a function of the severity of losses than of their frequency. A risk with the potential of a catastrophic loss, even though its frequency is rare, is far more serious than a risk that is expected to produce frequent but small losses.

    ☐ Two approaches to measuring loss severity include (1) the maximum loss approach and (2) the average loss approach. The *maximum loss* is the dollar loss associated with the worst-case scenario, while the *average loss* is the average dollar loss associated with a particular peril.

Property loss exposures involve both real property (land and buildings) and personal property.

■ *Physical, social, and economic perils* are the three categories most commonly associated with property losses.

■ *Direct* losses to property occur when it is destroyed, damaged, or lost. *Indirect* losses stem from direct loss: for example, the loss of profits during the time when fire damage is being repaired.

■ To measure a firm's potential exposure to property losses, the risk manager must attach a value to the firm's property. Property appraisers utilize several standards of measurement for assigning property values:
- ☐ *Original cost* is the dollar cost at acquisition.
- ☐ *Book value* is the original cost less the accumulated depreciation.
- ☐ *Market value* is the current value of an asset as set by supply and demand conditions in the marketplace.
- ☐ *Tax appraisal value* is often set at less than true market value to reduce valuation appeals.
- ☐ *Economic value* is the present value of the cash flows that it is expected to produce.
- ☐ *Replacement value* is the cost to replace the property at the time of the appraisal.

■ In general, property loss exposures are managed either by retaining the risk or by passing it to an insurer.

Businesses also face liability loss exposure. The term liability involves the concept of a penalty that can be imposed when a responsibility is not met. Companies risk liability losses through five categories of exposure: bailee exposure, ownership exposure, business operation exposure, employee actions exposure, and professional exposure.

■ A business may enter into a transaction called a *bailment*, in which a business takes possession of another's property to perform some service, and then returns the property to the owner. Businesses that act as *bailees*, then, must be fully aware of the liability exposure that such arrangements create.

■ Ownership of real and personal property brings with it significant liability exposure. For example, injuries that occur on a firm's real property or as a result of its personal property may give rise to liability losses.

■ Liability exposure that arises from business operations is often the most critical exposure that firms face. It can include the following types:
- ☐ *Nuisance* exposure involves activities, such as environmental pollution, which can harm third parties.
- ☐ *Patent and copyright infringement* are violations of invention or creative work protection laws.
- ☐ *Unfair trade practices* also create the potential for large liability exposures.
- ☐ *Product liability* stems from defects in the firm's goods and services provided.

■ *Improper actions* of employees, such as sexual harassment, is another type of liability exposure.

■ *Professional liability* can impact firms that provide services requiring advance training and licensing. The cost and number of malpractice lawsuits have increased dramatically in recent years.

Firms are subject to numerous risk exposures due to interest rate, stock price, and exchange rate fluctuations in the financial markets. There are a number of ways to limit financial loss exposure.

■ Price risk and reinvestment rate risk exposure can subject firms to financial losses. *Price risk* is the risk that the price of a debt security will fall as a result of increases in interest rates, and *reinvestment rate risk* is the risk of earning a return less than expected when debt principal or interest payments are reinvested at rates less than the original yield to maturity.
  □ If interest rates *fall*, and the portfolio is invested in relatively short-term bonds, then the reinvestment rate penalty exceeds the capital gains, so a net shortfall occurs.
  □ If interest rates *rise*, and the portfolio is invested in relatively short-term bonds, then gains from high reinvestment rates will more than offset capital losses, and the final portfolio value will exceed the required amount.

■ Zero coupon bonds and stripped Treasuries can be used to eliminate reinvestment rate risk.

■ Bond portfolios can be *immunized* against price and reinvestment rate risk. The immunization process involves selecting maturities for the bonds in a portfolio such that gains or losses from reinvestment exactly match gains or losses from price changes.
  □ The key to immunizing a portfolio is to buy bonds which have a *duration* equal to the years until the funds will be needed. Duration is to a bond somewhat like payback is to a capital budgeting project, because the longer the duration, the longer funds are tied up in the bond.

■ One of the most useful tools for reducing both *security and commodity price exposure* is to *hedge* in the futures markets.
  □ *Futures*, or *futures contracts*, call for the purchase or sale of a financial or real asset at some future date, but at a price which is fixed today.
  □ Futures contracts are divided into two classes, *commodity futures* and *financial futures*.
  □ When futures contracts are purchased, the purchaser does not have to put up the full amount of the purchase price; rather, the purchaser is required to post an initial *margin*. However, investors are required to maintain a certain value in the margin account, called a *maintenance margin*.
  □ An *option* is similar to a futures contract, but it merely gives someone the right to buy (call) or sell (put) an asset, but the holder of the option does not have to complete the transaction.

■ Firms are exposed to price losses when securities are being issued and when securities are held as part of investment portfolios. In addition, firms are exposed to risk when floating rate debt is used to finance an investment that has a more-or-less fixed income stream. These types of risk can be reduced by using *derivatives*, which are securities whose values stem, or are derived, from the values of other assets. *Futures and swaps* are two types of derivatives used to manage security price exposure.

☐ *Futures markets* are used for both speculation and hedging: *Speculation* involves betting on future price movements; *hedging* is done by a firm or individual engaged in a business where a price change could negatively affect profits.

▶ There are two basic types of hedges: (1) *long hedges*, in which futures contracts are bought in anticipation of (or to guard against) price increases, and (2) *short hedges*, where a firm or individual sells futures contracts to guard against price declines.

☐ The futures and options markets permit flexibility in the timing of financial transactions, because the firm can be protected partially against changes that occur between the present and the time when a particular transaction will be completed.

▶ Firms must weigh the benefit versus the cost of the commissions plus the opportunity cost of the margin money.

▶ A *swap* is another method for reducing financial risks. It is an exchange of cash payment obligations, in which each party to the swap prefers the payment type or pattern of the other party.

▶ Although the corporate use of derivatives to hedge risk is a relatively new phenomenon, it has caught on like wild fire. In fact, about 90 percent of the largest 200 companies in the U.S. currently use derivatives on a regular basis.

▶ There is, however, a downside to derivatives: Problems can quickly arise when hedges are improperly constructed or when corporate managers, eager to boost profits, use derivatives for speculation rather than hedging.

▶ While the use of derivatives to hedge risk is an important tool for risk managers, if used improperly, derivatives have the potential to create very large losses in very short periods.

SELF-TEST QUESTIONS

Definitional

1. _____ _____ generally involves the management of unpredictable events that have adverse financial consequences for the firm.

2. Firms often use a three-step approach to risk management: (1) _____ the risks faced by the firm, (2) _____ the potential impact of the risks identified, and (3) decide how each relevant risk should be _____.

3. _____-_____ means bearing the risk directly rather than paying to have another party bear the risk.

4. Risk management decisions, like all corporate decisions, should include a rigorous _____/_____ analysis for each feasible alternative.

5. _____ _____ are instruments that are created by outsiders rather than the firm, are bought and sold primarily by investors and speculators, and are of greater importance to individual investors than to financial managers.

6. When the exercise price exceeds the current stock price a call option is said to be _____-_____-_____-_____; however, when the exercise price is less than the current price of the underlying stock, a call option is _____-_____-_____.

7. In addition to the stock price and the exercise price, the price of an option depends on three other factors: (1) the option's term to _____, (2) the _____ of the stock price, and (3) the _____-_____ _____.

8. The _____-_____ _____ _____ _____ is widely used by option traders to estimate the value of a call option.

9. After the risks have been identified, it is necessary to measure the firm's degree of exposure to each risk. This involves estimating loss _____ (the probability of a loss) and loss _____ (the dollar value of each loss).

10. There are two approaches to measuring loss severity: (1) the _____ _____ approach and (2) the _____ _____ approach.

11. _____ losses to property occur when it is destroyed, damaged, or lost.

12. _____ _____ represents the present value of the cash flows the property is expected to produce, while _____ _____ represents the current value of an asset as set by supply and demand conditions.

13. _____ involves the concept of a penalty that can be imposed when a responsibility is not met. Companies risk this type of loss through five categories of exposure: _____ exposure, _____ exposure, business operation exposure, employee actions exposure, and _____ exposure.

14. _____ are contracts which require the holder to buy or sell something at a specified price on a specific future date.

15. The _____ process involves selecting maturities for the bonds in a portfolio such that gains or losses from reinvestment exactly match gains or losses from price changes.

16. Futures markets are used for both hedging and speculation: _____ involves betting on future price movements, while _____ is done by a firm or individual engaged in a business where a price change could negatively affect profits.

17. _____ are securities whose values stem, or are derived, from the values of other assets.

18. A(n) _____ is an exchange of cash payment obligations, in which each party to the transaction prefers the payment type or pattern of the other party.

19. A(n) _____ _____ often means a debt obligation which is derived from some other debt obligation, for example, collateralized mortgage obligations.

20. _____, _____, and _____ perils are the three categories most commonly associated with property losses.

Conceptual

21. Immunization is the process of eliminating, or at least minimizing, a bond portfolio's interest rate (price) risk and reinvestment rate risk. The process involves selecting securities such that the duration of each security in the portfolio matches the due date of some future cash outflow.

    a. True   b. False

22. The two basic types of hedges involving the futures market are long hedges and short hedges, where the words "long" and "short" refer to the maturity of the hedging instrument. For example, a long hedge might use stocks, while a short hedge might use 3-month T-bills.

   a. True   b. False

23. Which of the following statements about liability loss exposure, if any, is *incorrect*?

   a. The liability exposure that arises from business operations is often the most critical exposure that firms face.
   b. Professional liability applies to doctors, lawyers, and other service providers that require advance training and licensing.
   c. Liability exposures are typically handled by either self-insuring or passing the risk to an insurance company.
   d. Bailment is the act of taking possession of personal property owned by another person or business and performing some service on that property.
   e. Companies that do not produce consumer products have minimal liability exposure.

24. A swap is a method for reducing financial risk. Which of the following statements about swaps, if any, is *incorrect*?

   a. A swap involves the exchange of cash payment obligations.
   b. The earliest swaps were currency swaps, in which companies traded debt denominated in different currencies, say dollars and pounds.
   c. Swaps are generally arranged by a financial intermediary, who may or may not take the position of one of the counterparties.
   d. A problem with swaps is the lack of standardized contracts, which limits the development of a secondary market.
   e. All of the above statements are correct.

25. Which of the following statements about interest rate and reinvestment rate risk is *correct*?

    a. Variable, or floating rate, securities have a high degree of interest rate (price) risk.

    b. Price risk occurs because fixed-rate debt securities lose value when interest rates rise, while reinvestment rate risk is the risk of earning less than expected when interest payments or debt principal are reinvested.

    c. Reinvestment rate risk can be eliminated by purchasing zero coupon bonds.

    d. Reinvestment rate risk can be eliminated by purchasing variable, or floating, rate bonds.

    e. Statements b and c are both correct.

SELF-TEST PROBLEMS

1. What is the duration of a 5-year zero coupon bond?

    a. 0 years   **b.** 5 years   **c.** 10 years   **d.** undefined   **e.** infinity

2. What is the approximate duration of an 8 percent, 3-year, annual coupon bond selling at its $1,000 par value?

    a. 2 years   **b.** 2.2 years   **c.** 2.5 years   **d.** 2.8 years   **e.** 3.0 years

ANSWERS TO SELF-TEST QUESTIONS

1. Risk management
2. identify; measure; minimized
3. Self-insure
4. cost/benefit
5. pure options
6. out-of-the-money; in-the-money
7. maturity; variability; risk-free rate
8. Black-Scholes Option Pricing Model
9. frequency; severity
10. maximum loss; average loss

11. Direct
12. Economic value; market value
13. Liability; bailee; ownership; professional
14. Futures
15. immunization
16. speculation; hedging
17. Derivatives
18. swap
19. structured note
20. physical; social; economic

21. a. This statement is correct.

22. b. Long hedges are futures contracts bought to guard against price increases, while short hedges are futures contracts sold to guard against price declines.

23. e. Liability involves the concept of a penalty that can be imposed when a responsibility is not met. Thus, it has broad encompassing effects.

24. d.

25. e.

SOLUTIONS TO SELF-TEST PROBLEMS

1. b. For a zero coupon bond, duration is the same as maturity.

2. d.

t	CF	PVCF	PVCF/V	t(PVCF/V)
1	$80.00	$74.07	0.0741	0.0741
2	80.00	68.59	0.0686	0.1372
3	1,080.00	857.34	0.8573	2.5720

Duration = 2.7833 ≈ 2.8.

CHAPTER 24

BANKRUPTCY, REORGANIZATION, AND LIQUIDATION

OVERVIEW

The financial manager of a failing firm must know how to ward off his or her firm's total collapse and thereby reduce its losses. The ability to hang on during rough times often means the difference between the firm's forced liquidation versus its rehabilitation and eventual success. At the same time, an understanding of business failures and bankruptcies, their causes, and their possible remedies is also important to financial managers of successful firms, because they must know their firms' rights when their customers or suppliers go bankrupt.

OUTLINE

Financial distress experienced by firms can range from a vague uneasiness about future profitability to complete disintegration of the firm. Common definitions of financial distress include the following:

- *Economic failure* signifies that a firm's revenues do not cover its total costs, including its cost of capital. These firms can keep on operating as long as investors are willing to provide additional capital and their owners are willing to accept below-market rates of return.

- *Business failure* is a term defined by Dun & Bradstreet as any business that has terminated operations with a resultant loss to creditors, regardless of whether the firm has entered formal bankruptcy proceedings.

- A firm is considered *technically insolvent* if it cannot meet its current obligations as they fall due.

- A firm is *insolvent in bankruptcy* when its book value of total liabilities exceeds the true market value of its assets. This is a more serious condition than technical insolvency because it is a sign of economic failure, and it generally leads to liquidation of the business.

- *Legal bankruptcy* occurs when the firm has filed for bankruptcy under federal law.

A number of factors combine to cause business failures. Case studies show that financial difficulties are usually the result of a series of errors, misjudgments, and interrelated weaknesses that can be attributed directly or indirectly to management, and signs of potential financial distress are generally evident before the firm actually fails.

■ Although bankruptcies are more common among smaller firms, it is clear that large firms are not immune. It is interesting to note that whereas the failure rate per 10,000 businesses fluctuates with the state of the economy, the average liability per failure has tended to increase over time. This is due primarily to inflation, but it also reflects the fact that some very large firms have failed in recent years.

■ Government and industry seek to avoid failure among larger firms. For financial institutions the reason for this is to prevent an erosion of confidence and a consequent run on the banks. The fact that bankruptcy is a very expensive process gives private industry strong incentives to avoid outright bankruptcy.

Financial distress begins when a debtor is unable to meet scheduled payments to creditors or when the firm's cash flow projections indicate that it will soon be unable to do so.

■ Several questions arise as to how a firm should proceed:
  □ Is the situation temporary or a permanent problem?
  □ If temporary, can an agreement with creditors be worked out; if permanent, who should bear the losses?
  □ Is the company "worth more dead than alive"?
  □ Should the firm file for bankruptcy or use informal procedures?
  □ Who should control the firm while it is being liquidated or rehabilitated?

Because of the high costs of formal bankruptcy, it is desirable to reorganize or liquidate a firm outside formal bankruptcy through use of informal settlements.

■ *Informal reorganization* can be used in the case of an economically sound company in temporary distress. Voluntary plans, called *workouts,* usually require some type of *restructuring* of the firm's debt.
  □ A debt restructuring begins with a meeting between the failing firm's managers and creditors. An *adjustment bureau* run by the creditor managers' association often arranges the meeting. A great deal of negotiation is involved to reach a final debt restructuring agreement.

☐ At least three conditions are usually necessary to make an informal debt restructuring feasible: (1) The debtor must be a good moral risk, (2) the debtor must demonstrate a reasonable plan to solve its problems, and (3) general business conditions must be favorable to recovery.

☐ Creditors often prefer an *extension* because it promises eventual payment in full. In an extension, creditors postpone the dates of required interest or principal payments, or both.

☐ In a *composition*, creditors voluntarily reduce their fixed claims on the debtor by accepting a lower principal amount, by reducing the interest rate on the debt, by accepting equity in place of debt, or by accepting some combination of these changes.

☐ Such voluntary settlements are not only informal and simple but also relatively inexpensive because legal and administrative expenses are held to a minimum. Creditors often recover more money, and sooner, than if the firm were to file for bankruptcy.

☐ Perhaps the biggest problem in informal reorganizations is in getting all the parties to agree to the voluntary plan. This problem is called the *holdout problem*.

■ *Informal liquidation* is the result of determining that a firm is more valuable dead than alive. *Assignment* is an informal procedure for liquidating a firm, and it usually yields creditors a larger amount than they would receive in a formal bankruptcy liquidation. In an assignment, the title to the debtor's assets is transferred to a third party, known as an assignee or trustee, who is instructed to liquidate the assets through a private sale or public auction and then to distribute the proceeds among the creditors on a pro rata basis. Assignments are feasible only if the firm is small and its affairs are not too complex.

A firm is officially bankrupt when it files for bankruptcy with a federal court. Formal bankruptcy proceedings are designed to protect both the firm and its creditors. Chapter 11 of the 1978 Bankruptcy Reform Act deals with business reorganization.

■ If the problem is technical insolvency, then the firm may use bankruptcy proceedings to gain time to solve its cash flow problems without foreclosure by its creditors.

■ If the firm is bankrupt in the sense that liabilities exceed assets, the creditors can use bankruptcy procedures to attempt to ensure that the firm's owners do not siphon off assets which should go to creditors.

Two problems often arise to stymie informal reorganizations and thus force debtors into formal Chapter 11 bankruptcy.

■ The *common pool problem* occurs because individual creditors have an incentive to foreclose on the firm even though the firm is worth more collectively as an ongoing concern. A solution to the common pool problem is the Chapter 11 *automatic stay provision*, which limits the ability of creditors to foreclose unilaterally on the debtor to collect their individual claims.

■ *Fraudulent conveyance* statutes, which are part of debtor-creditor law in most states, protect creditors from unjustified transfers of property by a firm in financial distress.

■ The *holdout problem* can also make it difficult to reorganize a firm's debts. If all creditors agreed to a reorganization plan, it would benefit the creditors and the firm simultaneously. However, there is an advantage for a creditor to "hold out" since his or her claim would be higher than that of those who would agree to a lower settlement. Thus, it is likely that none of the creditors would accept the offer. Because of this problem, it is easier for a firm with few creditors to informally reorganize than it is for a firm with many creditors.

In bankruptcy, it is much easier to gain acceptance of a reorganization plan, because the bankruptcy court will lump the creditors into classes.

■ A *cramdown* is a procedure in which the court mandates a reorganization plan in spite of dissent.

Filing for bankruptcy under Chapter 11 has several benefits besides automatic stay and cramdown that are not inherent in informal restructurings.

■ Interest and principal payments may be delayed without penalty until a reorganization plan is approved.

■ The firm is permitted to issue *debtor in possession (DIP) financing* which enhances the ability of the firm to borrow funds for short-term liquidity purposes, because such loans are senior to all other unsecured debt.

■ The debtor firm's managers are given the exclusive right for 120 days after filing to submit a reorganization plan, plus another 60 days to obtain agreement on the plan from the parties affected.

■ Under the early bankruptcy laws, most formal reorganization plans were guided by the *absolute priority doctrine*. This doctrine holds that creditors should be compensated for their claims in a rigid hierarchical order, and that senior claims must be paid in full before junior claims can receive even a dime. An alternative position, the *relative priority doctrine*, holds that more flexibility should be allowed in a reorganization, and that balanced consideration should be given to all claimants. Current law represents a movement away from absolute priority and toward relative priority.

The primary role of the bankruptcy court in a reorganization is to determine the fairness and the feasibility of proposed plans of reorganization.

■ The *fairness* doctrine states that claims must be recognized in the order of their legal and contractual priority.

■ The primary test of *feasibility* in a reorganization is whether the fixed charges after reorganization will be adequately covered by earnings.

■ Recently a new type of reorganization called *prepackaged bankruptcy* combines the advantages of both the informal workout and formal Chapter 11 reorganization. Here the debtor firm gets all, or most of, the creditors to agree to the reorganization plan prior to filing for bankruptcy. Then, a reorganization plan is filed along with the bankruptcy petition. If enough creditors have signed on before the filing, a cramdown can be used to bring reluctant creditors along.
  □ The three primary advantages of a prepackaged bankruptcy are (1) reduction of the holdout problem, (2) preserving creditors' claims, and (3) taxes.

If a company is "too far gone" to be reorganized, then it must be liquidated.

■ Liquidation should occur when the business is worth more dead than alive, or when the possibility of restoring the firm to financial health is so remote that the creditors run a higher risk of greater loss if operations are continued.

■ Chapter 7 of the Federal Bankruptcy Reform Act addresses three important problems during a liquidation:
  □ It provides safeguards against fraud by the debtor.
  □ It provides for an equitable distribution of the debtor's assets among the creditors.
  □ It allows insolvent debtors to discharge all their obligations and thus be able to start new businesses unhampered by the burden of prior debt.

■ The distribution of assets in a liquidation under Chapter 7 is governed by the following priority of claims: (1) Secured creditors, (2) trustee's costs, (3) expenses incurred after an involuntary case has begun but before a trustee is appointed, (4) wages due workers if earned within 3 months prior to filing the bankruptcy petition, (5) claims for unpaid contributions to employee benefit plans, (6) unsecured claims for customer deposits, (7) taxes due, (8) unfunded pension plan liabilities, (9) general (unsecured) creditors, (10) preferred stockholders, and (11) common stockholders.

Normally, bankruptcy proceedings originate after a company cannot meet its current obligations. However, bankruptcy law also permits a company to file for bankruptcy if its financial forecasts indicate that a continuation of current conditions would lead to insolvency.

Many critics today claim that current bankruptcy laws are not doing what they were intended to do.

■ Before 1978, most bankruptcies ended quickly in liquidation. Then, Congress rewrote the laws giving companies more opportunity to stay alive, believing that this was best for managers, employees, creditors, and stockholders.

■ Critics believe that bankruptcy is good business for consultants, lawyers, and investment bankers, who reap hefty fees during bankruptcy proceedings, and for managers, who continue to collect their salaries and bonuses as long as the business is kept alive.

■ Bankruptcy cases can drag on in court for many years, depleting assets that could be sold to pay off creditors and shareholders. In effect, critics say, maintaining companies on life support does not serve the interests of the parties that bankruptcy laws were meant to protect.

Multiple Discriminant Analysis (MDA) is a statistical tool which can predict the possibility of bankruptcy, thus allowing firms to take steps to avoid bankruptcy or at least reduce its impact. MDA uses a set of economic variables, such as the current ratio and debt ratio, to establish the possibility of failure.

■ In a classic paper, Edward Altman applied MDA to a sample of corporations, and he developed the following discriminant function:

$$Z = 0.012X_1 + 0.014X_2 + 0.033X_3 + 0.006X_4 + 0.999X_5.$$

☐ Here, X_1 = net working capital divided by total assets; X_2 = retained earnings divided by total assets; X_3 = EBIT divided by total assets; X_4 = market value of common and preferred stock divided by book value of debt; and X_5 = sales divided by total assets.

☐ Altman's *zone of ignorance* was from Z = 1.81 to Z = 2.99; and the higher the Z score, the lower the probability of bankruptcy.

SELF-TEST QUESTIONS

Definitional

1. _____ _____ experienced by firms can range from a vague uneasiness about future profitability to complete disintegration of the firm.

2. _____ _____ signifies that a firm's revenues do not cover its total costs, including its cost of capital.

3. _____ _____ is defined as any business that has terminated operations with a resultant loss to creditors, regardless of whether the firm has entered formal bankruptcy proceedings.

4. A firm is considered _____ _____ if it cannot meet its current obligations as they fall due.

5. _____ _____ can be used in the case of an economically sound company in temporary distress. Voluntary plans, called _____, usually require some type of restructuring of the firm's debt.

6. Creditors often prefer a(n) _____ because it promises eventual payment in full.

7. In a(n) _____, creditors agree to reduce their fixed claims on the debtor.

8. _____ is an informal procedure for liquidating a firm, and it usually yields creditors a larger amount than they would receive in a formal bankruptcy liquidation.

9. Two problems often arise to stymie informal reorganizations and thus force debtors into formal Chapter 11 bankruptcy: the _____ _____ _____ and the _____ _____.

10. A(n) _____ is a procedure in which the court mandates a reorganization plan in spite of dissent.

11. _____ _____ _____ financing enhances the ability of the firm to borrow funds for short-term liquidity purposes, because such loans are senior to all other unsecured debt.

12. The _____ doctrine states that claims must be recognized in the order of their legal and contractual priority, while the primary test of _____ in a reorganization is whether the fixed charges after reorganization will be adequately covered by earnings.

13. _____ _____ _____ is a statistical tool which can predict the possibility of bankruptcy, thus allowing firms to take steps to avoid bankruptcy or at least reduce its impact.

Conceptual

14. Economic failure is the term used by Dun & Bradstreet to define any business that has terminated operations with a resultant loss to creditors.

    a. True   b. False

15. A firm is insolvent in bankruptcy when its book value of total liabilities exceeds the true market value of its assets.

    a. True   b. False

16. Financial distress begins when a firm is unable to meet scheduled payments to creditors, not when the firm's cash flow projections indicate that it will soon be unable to do so.

    a. True   b. False

17. Bankruptcies are more common among larger firms than smaller firms.

    a. True   b. False

18. Informal reorganization can be used in the case of an economically sound company in temporary distress. One type of voluntary plan is called a workout.

    a. True   b. False

19. Which of the following statements is most *correct*?

   a. In an extension, creditors voluntarily reduce their fixed claims on the debtor by accepting a lower principal amount, by reducing the interest rate on the debt, by accepting equity in place of debt, or by accepting some combination of these changes.
   b. Technical insolvency occurs when a firm's book value of total liabilities exceeds the true market value of its assets.
   c. Although many people use the term bankruptcy to refer to any firm that has "failed," a firm is not legally bankrupt unless it has filed for bankruptcy under federal law.
   d. Both statements a and c are true.
   e. All of the statements are false.

20. Which of the following statements is most *correct*?

   a. The automatic stay provision provided for in Chapter 11 is only granted to certain debtors in bankruptcy. It limits the ability of creditors to foreclose unilaterally on the debtor to collect their individual claims and, as a result, it provides a solution to the holdout problem.
   b. Fraudulent conveyance statutes, which are a part of debtor-creditor law in most states, protect creditors from unjustified transfers of property by a firm in financial distress.
   c. In a cramdown, creditors postpone the dates of required interest or principal payments, or both.
   d. The common pool problem occurs because individual creditors have an incentive to foreclose on the firm even though the firm is worth more collectively as an ongoing concern.
   e. Both statements b and d are true.

21. Which of the following statements is most *correct*?

   a. Chapter 11 of the Federal Bankruptcy Reform Act addresses liquidation, while Chapter 7 deals with business reorganization.
   b. Preferred stockholders have priority over general, or unsecured, creditors in the distribution of claims in a liquidation.
   c. In multiple discriminant analysis the higher the Z-score, the higher the probability of bankruptcy.
   d. Multiple discriminant analysis is a statistical tool which can predict the possibility of bankruptcy, thus allowing firms to take steps to avoid bankruptcy or at least reduce its impact.
   e. All of the above statements are true.

SELF-TEST PROBLEMS

1. The Stanton Marble Company has the following balance sheet:

Current assets	$15,120	Accounts payable	$ 3,240
		Notes payable (to bank)	1,620
		Accrued taxes	540
		Accrued wages	540
		Total current liabilities	$ 5,940
Fixed assets	8,100	First mortgage bonds	2,700
		Second mortgage bonds	2,700
		Total mortgage bonds	$ 5,400
		Subordinated debentures	3,240
		Total long-term debt	$ 8,640
		Preferred stock	1,080
		Common stock	7,560
Total assets	$23,220	Total liabilities and equity	$23,220

The debentures are subordinated only to the notes payable. Suppose Stanton Marble goes bankrupt and is liquidated with $5,400 being received from the sale of the fixed assets, which were pledged as security for the first and second mortgage bonds, and $8,640 received from the sale of current assets. The trustee's costs total $1,440. How much will the holders of subordinated debentures receive?

a. $2,052   b. $2,448   c. $3,240   d. $2,709   e. $3,056

(The following data apply to the next three problems.)

The Lockwood Corporation's 1996 balance sheet and income statement are as follows (in millions of dollars). Lockwood and its creditors have agreed upon a voluntary reorganization plan. In this plan, each share of the $6 preferred will be exchanged for one share of $2.40 preferred with a par value of $37.50 plus one 8 percent subordinated income debenture with a par value of $75. The $10.50 preferred issue will be retired with cash.

Balance Sheet:

Current assets	$336	Current liabilities	$ 84
Net fixed assets	306	Advance payments	156
Goodwill	30	Reserves	12
		$6 preferred stock, $112.50 par value	
		(2,400,000 shares)	270
		$10.50 preferred stock, no par, callable	
		at $150 (120,000 shares)	18
		Common stock, $1.50 par value	
		(12,000,000 shares)	18
		Retained earnings	114
Total assets	$672	Total claims	$672

Income Statement:

Net sales	$1,080.0
Operating expense	1,032.0
Net operating income	$ 48.0
Other income	6.0
EBT	$ 54.0
Taxes (50%)	27.0
Net income	$ 27.0
Dividends on $6 preferred	14.4
Dividends on $10.50 preferred	1.3
Income available to common stockholders	$ 11.3

2. What is the value (in millions of dollars) of total assets on the balance sheet?

a. $680   b. $620   c. $636   d. $654   e. $645

3. What is the value (in millions of dollars) of the new preferred stock?

   a. $105   **b.** $90   **c.** $110   **d.** $80   **e.** $95

4. What is the net income available to common stockholders (in millions of dollars) after the proposed recapitalization takes place?

   a. $17   **b.** $11   **c.** $14   **d.** $13   **e.** $16

(The following data apply to the next six problems.)

At the time it defaulted on its interest payments and filed for bankruptcy, the Southeastern Manufacturing Company (SMC) had the following balance sheet (in thousands of dollars). The court, after trying unsuccessfully to reorganize the firm, decided that the only recourse was liquidation under Chapter 7. Sale of the fixed assets, which were pledged as collateral to the mortgage bondholders, brought in $1,600,000, while the current assets were sold for another $800,000. Thus, the total proceeds from the liquidation sale were $2,400,000. Trustee's costs amounted to $200,000; no single worker was due more than $2,000 in wages; and there were no unfunded pension plan liabilities.

Current assets	$1,600	Accounts payable	$ 200
		Accrued taxes	160
		Accrued wages	120
		Notes payable	720
		Total current liabilities	$1,200
Net fixed assets	2,400	First mortgage bonds[a]	1,200
		Second mortgage bonds[a]	800
		Debentures	800
		Subordinated debentures[b]	400
		Common stock	200
		Retained earnings	(600)
Total assets	$4,000	Total claims	$4,000

Notes:

[a]All fixed assets are pledged as collateral to the mortgage bonds.
[b]Subordinated to notes payable.

5. How much of the proceeds (in thousands of dollars) from the sale of assets remain to be distributed to general creditors after distribution to priority claimants?

   a. $432   **b.** $500   **c.** $375   **d.** $300   **e.** $320

6. How much of the proceeds (in thousands of dollars) do the second mortgage holders receive after distribution to general creditors and subordination adjustments are made?

   a. $400   **b.** $451   **c.** $51   **d.** $375   **e.** $500

7. How much of the proceeds (in thousands of dollars) do the holders of the subordinated debentures receive after distribution to general creditors and subordination adjustments are made?

   a. $51   **b.** $102   **c.** $142   **d.** $0   **e.** $25

8. How much of the proceeds (in thousands of dollars) from the liquidation do the common stockholders receive?

   a. $0   **b.** $51   **c.** $25   **d.** $102   **e.** $142

9. SMC's EBIT was $320,000 based on sales of $4,800,000, and its common stock market value was $800,000. What Z-score is obtained when using Altman's multiple discriminant function, $Z = 0.012X_1 + 0.014X_2 + 0.033X_3 + 0.006X_4 + 0.999X_5$.

   a. 1.22   **b.** 1.72   **c.** 1.48   **d.** 1.33   **e.** 1.66

10. Assume that you used Altman's multiple discriminant function in Self-Test Problem 9 and calculated a Z-score of 1.1. What does this score mean?

   a. The Z-score falls in the zone of ignorance, which means that we are uncertain about how the firm should be classified.

   b. Because the Z-score falls below 1.81, there is a likelihood that the firm will not go bankrupt: the lower the Z-score, the lower the probability of bankruptcy.

   c. Because the Z-score falls below 1.81, there is a likelihood that the firm will go bankrupt: the higher the Z-score, the lower the probability of bankruptcy.

   d. All the statements are false.

ANSWERS TO SELF-TEST QUESTIONS

1. Financial distress
2. Economic failure
3. Business failure
4. technically insolvent
5. Informal reorganization; workouts
6. extension
7. composition

8. Assignment
9. common pool problem; holdout problem
10. cramdown
11. Debtor in possession
12. fairness; feasibility
13. Multiple discriminant analysis

14. b. This is the definition for business failure, not economic failure.

15. a. This statement is correct.

16. b. Financial distress also begins when the firm's cash flow projections indicate that it will soon be unable to meet scheduled payments to creditors.

17. b. Just the reverse is true; however, large firms are not immune to bankruptcy.

18. a. This statement is correct.

19. c. Statement a is false; it describes a composition, not an extension. Statement b is false; a firm is considered technically insolvent if it cannot meet its current obligations as they fall due. Statement c is true. Thus, statements d and e are both incorrect.

20. e. Statement a is false; automatic stay is granted to all debtors in bankruptcy and it is a solution for the common pool problem. Statement b is true. Statement c describes an extension, not a cramdown. Statement d is true; thus, statement e is correct.

21. d. Statement a is false; the chapters have been reversed. Statement b is false; general, or unsecured, creditors have priority over preferred stockholders in the distribution of claims. Statement c is false; the higher the Z score, the lower the probability of bankruptcy. Statement d is true. Thus, statement e is false.

SOLUTIONS TO SELF-TEST PROBLEMS

1. a.

Claimant	Claim Amount (1)	Priority Distribution and General Creditor (2)	Subordinate Adjustment (3)	Percent of Claim (4)
Accounts payable	$ 3,240	$ 2,448	$ 2,448	75.56%
Notes payable	1,620	1,224	1,620	100.00
Accrued taxes	540	540	540	100.00
Accrued wages	540	540	540	100.00
1st mortgage bonds	2,700	2,700	2,700	100.00
2nd mortgage bonds	2,700	2,700	2,700	100.00
Subordinated debentures	3,240	2,448	2,052	63.33
Preferred stock	1,080	0	0	0.00
Common stock	7,560	0	0	0.00
Trustee	1,440	1,440	1,440	100.00
Total	$24,660	$14,040	$14,040	56.93%

Explanation of the columns:

(1) Values are taken from the balance sheet.

(2) Since the firm's total debt obligations (including trustee costs) equals $16,020 and only $14,040 is received from the sale of assets, the preferred and common stockholders are wiped out. These stockholders receive nothing.

    The $5,400 from the sale of fixed assets is immediately allocated to the mortgage bonds. The holders of the first mortgage bonds are paid off first, so they receive $2,700. The remaining $2,700 from the sale of fixed assets is allocated to the second mortgage bonds, so these bondholders are also paid off.

    By law, trustee expenses have first claim on the remaining available funds, wages have second priority, and taxes have third priority. Thus, these claims are paid in full.

    We now have $6,120 remaining and claims of $8,100, so the general creditors will receive 75.56 cents on the dollar:

$$\frac{\text{Funds available}}{\text{Unsatisfied debt}} = \frac{\$14,040 - \$5,400 - \$1,080 - \$1,440}{\$3,240 + \$1,620 + \$3,240} = 0.7556.$$

General creditors are now initially allocated 75.56 percent of their original claims.

(3) This column reflects a transfer of funds from the subordinated debentures to the notes payable to the bank. Since subordinated debentures are subordinate to bank debt, notes payable to the bank must be paid in full before the debentures receive anything. The notes are paid in full by transferring the difference between their book value and initial allocation ($1,620 − $1,224 = $396) from subordinated debentures to notes payable. This reduces the allocation to subordinated debentures and increases the allocation to notes payable by $396.

(4) Column 3 ÷ Column 1.

2. d. The pro forma balance sheet follows (in millions of dollars):

Current assets[a]	$318	Current liabilities	$ 84
Net fixed assets	306	Advance payments	156
Goodwill	30	Reserves	12
		Subordinated debentures[b]	180
		$2.40 preferred stock, $37.50 par value (2,400,000 shares)[c]	90
		Common stock, $1.50 par value (12,000,000 shares)	18
		Retained earnings	114
Total assets	$654	Total claims	$654

Notes:

[a]$336 million - $18 million = $318 million used to retire the $10.50 preferred stock.

[b]2,400,000 shares × $75 par value = $180 million.

[c]2,400,000 shares × $37.50 par value = $90 million.

3. b. See the balance sheet shown in response to Self-Test Problem 2.

4. c. The pro forma income statement (in millions of dollars) follows:

Net sales	$1,080.0
Operating expense	1,032.0
Net operating income	$ 48.0
Other income	6.0
EBIT	$ 54.0
Interest expense[a]	14.4
EBT	$ 39.6
Taxes (50%)	19.8
Net income	$ 19.8
Dividends on $2.40 preferred[b]	5.8
Income available to common stockholders	$ 14.0

Notes:

[a]0.08($180 million par value) = $14.4 million.

[b]$2.40(2,400,000 shares) = $5.76 million ≈ $5.8 million.

5. e. Distribution to priority claimants (in thousands of dollars):

Proceeds from the sale of assets	$2,400
Less:	
1. First mortgage (paid from sale of fixed assets)	1,200
2. Second mortgage (paid from sale of fixed assets)	400
3. Fees and expenses of bankruptcy	200
4. Wages due to workers	120
5. Taxes due	160
Funds available for distribution to general creditors	$ 320

Distribution to general creditors (in thousands of dollars):

General Creditor Claims	Amount of Claim	Pro Rata Distribution[a]	Distrib. After Subord. Adj.[b]	% of Orig. Claim Received
Unsatisfied 2nd mortgage	$ 400	$ 51	$ 51	56%[c]
Accounts payable	200	25	25	13
Notes payable	720	91	142	20
Debentures	800	102	102	13
Subord. debentures	400	51	0	0
Total	$2,520	$320	$320	

Notes:
[a]Pro rata distribution: $320/$2,520 = 0.127 = 12.7%.
[b]Subordinated debentures are subordinated to notes payable. Unsatisfied portion of notes payable is greater than subordinated debenture distribution so subordinated debentures receive $0.
[c]Includes $400 from sale of fixed assets received in priority distribution.

6. b. See the distribution worksheet shown in response to Self-Test Problem 5.

7. d. See the distribution worksheet shown in response to Self-Test Problem 5.

8. a. Because the amount of funds available for distribution to general creditors is $320,000 and the total claims of these general creditors is $2,520,000, the common stockholders will receive nothing.

9. c. First, compute the five variables required in the Altman model (in thousands of dollars):

X_1 = Net working capital/Total assets = ($1,600 - $1,200)/$4,000 = 0.10 = 10%.

X_2 = Retained earnings/Total assets = -$600/$4,000 = -0.15 = -15%.

X_3 = EBIT/Total assets = $320/$4,000 = 0.08 = 8%.

X_4 = Mkt. value of common stk./Book value of debt = $800/$4,400 = 0.18 = 18%.

X_5 = Sales/Total assets = $4,800/$4,000 = 1.20.

Next, determine the Z-score:

Z = 0.012(10) + 0.014(-15) + 0.033(8) + 0.006(18) + 0.999(1.2) = 1.48.

10. c. Finally, compare the Z-score of 1.48 with Altman's standard:

Bankrupt		Zone of Ignorance		Nonbankrupt
	1.81		2.99	

A Z-score of 1.48 indicates a likelihood of bankruptcy—the higher the Z-score, the lower the probability of bankruptcy.

CHAPTER 25

MERGERS, LBOs, DIVESTITURES, AND HOLDING COMPANIES

OVERVIEW

Most corporate growth occurs by internal expansion, which takes place when a firm's existing divisions grow through normal capital budgeting activities. However, the most dramatic examples of growth, and often the largest increases in stock prices, result from *mergers*, the first topic covered in this chapter. *Leveraged buyouts*, or *LBOs*, occur when a firm's stock is acquired by a small group of investors rather than by another operating company.

Since LBOs are similar to mergers in many respects, they are also covered in this chapter. Conditions change over time, and, as a result, firms often find it desirable to sell off, or *divest* major divisions to other firms that can better utilize the divested assets. *Divestitures* are also discussed in the chapter. Finally, we discuss the *holding company* form of organization, wherein one corporation owns the stock of one or more other companies.

OUTLINE

Several reasons have been proposed to justify corporate mergers.

- One major reason for mergers is *synergy*.
  - ☐ If Companies A and B merge to form Company C, and if C's value exceeds that of A and B taken separately, then synergy is said to exist.
  - ☐ Synergism can arise from four sources:
    - ▸ Operating economies
    - ▸ Financial economies
    - ▸ Differential management efficiency
    - ▸ Increased market power
  - ☐ Operating and financial economies, as well as increases in managerial efficiency, are socially desirable. However, mergers that reduce competition are both undesirable and illegal.

- *Tax considerations* can provide an incentive for mergers.

□ A highly profitable firm might merge with a firm which has accumulated tax losses so as to put these losses to immediate use.

□ A firm with excess cash and a shortage of internal investment opportunities might seek a merger rather than pay the cash out as dividends, which would result in the shareholders paying immediate taxes on the distribution.

■ Occasionally, a firm will merge with another because it thinks it has found a "bargain," that is, *assets can be purchased below their replacement cost.*

□ However, if the capital markets are efficient, stock prices represent the fair market value of the underlying assets.

□ The fact that a firm's market value is far below its replacement or book value does not, in itself, make the firm an attractive acquisition candidate.

■ *Diversification* is often cited by managers as a rationale for mergers.

□ Diversification may bring some real benefits to the firm, especially by reducing the variability of the firm's earnings stream, which benefits the firm's managers, creditors, and other stakeholders.

□ However, by simply holding portfolios of stocks, stockholders can generally diversify more easily and efficiently than can firms.

■ Financial economists like to think that business decisions are based only on economic considerations. However, some business decisions are based more on managers' personal motivations than on economic factors.

□ Some mergers occur because managers want to increase the size of their firms, and hence gain more power, prestige, and monetary compensation.

□ Other mergers occur because managers want to keep their jobs, so they merge with other firms to make the firm less attractive to hostile suitors. This type of merger is called a *defensive merger.*

■ Firms are generally valued in the markets as ongoing firms. However, some firms are worth more if they are broken up and then sold off in pieces. Thus, some acquisitions are motivated by the fact that a firm's *breakup value* is greater than its current market value.

There are four primary types of mergers.

■ A *horizontal merger* occurs when one firm combines with another in the same line of business.

■ A *vertical merger* exists when firms combine in a producer-supplier relationship.

■ A *congeneric merger* occurs when the merging companies are somewhat related, but not to the extent required for a horizontal or vertical merger.

■ A *conglomerate merger* occurs when completely unrelated enterprises combine.

The high level of merger activity in the 1980s was sparked by several factors.

■ The relatively depressed condition of the stock market that existed at the beginning of the decade.

■ The unprecedented level of inflation that existed during the 1970s and early 1980s, which increased the replacement value of firms' assets.

■ The Reagan administration's view that "bigness is not necessarily badness."

■ The general belief among the major natural resource companies that it is cheaper to "buy reserves on Wall Street" than to explore and find them in the field.

■ The development of an active junk bond market which helped finance many takeovers.

■ Attempts to ward off raiders by use of defensive mergers.

■ The decline of the dollar, which made U.S. companies relatively cheap to foreign acquirers.

■ Technological developments which led to "strategic mergers."

In most mergers, one company, the target company, is acquired by another, the acquiring company.

■ In a *friendly merger*, the management of the target company approves the merger and recommends it to their stockholders.
   □ Under these circumstances a suitable price is determined, and the acquiring company will simply buy the target company's shares through a friendly *tender offer*.
   □ Payment will be made either in cash, or in the stock or debt of the acquiring firm.

■ A *hostile merger* is one in which the target firm's management resists the takeover. The target firm's management either believes the price offered is too low, or it may simply want to remain independent.

   ☐ Under these circumstances, the acquiring company may make a hostile tender offer for the target company's shares. This is a direct appeal to the target firm's stockholders asking them to exchange their shares for cash, bonds, or stock in the acquiring firm.

   ☐ The number of hostile tender offers has increased greatly during the past several years.

Mergers are regulated by both the state and federal governments.

■ Federal laws place three major restrictions on acquiring firms.

   ☐ Acquirers must disclose their current holdings and future intentions within 10 days of amassing at least 5 percent of a company's stock, and they must disclose the source of the funds to be used in the acquisition.

   ☐ Target shareholders must be given at least 20 days to tender their shares.

   ☐ If the tender price is increased during the 20-day open period, all shareholders who tendered prior to the new offer must receive the higher price.

■ Many states now have merger laws which restrict the actions that can be taken by raiders.

   ☐ One such law restricts the ability of a raider to vote the shares they have acquired; that is, the merger must be approved by disinterested shareholders.

   ☐ Other state laws limit the use of *golden parachutes,* onerous debt-financing plans, and some types of *poison pills* to protect target stockholders from their own managers.

While merger analysis may appear simple, there are a number of complex issues involved.

■ The acquiring firm must perform a capital budgeting-type analysis. If it appears that the target firm can be purchased for less than its intrinsic value, then the offer should be made.

■ However, the target firm's shareholders must believe that a "fair" price is being offered. Otherwise, they will not tender their shares.

■ Several methodologies are used to value firms. Two commonly -used methods are *discounted cash flow analysis* and *earnings multiple analysis.* Regardless of the valuation methodology, two factors must be recognized.

   ☐ Any changes in operations occurring as a result of the proposed merger that will impact the value of the business must be considered in the analysis.

- ☐ The goal of merger valuation is to set the value of the target business's equity, or ownership position.

- ■ The *discounted cash flow approach* to valuing a business involves the application of classical capital budgeting procedures to an entire firm rather than to a single project.
  - ☐ To apply this method, two key items are needed: (1) a set of pro forma statements that develop the incremental cash flows expected to result from the merger, and (2) a discount rate, or cost of capital, to apply these projected cash flows.
  - ☐ In a pure *financial merger*, in which no synergies are expected, the incremental postmerger cash flows are simply the expected cash flows of the target firm if it were to continue to operate independently.
  - ☐ In an *operating merger*, in which the two firms' operations are to be integrated, or if the acquiring firm plans to change the target firm's operations to get better results, then forecasting future cash flows is even more complex.

- ■ Merger cash flows, unlike capital budgeting cash flows, *must include* interest expense.
  - ☐ The target firm usually has embedded debt that will be assumed by the acquiring company.
  - ☐ The acquisition is often financed partially by debt.
  - ☐ If the subsidiary is expected to grow in the future, new debt will have to be issued over time to support its expansion. Thus, debt costs must be explicitly included in the cash flow analysis.

- ■ With debt costs included in the cash flow analysis, the resulting net cash flows accrue solely to the equity holders of the acquiring firm; thus, we are using the *equity residual method*. Thus, the *appropriate discount rate is a cost of equity* rather than an overall cost of capital. The cost of equity used must reflect the underlying riskiness of the target company's assets and the riskiness of the financing mix used for the acquisition.

- ■ Hamada's equation, which was developed in Chapter 14, can be used to adjust the beta of the target firm to reflect the tax and leverage consequences of the merger. The Security Market Line can then be used to determine the target firm's post-merger cost of equity.

- ■ The present value of the incremental merger cash flows is the maximum price that the acquiring firm should pay for the target company.

- ■ Another method of valuing a target company is *market multiple analysis*, which applies a market-determined multiple to some measure of earnings such as net income or earnings per share. The basic premise is that the value of any business depends on the earnings that the business produces.

☐ Note that earnings (or cash flow) measures other than net income can be used in the market multiple approach. Another commonly used measure is *earnings before interest, taxes, depreciation, and amortization (EBITDA)*.

■ Although the DCF method has strong theoretical support, one has to be very concerned over the validity of the estimated cash flows and the discount rate applied to those flows.

■ The market multiple method is more ad hoc, but its proponents argue that earnings estimates for a single year, or for a few years, are much more likely to be accurate than the many years of cash flows that must be estimated in the DCF approach and it avoids the problem of having to estimate a discount rate.

☐ The market multiple method has problems of its own. One concern is the comparability between the firm being analyzed and the firm (or firms) that set the market multiple. Another concern is how well does one year of earnings capture the value of a firm that will be operated for many years into the future, and whose earnings could soar due to merger-related synergies.

■ The terms of a merger include three important elements:

☐ *The price to be paid* determines whether the shareholders of the acquiring company or the shareholders of the target company reap the greater benefits from the merger.

▸ If there were no synergistic benefits, the maximum bid would be equal to the current value of the target company. The greater the synergistic gains, the greater the gap between the target's current price and the maximum the acquiring company could pay.

▸ The greater the synergistic gains, the more likely a merger is to be consummated.

▸ The issue of how to divide the synergistic benefits is critically important in any merger analysis.

▸ Where in the range the actual price will be set depends on the negotiating skills of the two management teams and on the bargaining positions of the two parties as determined by fundamental economic conditions.

☐ *Postmerger control of the firm*, which is of great interest to managers due to their concern for their jobs.

☐ *The structure of the offer* is how to pay for the merger--in cash, in securities of the acquiring firm, or in some combination of the two.

Once the value of the target is estimated, the acquiring firm must decide on the structure of the takeover bid.

■ The structure of the bid is extremely important since it affects:
   ☐ The capital structure of the postmerger firm.
   ☐ The tax treatment of both the acquiring firm and the target firm's stockholders.
   ☐ The ability of the target firm's stockholders to reap the rewards of future merger-related gains.
   ☐ The types of federal and state regulations that apply to the merger.

■ Target shareholders do not have to pay taxes on the their takeover proceeds if their shares are paid for by stock in the acquiring firm (at least 50 percent of the payment must be in stock). If the offer is predominantly cash or debt securities, taxes will have to be paid.

■ If the acquiring firm elects to write up the target company's assets for tax purposes, the target company must pay a capital gains tax on the write-up. However, it can then depreciate the assets from their new, higher value.

Investment bankers play an important role in merger activities.

■ The major investment banking firms have merger and acquisition (M&A) departments which help to match merger partners.

■ These same investment bankers can also help a firm fend off an unwanted suitor.
   ☐ Sometimes a *white knight* will be lined up to acquire a firm that is trying to avoid being taken over by an unfriendly suitor.
   ☐ In other situations, a *white squire* may be sought to buy shares in the target firm, hold them, and then vote in favor of current management.
   ☐ Investment bankers can also recommend *poison pills*, which are actions that effectively destroy the value of the firm in the event of merger, and hence drive off unwanted suitors.

■ Investment bankers are often used to help establish the offering price. Generally, both the acquiring and target firms will use investment bankers to help establish a price and also to participate in the negotiations.

■ Investment banking firms also engage in *risk arbitrage*, which means speculating in the stocks of companies that are likely takeover targets.

■ They help finance mergers too.

The latest merger wave has sparked a great deal of research to answer this question: Do corporate acquisitions really create value, and if so, how is this value shared between the parties involved?

■ Researchers attempt to answer questions such as this by examining the relative stock price performance of merging firms around the merger announcement date.

■ On average, the stock prices of target companies have increased by 20-30 percent upon the merger announcement.

■ However, the stock prices of acquiring firms have tended to remain unchanged.

■ Thus, the evidence strongly indicates that acquisitions do create value, but that shareholders of target firms reap virtually all of the benefits.

Mergers are one way for two companies to completely join assets and management, but many firms are striking cooperative deals which fall short of merging. Such cooperative amalgamations are called corporate alliances, and they occur in many forms.

■ *Joint ventures* are an important type of alliance.
  □ Joint ventures are controlled by a combined management team formed by the parent companies.
  □ Joint ventures are operated independently from the parent companies.

■ Other types of alliances include cross-licensing, consortia, joint bidding, and franchising.

In a leveraged buyout (LBO), a small group of equity investors, usually including current top management, acquires a firm in a transaction financed largely by debt.

■ The debt is serviced by the cash flows generated by the acquired company's operations and by the sale of some of its assets.
  □ Often, some of the assets must be sold to service the debt.
  □ The heavy debt burden forces management to operate very efficiently.

■ Usually, after several years of being privately held, the firm has been streamlined and made more efficient. Then, the owners recover their equity investment by going public again.

Although corporations do more buying than selling of productive assets, selling, or divestiture, does take place.

■ There are three primary types of *divestitures*:
  □ A division may be *sold to another firm*. This is the most common form of divestiture.
  □ In a *spin-off*, a division may be set up as a corporation, with the parent firm's stockholders then being given stock in the new corporation on a pro rata basis.
  □ In a *liquidation*, the assets of a division are sold off piecemeal, rather than as a single entity.

■ There are a variety of reasons cited for divestitures:
  □ It appears that, on occasion, investors do not properly value some assets when they are part of a large conglomerate. Thus, divestiture can occur to enhance firm value.
  □ Often, firms will need to raise large amounts of cash to finance expansion in their core business, or to reduce an onerous debt burden, and divestitures can raise the needed cash.
  □ Sometimes, assets are just no longer profitable and must be liquidated.
  □ Firms that are struggling against bankruptcy often have to divest profitable divisions just to stay alive.
  □ The government sometimes mandates divestiture on antitrust grounds.

A holding company is a firm that holds large blocks of stock in other companies and exercises control over those firms. The holding company is often called the parent company and the controlled companies are known as subsidiaries or operating companies. Holding companies may be used to obtain some of the same benefits that could be achieved through mergers and acquisitions. However, the holding company device has some unique disadvantages as well as unique advantages.

■ Advantages of holding companies include the following:
  □ *Control with fractional ownership.* Effective control of a company may be achieved with far less than 50 percent ownership of the common stock.
  □ *Isolation of risks.* Claims on one unit of the holding company may not be liabilities to the other units. Each element of the holding company organization is a separate legal entity.

■ Disadvantages of holding companies include the following:
  □ *Partial multiple taxation.* Consolidated tax returns may be filed only if the holding company owns 80 percent or more of the voting stock of the subsidiary. Otherwise, intercorporate dividends will be taxed. Note, though, that firms that own over 20 percent but less than 80 percent of another corporation can deduct 80 percent of the dividends received from taxable

income, while firms that own less than 20 percent may deduct only 70 percent of the dividends received.

☐ *Ease of enforced dissolution.* It is much easier for the Justice Department to require disposal of a stock position than to demand the separation of an integrated business operation.

■ The holding company device can be used to control large amounts of assets with a relatively small equity investment. The substantial leverage involved in such an operation may result in high returns, but it also involves a high degree of risk.

SELF-TEST QUESTIONS

Definitional

1. If the value of two firms, in combination, is greater than the sum of their separate values, then _____ is said to exist.

2. Synergistic effects may result from either _____ economies or _____ economies.

3. The Justice Department may be concerned about the _____ implications of a proposed merger.

4. A(n) _____ merger takes place when two firms in the same line of business combine, while the combination of a steel company with a coal company would be an example of a(n) _____ merger.

5. The merger of two completely unrelated enterprises is referred to as a(n) _____ merger.

6. A firm which seeks to take over another company is commonly called the _____ company, while the firm it seeks to acquire is referred to as the _____ company.

7. A merger may be described as "friendly" or "hostile," depending upon the attitude of the _____ of the target company.

8. A(n) _____ _____ is a request by the acquiring company to the target company's _____ to submit their shares in exchange for a specified price or specified number of shares of stock.

9. A(n) _____ merger combines the business activity of the two firms with the expectation of _____ benefits.

10. _____ mergers do not combine the business operations of two firms, and no operating economies are expected.

11. Merger analysis is very similar to _____ _____ analysis.

12. In valuing the target firm, the analysis focuses on the cash flows that accrue to the stockholders of the _____ firm.

13. A(n) _____ _____ occurs when two firms combine parts of their companies to accomplish specific, limited objectives.

14. A(n) pro rata distribution of stock in a new firm which was formerly a subsidiary is called a _____.

15. Unless a holding company owns at least _____ percent of the shares of a subsidiary company, it may be subject to multiple _____ on a portion of any intercorporate _____.

Conceptual

16. In a financial merger, the expected post-merger cash flows are generally the sum of the cash flows of the separate companies.

    a. True   b. False

17. Interest expense must be explicitly included in the incremental cash flow analysis for a merger.

    a. True   b. False

18. The holding company device can be used to take advantage of the principle of financial leverage. Thus, the holding company can control a great deal of assets with a limited amount of top-tier equity.

    a. True   b. False

SELF-TEST PROBLEMS

(The following data apply to the next four problems.)

TransCorp, a large conglomerate, is evaluating the possible acquisition of the Chip Company, a transistor manufacturer. TransCorp's analyst projects the following postmerger incremental cash flows (in millions of dollars):

	1997	1998	1999	2000
Net sales	$200	$230	$250	$270
Cost of goods sold	130	140	145	150
Selling/administrative expense	20	25	30	32
EBIT	$ 50	$ 65	$ 75	$ 88
Interest	10	12	13	14
EBT	$ 40	$ 53	$ 62	$ 74
Taxes (40%)	16	21	25	30
Net income	$ 24	$ 32	$ 37	$ 44
Retained earnings	12	13	14	15
Cash available to stockholders	$ 12	$ 19	$ 23	$ 29
Terminal value				400
Net CF	$ 12	$ 19	$ 23	$429

The acquisition, if made, would occur on January 4, 1997. All cash flows above are assumed to occur at end-of-year. Chip currently has a market value capital structure of 10 percent debt, but TransCorp would increase the debt to 50 percent if the acquisition were made. Chip, if independent, pays taxes at 30 percent, but its income would be taxed at 40 percent if consolidated. Chip's current market-determined beta is 1.80.

The cash flows above include the additional interest payments due to increased leverage and asset expansion, and the full taxes paid by TransCorp on the Chip income stream. Depreciation-generated funds would be used to replace worn-out equipment, so they would not be available to TransCorp's shareholders. Retained earnings would be used, in addition to new debt, to finance required asset expansion. Thus, the net cash flows are the flows that would accrue to TransCorp's stockholders. The risk-free rate is 10 percent and the market risk premium is 5 percent.

1. What is the appropriate discount rate for valuing the acquisition?

   a. 10.00%   **b.** 15.00%   **c.** 19.00%   **d.** 21.75%   **e.** 23.35%

2. What is the value of the Chip Company to TransCorp?

   a. $197.73 million   d. $322.85 million
   b. $206.42 million   e. $429.00 million
   c. $219.78 million

3. Chip has 5 million shares outstanding. Chip's current market price is $32.50. What is the maximum price per share that TransCorp should offer?

   a. $32.50   b. $37.50   c. $41.37   d. $43.96   e. $46.93

4. TransCorp should offer Chip's stockholders $32.625 per share.

   a. True   b. False

ANSWERS TO SELF-TEST QUESTIONS

1. synergy
2. operating; financial
3. antitrust
4. horizontal; vertical
5. conglomerate
6. acquiring; target
7. management
8. tender offer; stockholders
9. operating; synergistic
10. Financial
11. capital budgeting
12. acquiring
13. joint venture
14. spinoff
15. 80; taxation; dividends

16. a. In a financial merger, no synergistic effects are anticipated.

17. a. The target firm generally has embedded debt that is being assumed by the acquiring firm. Since these costs are not marginal, they must be specifically included in the analysis.

18. a. This statement is true, but the leveraging which occurs in a holding company organization significantly increases the riskiness of the firm.

SOLUTIONS TO SELF-TEST PROBLEMS

1. e. $b_U = \dfrac{b_L}{1 + (1 - T)(D/E)} = \dfrac{1.80}{1 + (1 - 0.30)(0.1/0.9)} = \dfrac{1.80}{1.08} = 1.67.$

$b_L = b_U[1 + (1 - T)(D/E)] = 1.67[1 + (1 - 0.40)(0.5/0.5)]$

$\qquad = 1.67(1.6) = 2.67.$

$k_s = 10\% + (5\%)\,2.67 = 23.35\%.$

2. c. $V = \dfrac{\$12 \text{ million}}{(1.2335)^1} + \dfrac{\$19 \text{ million}}{(1.2335)^2} + \dfrac{\$23 \text{ million}}{(1.2335)^3} + \dfrac{\$429 \text{ million}}{(1.2335)^4} = \$219.78 \text{ million}.$

3. d. \$219.78 million/5 million = \$43.96.

4. b. It does not make sense to offer Chip's shareholders just a little above the current market price. Not enough shares would be tendered to gain control, the expenses would be for nought, and other firms could be induced to make competing bids.

CHAPTER 26

MULTINATIONAL
FINANCIAL MANAGEMENT

OVERVIEW

As the world economy becomes more integrated, the role of multinational firms is increasing. Although the same basic principles of financial management apply to multinational corporations as well as to domestic ones, the financial managers of multinational firms face a much more complex task. The primary problem, from a financial standpoint, is the fact that the cash flows must cross national boundaries.

These flows may be constrained in various ways, and, equally important, their values in dollars may rise or fall depending on exchange rate fluctuations. This means that the multinational financial manager must be constantly aware of the many complex interactions among national economies and their effects on international operations.

OUTLINE

A multinational, or global, corporation is one that operates in an integrated fashion in two or more countries. The growth of multinationals has greatly increased the degree of worldwide economic and political interdependence.

■ Companies, both U.S. and foreign, go "international" for six primary reasons:
  □ After a company has saturated its home market, growth opportunities are often better in foreign markets.
  □ Many of the present multinational firms began their international operations because raw materials were located abroad.
  □ Because no single nation holds a commanding advantage in all technologies, companies are scouring the globe for leading scientific and design ideas.
  □ Still other firms have moved their manufacturing facilities overseas to take advantage of cheaper production costs in low-cost countries.
  □ Firms can avoid political and regulatory hurdles by moving production to other countries.
  □ Finally, firms go international so that they can diversify, and consequently, cushion the impact of adverse economic trends in any single country.

■ The past decade has seen an increasing amount of investment in the U.S. by foreign corporations. This "reverse" investment has been growing at a higher rate than U.S. investment abroad. These developments suggest an increasing degree of mutual influence and interdependence among business enterprises and nations.

In theory, financial concepts and procedures are valid for both domestic and multinational operations. However, there are several factors which distinguish financial management as practiced by firms operating entirely within a single country from management by firms that operate in several different countries.

■ Cash flows will be denominated in different currencies, making exchange rate analysis necessary for all types of financial decisions.

■ Economic and legal differences among countries can cause significant problems when the corporation tries to coordinate and control worldwide operations of its subsidiaries.

■ The ability to communicate is critical in all business transactions. U.S. citizens are often at a disadvantage because we are generally fluent only in English.

■ Values and the role of business in society reflect the cultural differences that may vary dramatically from one country to the next.

■ Financial models based on the traditional assumption of a competitive marketplace must often be modified to include political (governmental) and other noneconomic facets of the decision.

■ *Political risk*, which is seldom negotiable and may be as extreme as *expropriation*, must be explicitly addressed in financial analysis.

An exchange rate specifies the number of units of a given currency that can be purchased for one unit of another currency.

■ An exchange rate listed as the number of U.S. dollars required to purchase one unit of foreign currency is called a *direct quotation*. The number of units of foreign currency that can be purchased for one U.S. dollar is called an *indirect quotation*. Normal practice in the U.S. is to use indirect quotations for all currencies *other than British pounds, for which direct quotations are given.*

- Converting from one foreign currency to another foreign currency may require the use of *cross rates*. For example, if the direct quotation between pounds and dollars is $1.7875 and the indirect quotation between francs and dollars is FF5.6344, the cross rate between pounds and francs can be calculated as follows:

$$\text{Cross rate} = \frac{\text{Dollars}}{\text{Pound}} \times \frac{\text{Francs}}{\text{Dollar}} = \frac{\text{Francs}}{\text{Pound}}$$
$$= 1.7875 \text{ dollars per pound} \times 5.6344 \text{ francs per dollar}$$
$$= 10.0715 \text{ francs per pound.}$$

The International Monetary Fund (IMF) was the center of a fixed exchange rate system that operated for 25 years after World War II.

- Under this system, the U.S. dollar, which was linked to gold by a fixed price of $35 per ounce, was the base currency, and the relative values of all other currencies to the dollar were controlled within narrow limits, but then adjusted periodically.
    - Currency fluctuations depend on supply and demand, capital movements, and the activities of international speculators. However, these fluctuations were kept within limits by the actions of the various central banks, which bought or sold currency to maintain specific prices.
    - If a country *devalued* its currency, then fewer units of another currency would be required to buy one unit of the devalued currency. Its "price" would be reduced, making the country's goods cheaper and thus stimulating exports and discouraging imports. A country could devalue its currency only with the approval of the IMF.

- In 1971, the *fixed exchange rate system* was replaced by a system under which the U.S. dollar was permitted to "float."
    - A *floating exchange rate system* is one under which currency prices are allowed to reach their own levels without much governmental intervention.
    - The present managed floating system permits currency rates to move without any specific limits, but central banks do buy and sell currencies to smooth out exchange rate fluctuations.

- The inherent volatility of exchange rates under a floating system increases the uncertainty of the cash flows for a multinational corporation. This uncertainty is known as *exchange rate risk*, and it is a major factor differentiating the multinational corporation from a purely domestic one.

- Not all currencies are *convertible*. A currency is convertible when the issuing nation allows it to be traded in the currency markets and is willing to redeem the currency at market rates.

Importers, exporters, and tourists, as well as governments, buy and sell currencies in the foreign exchange market, which consists of a network of brokers and banks based in New York, London, Tokyo, and other financial centers.

■ The rate paid for delivery of currency no more than one day after the day of trade is called the *spot rate*.

■ When currency is bought or sold and is to be delivered at some agreed-upon future date, usually 30, 90, or 180 days into the future, a *forward exchange rate* is used.
   □ If one can obtain more of the foreign currency for a dollar in the forward market than in the spot market, then the forward currency is less valuable than the spot currency, and the forward currency is said to be selling at a *discount*.
   □ If a dollar will buy fewer units of a currency in the forward market than in the spot market, then the forward currency is worth more dollars than the spot currency, and the forward currency is said to be selling at a *premium*.

■ Individuals and firms buy or sell forward currencies to *hedge* against unwanted changes in exchange rates by using *futures or forward contracts*.

Relative inflation rates have many implications for multinational financial decisions. Equally important, they have a dominant influence on relative interest rates as well as exchange rates.

■ A foreign currency on average will depreciate at a percentage rate approximately equal to the amount by which its country's inflation rate exceeds the U.S. inflation rate. Conversely, foreign currencies in countries with less inflation than the U.S. will, on average, appreciate relative to the U.S. dollar.

■ Countries experiencing higher rates of inflation tend to have higher interest rates.

■ Gains from borrowing in countries with low interest rates can be offset by losses from currency appreciation in those countries.

There exists a well developed system of international capital markets.

■ Americans can invest in world markets by investing in the stock of U.S. multinational corporations or by buying the bonds and stocks of large corporations (or governments) headquartered outside the United States.
   □ Investment by U.S. firms in foreign operating assets is called *direct investment*.

- ☐ Investment in foreign stocks and bonds is called *portfolio investment.*

- ■ The *Eurodollar market* is essentially a short-term market for handling dollar-denominated loans and deposits made outside the United States.
  - ☐ A *Eurodollar* is a U.S. dollar placed on deposit in a foreign (normally European) bank, including foreign branches of U.S. banks.
  - ☐ The major difference between a dollar on deposit in Chicago and a dollar on deposit in London is the geographic location. The deposits do not involve different currencies, so exchange rate considerations do not apply. However, Eurodollars are outside the direct control of the U.S. monetary authorities, so U.S. banking regulations, such as fractional reserves and FDIC insurance premiums, do not apply.
  - ☐ If interest rates in the United States are above Eurodollar rates, these funds will be sent back and invested in the United States, while if Eurodollar deposit rates are significantly above U.S. interest rates, more dollars will be sent out of the United States.
  - ☐ Interest rates on Eurodollar deposits (and loans) are tied to a standard rate known as the *London Interbank Offer Rate (LIBOR)*, the rate of interest offered by the largest and strongest London banks on dollar deposits of significant size.

- ■ Two international bond markets have developed which trade in long-term funds.
  - ☐ *Foreign bonds* are bonds sold by a foreign borrower but denominated in the currency of the country in which the issue is sold.
  - ☐ *Eurobonds* are bonds sold in a country other than the one in whose currency the issue is denominated.

- ■ More and more, European financial transactions are being made in *European currency units*, or *ECUs*, units of account that are made up of the currencies of the twelve countries that belong to the European monetary system.

- ■ New issues of stock are sold in international markets for a variety of reasons.
  - ☐ Firms are able to tap a much larger source of capital than their home countries.
  - ☐ Firms want to create an equity market presence to accompany operations in foreign countries.
  - ☐ Large multinational companies also occasionally issue new stock simultaneously in multiple countries.

- ■ In addition to direct listing, U.S. investors can invest in foreign companies through *American depository receipts (ADRs)*, which are certificates representing ownership of foreign stock held in trust.

There are several important differences in capital budgeting analysis of foreign versus domestic operations.

■ Cash flow analysis is much more complex for overseas investments.
  □ Usually a firm will organize a separate subsidiary in each foreign country in which it operates.
  □ Any dividends or royalties repatriated by the subsidiary must be converted to the currency of the parent company and thus are subject to exchange rate fluctuations.
  □ Dividends and royalties received are normally taxed by both foreign and domestic governments.
  □ Some governments place restrictions, or exchange controls, on the amount of cash that may be remitted to the parent company in order to encourage reinvestment of earnings in the foreign country.
  □ The only relevant cash flows for analysis of an international investment are the financial cash flows that the subsidiary can legally send back to the parent.

■ The cost of capital may be higher for foreign investments because they may be riskier than domestic investments.
  □ *Exchange risk* refers to the fact that exchange rates may fluctuate, increasing the uncertainty about cash flows to the parent company.
  □ *Political risk* refers to the possibility of *expropriation* and to restrictions on cash flows to the parent company.

Significant differences have been observed in the capital structures of U.S. corporations in comparison to their German and Japanese counterparts. An analysis of both bankruptcy and equity reporting costs leads to the conclusion that U.S. firms use more equity and less debt than firms in Japan and Germany.

The objectives of working capital management in the multinational corporation are similar to those in the domestic firm but the task is more complex.

■ The objectives of cash management in the multinational corporation are to speed up collections and to slow disbursements, to shift cash rapidly from those parts of the business that do not need it to those parts that do, and to obtain the highest possible risk-adjusted rate of return on temporary cash balances. The same general procedures are used by multinational firms as those used by domestic firms, but because of longer distances and more serious mail delays, lockbox systems and electronic funds transfers are especially important.

■ Granting credit is more risky in an international context because, in addition to the normal risks of default, the multinational corporation must also worry about exchange rate changes between the time a sale is made and the time a receivable is collected. Credit policy is generally more important for a multinational firm than for a domestic firm.

  □ Much of the U.S.'s trade is with poorer, less-developed countries; thus, granting credit is generally a necessary condition for doing business.

  □ Nations whose economic health depends upon exports often help their manufacturing firms compete internationally by granting credit to foreign countries.

■ The physical location of inventories is a complex consideration for the multinational firm. The multinational firm must weigh a strategy of keeping inventory concentrated in a few areas from which they can be shipped, and thus minimize the total amount of inventory needed to operate the global business, with the possibility of delays in getting goods from central locations to user locations around the world. Exchange rates, import/export quotas, the threat of expropriation, and taxes all influence inventory policy.

SELF-TEST QUESTIONS

Definitional

1. The _____ _____ determines the number of units of one currency that can be exchanged for another.

2. International financial transactions were carried out under a(n) _____ _____ _____ system from the end of World War II until 1971.

3. The organization which controlled the fixed exchange rate system was the _____ _____ _____, which served as a world central bank.

4. Under the fixed rate system, the relative values of various currencies were based on the _____ _____ _____, and were controlled within narrow limits, but then adjusted periodically.

5. Countries with export surpluses and a strong currency might have to _____ their currencies upward.

6. In 1971, the _____ rate system was replaced by one that permitted the U.S. dollar to _____ against other currencies.

7. Evaluation of foreign investments involves the analysis of dividend and royalty cash flows that are _____ to the parent company.

8. Some foreign governments restrict, or block, the amount of income that can be repatriated to encourage _____ in the foreign country.

9. _____ risk refers to the possibility of restrictions on cash flows or the outright _____ of property by a foreign government.

10. A dollar deposited in a non-U.S. bank is often called a(n) _____.

11. Firms can hedge against exchange rate movements by buying or selling _____ or _____ contracts.

12. Investment by U.S. firms in foreign operations is called _____ investment, while the purchase of foreign bonds and stock by U.S. citizens or firms is called _____ investment.

13. _____ bonds are bonds sold by a foreign borrower but denominated in the currency of the country in which the issue is sold.

Conceptual

14. Financial analysis is not able to take into account political risk.

    a. True   b. False

15. When a central bank of a country buys and sells its currency to smooth out fluctuations in the exchange rate, the system is referred to as a managed floating system.

    a. True   b. False

16. A foreign currency will, on average, appreciate at a percentage rate approximately equal to the amount by which its inflation rate exceeds the inflation rate in the United States.

    a. True   **b.** False

17. The cost of capital is generally lower for a foreign project than for an equivalent domestic project since the possibility of exchange gains exists.

    a. True   **b.** False

18. Which of the following statements concerning multinational cash flow analysis is *not* correct?

    a. The relevant cash flows are the dividends and royalties repatriated to the parent company.
    b. The cash flows must be converted to the currency of the parent company and, thus, are subject to future exchange rate changes.
    c. Dividends and royalties received are normally taxed only by the government of the country in which the subsidiary is located.
    d. Foreign governments may restrict the amount of the cash flows that may be repatriated.

SELF-TEST PROBLEMS

1. The "spot rate" for Greek drachmas is 0.0313 U.S. dollars per drachma. What would the exchange rate be expressed in drachmas per dollar?

    a. 0.0313 drachmas per dollar   **d.** 319.4890 drachmas per dollar
    b. 3.1300 drachmas per dollar   **e.** 400.0000 drachmas per dollar
    c. 31.9489 drachmas per dollar

2. The U.S. dollar can be exchanged for 942.1432 Italian lire today. The Italian currency is expected to appreciate by 10 percent tomorrow. What is the expected exchange rate tomorrow expressed in lire per dollar?

    a. 836.1935 lire per dollar   **d.** 958.2334 lire per dollar
    b. 841.3167 lire per dollar   **e.** 965.9813 lire per dollar
    c. 847.9289 lire per dollar

3. You are considering the purchase of a block of stock in Galic Steel, a French steel producer. Galic just paid a dividend of 10 francs per share; that is, $D_0 = 10$ francs. You expect the dividend to grow indefinitely at a rate of 15 percent per year, but because of a higher expected rate of inflation in France than in the United States, you expect the franc to depreciate against the dollar at a rate of 5 percent per year. The exchange rate is currently 5 francs per U.S. dollar, but this ratio will change as the franc depreciates. For a stock with this degree of risk, including exchange rate risk, you feel that a 20 percent rate of return is required. What is the most, in dollars, that you should pay for the stock?

   a. $20.90   **b.** $31.70   **c.** $46.00   **d.** $53.60   **e.** $60.34

4. Refer to Self-Test Problem 3. Now assume that the franc is expected to appreciate against the dollar at the rate of 1 percent per year. All other facts are unchanged. Under these conditions, what should you be willing to pay for the stock?

   a. $20.90   **b.** $31.70   **c.** $46.00   **d.** $53.60   **e.** $60.34

ANSWERS TO SELF-TEST QUESTIONS

1. exchange rate
2. fixed exchange rate
3. International Monetary Fund (IMF)
4. U.S. dollar
5. revalue
6. fixed; "float"
7. repatriated

8. reinvestment
9. Political; expropriation
10. Eurodollar
11. forward; futures
12. direct; portfolio
13. Foreign

14. b. Political risk must be explicitly addressed by international financial managers.

15. a. This statement is correct.

16. b. The foreign currency will depreciate if its inflation rate is higher than that of the United States.

17. b. The cost of capital is generally higher because of exchange risk and political risk.

18. c. Dividends and royalties received will generally also be taxed by the U.S. government, but the total taxes paid to both governments will not exceed that which would be paid had the earnings occurred in the United States.

SOLUTIONS TO SELF-TEST PROBLEMS

1. c. The exchange rate for drachmas per dollar would be the reciprocal of the exchange rate of dollars per drachma: 1/(0.0313 dollars per drachma) = 31.9489 drachmas per dollar.

2. c. 942.1432(0.90)/$1.00 = 847.9289 lire per dollar.

3. a. First, the valuation equation must be modified to convert the expected dividend stream to dollars:

$$D_t = D_0(1 + g)(ER),$$

where ER = exchange ratio. ER = 1/5 today, but if francs depreciate at a rate of 5 percent, it will take more francs to buy a dollar in the future. The value of ER at some future time (t) will be

$$ER_t = \frac{Dollars}{Francs} = \frac{1}{5(1.05)^t}.$$

Therefore, D_t in dollars may be calculated as follows:

$$
\begin{aligned}
D_t \text{ (in dollars)} &= (10 \text{ francs})(1 + g)^t(ER_t) \\
&= \frac{\$10(1.15)^t}{5(1.05)^t} \\
&= \frac{\$2(1.15)^t}{(1.05)^t} \\
&= \$2\left(\frac{1.15}{1.05}\right)^t \\
&= \$2(1.0952)^t.
\end{aligned}
$$

Thus, if the dividend in francs is expected to grow at a rate of 15 percent per year, but the franc is expected to depreciate at a rate of 5 percent per year against the dollar, then the growth rate, in dollars, of dividends received will be 9.52 percent. We can now calculate the value of the stock in dollars:

$$\hat{P}_0 = \frac{D_1}{k_s - g} = \frac{\$2(1.0952)}{0.20 - 0.0952} = \frac{\$2.1904}{0.1048} = \$20.90.$$

4. e. Solve the problem as above: $ER_t = 1(1.01)^t/5$.

$$D_t \text{ (in dollars)} = (10 \text{ francs})(1 + g)^t \left(\frac{(1.01)^t}{5} \right)$$
$$= (\$10/5)(1.15)^t(1.01)^t$$
$$= \$2(1.1615)^t.$$

Thus, the franc dividend is expected to increase at a rate of 15 percent per year, and the value of these francs is expected to rise at the rate of 1 percent per year, so the expected annual growth rate of the dollar dividend is 16.15 percent. We can now calculate the stock price:

$$\hat{P}_0 = \frac{D_1}{k_s - g} = \frac{\$2(1.1615)}{0.20 - 0.1615} = \frac{\$2.3230}{0.0385} = \$60.34.$$

CHAPTER 27

PENSION PLAN
MANAGEMENT

OVERVIEW

Pension plans are an important component of the U.S. financial system for five reasons: (1) Pension funds, which have an aggregate market value of about $5 trillion, are important participants in the financial markets. (2) Pension plans provide employees with the majority of their retirement income. (3) Contributions to pension plans are an important component of most compensation plans, and thus they affect both labor productivity and economic stability.

(4) The rate of return on private pension plan assets can have a major effect on corporate earnings, employees' retirement incomes, or both. Similarly, the return on public pension plan assets can affect both taxes and employees' retirement incomes. (5) Because pension plans are large and concentrated owners of corporate stocks, their managers play an important role in corporate governance.

OUTLINE

Most companies, and practically all government units, have some type of employee pension plan.

■ The *chief financial officer (CFO)* typically administers the plan. He or she must decide on the general nature of the plan, determine the required annual payments into the plan, and manage the plan's assets.

■ The company does not have total control over these decisions. Employees and the federal government have a major say about the plan's structure and rules on certain aspects of the plan.

■ Under a typical plan, the company (or governmental unit) agrees to provide some type of retirement payments for employees. These promised payments constitute a liability, and the employer is required to establish a *pension fund* and place money in it each year, with the idea being to have sufficient assets to meet the pension payments as they come due.

■ Pension plan assets represent a very large pool of value for many firms.

■ Because pension fund administration requires so much specialized technical knowledge, companies typically hire specialists as consultants to help design, modify, and administer their plans.

The following concepts are used frequently in pension plan management.

■ A *defined contribution plan* is one in which a company agrees to make specific payments into a retirement fund and then retirees receive benefits from the plan that depend on the plan's investment success.
  □ The firm is obligated, in bad times as well as in good times, to make specified contributions on behalf of participating employees.
  □ Such plans are *portable* in that assets belong to the employee whenever he or she terminates employment.
  □ Because the sponsoring firm does not guarantee any specific dollar payments to participants upon retirement, participants in a defined contribution plan bear all of the investment risk associated with poor portfolio performance. However, participants can often choose among several investment alternatives so each individual can match his or her own risk preference.

■ Under a *defined benefit plan*, the employer agrees to give retirees a specifically defined benefit, such as $500 per month or 50 percent of the average salary over the five years preceding retirement.
  □ The sponsoring firm, not the participants, bears the risk of poor portfolio performance. Thus, the firm has a debt obligation to its retirees that must be met regardless of how well or poorly the pension plan assets are managed.
  □ Most defined benefit participants still bear purchasing power risk because inflation could eat away at the purchasing power of a fixed pension payment.

■ A *profit sharing plan* calls for the employer to make payments into the retirement fund, but with the payments varying with the level of corporate profits. These plans are operated like defined contribution plans in the sense that each employee's funds are maintained in a separate account, and benefits depend on the plan's performance. These plans can be operated separately or in conjunction with defined benefit or defined contribution plans.

■ If employees have a right to receive pension benefits even if they leave the company prior to retirement, then their pension rights are said to be *vested*; if the employee loses pension rights if he or she leaves the company prior to retirement, the rights are said to be *nonvested*.

☐ Most defined benefit plans today have *deferred vesting,* where pension rights are nonvested for the first few years, but become fully vested if the employee remains with the company for a prescribed period.

☐ Companies with defined benefit plans are required to vest participants at least as fast as either the five-year rule (*cliff vesting*) or the 3-to-7-year rule (*partial vesting*).

■ A *portable* pension plan is one that an employee can carry from one firm to another. It is extremely important in occupations such as construction where workers move from one employer to another fairly frequently.

☐ Defined contribution plans are always portable, because the plan's assets are held in the employees' names. For a defined benefit plan to be portable, both the old employer and the new employer must be part of the same plan.

■ A plan is said to be *fully funded* if the present value of expected retirement benefits is equal to assets on hand. If assets exceed the present value of benefits, the plan is *overfunded.* Conversely, if the present value of benefits exceeds assets, the plan is *underfunded,* and an *unfunded pension liability* exists.

■ The discount rate used to determine the present value of future benefits under a defined benefit plan is called the *actuarial rate of return.* Higher actuarial rate assumptions lead to lower current contribution requirements for two reasons: (1) the present value of benefits will be lower, and (2) the plan's assets will be assumed to earn more, hence to grow at a faster rate. Thus, the actuarial rate of return has a significant impact on the plan's annual contributions.

■ The *Employee Retirement Income Security Act of 1974 (ERISA)* is the basic federal law governing the structure and administration of corporate pension plans. ERISA requires, among other things, that companies fully fund their defined benefit pension plans, although it gives them up to 30 years to correct for underfunding of past service benefits.

☐ ERISA mandates that pension funds be managed according to the "prudent man" rule, which focuses on diversification as the cornerstone of portfolio management.

☐ ERISA sets the mandatory vesting requirements so situations where long-term employees are fired or laid off just before their benefits are vested are avoided.

■ The Pension Benefit Guarantee Corporation (PBGC) was established by ERISA to insure corporate defined benefit pension funds. The PBGC steps in and takes over payments to retirees of bankrupt companies with underfunded pension plans. However, a number of restrictions apply:

☐ PBGC does not cover company-promised health insurance for retirees.

- □ PBGC payments are capped at about $28,000 per year per plan, which for some highly paid hourly workers, is considerably less than their plan originally promised.
- □ PBGC does not guarantee pensions that are paid by annuities purchased by plans from insurance companies.

■ Both the Financial Accounting Standards Board (FASB) and the SEC have established rules that require firms operating pension plans to report specific information in its annual report. While the reporting of defined contribution plans is relatively straightforward, the reporting of defined benefit plans is much more complex.

The calculation of the present value of expected future benefits is of primary importance in defined benefit pension plans. This calculation determines both the required contribution to the fund for the year and the reported unfunded liability or surplus.

■ The assumed rate of return can make a substantial difference in the annual contribution. Assumptions about how long the worker will live, years before retirement, and, if the payment is based on salary, annual raises will have similarly large effects on the required annual contribution.

Different types of plans differ with regard to the certainty of cash contributions, investment earnings, and promised benefits at retirement.

■ In a *defined contribution plan*, the corporation, or plan sponsor, contributes a guaranteed amount which will be invested for eventual retirement payments to the beneficiaries of the plan. No guarantee is made about either the rate of return earned on the funds contributed or the final payments. Thus, the beneficiaries assume the risk of fluctuations in the rate of return on the invested money.

■ A *profit sharing plan* is similar, except that the sponsor's cash contributions are also uncertain, thus increasing the risk to the beneficiaries. Retirees' incomes could be quite large or quite small, depending on how profitable the corporation is and how well the plan's assets are managed.

■ In a *defined benefit plan*, the corporate sponsor assumes all risks of unexpected variations in rates of return on investment. The resulting annual contributions, however, could vary if the defined benefits are based on some average of the final years' salaries. Further, these contributions cannot be reduced if the corporation's profits fall, as they could be with a profit sharing plan.

■ Therefore, a defined benefit plan is by far the riskiest from the standpoint of the sponsoring corporation, but the least risky from the standpoint of the employees, although employees still bear purchasing power risk.

■ Risks to a corporation under a defined benefit plan can be divided into (1) uncertainty about the annual cash contribution and (2) uncertainty about the firm's obligations in the event it goes bankrupt.

    □ The *minimum annual cash contribution* is the sum of the amount needed to fund projected future benefit payments that were accrued during the current period, the amount that must be contributed to make up for not having funded all benefits for service that occurred prior to the current period, and an additional amount required to offset unexpected deviations from the plan's actuarial assumptions, especially deviations in the earned rate of return and in employee turnover and wage rates.

    □ There are three key types of actuarial assumptions which reflect real-world risks:

        ▶ *decrement assumptions,* which allow the actuary to adjust annually for the probability that any employee will leave the company;

        ▶ *future salary assumptions,* which take into account expected future average wage increases, which will affect the final salary and hence defined benefit payments based on the final salary; and

        ▶ *discount rate assumptions,* which explicitly forecast the portfolio's expected future rate of return, which is used both to compound the fund's growth from investment and to discount and thus find the present value of future benefits.

    □ At the end of each year, the assumptions are examined and modified if necessary, and actuaries determine the present value of expected future benefits.

    □ Prior to the passage of ERISA, employees had no claim against a corporation's assets in the event of bankruptcy. By passing ERISA, Congress elevated the priority of unfunded vested pension liabilities in the event of bankruptcy. In the event of a pension plan termination due to bankruptcy, unfunded vested liabilities have a lien on a par with federal taxes on up to 30 percent of the stockholders' equity.

    □ The value of a firm's stock is affected by the financial condition of its pension plan. However, devising a reasonable set of accounting procedures for reporting both the annual pension expense and the corporation's pension liabilities has proved to be quite difficult.

■ Not all risks associated with defined benefit pension plans are borne by the PBGC or corporate sponsor; its participants can also face uncertainties. For example, bankruptcy of a firm still imposes hardships on workers; it has been a major factor in unions' acceptance of reduced wages and benefits in situations where corporate bankruptcy with corresponding layoffs would otherwise have occurred.

As an employee, choosing between a defined benefit or a defined contribution plan is not an easy decision to make. It depends on both the specifics of the plans being offered and the unique situation of the individual making the decision.

■ A young employee who has a high probability of moving would be better off under a defined contribution plan. The economic consequences of changing jobs are much worse under the defined benefit plan because benefits are frozen rather than increased with inflation.

■ It is much more costly to a firm to hire older workers if it operates under a defined benefit plan than if it operates under a defined contribution plan.

■ Employees are generally exposed to more risks under a defined contribution plan, while employers face more risks under a defined benefit plan.

The actual choice of a plan type is often dictated by competitive conditions in the labor market.

■ Unions generally seek defined benefit plans in order to cushion the beneficiaries from the investment risks that would exist under a defined contribution or a profit sharing plan.

■ A defined benefit plan provides tax-planning flexibility because firms can vary the fund contribution from year to year. Thus, in highly profitable years, firms can make large contributions, which decrease taxable income and hence reduce taxes. Defined contribution plans do not afford such flexibility because the specified contributions must be made each year regardless of the firm's profitability.

■ In recent years, small firms have tended to adopt defined contribution or profit sharing plans, while larger firms tend to adopt defined contribution plans. The regulatory burden of ERISA has in fact driven many firms to terminate their defined benefit plans.

■ Assuming that a firm had decided on a defined benefit plan, proper strategic planning requires integrating the plan's funding and investment policies into the company's general corporate policies.
  □ The *funding strategy* involves deciding how fast should any unfunded liability be reduced, and what rate of return should be assumed in the actuarial calculations.
  □ The *investment strategy* must determine how should a portfolio that minimizes the risk of not achieving an assumed actuarial rate of return be structured.

☐ Pension fund managers use *asset allocation models* to help plan funding and investment strategies. Several conclusions emerge from such model runs.
  ▸ The safety of principal is a paramount consideration, so pension fund managers ought not to "reach" for the highest possible returns.
  ▸ For a given level of return, the inclusion of more types of assets generally reduces the portfolio's risk, because asset types are not perfectly correlated.
  ▸ Choices among the possible portfolios are limited by the introduction of managerial constraints.

Pension fund investment tactics depend on three characteristics: (1) the dollar size of a fund's investable assets, (2) the mix of the funds' liabilities between those attributable to active workers and those attributable to retired beneficiaries, and (3) the tax situation facing the corporate sponsor.

■ A common investment tactic involves segregating pension fund assets into two parts: a "retiree portfolio" that provides income to current retirees and a "worker portfolio" that builds value for current workers. Then, as current workers retire, the assets of the fund are shifted from the worker portfolio to the retiree portfolio.
  ☐ The retiree portfolio is usually invested in fixed-income securities that are chosen to produce a cash payment stream that matches the required retiree pension payments. In managing the retiree portfolio, fund managers often use *immunization techniques* such as *duration* to eliminate, or at least significantly reduce, the risk associated with rising and falling interest rates.
  ☐ The active worker portfolio usually includes some relatively risky assets such as stocks and real estate. To reduce the risk inherent in such a portfolio, pension fund managers often use a hedging technique called *portfolio insurance*, which does not appreciably affect upside potential but limits the downside risk.

■ Pension fund sponsors need to evaluate the performance of their portfolio managers on a regular basis and then use this performance evaluation information as a basis for allocating the fund's assets among portfolio managers.
  ☐ *Alpha analysis* adds substantially to a pension manager's knowledge about his or her equity portfolio's results. Alpha measures the vertical distance of a portfolio's return above or below the Security Market Line.

■ In general, a fund's assets are invested on either an *active* or a *passive* basis. Active managers select stocks with the idea of "beating the market," while passive management is based on the idea of achieving average returns while minimizing transactions costs and management fees.

There is an ongoing debate about whether excess assets in a defined benefit plan belong to the sponsoring company or to the employees. Legally, they belong to the company, but a number of union leaders have argued that they ought to belong to the workers.

Sixty-five percent of all companies, especially medium-size and small firms, have scrapped or cut back on their retiree health benefits, which are normally a part of the retirement package. Surging healthcare costs, an aging population, and new accounting rules have all put pressure on sponsoring firms to reduce or eliminate health benefits for its beneficiaries.

SELF-TEST QUESTIONS

Definitional

1. The _____ _____ _____ typically administers the pension plan.

2. A(n) _____ _____ plan is one in which a company agrees to make specific payments into a retirement fund and then retirees receive benefits from the plan that depend on the plan's investment success.

3. Under a(n) _____ _____ plan the employer agrees to give retirees a specific amount, such as $500 per month or 50 percent of the individual's average salary over the five years preceding retirement.

4. A(n) _____ _____ plan calls for the employer to make payments into the retirement fund, but with the payments varying with the level of corporate profits.

5. If employees have a right to receive pension benefits even if they leave the company prior to retirement, then their pension rights are said to be _____; if the employee loses pension rights if he or she leaves the company prior to retirement, the rights are said to be _____.

6. Most defined benefit plans today have _____ _____, where pension rights are nonvested for the first few years, but become fully vested if the employee remains with the company for a prescribed period.

7. A(n) _____ pension plan is one that an employee can carry from one firm to another.

8. A plan is said to be _____ _____ if the present value of expected retirement benefits is equal to assets on hand.

9. If assets exceed the present value of benefits, the plan is _____.

10. If the present value of benefits exceeds assets, the plan is _____, and a(n) _____ _____ _____ exists.

11. The _____ _____ _____ _____ _____ of 1974 is the basic federal law governing the structure and administration of corporate pension plans.

12. The _____ _____ _____ _____ was established to insure corporate defined benefit pension funds.

13. In a defined benefit plan, the _____ _____ assumes all risks of unexpected variations in rates of return on investment.

14. The _____ _____ _____ _____ is the sum of the amount needed to fund projected future benefit payments that were accrued during the current period, the amount that must be contributed to make up for not having funded all benefits for service that occurred prior to the current period, and an additional amount required to offset unexpected deviations from the plan's actuarial assumptions.

15. There are three key types of actuarial assumptions which reflect real-world risks: _____ assumptions, which allow the actuary to adjust annually for the probability that any employee will leave the company, _____ _____ assumptions, and _____ _____ assumptions.

16. In general, a fund's assets are invested on either a(n) _____ or a(n) _____ basis. _____ managers select stocks with the idea of "beating the market," while _____ management is based on the idea of achieving average returns while minimizing transactions costs and management fees.

17. Pension fund investment tactics depend on three characteristics: (1) the _____ _____ of a fund's investable assets, (2) the _____ of the fund's liabilities between those attributable to active workers and those attributable to retired beneficiaries, and (3) the _____ situation facing the corporate sponsor.

Conceptual

18. Under a defined benefit plan, employees agree to contribute some percentage of their salaries, up to 20 percent, to the firm's pension fund.

   a. True   **b.** False

19. If employees have a right to receive pension benefits even if they leave the company prior to retirement, their pension rights are said to be deferred.

   a. True   **b.** False

20. From a pure cost standpoint, a firm with a defined benefit plan would be more likely to hire older workers than a firm with a defined contribution plan.

   a. True   **b.** False

21. The performance measurement of stock portfolio managers must recognize the risk inherent in the investment portfolio. One way to incorporate risk into performance measurement is to examine the portfolio's z-score, which measures the vertical distance of the portfolio's return above or below the Security Market Line.

   a. True   **b.** False

22. Which of the following statements about pension plans, if any, is most *correct*?

   a. A defined contribution plan is, in effect, a savings plan that is funded by employers, although many plans also permit additional contributions by employees.
   b. Under a defined benefit plan, the employer agrees to give retirees a specifically defined benefit, such as $500 per month or 50 percent of the employees final salary.
   c. A portable pension plan is one that an employee can carry from one employer to another.
   d. An employer's obligation is satisfied under a defined benefit plan when it makes the required contributions to the plan. The risk of inadequate investment returns is borne by the employee.
   e. Statements a, b, and c are all correct.

23. Which of the following statements about defined contribution plans, if any, is *incorrect*?

   a. A defined contribution plan places the risk of poor pension portfolio performance on the employee.
   b. In general, employees can choose the investment vehicle under a defined contribution plan. Thus, highly risk-averse employees can choose low-risk investments, while more risk-tolerant employees can choose high-risk investments.
   c. In a defined contribution plan, the employer must make larger-than-average contributions to the pension plan when investment returns have been below expectations.
   d. Large corporations tend to use defined benefit plans, while small corporations tend to use defined contribution plans.
   e. All of the above statements are correct.

24. Which of the following statements about pension plan portfolio performance, if any, is *incorrect*?

   a. Pension fund sponsors must evaluate the performance of their portfolio managers periodically as a basis for future asset allocations.
   b. Alpha analysis, which relies on the Capital Asset Pricing Model, considers the risk of the portfolio when measuring performance.
   c. Peer comparison examines the relative performance of portfolio managers with different investment objectives.
   d. A portfolio annual return of 12 percent from one investment advisor is not necessarily better than a return of 10 percent from another advisor.
   e. Index fund managers are evaluated against the index whose returns they attempt to match.

SELF-TEST PROBLEMS

1. The Apex Company has just hired Mr. Smith, who is age 25 and is expected to retire at age 60. Mr. Smith's current salary is $30,000 per year, but his wages are expected to increase by 5 percent annually over the next 35 years. Apex has a defined benefit pension plan in which workers receive 1.5 percent of their final year's wages for each year of employment. Assume a world of certainty. Further, assume that all payments occur at year-end. What is Mr. Smith's approximate expected annual retirement benefit?

   a. $35,000   b. $57,000   c. $87,000   d. $116,000   e. $132,000

2. Midwest Investment Consultants (MIC) operates several stock investment portfolios that are used by firms for investment of pension plan assets. Last year, one portfolio had a realized return of 12.6 percent and a beta coefficient of 1.25. The average T-bond rate was 7 percent and the realized rate of return on the S&P 500 was 12 percent. What was the portfolio's alpha?

    a. -0.65%   **b.** -0.25%   **c.** 0%   **d.** +0.25%   **e.** +0.65%

3. The Ritz Company has a 40-year old employee that will retire at age 60 and live to age 75. The firm has promised a retirement income of $20,000 at the end of each year following retirement until death. The firm's pension fund is expected to earn 7 percent annually on its assets. What is Ritz's annual pension contribution for this employee? (Assume certainty and end-of-year cash flows.)

    a. $2,756   **b.** $3,642   **c.** $4,443   **d.** $4,967   **e.** $5,491

ANSWERS TO SELF-TEST QUESTIONS

1. chief financial officer
2. defined contribution
3. defined benefit
4. profit sharing
5. vested; nonvested
6. deferred vesting
7. portable
8. fully funded
9. overfunded

10. underfunded; unfunded pension liability
11. Employee Retirement Income Security Act
12. Pension Benefit Guarantee Corporation
13. corporate sponsor
14. minimum annual cash contribution
15. decrement; future salary; discount rate
16. active; passive; Active; passive
17. dollar size; mix; tax

18. b. Under a defined benefit plan, the employer agrees to give retirees a specifically defined benefit.

19. b. The employee's pension rights are vested.

20. b. It is much more costly to a company to hire older workers if it operates under a defined benefit plan than if it operates under a defined contribution plan.

21. b. Alpha analysis adds substantially to a pension manager's knowledge about his or her equity portfolio's results. Alpha measures the vertical distance of a portfolio's return above or below the Security Market Line.

22. e. The risk of inadequate investment returns in a defined benefit plan are borne by the corporate sponsor.

23. c. In a defined contribution plan, the corporate sponsor agrees to make *specific* payments.

24. c. Peer comparison examines the relative performance of portfolio managers with similar investment objectives.

SELF-TEST PROBLEMS

1. c. Final year's salary = $30,000(1.05)^{35} = $165,480.46.
Salary multiplier = 35(1.5%) = 52.5%.
Pension benefit = 0.525($165,480.46) = $86,877.24.

2. a. Portfolio's required rate of return = $k_{RF} + (k_M - k_{RF})b$
$$= 7\% + (12\% - 7\%)1.25$$
$$= 7\% + (5\%)1.25 = 13.25\%.$$

Alpha = 12.6% - 13.25% = -0.65%.

3. c. Find the PV (at retirement) of the 15-year pension payment:

$$\$20,000(\text{PVIFA}_{7\%, \ 15 \ years}) = \$182,158.28.$$

Alternatively, using a financial calculator input the following: N = 15, I = 7, PMT = 20,000, FV = 0, and then solve for PV = $182,158.28.

Find the annual payment needed to accumulate the above amount over 20 years:

$$\text{Annual payment} = \$182,158.28(\text{FVIFA}_{7\%, \ 20 \ years}) = \$4,443.37.$$

Alternatively, using a financial calculator input the following: N = 20, I = 7, PV = 0, FV = 182,158.28, and then solve for PMT = $4,443.37.